RETROSYNTHETIC ANALYSIS AND SYNTHESIS OF DRUGS
The Disconnection Approach

Prof. (Dr.) N. J. Gaikwad
M. Pharm., Ph. D., DBM., LLB., BJ.,
Professor and Head,
University Department of Pharmaceutical Sciences,
RTM Nagpur University, Nagpur.

Prof. (Dr.) V. R. Patil
M. Pharm., Ph. D.
Professor and Principal,
Hon. Loksevak Madhukarrao Chaudhari
College of Pharmacy, Faizpur.

Prof. (Dr.) R. Y. Chaudhari
M. Pharm., Ph. D.
Professor and Vice-Principal,
Hon. Loksevak Madhukarrao Chaudhari
College of Pharmacy, Faizpur.

NIRALI PRAKASHAN

RETROSYNTHETIC ANALYSIS AND SYNTHESIS OF DRUGS   **ISBN 978-93-80064-93-2**

Second Edition : September, 2012

© : Authors

The text of this publication, or any part thereof, should not be reproduced or transmitted in any form or stored in any computer storage system or device for distribution including photocopy, recording, taping or information retrieval system or reproduced on any disc, tape, perforated media or other information storage device etc., without the written permission of Authors with whom the rights are reserved. Breach of this condition is liable for legal action.

Every effort has been made to avoid errors or omissions in this publication. In spite of this, errors may have crept in. Any mistake, error or discrepancy so noted and shall be brought to our notice shall be taken care of in the next edition. It is notified that neither the publisher nor the authors or seller shall be responsible for any damage or loss of action to any one, of any kind, in any manner, therefrom.

Published By :
NIRALI PRAKASHAN
Abhyudaya Pragati, 1312, Shivaji Nagar,
Off J.M. Road, PUNE – 411005
Tel - (020) 25512336/37/39, Fax - (020) 25511379
Email : niralipune@pragationline.com

Printed By :
Repro Knowledgecast Limited,
Thane

DISTRIBUTION CENTRES

PUNE
Nirali Prakashan
119, Budhwar Peth, Jogeshwari Mandir Lane
Pune 411002, Maharashtra
Tel : (020) 2445 2044, 66022708
Fax : (020) 2445 1538
Email : bookorder@pragationline.com

MUMBAI
Nirali Prakashan
385, S.V.P. Road, Rasdhara Co-op. Hsg. Society Ltd.,
Girgaum, Mumbai 400004, Maharashtra
Tel : (022) 2385 6339 / 2386 9976,
Fax : (022) 2386 9976
Email : niralimumbai@pragationline.com

DISTRIBUTION BRANCHES

NAGPUR
Pratibha Book Distributors
Above Maratha Mandir, Shop No. 3, First Floor,
Rani Jhanshi Square, Sitabuldi, Nagpur 440012,
Maharashtra, Tel : (0712) 254 7129

BENGALURU
Pragati Book House
House No. 1, Sanjeevappa Lane, Avenue Road Cross,
Opp. Rice Church, Bengaluru – 560002.
Tel : (080) 64513344, 64513355,
Mob : 9880582331, 9845021552
Email:bharatsavla@yahoo.com

JALGAON
Nirali Prakashan
34, V. V. Golani Market, Navi Peth, Jalgaon 425001,
Maharashtra, Tel : (0257) 222 0395
Mob : 94234 91860

KOLHAPUR
Nirali Prakashan
New Mahadvar Road,
Kedar Plaza, 1st Floor Opp. IDBI Bank
Kolhapur 416 012, Maharashtra. Mob : 9855046155

CHENNAI
Pragati Books
9/1, Montieth Road, Behind Taas Mahal, Egmore,
Chennai 600008 Tamil Nadu, Tel : (044) 6518 3535,
Mob : 94440 01782 / 98450 21552 / 98805 82331
Email : bharatsavla@yahoo.com

RETAIL OUTLETS
PUNE

Pragati Book Centre
157, Budhwar Peth, Opp. Ratan Talkies,
Pune 411002, Maharashtra
Tel : (020) 2445 8887 / 6602 2707, Fax : (020) 2445 8887

Pragati Book Centre
Amber Chamber, 28/A, Budhwar Peth,
Appa Balwant Chowk, Pune : 411002, Maharashtra
Tel : (020) 20240335 / 66281669
Email : pbcpune@pragationline.com

Pragati Book Centre
676/B, Budhwar Peth, Opp. Jogeshwari Mandir,
Pune 411002, Maharashtra
Tel : (020) 6601 7784 / 6602 0855

Pragati Book Centre
917/22, Sai Complex, F.C. Road, Opp. Hotel Roopali,
Shivajinagar, Pune 411004, Maharashtra
Tel : (020) 2566 3372 / 6602 2728

PBC Book Sellers & Stationers
152, Budhwar Peth, Pune 411002, Maharashtra
Tel : (020) 2445 2254 / 6609 2463

MUMBAI
Pragati Book Corner
Indira Niwas, 111 - A, Bhavani Shankar Road, Dadar (W), Mumbai 400028, Maharashtra
Tel : (022) 2422 3526 / 6662 5254
Email : pbcmumbai@pragationline.com

Preface

It gives us great pleasure to offer our students and the research chemists the first edition of our "**Reterosynthetic Analysis and Synthesis of Drugs- the Disconnection Approach**". The synthesis of organic compounds is central to area of pharmaceutical research, from the most applied to the most academic and is not limited to pharmaceutical chemists. Any research which uses new organic chemicals, which are not available commercially, or those which are very costly, will require the synthesis of such compounds at laboratory level.

This book continues to cover the most up-to-date reterosynthetic analysis and synthesis of commonly used drug molecules. It is not claimed to be a comprehensive compilation of information to meet all possible needs and circumstances; rather the intention has been to provide sufficient guidance to allow the researchers to workout synthesis of organic molecules which offer highest chance of success and will fulfill needs of Research and Development. The book is written for postgraduate and advanced level undergraduate pharmaceutical chemists and for chemists in industry.

Our special thanks are due to Mr. J. D. Fegade, who gave valuable assistance for the construction of structures of organic compounds. We are heartley thankful to our publisher Mr. D. K. Furia and Jignesh Furia for their kind co-operation. We extend our thanks to Mr. P.M More for his kind co-operation and moral support throught the work. We are much indebted to number of friends, most of them on this side of water, who have in various ways shared with us the task of preparing the present manuscript. It seems hardly necessary to say that our colleagues here have contributed largely in the preparation of this manuscript.

We sincerely hope this book will continue to find favor with the students it is meant for.

Suggestions for the improvement of the book will be greatfully acknowledged and incorporated, from any corner of profession are always welcome.

Faizpur: September, 2012

N. J. Gaikwad
V. R. Patil
R.Y. Chaudhari

General Nomenclature

R	alkyl
Ac or Me-CO-	acetyl
Bn or Ph-CH$_2$-	benzyl
Boc or Me$_3$C-O-CO-	t-butoxycarbonyl
Bu or C$_4$H$_9$-	n-butyl
Bu^i or (CH$_3$)$_2$CH-CH$_2$-	isobutyl
Bu^s or CH$_3$-CH$_2$-CH(CH$_3$)-	s-butyl (1-methylpropyl)
Bu^t or (CH$_3$)$_3$C-	t-butyl (1,1-dimethylethyl)
Bz or Ph-CO-	benzoyl
Cbz or Ph-CH$_2$-O-CO-	benzyloxycarbonyl
Et or C$_2$H$_5$	ethyl
i	iso
Me or CH$_3$-	methyl
MEM or Me-O-CH$_2$-CH$_2$-O-CH$_2$-	2-methoxyethoxymethyl
Ms or Me-SO$_2$-	methanesulphonyl (mesyl)
n	straight chain
Ph or C$_6$H$_5$	phenyl
Pr or C$_3$H$_7$-	n-propyl
Pr^i or (CH$_3$)$_2$CH-	isopropyl (1-methylethyl)
s	secondary
Sia or (CH$_3$)$_2$CH-CH(CH$_3$)-	s-isoamyl (1,2-dimethylpropyl)
t	tertiary
THP	tetrahydropyranyl
Ts or p-Me-C$_6$H$_4$-SO$_2$-	toluene-p-sunphonyl (tosyl)

•••

Reagents and Solvents

AIBN	α, α'-azobisisobutyronitrile
9-BBN	9-borabicyclo[3.3.1]nonane
BDSC	t-butyldimethylchlorosilane
BTMSA	N,O-bis(trimethylsilyl)acetamide
DBU	1,8-diazabicyclo[5.4.0]undac-7-ene
DCC	dicyclohexylcarbobiimide
DDQ	2,3-dichloro-5-6-dicyno-1,4-benzoquinone
DEG	diethylene gylcol
DET	diethyl tartarate
DIBAL	diisobutylaluminium hydride
DME	1,2-dimethoxyethane (glyme)
DMF	dimethylformamide
DMSO	dimethyl sulphoxide
DNFB	2,4-dinitroflurobenzene
DSS	sodium 3-(trimethylsilyl)-1-propanesulphonate
EAA	ethyl acetoacetate
HMDS	hexamethyldisilazane [bis(trimethylsilyl)amine]
HMPT	N,N,N',N',N'',N''-hexamethylphosphotriamide
LAH	lithium aluminium hydride
LDA	lithium isopropylamide
MCPBA	m-chloroperbenzoic acid

MEK	ethyl methyl ketone
MVK	methyl vinyl ketone
NBS	N-bromosuccinimide
NCS	N-chlorosuccinimide
PCC	pyridinium chlorochromate
PDC	pyridinium dichromate
PEG	polyethylene glycol
PPA	polyphosphoric acid
PPTSA	pyridinium toluene-p-sulphonate
Py	pyridine
SBH	sodium borohydride
TEG	triethylene glycol
TFA	trifluroacetic acid
THF	tetrahydrofuran
TMEDA	N,N,N',N'-tetramethylethylenediamine
TMCS	chlorotrimethylsilane
TMS	tetramethylsilane

•••

SYNTHON APPROACH

Introduction :
The synthon approach provides new and innovative synthetic strategies for organic molecules. Specifically new synthetic strategies and improvements in processes for manufacture of drugs, perfumery and fine chemicals are constantly required in industry. Terms used in synthon approach are given below:

Disconnection :
An operation which involves breaking a bond between two atoms.

Synthon :
Positively or negatively charged ions and/or radicals (neutral) obtained by disconnection.

Abbreviations :
FGE or FGC – Functional Group Equivalent or Functional Group Conversion. FGE or FGC operation involves substitution of one functional group by another from which it could be derived.

Example :

CH_3COO- $\xrightarrow{FGC}$ $N\equiv C-$

$-NH_2$ $\xrightarrow{FGC}$ $-NO_2$

$-Cl$ $\xrightarrow{FGC}$ $-OH$

Symbols :

⇒	Means bond breaking operation is carried out.
→	Denotes a chemical reaction.
↷	Indicates which bond being broken and the curve arrow on top of it.
C-N ⇒	Indicates which fragment will carry the negative charge in a heterocyclic disconnection.
C-C ⇒	Refers to particular bonds which are broken.

Basic Rules of Disconnection :

For synthesis of a molecule by synthon approach disconnection of a molecule is necessary. The basic rules of disconnection are :

1. **Disconnection of a bond should be done such that stable ion fragments are obtained. When disconnection is carried out, the molecule is generally broken down by one bond at a time.**

   Frequently a heterocyclic disconnection is done so that each disconnection will generate two fragments, one a positively charged and other negatively charged fragment.

   Disconnection of C-C bond in the following example give two types of fragments depending on mode I or mode II.

   (Mode-I)

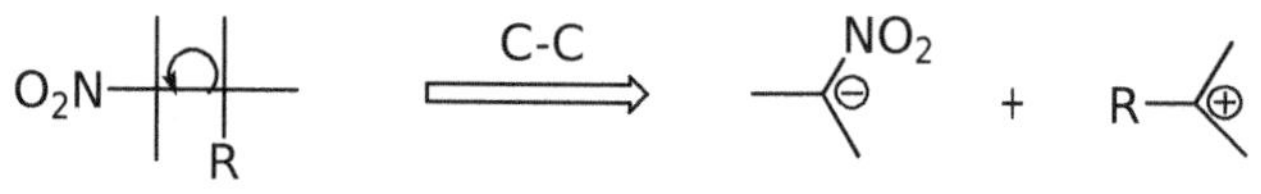

   $$O_2N-C(R)- \quad \xrightarrow{C-C} \quad -C(NO_2)^{\ominus} \ + \ R^{\oplus}$$

   (Mode-II)

   $$O_2N-C(R)- \quad \xrightarrow{C-C} \quad -C(NO_2)^{\oplus} \ + \ R^{\ominus}$$

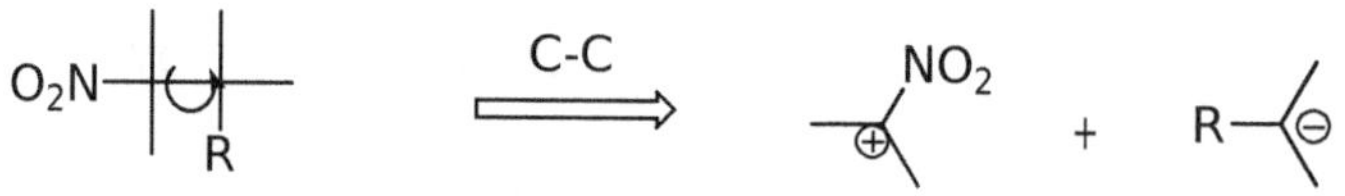

   The carbanion fragment generated is always stabilized by an electron withdrawing group. **e.g.** CN, NO_2, COOEt. While the carbonium ion fragment is stabilized by an electron releasing alkyl (-R) or alkoxy (-OR) group.

   Thus in above example, mode-I is preferred mode of disconnection since it generates stabilized ion fragments.

2. **The number of fragments generated from a disconnection should be as small as possible so that the synthesis of target molecule should be carried out in as few steps as possible.**

   (Mode-I)

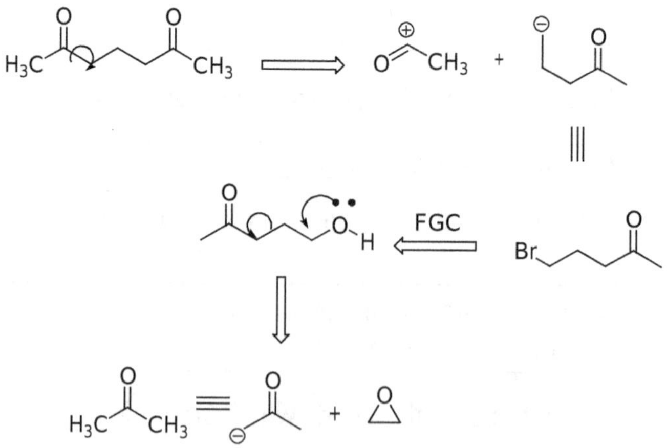

   $$H_3C-CO-CH_2-CH_2-CO-CH_3 \implies {}^{\oplus}O=CH-CH_3 \ + \ {}^{\ominus}CH_2-CO-CH_3$$

   $$\Updownarrow$$

   $$CH_3-CO-CH_2-CH_2-\ddot{O}-H \quad \xleftarrow{FGC} \quad Br-CH_2-CH_2-CO-CH_3$$

   $$\Downarrow$$

   $$H_3C-CO-CH_3 \equiv H_3C-CO-CH_2^{\ominus} \ + \ \triangle\!\!\!O$$

(**Mode-II**)

$$H_3C-CO-CH_2-CH_2-CH_2-CO-CH_3 \implies CH_3-CO-CH_3 + H_2C=CH-CO-CH_3$$

heptane-2,6-dione

The latter mode of disconnection is preferred since the target compound, heptane-2,6-dione can be synthesized in one step from readily available material.

Thus, whole molecule as well as the various functional groups present and the positional relationship between various functional grouping should be considered before beginning of the disconnection operation.

3. **The bond joining a carbon to a heteroatom (O, N and S) is always broken with the electron pair being transferred to the heteroatom.**

During the above disconnection, principle of electronegativity is followed i.e. O, N and S are more electronegative than carbon.

4. **Sometimes a disconnection carried out doesn't generate stabilized fragments but such fragments can be obtained by using FGC or by introducing an additional electron withdrawing group and then removing it after synthesis.**

Analysis:

Synthesis:

$$CH_3\text{-}NO_2 \xrightarrow[R\diagdown\diagdown Cl]{\text{base}} O_2N\diagdown\diagdown R \xrightarrow{\text{reduction}} H_2N\diagdown\diagdown R$$

Analysis:

$$\diagdown\diagdown\overset{O}{\underset{R}{\diagdown}} \Longrightarrow R\overset{O}{\underset{\|\|\|}{\diagdown}}\overset{\ominus}{CH_2} + \diagdown\diagdown^{\oplus} \equiv Cl\diagdown\diagdown$$

$$EtO\overset{O}{\diagdown}\overset{O}{\diagdown}R$$

Synthesis:

$$EtO\overset{O}{\diagdown}\overset{O}{\diagdown}R \xrightarrow[Cl\diagdown\diagdown]{\text{base}} EtO\overset{O}{\diagdown}\overset{R\diagdown\diagdown =O}{\diagdown} \xrightarrow[\substack{-CO_2\\-OEt}]{H^{\oplus}} \diagdown\diagdown\overset{O}{\diagdown}R$$

5. In the synthon approach +ve and –ve charged fragments are replaced by recognizable and meaningful chemical entities.

In most cases a positively charged alkyl fragment is considered equivalent to halo, hydroxyl or an alkoxy compounds.

$$\underset{\oplus}{\overset{R}{\underset{|}{CH_2}}} \equiv R-CH_2Cl$$

$$\equiv R-CH_2OH$$

$$\equiv R-CH_2OEt$$

In most cases a positively charged acyl fragment is considered equivalent to acid chloride, acid or ester.

$$\overset{\oplus}{O}\diagdown R \equiv R\overset{O}{\diagdown}Cl$$

$$\equiv R\overset{O}{\diagdown}OH$$

$$\equiv R\overset{O}{\diagdown}OEt$$

In most cases a negatively charged fragment is considered equivalent to corresponding protonated species.

$$O_2N-\overset{\ominus}{HC}R \equiv O_2N-\overset{R}{CH_2}$$

$$Ph^{\ominus} \equiv Ph-H$$

$$R-\overset{\ominus}{CH}-C(O)OEt \equiv R-CH_2-C(O)OEt$$

$$H-\overset{\ominus}{N}-R \equiv H-\overset{R}{N}-H$$

$$R-\overset{\ominus}{O} \equiv R-OH$$

6. **The ion fragments generated in a retrosynthetic scheme will be real intermediates if a synthesis is carried out using the scheme**.

Thus, the knowledge of various name reactions help in terms of predicting whether such ionic intermediates can be generated in a reaction vessel. Rationalization of various steps in the scheme is required to be done by using basic principles of organic chemistry.

Once the disconnection operation is completed and fragments have been converted to readily recognizable chemical entities, the next step is to write a synthesis of the target molecule.

Analysis:

Synthesis:

Toluene + CH₃COCl / AlCl₃ → 4′-methylacetophenone → (epoxide, base) → 1-(4-methylphenyl)-4-hydroxybutan-1-one

Table No. 1 : Benzene Ring Activating and Deactivating Substituents

Sr. No.	Activating Substituents (*ortho, para*-Directors)	Deactivating Substituents (*meta* Directors)	Deactivating Substituents (*ortho, para* Directors)
1	$-NH_2$	$-NR_3$	$-F$
2	$-NHR$	$-NO_2$	$-Cl$
3	$-OH$	$-CN$	$-Br$
4	$-OR$	$-SO_3H$	$-I$
5	$-NHCOR$	$-COH$	-
6	$-COR$	$-COR$	-
7	$-R$	$-COOR$	-
8	$-Ar$	$-COOH$	-
9	-	$-CONH_2$	-

Table No. 2 : Reagents for Aromatic Electrophilic Substitution Reaction

Sr. No.	Reaction	Synthon	Reagent
1	Friedel-Craft alkylation	R^+	$RBr+AlCl_3$, $ROH+H^+$
2	Friedel-Craft acylation	RC^+O	$RCOCl+AlCl_3$
3	Nitration	$^+NO_2$	$HNO_3+H_2SO_4$
4	Chlorination	Cl^+	Cl_2+FeCl_3
5	Bromination	Br^+	Br_2+Fe
6	Sulphonation	$^+SO_2OH$	H_2SO_4
7	Chlorosulphonation	$^+SO_2Cl$	$ClSO_2OH$
8	Choromethylation	$-CH_2Cl$	$CH_2O+HCl+ZnCl_2$
9	Reamer-Tiemann	$-CHO$	$CHCl_3+OH$

Table No. 3: Functional Group Interconversion and Reagents

Y—⟨Ar⟩—R →(Reagent)→ X—⟨Ar⟩—R

Reaction	Y	X	Reagent
Reduction	$-NO_2$	$-NH_2$	H_2, Pd, Sn, Con. hydrochloric acid
	$-COR$	$-CH(OH)R$	$NaBH_4$
	$-COR$	$-CH_2R$	Zn/Hg, Con. hydrochloric acid
Oxidation	$-CH_2Cl$	$-CHO$	Hexamine
	$-CH_2R$	$-COOH$	$KMnO_4, K_2Cr_2O_7$
	$-CH_3$	$-COOH$	$KMnO_4, K_2Cr_2O_7$
Substitution	$-CH_3$	$-CCl_3$	Cl_2, PCl_5
	$-CCl_3$	$-CR_3$	SbR_4
	$-CN$	$-COOH$	$^-OH/H_2O$

Table No. 4: Protecting Groups and Reagents for Formation and Removal

Functional Group	Protecting Group	Reagents	
		Formation	Removal
R-CHO	$RCH(OR')_2$	ROH, H^+	H^+/H_2O
R-COOH	$RCOOCH_3$	CH_2N_2	---
	$RCOOC_2H_5$	$EtOH/H^+$	$^-OH/H_2O$
	$RCOOC_2Ph$	$PhCH_2OH/H^+$	H_2/HBr
	$RCOO^-$	Base	Acid
ROH	$ROCH_2Ph$	$PhCH_2Br$	$H_2/HBr, H^+/H_2O$
	$RCOOR'$	$R'COCl$	$NH_3/MeOH$
ArOH	ArOMe	Me_2SO_4	HI, HBr
	$ArOCH_2OCH_3$	$MeOCH_2Cl$	$AcOH, H_2O$
RNH_2	$NHCOR'$	$R'COCl$	$^-OH/H_2O, H^+/H_2O$
	$RNHCOOR'$	$R'OCOCl$	H_2/HBr
RSH	AcSR	RSH + AC-Cl + Base	OH/H_2O

ACEPROMAZINE

Use: neuroleptic

Analysis:

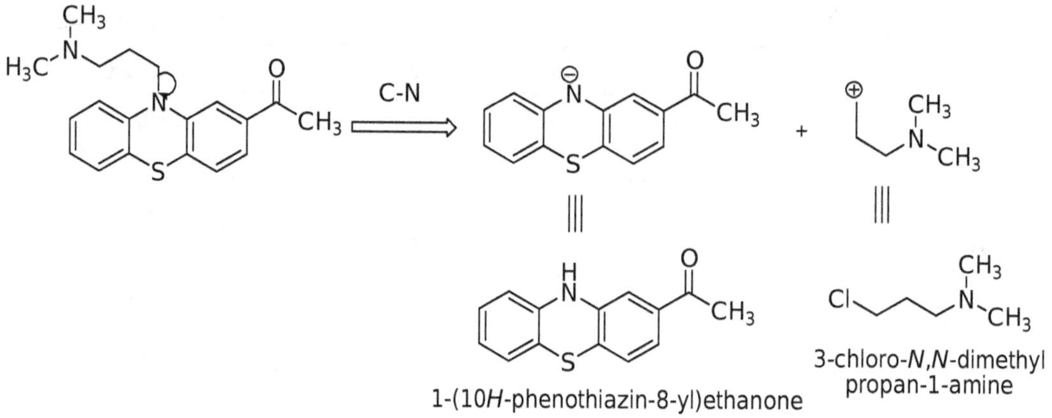

[Retrosynthetic scheme: acepromazine ⇒ (C-N disconnection) phenothiazine anion + 2-acetyl group ≡ 1-(10H-phenothiazin-8-yl)ethanone + 3-chloro-N,N-dimethylpropan-1-amine]

Synthesis:

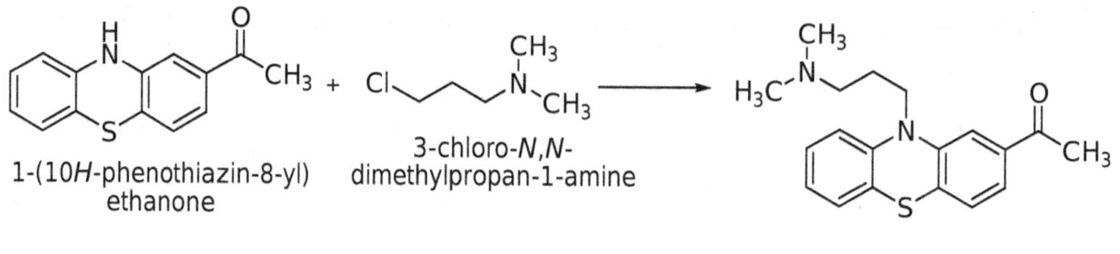

1-(10H-phenothiazin-8-yl)ethanone + 3-chloro-N,N-dimethylpropan-1-amine → **Acepromazine**

ACETOPHENAZINE

Use: neuroleptic, antipsychotic

Analysis:

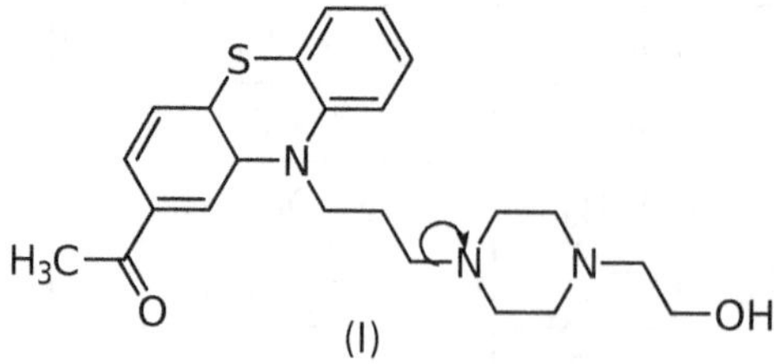

[Structure (I): phenothiazine with 2-acetyl group and N-(3-(4-(2-hydroxyethyl)piperazin-1-yl)propyl) substituent]

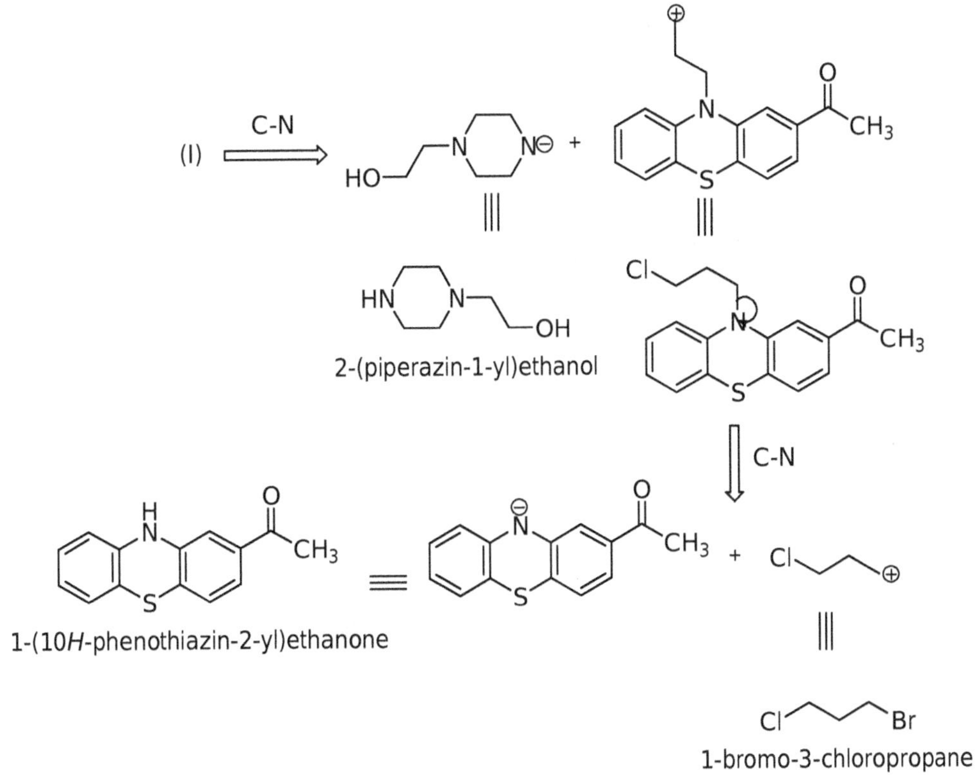

Retrosynthetic Analysis and Synthesis of Drugs

(I) ⟹ C-N

2-(piperazin-1-yl)ethanol

⟹ C-N

1-(10H-phenothiazin-2-yl)ethanone

1-bromo-3-chloropropane

Synthesis:

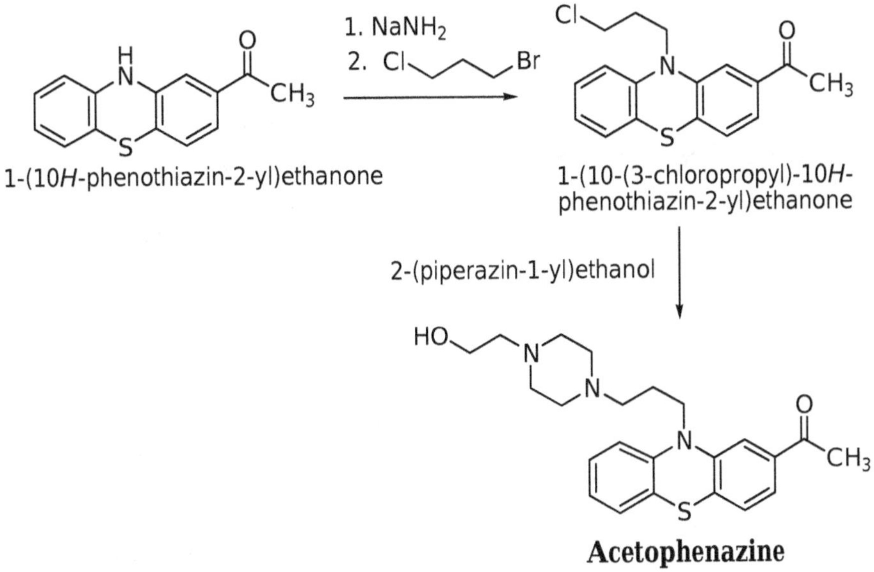

1-(10H-phenothiazin-2-yl)ethanone → (1. NaNH$_2$; 2. Cl(CH$_2$)$_3$Br) → 1-(10-(3-chloropropyl)-10H-phenothiazin-2-yl)ethanone

→ (2-(piperazin-1-yl)ethanol) →

Acetophenazine

ACETYLCHOLINE CHLORIDE

Use: parasympathomimetic

Analysis:

[Retrosynthetic analysis: Acetylcholine chloride disconnected at C-O bond to give acetyl cation (≡ acetyl chloride, $H_3C\text{-COCl}$) and choline (≡ HO-CH$_2$CH$_2$-N$^+$(CH$_3$)$_3$ Cl$^-$). Further C-N disconnection of choline gives Cl$^-$ + HO-CH$_2^+$ (≡ 2-chloroethanol, HO-CH$_2$CH$_2$-Cl) + trimethylamine, (CH$_3$)$_3$N.]

Synthesis:

trimethylamine + 2-chloroethanol $\longrightarrow$ HO-CH$_2$CH$_2$-N$^+$(CH$_3$)$_3$ Cl$^-$

$\xrightarrow{\text{CH}_3\text{COCl}}$

Acetylcholine chloride

ADIPHENINE

Use: antispasmodic, anticholinergic

Analysis:

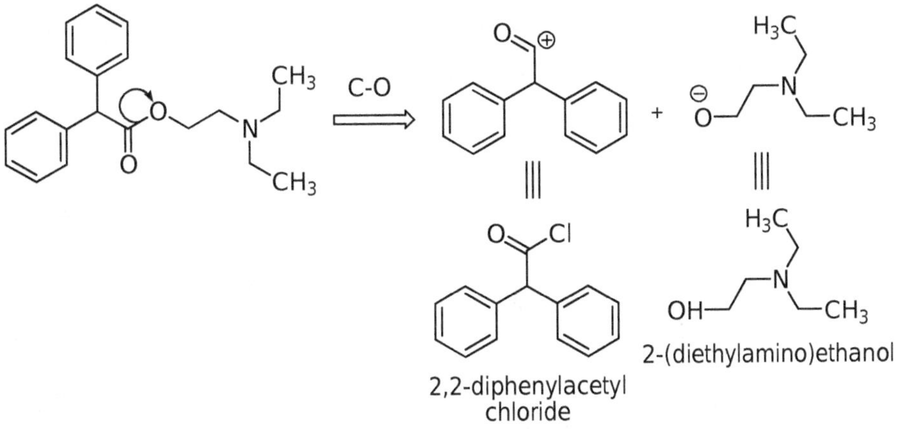

2,2-diphenylacetyl chloride

2-(diethylamino)ethanol

Synthesis:

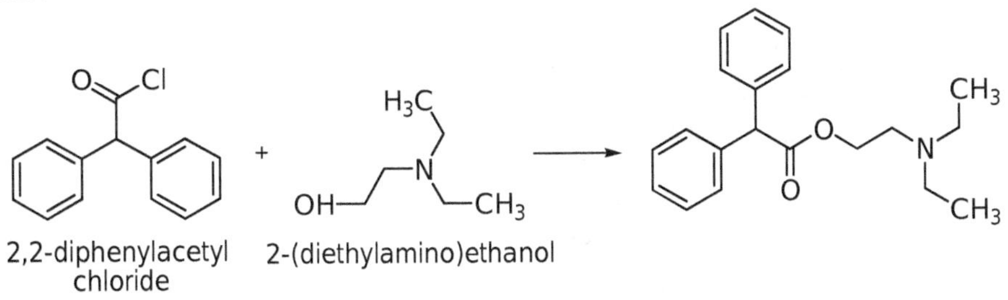

2,2-diphenylacetyl chloride + 2-(diethylamino)ethanol → **Adiphenine**

ALMITRINE

Use: analeptic

Analysis:

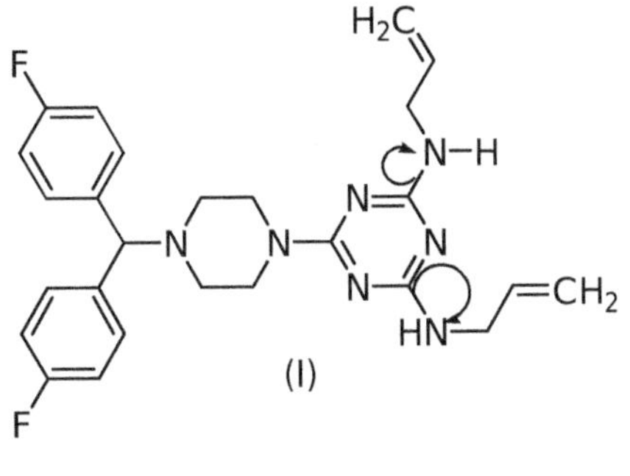

(I)

Retrosynthetic Analysis and Synthesis of Drugs

[Retrosynthetic analysis scheme showing target (I) disconnected via C-N/C-N bonds to 2 equivalents of but-3-en-1-amine (≡ prop-2-en-1-amine, H₂N–CH₂–CH=CH₂) plus a dicationic triazine-piperazine-bis(4-fluorophenyl)methyl intermediate, which is further disconnected via C-N to 2,4,6-trichloro-1,3,5-triazine and 1-(bis(4-fluorophenyl)methyl)piperazine.]

Synthesis:

1-(bis(4-fluorophenyl)methyl)piperazine + 2,4,6-trichloro-1,3,5-triazine $\xrightarrow{\text{NaOH}}$ (I)

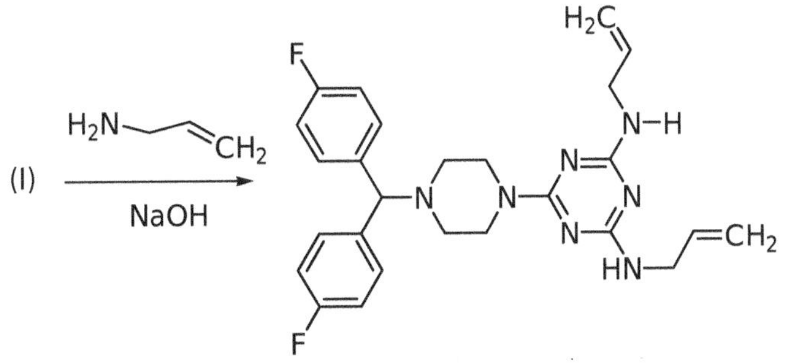

Retrosynthetic Analysis and Synthesis of Drugs

Almitrine

AMINOPROMAZINE

Use: antispasmodic

Analysis:

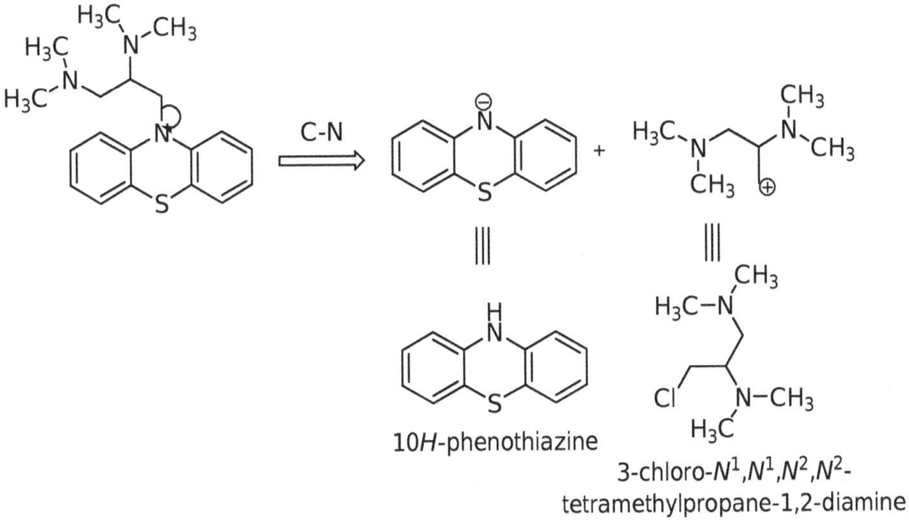

(retrosynthetic disconnection at C–N bond yielding 10H-phenothiazine and 3-chloro-N^1,N^1,N^2,N^2-tetramethylpropane-1,2-diamine)

10H-phenothiazine

3-chloro-N^1,N^1,N^2,N^2-tetramethylpropane-1,2-diamine

Synthesis:

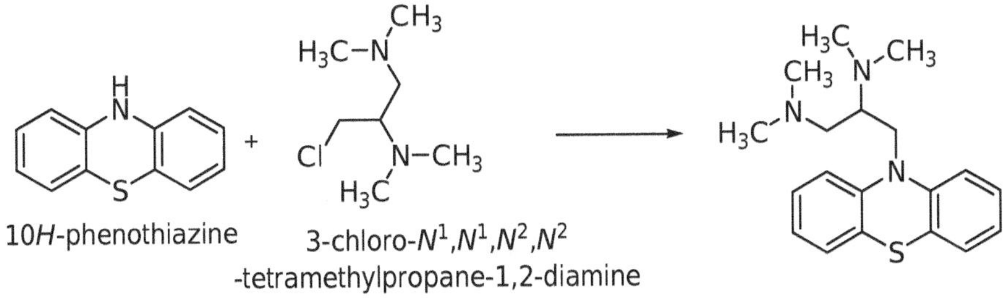

10H-phenothiazine + 3-chloro-N^1,N^1,N^2,N^2-tetramethylpropane-1,2-diamine → **Aminopromazine**

AMOBARBITAL
Use: hypnotic
Analysis:

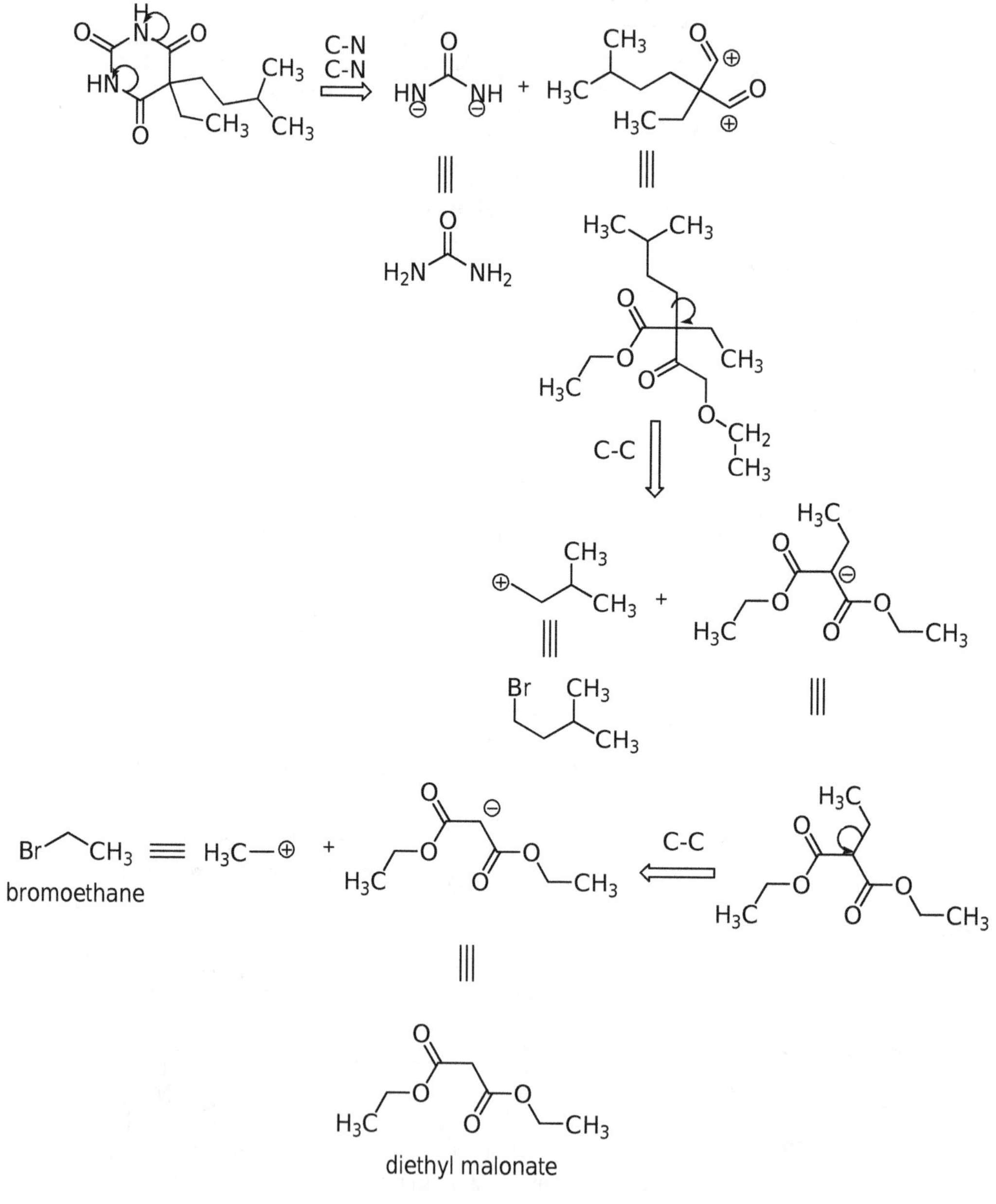

[Retrosynthetic analysis scheme: Amobarbital is disconnected via C-N bonds to urea (H₂N-CO-NH₂) and a diester synthon. The diester intermediate (diethyl 2-ethyl-2-isopentylmalonate) is disconnected via C-C bond to isopentyl cation (from 1-bromo-3-methylbutane) and diethyl 2-ethylmalonate anion. That intermediate is disconnected via C-C bond to ethyl cation (from bromoethane) and diethyl malonate anion, derived from diethyl malonate.]

bromoethane

diethyl malonate

Synthesis:

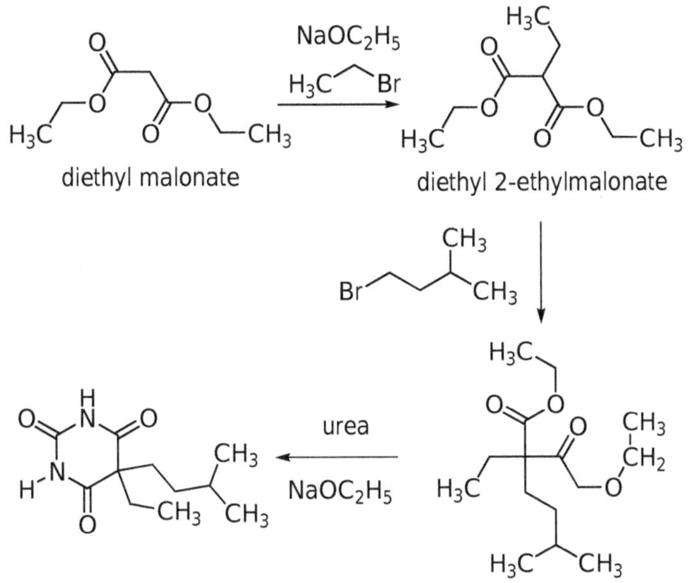

[Scheme: diethyl malonate → (NaOC₂H₅, H₃C-Br) → diethyl 2-ethylmalonate → (Br-CH₂CH₂CH(CH₃)₂) → intermediate → (urea, NaOC₂H₅) → Amobarbital]

Amobarbital

AMODIAQUINE

Use: antimalarial

Analysis:

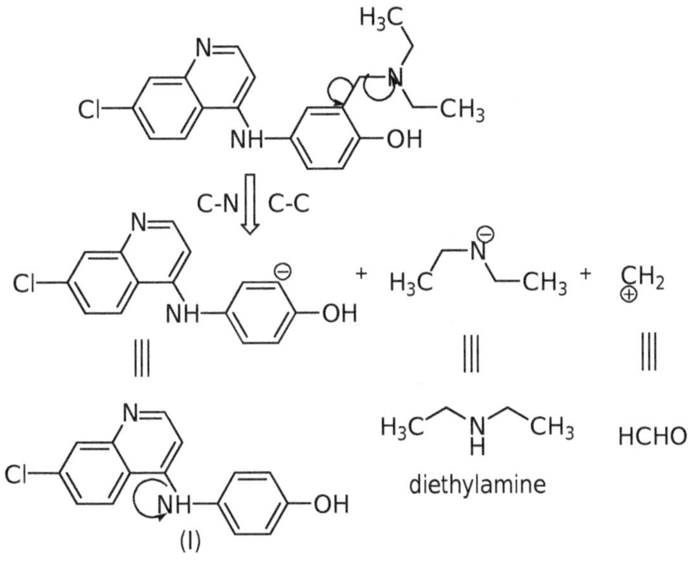

[Retrosynthetic scheme showing amodiaquine disconnection: C–N and C–C bonds break to give 7-chloro-4-aminoquinoline phenol intermediate + diethylamine + HCHO; intermediate (I) further disconnects to 4-aminophenol and 4,7-dichloroquinoline]

diethylamine   HCHO

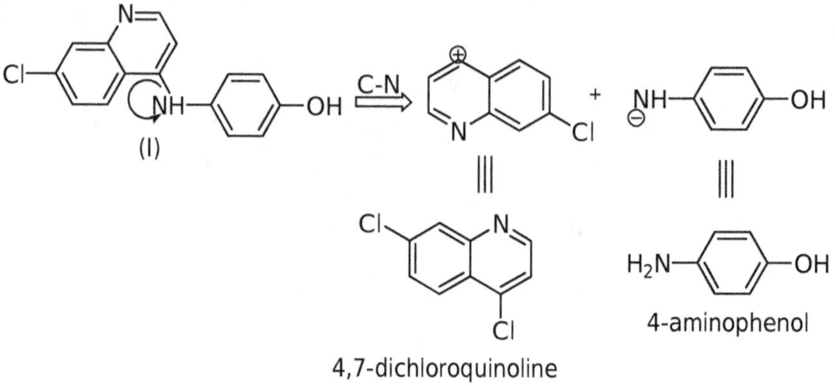

Synthesis:

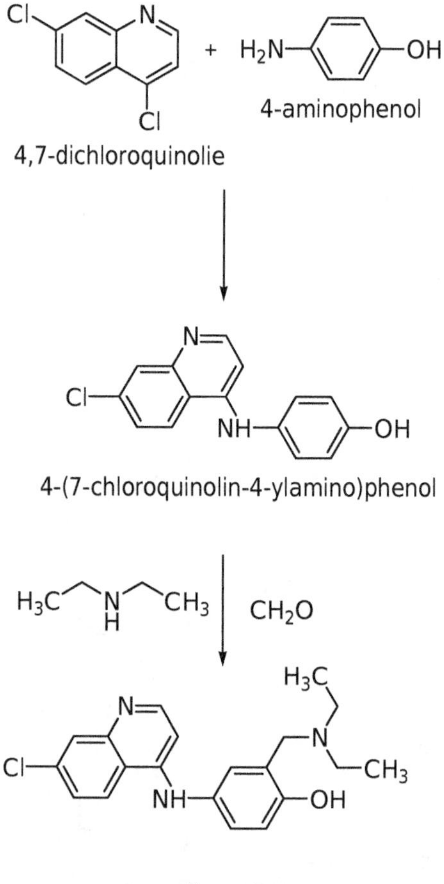

4,7-dichloroquinoline + 4-aminophenol

↓

4-(7-chloroquinolin-4-ylamino)phenol

↓ H₃C–NH–CH₃ (diethylamine), CH₂O

Amodiaquine

AMOXYCILLIN

Use: antibiotic

Analysis:

Synthesis:

Amoxycillin

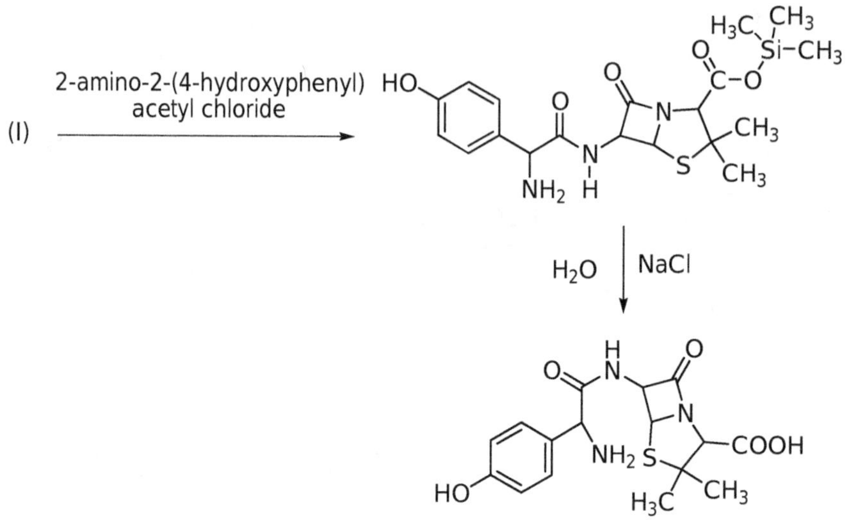

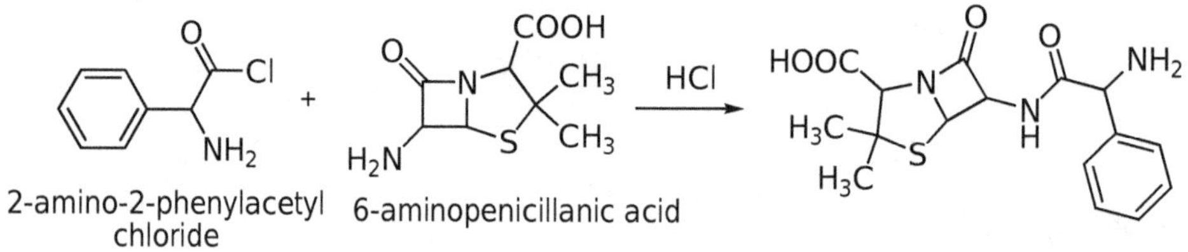

AMPICILLIN

Use: antibiotic

Analysis:

Synthesis:

Ampicillin

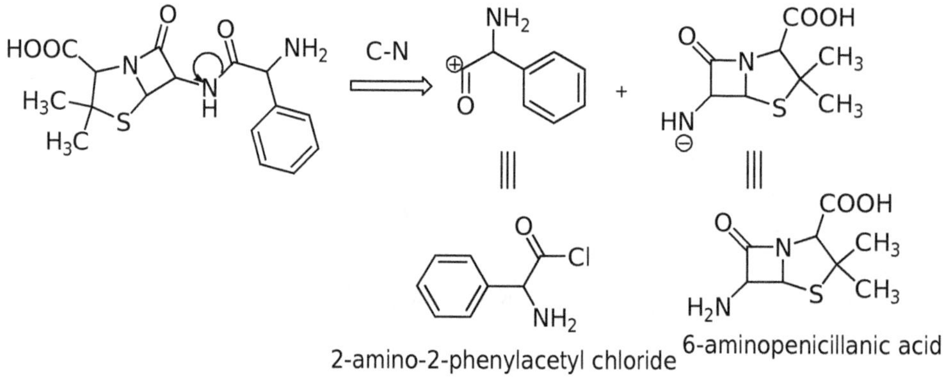

ANILERIDINE
Use: analgesic
Analysis:

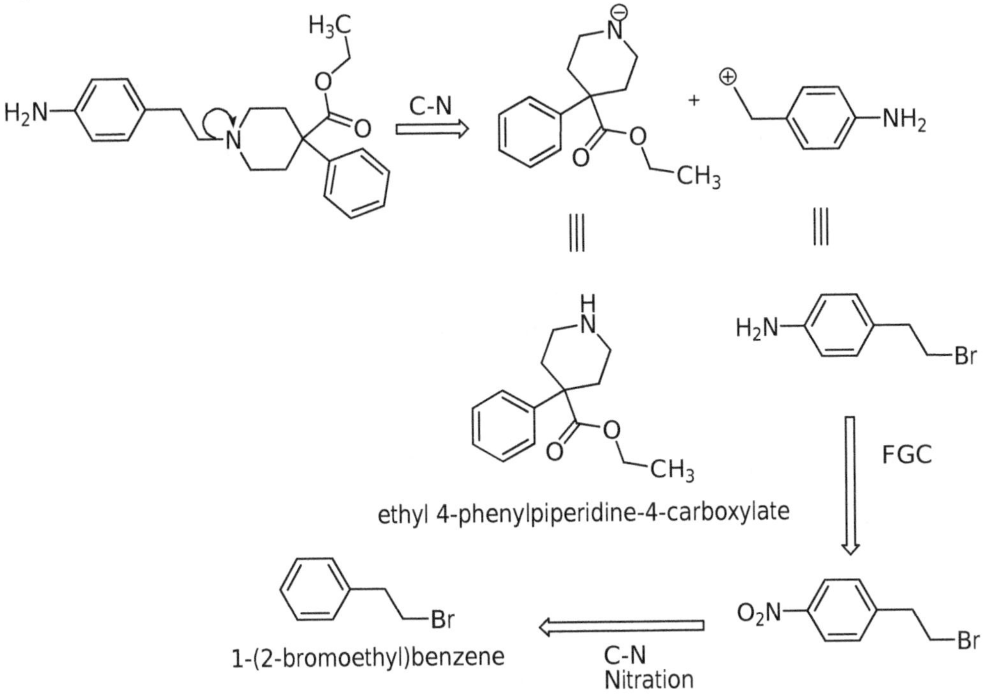

[Retrosynthetic scheme: Anileridine ⇒ (C-N disconnection) ethyl 4-phenylpiperidine-4-carboxylate anion + 4-aminobenzyl cation; the electrophile equates to H₂N-C₆H₄-CH₂CH₂-Br (FGC) ⇐ O₂N-C₆H₄-CH₂CH₂-Br ⇐ (C-N, Nitration) 1-(2-bromoethyl)benzene]

ethyl 4-phenylpiperidine-4-carboxylate

1-(2-bromoethyl)benzene

Synthesis:

1-(2-bromoethyl)benzene →(HNO₃)→ 1-(2-bromoethyl)-4-nitrobenzene →(SnCl₂, HCl)→ 4-(2-bromoethyl)benzenamine →(ethyl 4-phenylpiperidine-4-carboxylate)→ **Aniledine**

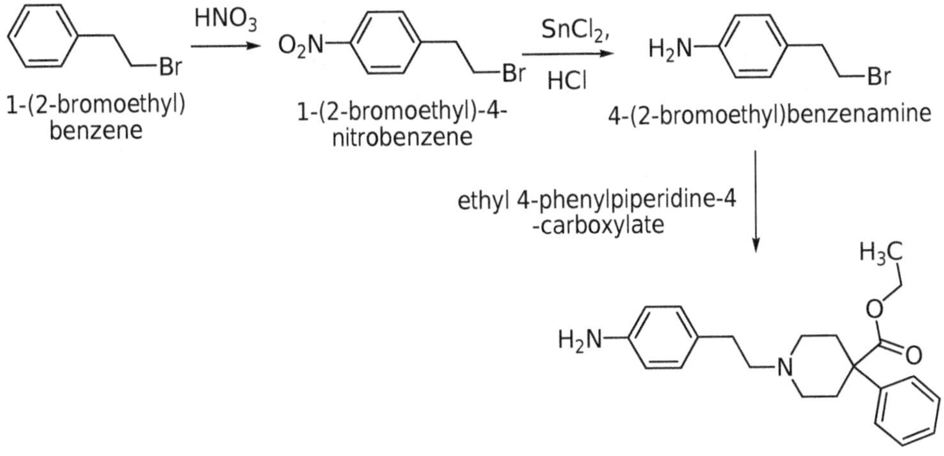

Anileridine

ANTAZOLINE
Use: antihistaminic
Analysis:

[Retrosynthetic scheme: Antazoline ⇒ (C-N disconnection) 4,5-dihydro-1H-imidazol-2-yl cation + N-benzylbenzenamine anion ≡ 2-(chloromethyl)-4,5-dihydro-1H-imidazole + N-benzylbenzenamine]

Synthesis:

N-benzylbenzenamine + 2-(chloromethyl)-4,5-dihydro-1H-imidazole → **Antazoline**

ASPIRIN
Use: analgesic, antipyretic
Analysis:

[Retrosynthetic scheme: Aspirin ⇒ (C-O disconnection) acetyl cation + 2-hydroxybenzoate anion ≡ acetic anhydride + 2-hydroxybenzoic acid]

Synthesis:

2-hydroxybenzoic acid + Acetic anhydride → **Aspirin**

AZAPETINE

Use: sympatholytic, vasodilator

Analysis:

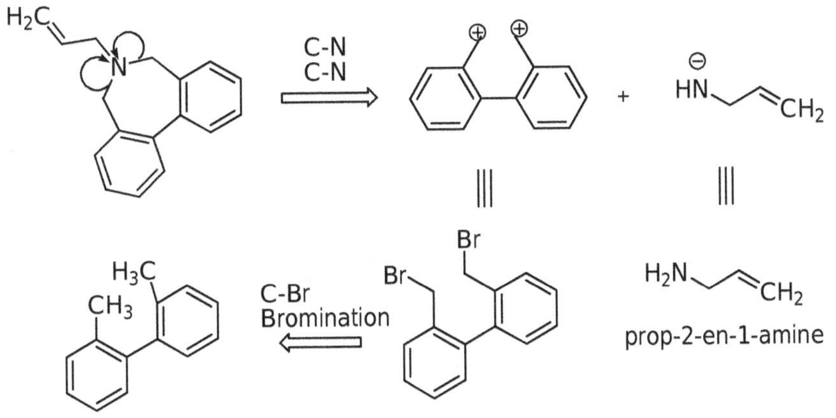

Synthesis:

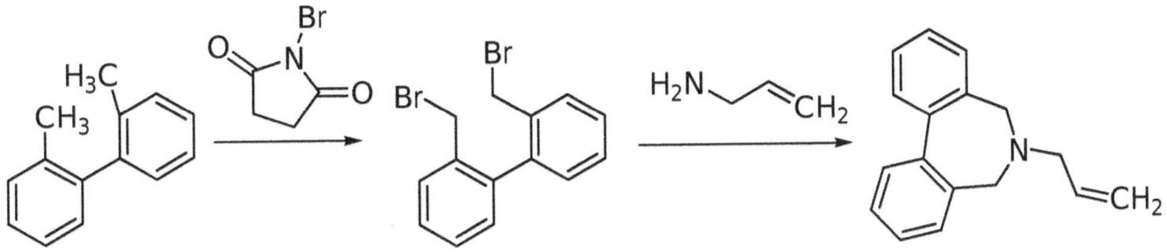

Azapetine

BAMIFYLLINE

Use: bronchodilator

Analysis:

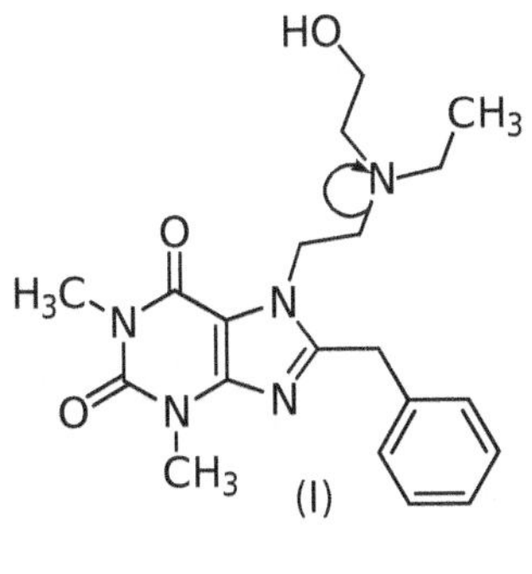

(I)

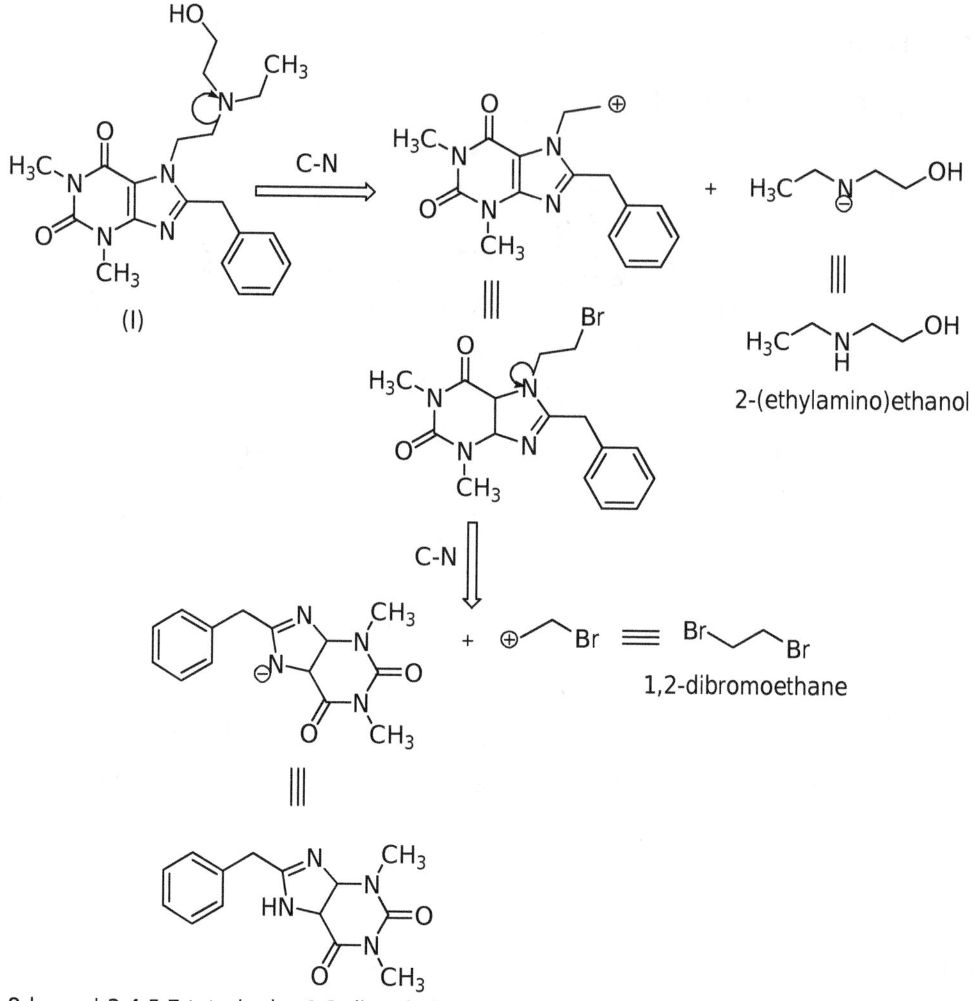

Retrosynthetic Analysis and Synthesis of Drugs

Synthesis:

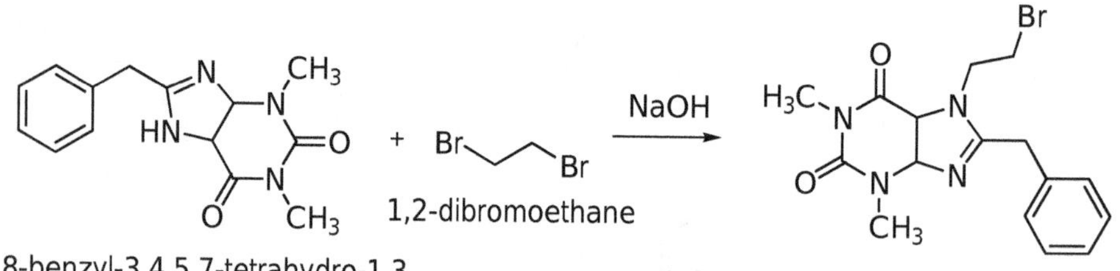

8-benzyl-3,4,5,7-tetrahydro-1,3-dimethyl-1H-purine-2,6-dione + 1,2-dibromoethane →(NaOH) 8-benzyl-7-(2-bromoethyl)-3,4,5,7-tetrahydro-1,3-dimethyl-1H-purine-2,6-dione (I)

Retrosynthetic Analysis and Synthesis of Drugs

Bamifylline

(I) + H₃C-NH-CH₂CH₂-OH → Bamifylline

BECLOBRATE

Use: hyperlipidemic

Analysis:

Retrosynthetic disconnections:

- C-O disconnection yields 4-chloro-4'-hydroxydiphenylmethane anion + ethyl 2-methyl-2-butyl cation (ethyl ester of 2-methylbutanoic acid)
- C-C disconnection of 4-chloro-4'-hydroxydiphenylmethane yields 4-chlorophenyl cation + phenolate

Starting materials:
- 1-chloro-4-(chloromethyl)benzene
- phenol

Bromination (C-Br) of ethyl 2-methylbutanoate gives ethyl 2-bromo-2-methylbutanoate.

C-O disconnection of ethyl 2-methylbutanoate yields:
- 2-methylbutanoic acid (H₃C-CH₂-CH(CH₃)-COOH) ≡ 2-methylbutanoyl cation
- ethoxide / ethanol

Synthesis:

[Scheme: 2-methylbutanoic acid + ethanol → 3-methylheptan-4-one → (Br₂) → ethyl 2-bromo-2-methylbutanoate (I)]

[Scheme: 1-chloro-4-(chloromethyl)benzene + Phenol → (ZnCl) → 4-(4-chlorobenzyl)phenol (II)]

[Scheme: (I) + (II) → (NaH) → **Beclobrate**]

BENAPRIZINE

Use: antiparkinsonian

Analysis:

[Retrosynthetic scheme showing C-O disconnection of benaprizine into 2-(N-ethyl-N-propylamino)ethanol and methyl 2-hydroxy-2,2-diphenylacetate via acyl cation equivalent]

Synthesis:

methyl 2-hydroxy-2,2-diphenylacetate + 2-(N-ethyl-N-propylamino)ethanol → (NaOCH₃) → **Benaprizine**

BENORYLATE

Use: analgesic, antirheumatic

Analysis:

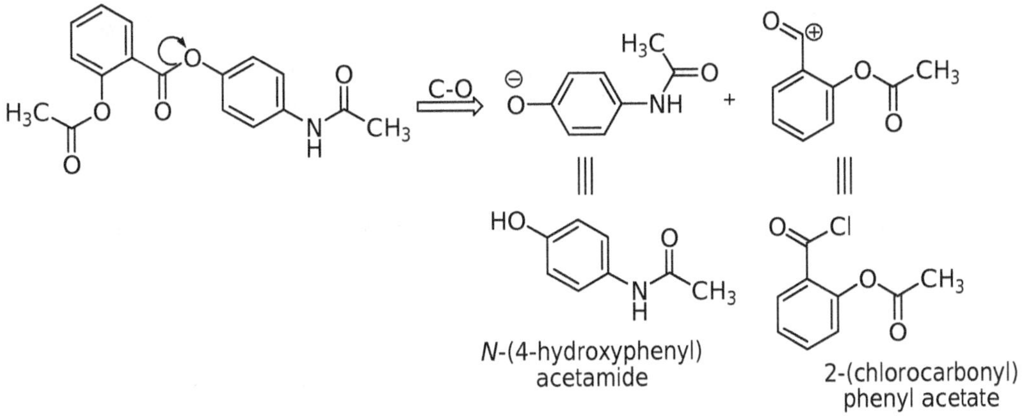

[Retrosynthetic scheme: Benorylate is disconnected at the C–O ester bond to give an acetamidophenoxide anion and an acylium cation of 2-acetoxybenzoyl, corresponding to the synthons N-(4-hydroxyphenyl)acetamide and 2-(chlorocarbonyl)phenyl acetate.]

N-(4-hydroxyphenyl) acetamide

2-(chlorocarbonyl) phenyl acetate

Synthesis:

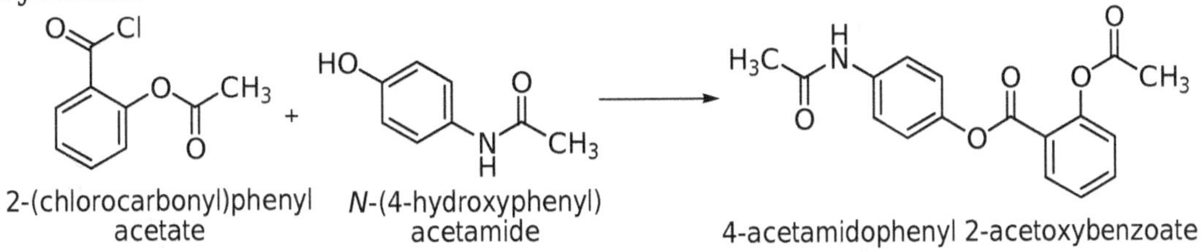

2-(chlorocarbonyl)phenyl acetate + N-(4-hydroxyphenyl) acetamide → 4-acetamidophenyl 2-acetoxybenzoate

Benorylate

BENSERAZIDE

Use: antiparkinsonian

Analysis:

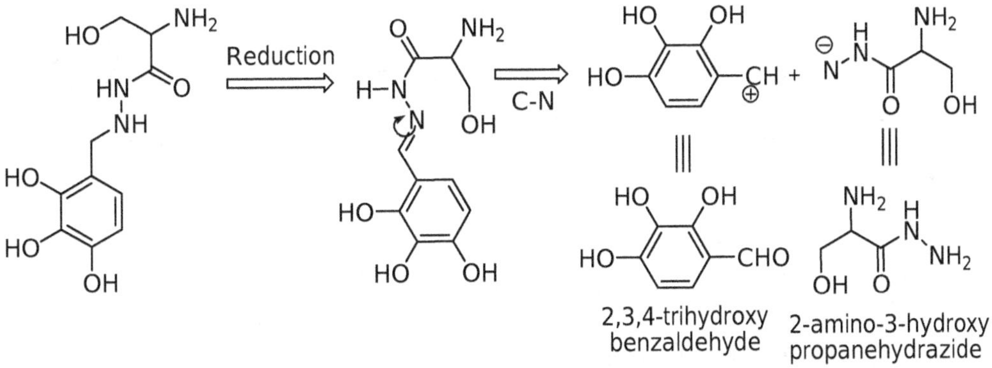

[Retrosynthetic scheme: Benserazide is analyzed by Reduction of the C=N imine to give an intermediate hydrazone, then disconnected at the C–N bond to give 2,3,4-trihydroxybenzaldehyde and 2-amino-3-hydroxy propanehydrazide.]

2,3,4-trihydroxy benzaldehyde

2-amino-3-hydroxy propanehydrazide

Synthesis:

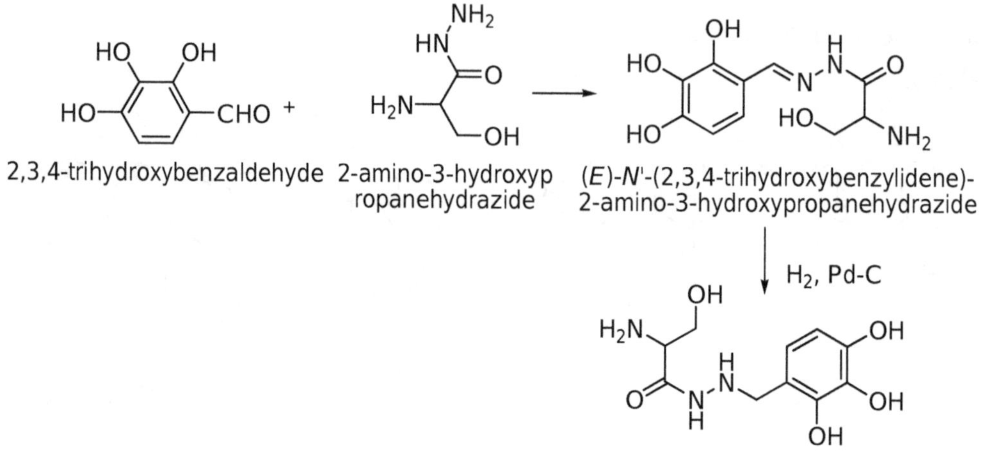
2,3,4-trihydroxybenzaldehyde
2-amino-3-hydroxyp ropanehydrazide
(*E*)-*N'*-(2,3,4-trihydroxybenzylidene)-2-amino-3-hydroxypropanehydrazide
H2, Pd-C

Benserazide

BENTIROMIDE

Use: pancrease function diagnostic

Analysis:

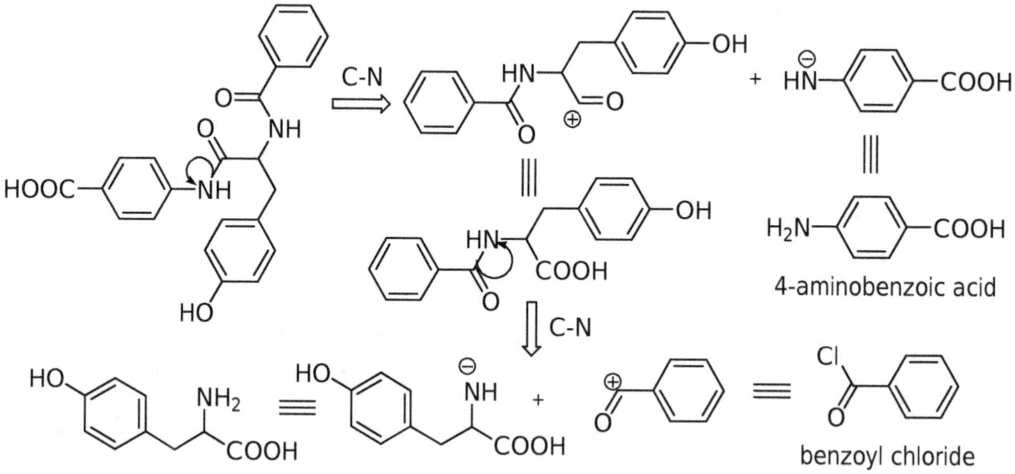
C-N
C-N
4-aminobenzoic acid
benzoyl chloride

Synthesis:

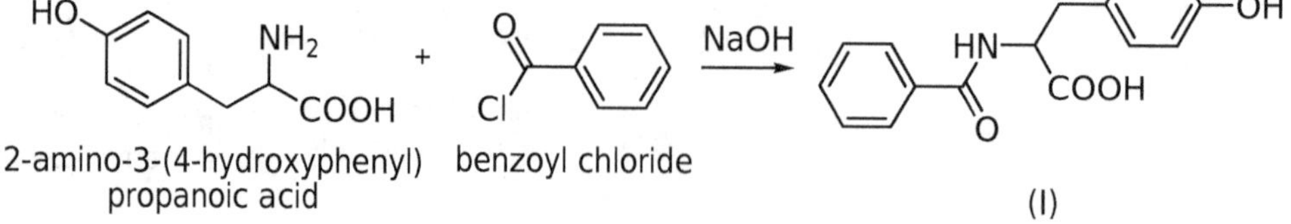
NaOH
2-amino-3-(4-hydroxyphenyl) propanoic acid
benzoyl chloride

(I)

Retrosynthetic Analysis and Synthesis of Drugs

(I) H₂N—C₆H₄—COOH + N-methylmorpholine, ClCOOC₂H₅ → **Bentiromide**

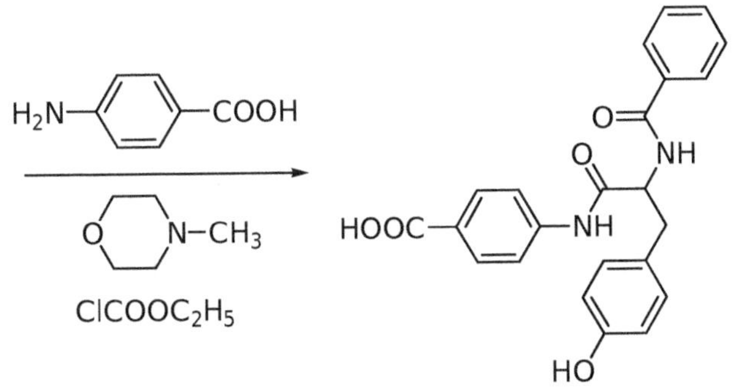

BENZPHETAMINE

Use: appetite depressant

Analysis:

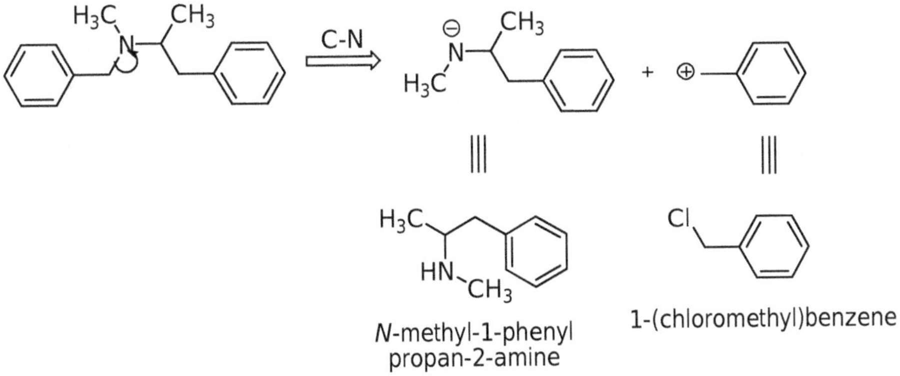

Benzphetamine ⇒ (C-N) N-methyl-1-phenylpropan-2-amine (anion) + phenyl cation

≡ N-methyl-1-phenylpropan-2-amine + 1-(chloromethyl)benzene

Synthesis:

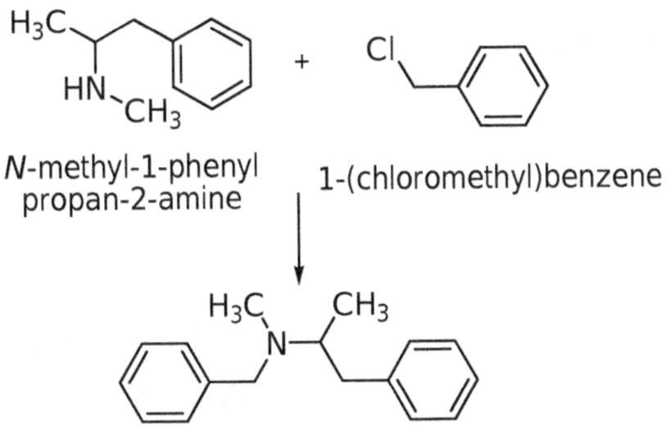

N-methyl-1-phenylpropan-2-amine + 1-(chloromethyl)benzene → **Benzphetamine**

BETHANECHOL

Use: parasympathomimetic

Analysis:

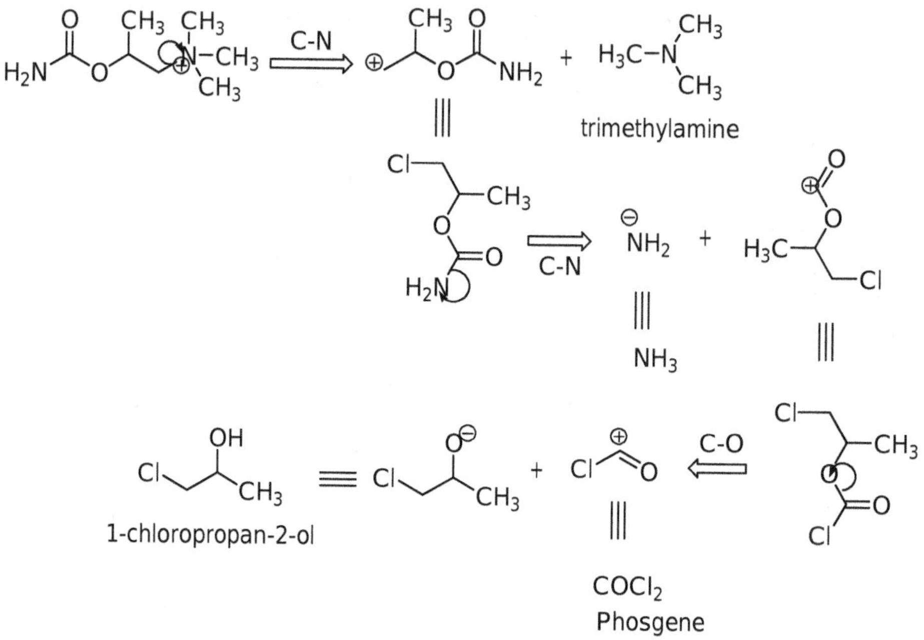

[Retrosynthetic analysis showing bethanechol broken down via C-N disconnection to a carbamate cation and trimethylamine; the carbamate (1-chloropropan-2-yl carbamate) broken via C-N to give NH₃ and a chloropropyl chloroformate; then via C-O disconnection to 1-chloropropan-2-ol and phosgene (COCl₂).]

1-chloropropan-2-ol

trimethylamine

NH₃

COCl₂
Phosgene

Synthesis:

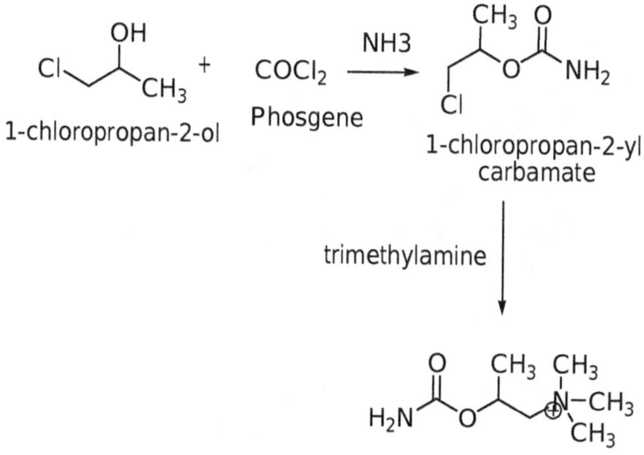

1-chloropropan-2-ol + COCl₂ (Phosgene) →[NH₃] 1-chloropropan-2-yl carbamate →[trimethylamine] **Bethanechol**

BEVANTOLOL

Use: cardioselctive β_1-adrenoreceptor blocker

Analysis:

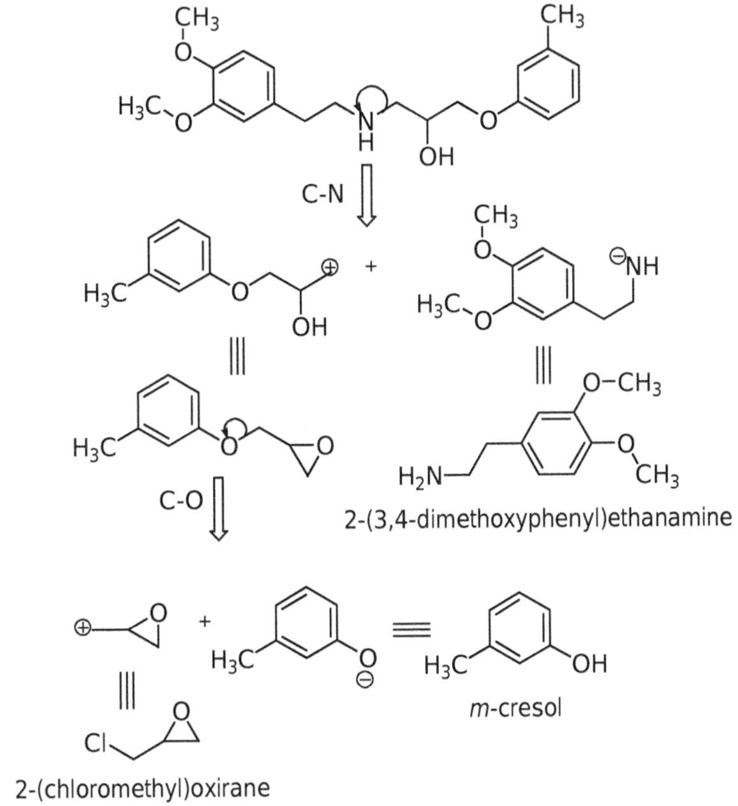

The target molecule is disconnected at the C–N bond to give a cation fragment derived from 1-(m-tolyloxy)-3-hydroxypropane and an amide anion from 2-(3,4-dimethoxyphenyl)ethanamine. The cation synthon corresponds to 2-((m-tolyloxy)methyl)oxirane, and the amide synthon corresponds to 2-(3,4-dimethoxyphenyl)ethanamine.

Further C–O disconnection of the oxirane gives 2-(chloromethyl)oxirane (epichlorohydrin) and m-cresol.

Synthesis:

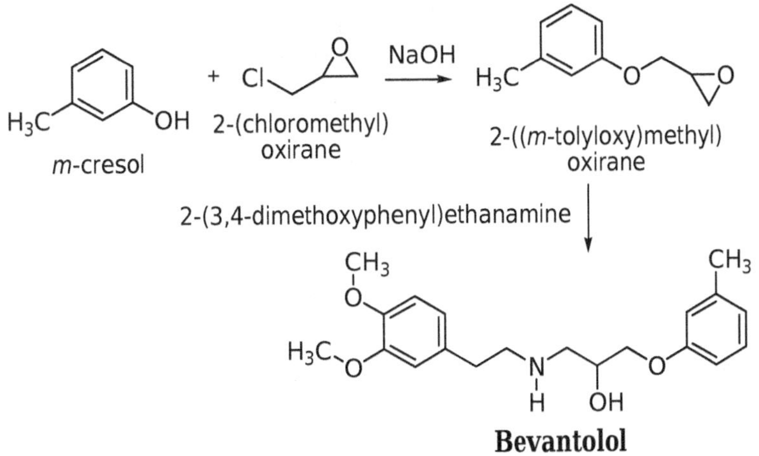

m-cresol + 2-(chloromethyl)oxirane $\xrightarrow{\text{NaOH}}$ 2-((m-tolyloxy)methyl)oxirane

2-((m-tolyloxy)methyl)oxirane + 2-(3,4-dimethoxyphenyl)ethanamine $\longrightarrow$ **Bevantolol**

BISACODYL

Use: laxative

Analysis:

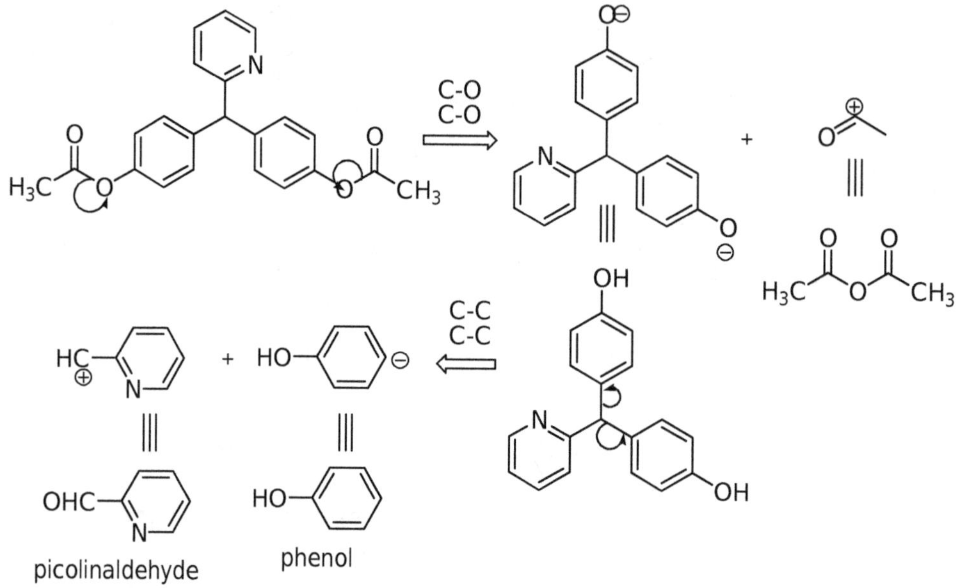

[Retrosynthetic analysis showing bisacodyl disconnecting via C-O/C-O cleavage to give the bis-phenol intermediate plus acetic anhydride, then via C-C/C-C disconnection to give 2-picolyl cation (from picolinaldehyde) and phenol.]

picolinaldehyde + phenol

Synthesis:

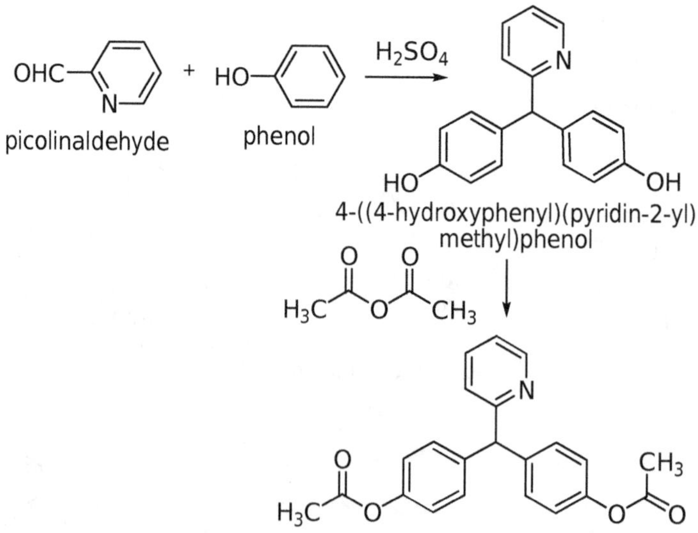

picolinaldehyde + phenol →(H₂SO₄) 4-((4-hydroxyphenyl)(pyridin-2-yl)methyl)phenol

→ (acetic anhydride) **Bisacodyl**

BITOLTEROL

Use: bronchodilator

Analysis:

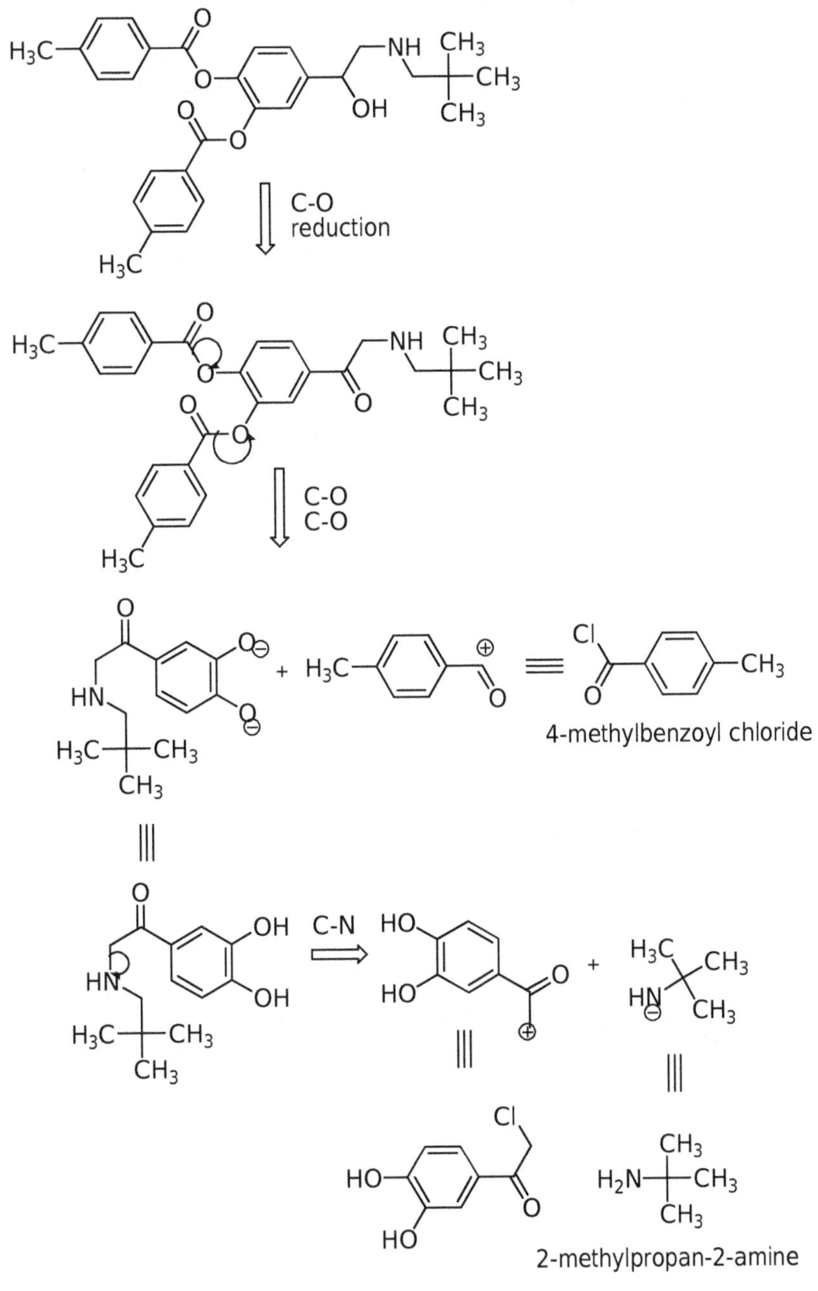
C-O
reduction
C-O
C-O
C-N
4-methylbenzoyl chloride
2-methylpropan-2-amine

Synthesis:

[Scheme: 2-chloro-1-(3,4-dihydroxyphenyl)ethanone + 2-methylpropan-2-amine → 1-(3,4-dihydroxyphenyl)-2-(neopentylamino)ethanone → (with ClOC-C₆H₄-CH₃) bis(4-methylbenzoate) intermediate → (NaBH₄) **Bitolterol**]

BROMDIPHENHYDRAMINE

Use: antihistaminic

Analysis:

[Retrosynthetic scheme: bromdiphenhydramine ⇒ (C–O disconnection) (4-bromophenyl)(phenyl)methyl cation + 2-(dimethylamino)ethanol; alternatively via FGC from (4-bromophenyl)(phenyl)methanol ⇐ the corresponding bromide (4-bromophenyl)(phenyl)methyl bromide]

2-(dimethylamino)ethanol

Retrosynthetic Analysis and Synthesis of Drugs

Synthesis:

(4-bromophenyl)(phenyl)methanol → [PBr, CCl$_4$] → 1-bromo-4-(bromo(phenyl)methyl)benzene → [2-(dimethylamino)ethanol] → **Bromdiphenhydramine**

BROMHEXINE
Use: expectorant

Analysis:

Bromhexine ⇒ [C-Br bromination] ⇒ debrominated aniline intermediate ⇒ [FGC] ⇒ nitro intermediate ⇒ [C-N] ⇒ N-methylcyclohexanamine + 1-(bromomethyl)-2-nitrobenzene

Synthesis:

1-(bromomethyl)-2-nitrobenzene + N-methylcyclohexanamine → N-(2-nitrobenzyl)-N-methylcyclohexanamine → [Raney-Ni, hydrazine] → (I)

(I) → [Br$_2$, CH$_3$COOH] → **Bromhexine**

BUCLOSAMIDE
Use: fungicide
Analysis:

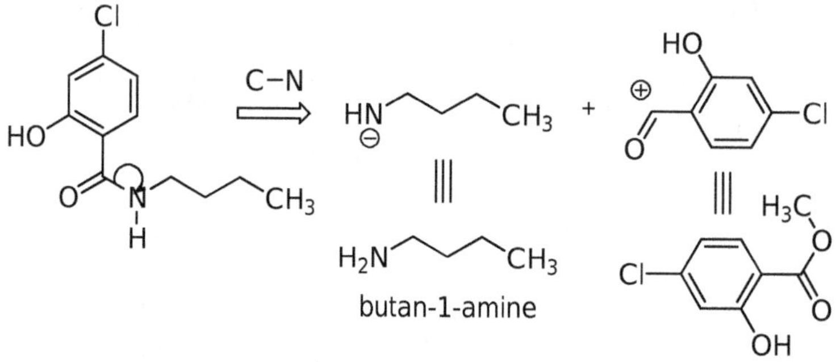

Reagents from retrosynthesis: butan-1-amine; methyl 4-chloro-2-hydroxybenzoate

Synthesis:

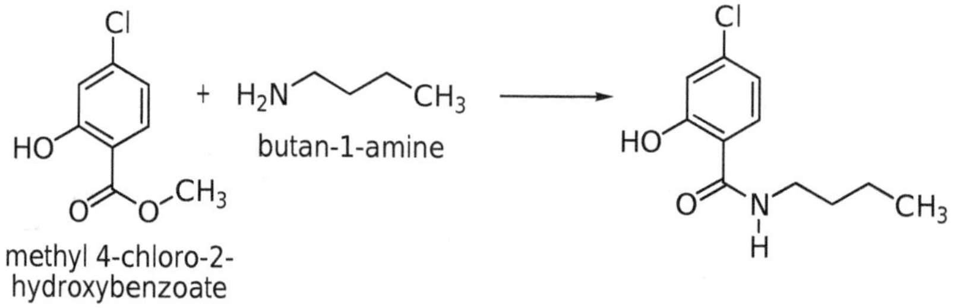

methyl 4-chloro-2-hydroxybenzoate + butan-1-amine → **Buclosamide**

BUDRALAZINE
Use: antihypertensive
Analysis:

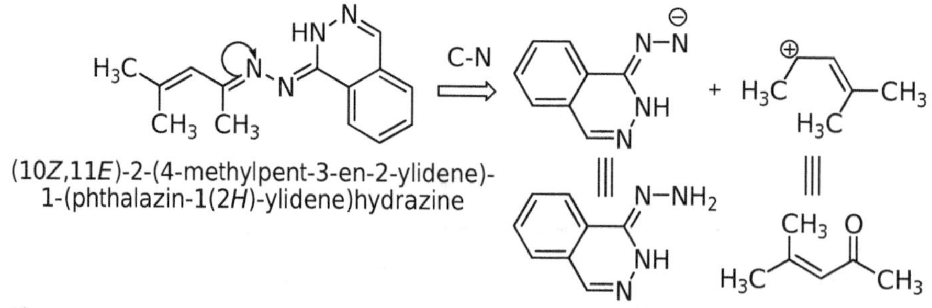

(10Z,11E)-2-(4-methylpent-3-en-2-ylidene)-1-(phthalazin-1(2H)-ylidene)hydrazine

Synthesis:

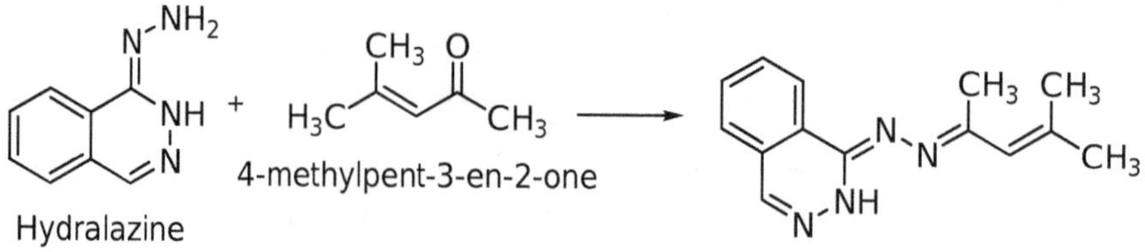

Hydralazine + 4-methylpent-3-en-2-one → **Budralazine**

BUFETOLOL
Use: β-blocking agent
Analysis:

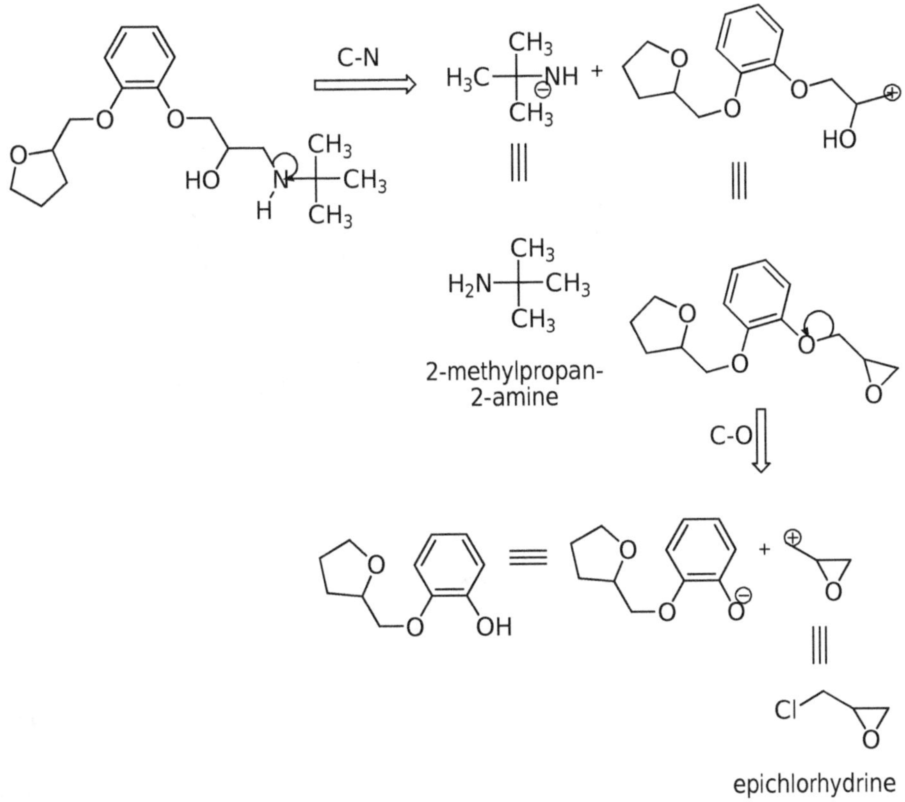

[Retrosynthetic analysis scheme showing C-N disconnection of bufetolol into 2-methylpropan-2-amine and an epoxide intermediate, followed by C-O disconnection into 2-(tetrahydrofuran-2-ylmethoxy)phenol and epichlorhydrine]

Synthesis:

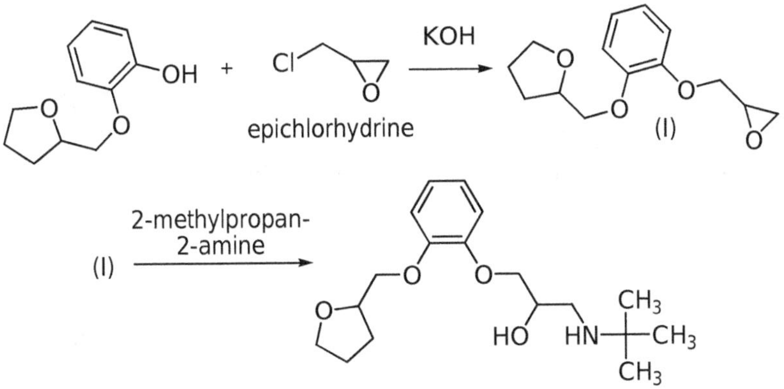

[Synthesis scheme: 2-(tetrahydrofuran-2-ylmethoxy)phenol + epichlorhydrine with KOH → intermediate (I) (epoxide); (I) + 2-methylpropan-2-amine → Bufetolol]

Bufetolol

BUFLOMEDIL

Use: vasodilator

Analysis:

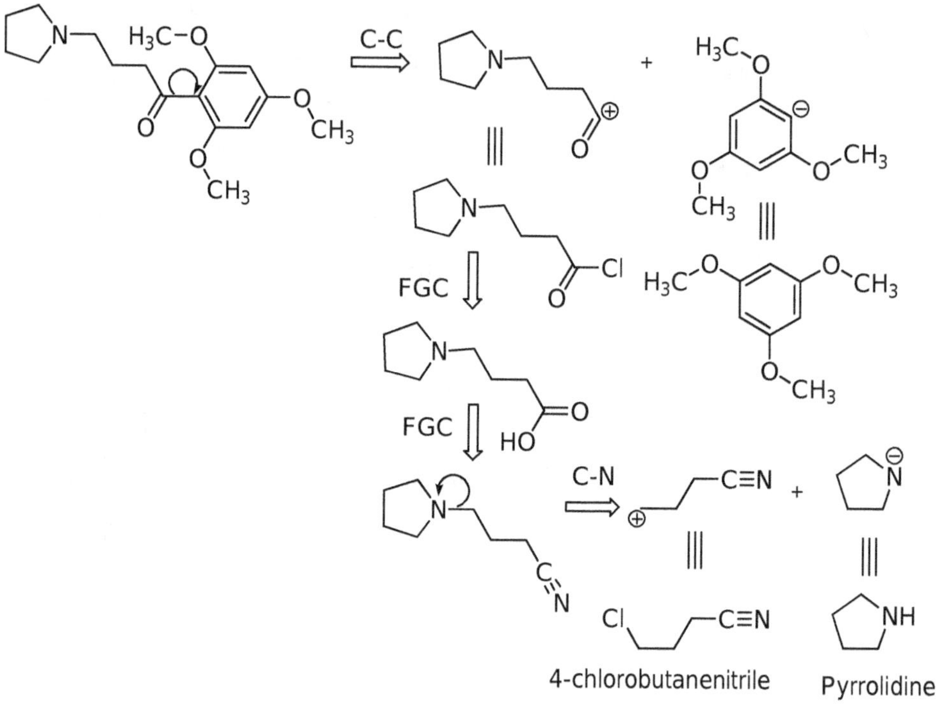
C-C
FGC
FGC
C-N
4-chlorobutanenitrile
Pyrrolidine

Synthesis:

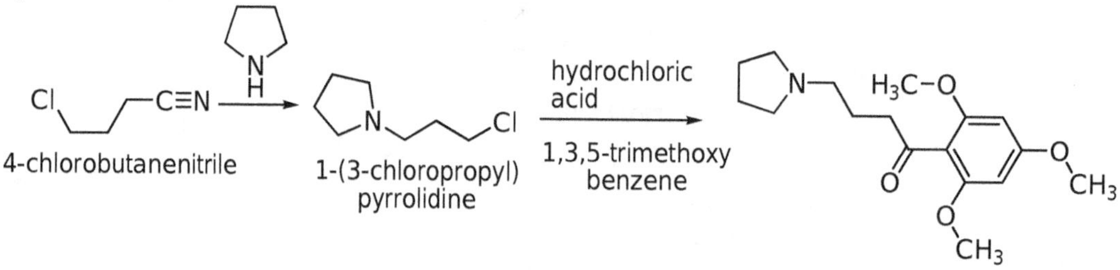
4-chlorobutanenitrile
1-(3-chloropropyl) pyrrolidine
hydrochloric acid
1,3,5-trimethoxy benzene

Buflomedil

BUNITROLOL

Use: β-blocking agent

Analysis:

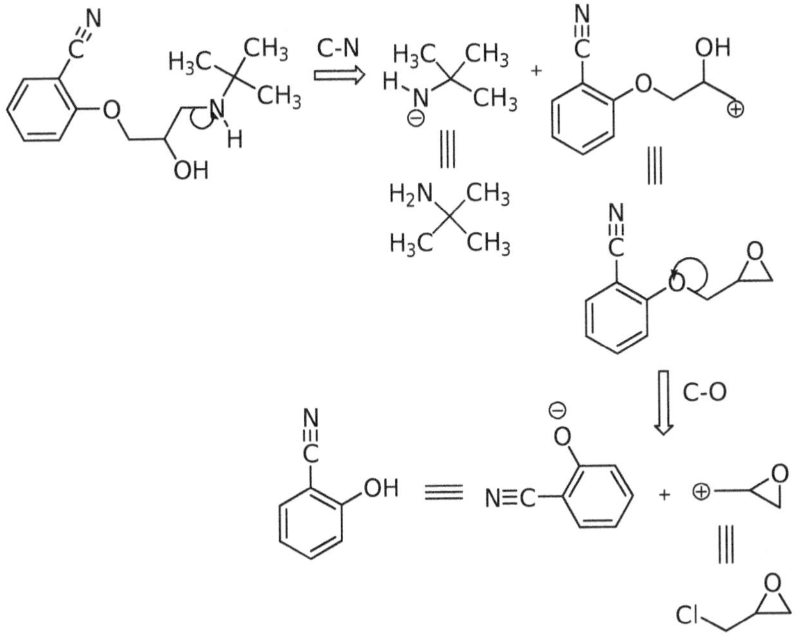

Synthesis:

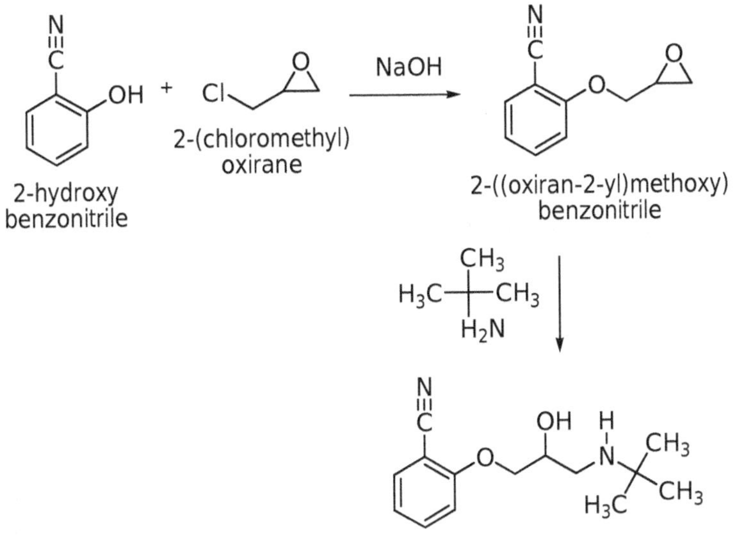

2-hydroxy benzonitrile + 2-(chloromethyl)oxirane →(NaOH) 2-((oxiran-2-yl)methoxy)benzonitrile →(tert-butylamine) **Bunitrolol**

BUSULFAN

Use: antineoplastic

Analysis:

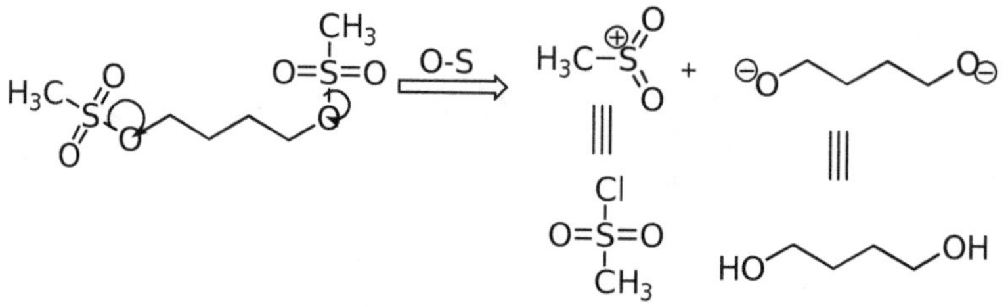

Synthesis:

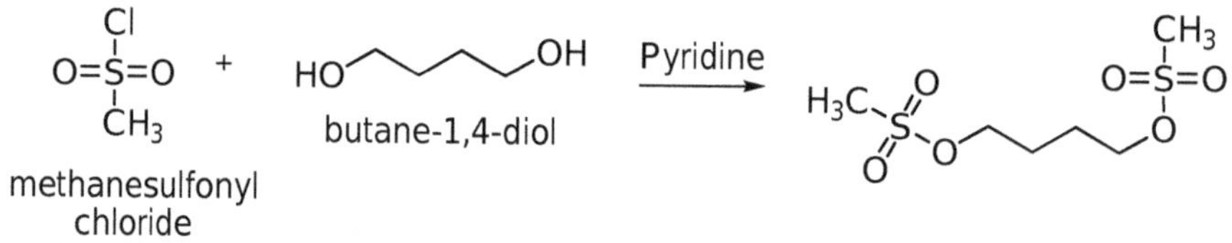

methanesulfonyl chloride + butane-1,4-diol → (Pyridine) → Busulfan

BUTACAINE

Use: local anaesthetic

Analysis:

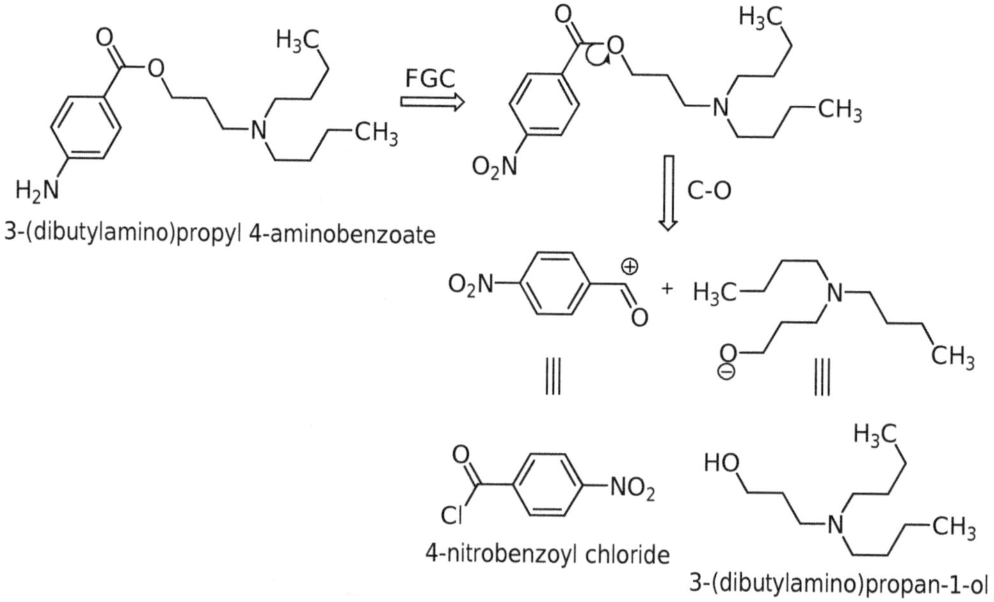

3-(dibutylamino)propyl 4-aminobenzoate

4-nitrobenzoyl chloride + 3-(dibutylamino)propan-1-ol

Synthesis:

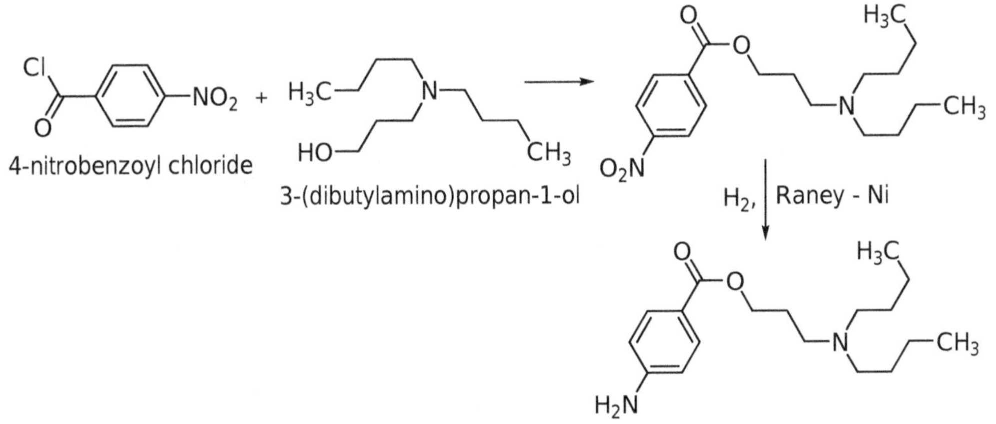

4-nitrobenzoyl chloride + 3-(dibutylamino)propan-1-ol → (intermediate) →[H$_2$, Raney-Ni] **Butacaine**

BUTALAMINE

Use: vasodilator

Analysis:

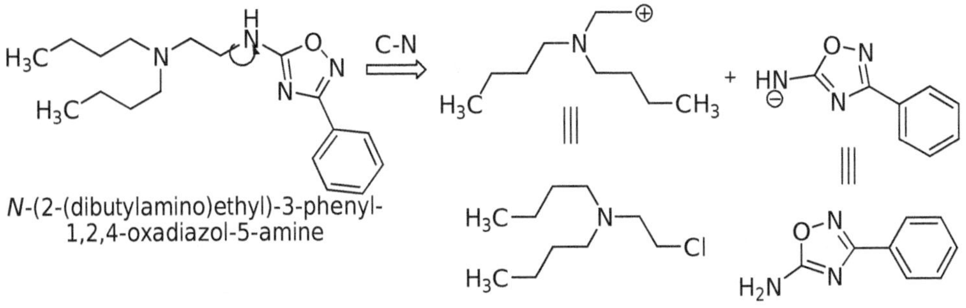

N-(2-(dibutylamino)ethyl)-3-phenyl-1,2,4-oxadiazol-5-amine ⇒[C-N] dibutylaminomethyl cation + 5-amino-3-phenyl-1,2,4-oxadiazole anion

≡ N-butyl-N-(2-chloroethyl)butan-1-amine + 3-phenyl-1,2,4-oxadiazol-5-amine

Synthesis:

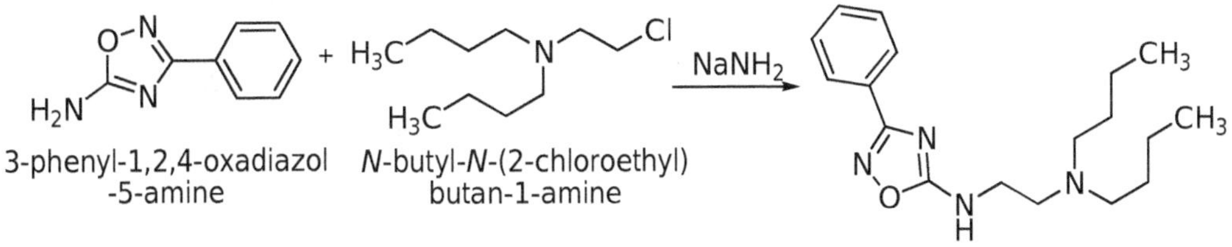

3-phenyl-1,2,4-oxadiazol-5-amine + N-butyl-N-(2-chloroethyl)butan-1-amine →[NaNH$_2$] **Butalamine**

BUTALBITAL
Use: sedative
Analysis:

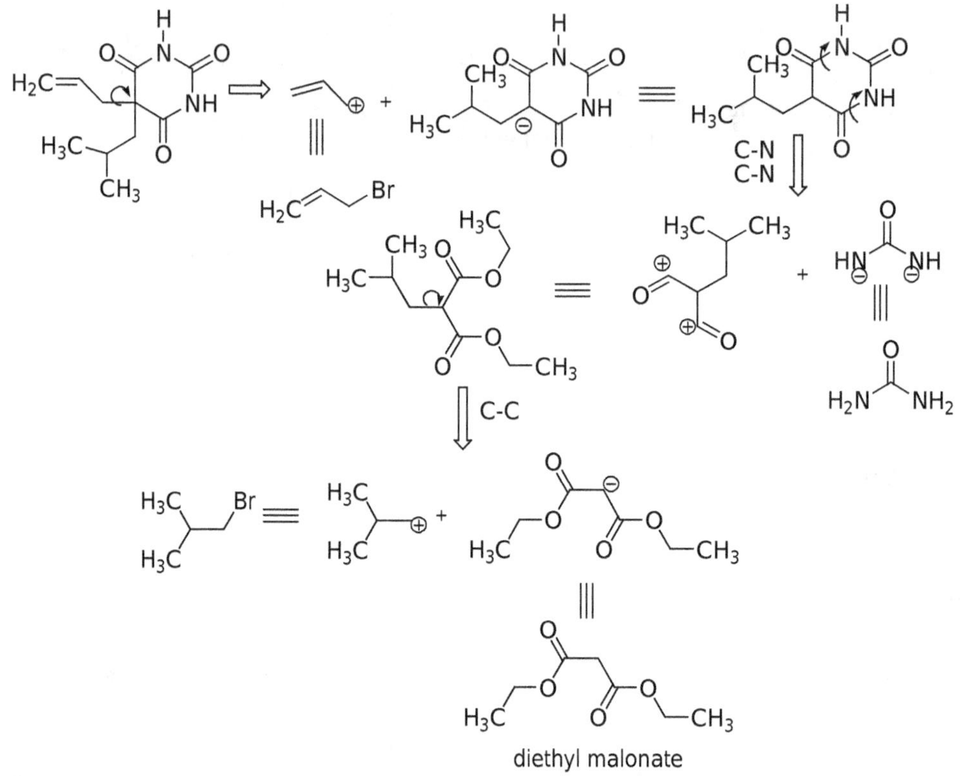

Synthesis:

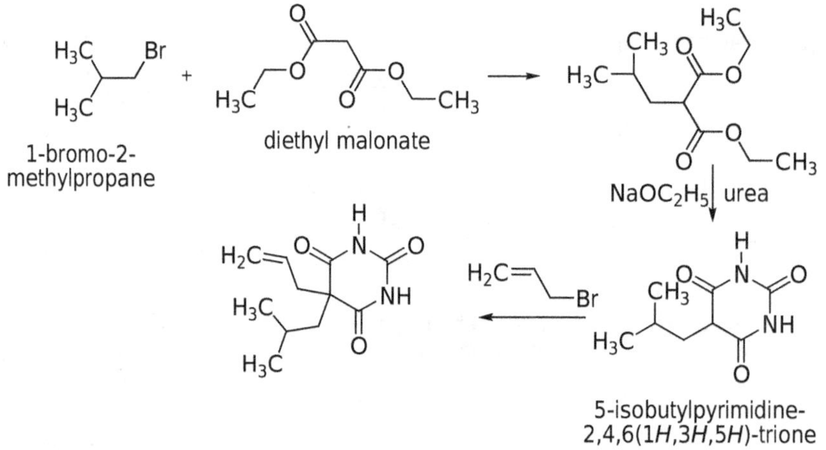

1-bromo-2-methylpropane + diethyl malonate → [alkylated diethyl malonate]

NaOC$_2$H$_5$, urea ↓

5-isobutylpyrimidine-2,4,6(1H,3H,5H)-trione

H$_2$C=CHCH$_2$Br →

Butalbital

BUTAMIRATE
Use: antitussive
Analysis:

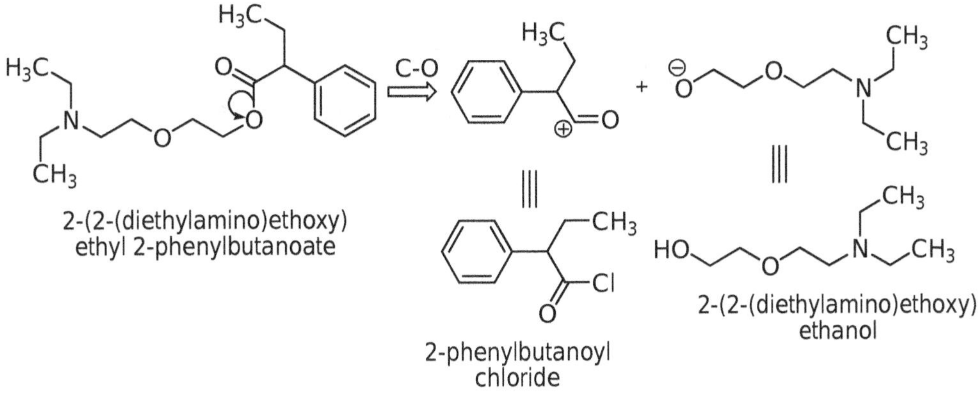

2-(2-(diethylamino)ethoxy)ethyl 2-phenylbutanoate

2-phenylbutanoyl chloride

2-(2-(diethylamino)ethoxy)ethanol

Synthesis:

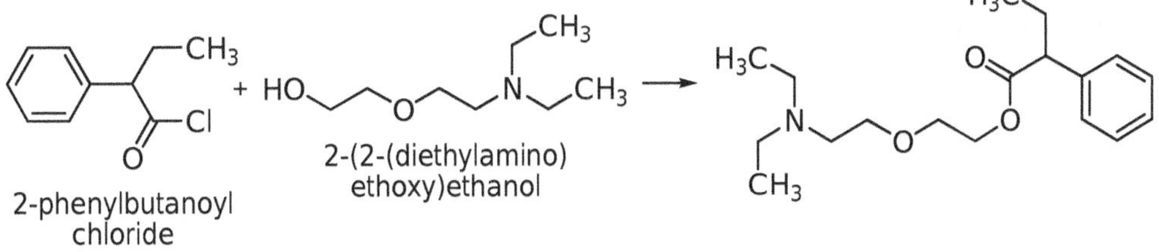

2-phenylbutanoyl chloride + 2-(2-(diethylamino)ethoxy)ethanol → Butamirate

BUTANILICAINE
Use: local anaesthetic
Analysis:

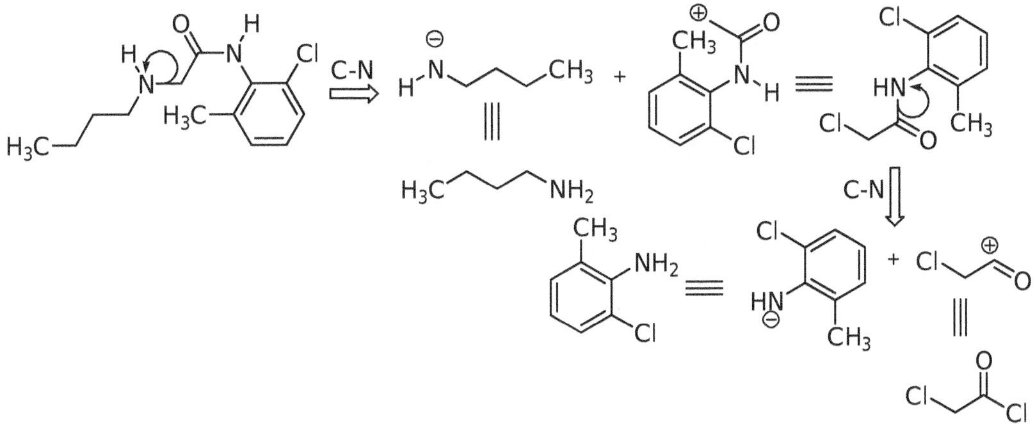

Synthesis:

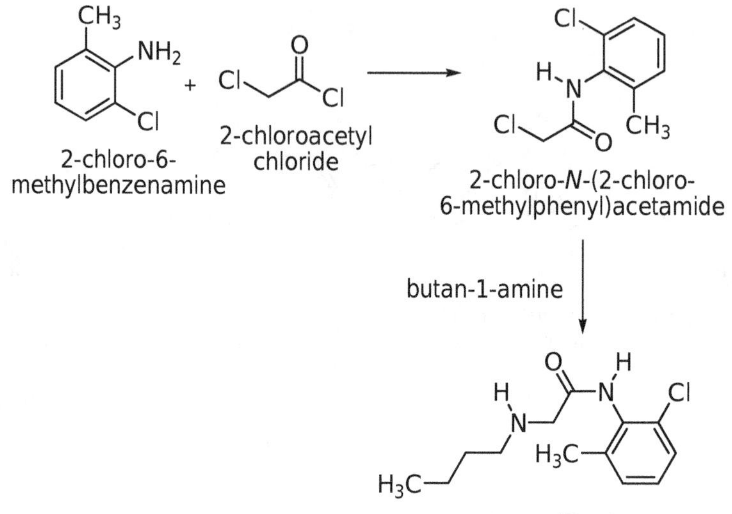

2-chloro-6-methylbenzenamine + 2-chloroacetyl chloride → 2-chloro-N-(2-chloro-6-methylphenyl)acetamide

butan-1-amine ↓

Butanilicaine

BUTETHAMINE
Use: local anaesthetic
Analysis:

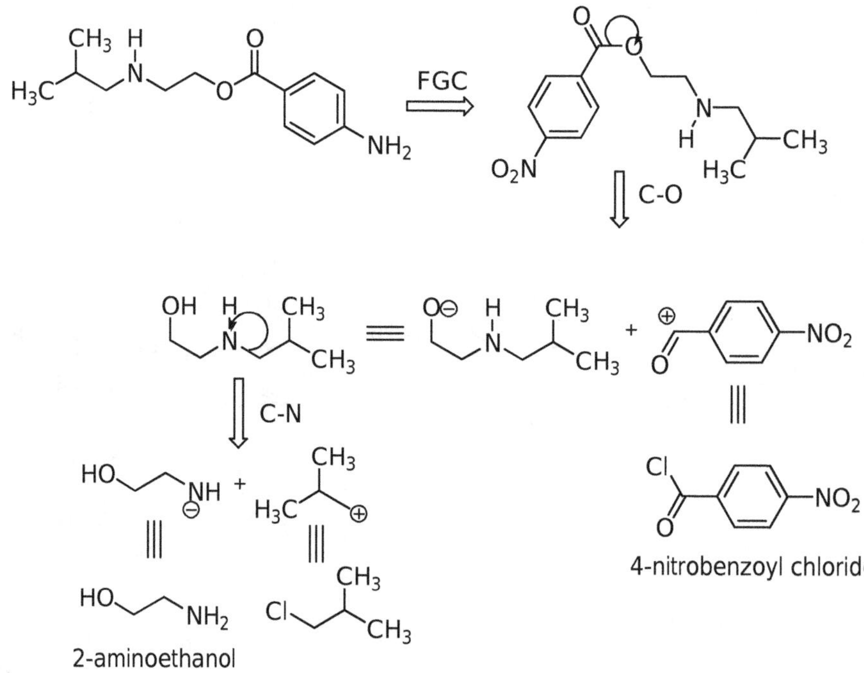

FGC ⇒

⇓ C-O

⇓ C-N

2-aminoethanol

4-nitrobenzoyl chloride

Synthesis:

[Scheme: 2-aminoethanol (HO-CH2-CH2-NH2) + 1-chloro-2-methylpropane (Cl-CH2-CH(CH3)-CH3) →(C2H5OH) 2-(isobutylamino)ethanol (HO-CH2-CH2-NH-CH2-CH(CH3)2) →(NaOH, O2N-C6H4-COCl) 2-(isobutylamino)ethyl 4-nitrobenzoate →(Sn, hydrochloric acid) Butethamine (4-aminobenzoate ester of 2-(isobutylamino)ethanol)]

Butethamine

BUTOFILOLOL

Use: β-blocking agent

Analysis:

[Retrosynthetic scheme for Butofilolol:
- Target: 1-(5-fluoro-2-(2-hydroxy-3-(tert-butylamino)propoxy)phenyl)butan-1-one
- C–N disconnection → epoxide intermediate + tert-butylamine (HN⁻C(CH3)3 ≡ H2N-C(CH3)3)
- C–O disconnection → phenoxide + 2-(chloromethyl)oxirane (Cl-CH2-epoxide)
- C–C disconnection → butyryl cation (CH3-CH2-CH2-CO⁺) ≡ butyryl chloride (CH3-CH2-CH2-COCl) + 4-fluorophenoxide ≡ 4-fluorophenol (HO-C6H4-F)]

Synthesis:

[Scheme: 4-fluorophenol + butyryl chloride → (AlCl₃) → 1-(5-fluoro-2-hydroxyphenyl)butan-1-one → (NaOH, chloromethyloxirane) → 1-(2-((oxiran-2-yl)methoxy)-5-fluorophenyl)butan-1-one → (tert-butylamine, H₂N-C(CH₃)₃) → **Butofilolol**]

CADRALAZINE

Use: antihypertensive, vasodilator

Analysis:

[Retrosynthetic scheme: Cadralazine ⇒ (C-N disconnection) → cation fragment + ethyl carbazate anion; equivalents shown as 1-(N-(6-chloropyridazin-3-yl)-N-ethylamino)propan-2-ol (I) and Ethyl carbozate]

Retrosynthetic Analysis and Synthesis of Drugs

1-(N-(6-chloropyridazin-3-yl)-N-ethylamino)propan-2-ol (I)

Retrosynthetic analysis: C–N disconnection gives H$_3$C-CH$_2$-N$^-$(CH$_2$CH(OH)CH$_3$)(CH$_2$CH$_3$) + 3-chloro-6-pyridazinyl cation (≡ 3,6-dichloropyridazine).

Further C–N disconnection of the aminoalcohol gives 2-methyloxirane (≡ H$_3$C-CH(OH)-CH$_2^+$) + H$_3$C-CH$_2$-NH$^-$ (≡ ethanamine, CH$_3$CH$_2$NH$_2$).

Synthesis:

2-methyloxirane + ethanamine (H$_3$C-CH$_2$-NH$_2$) → **1-(ethylamino)propan-2-ol**

+ 3,6-dichloropyridazine (Cl-C$_4$H$_2$N$_2$-Cl) ↓

1-(N-(6-chloropyridazin-3-yl)-N-ethylamino)propan-2-ol

+ H$_2$N-NH-C(O)-O-CH$_2$CH$_3$ ↓

Cadralazine

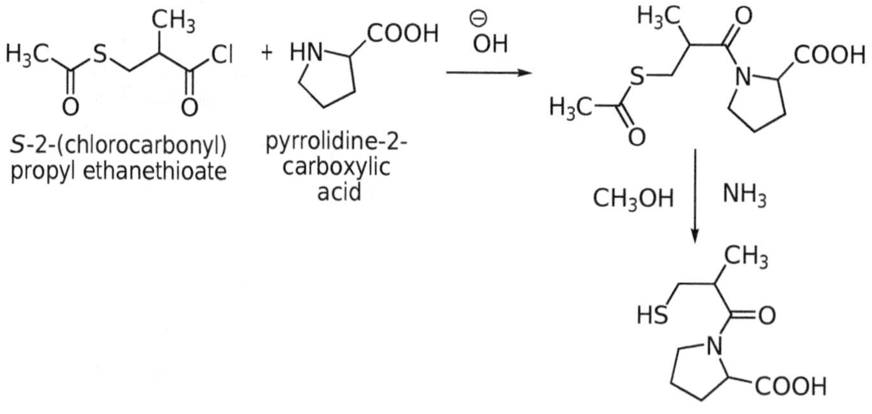

CAPTOPRIL

Use: antihypertensive

Analysis:

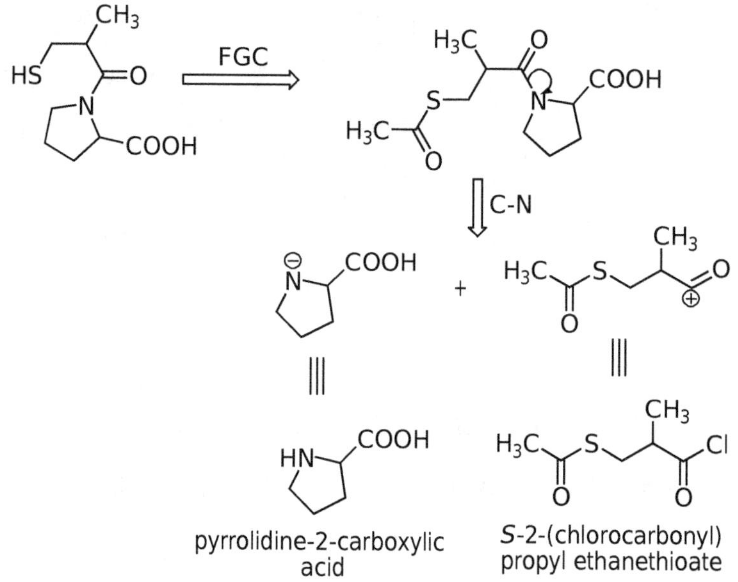

Synthesis:

CARBACHOL

Use: parasympathomimetic

Analysis:

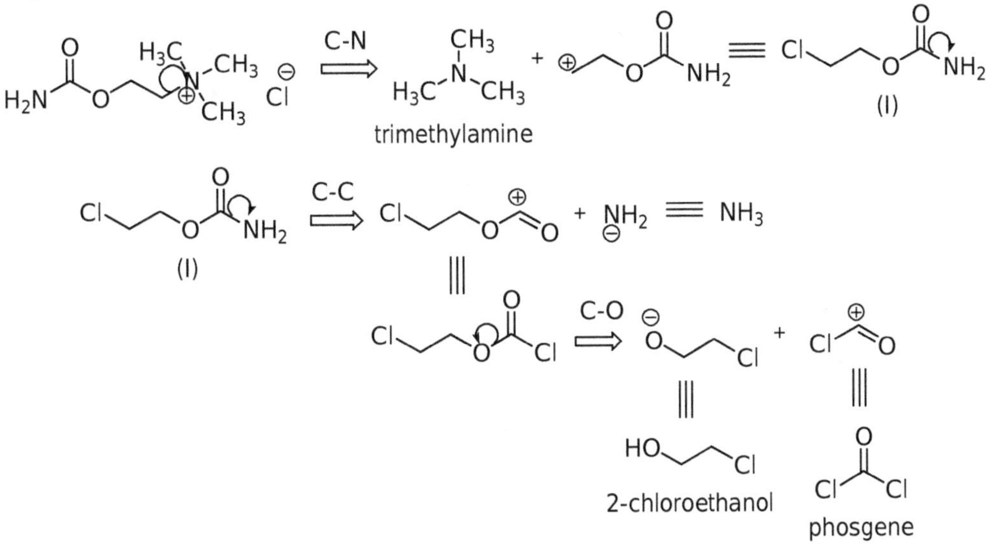

[Retrosynthetic analysis scheme: Carbachol is disconnected at C-N bond to give trimethylamine and 2-chloroethyl carbamate (I). Compound (I) is disconnected at C-C to give 2-chloroethyl chloroformate and ammonia. The chloroformate is disconnected at C-O to give 2-chloroethanol and phosgene.]

Synthesis:

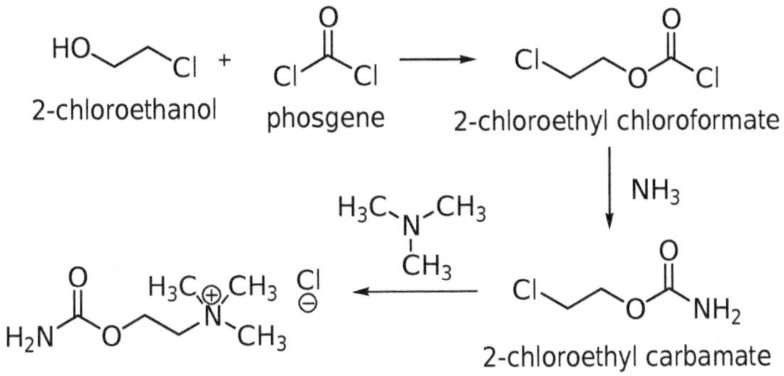

2-chloroethanol + phosgene → 2-chloroethyl chloroformate

$\xrightarrow{NH_3}$ 2-chloroethyl carbamate

$\xrightarrow{(CH_3)_3N}$ **Carbachol**

CARBAMAZEPINE

Use: anticonvulsant

Analysis:

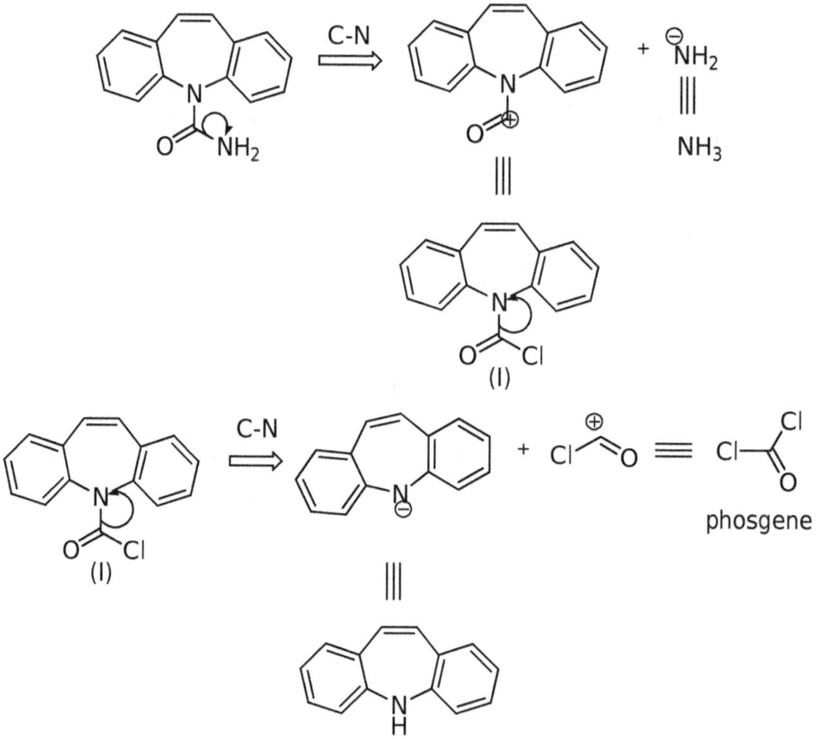
C-N
NH2
NH3
Cl
(I)
C-N
Cl
phosgene
N
H

Synthesis:

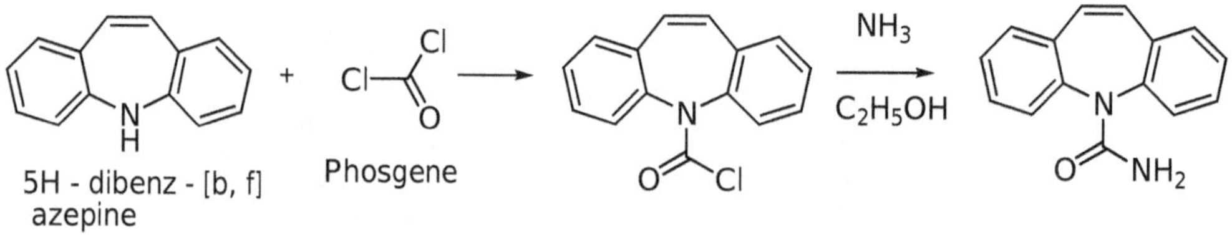
Cl
5H - dibenz - [b, f]
azepine
Phosgene
NH3
C2H5OH
NH2

Carbamazepine

CARBENICILLIN

Use: antibiotic

Analysis:

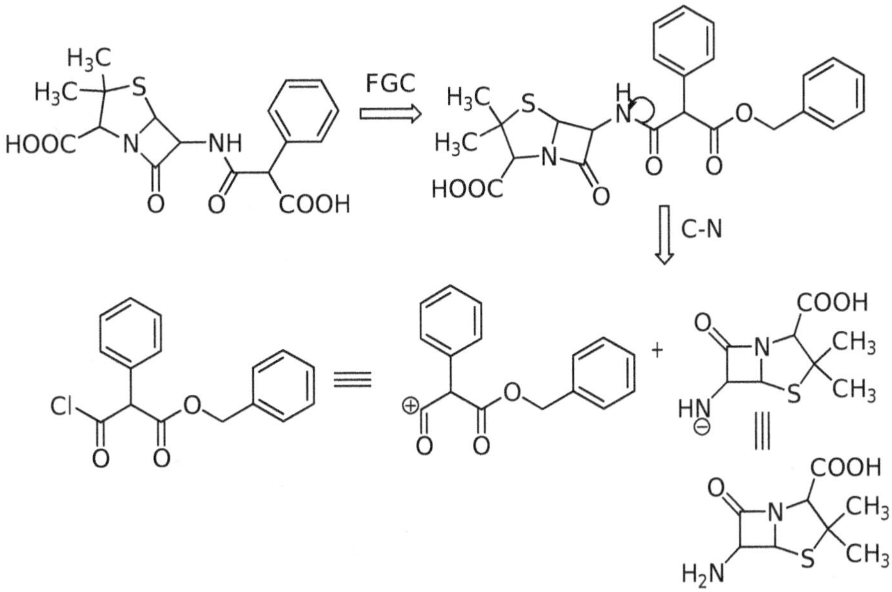

Synthesis:

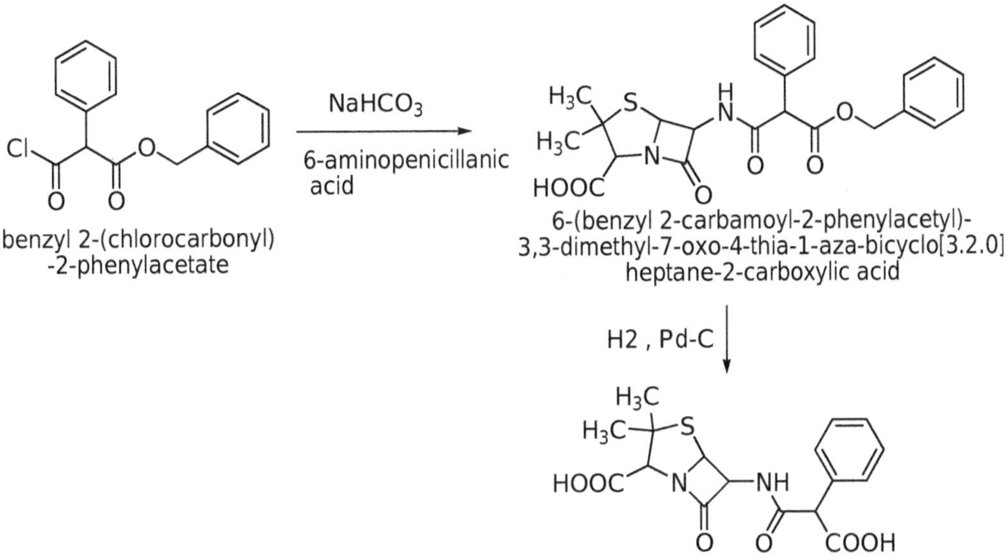

benzyl 2-(chlorocarbonyl)-2-phenylacetate

$\xrightarrow[\text{6-aminopenicillanic acid}]{\text{NaHCO}_3}$

6-(benzyl 2-carbamoyl-2-phenylacetyl)-3,3-dimethyl-7-oxo-4-thia-1-aza-bicyclo[3.2.0]heptane-2-carboxylic acid

$\xrightarrow{\text{H}_2,\ \text{Pd-C}}$

Carbenicillin

CARFECILLIN

Use: antibiotic

Analysis:

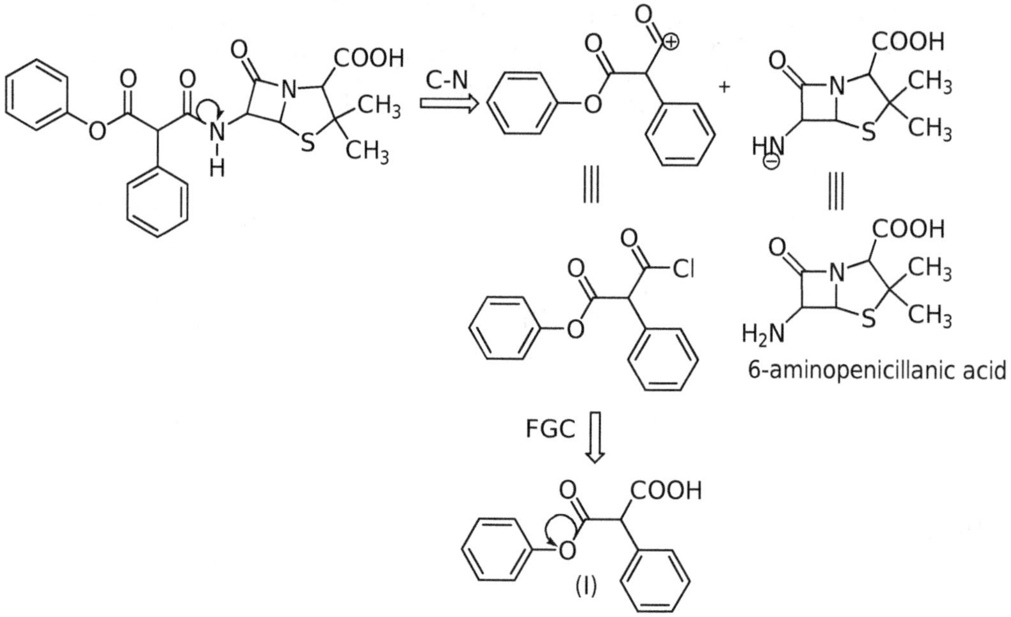
COOH
C-N
CH3
Cl
6-aminopenicillanic acid
FGC
(I)

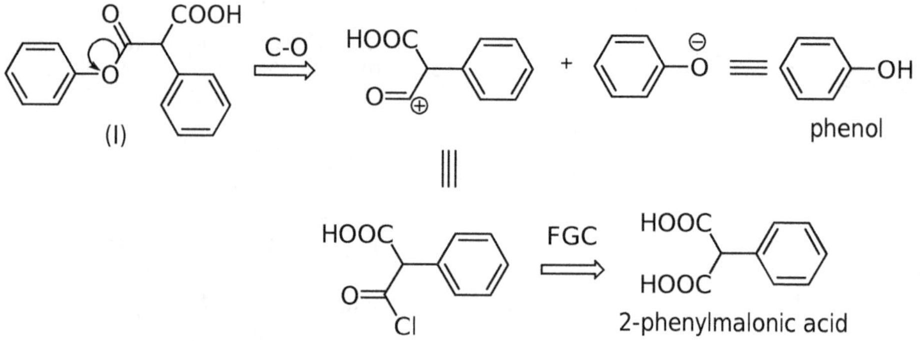
COOH
C-O
HOOC
OH
phenol
(I)
FGC
2-phenylmalonic acid

Synthesis:

[Scheme: 2-phenylmalonic acid → (SOCl₂, DMF) → 2-(chlorocarbonyl)-2-phenylacetic acid → (PhOH, NaHCO₃) → 2-(phenoxycarbonyl)-2-phenylacetic acid → (SOCl₂) → acid chloride → (6-aminopenicillanic acid) → **Carfecillin**]

CARMOFUR
Use: antineoplastic
Analysis:

[Retrosynthetic analysis: Carmofur ⇒ (C–N disconnection) acylated fluorouracil cation + hexan-1-amine; further ⇒ phosgene (Cl–CO–Cl) + 5-fluoropyrimidine-2,4(1H,3H)-dione]

Synthesis:

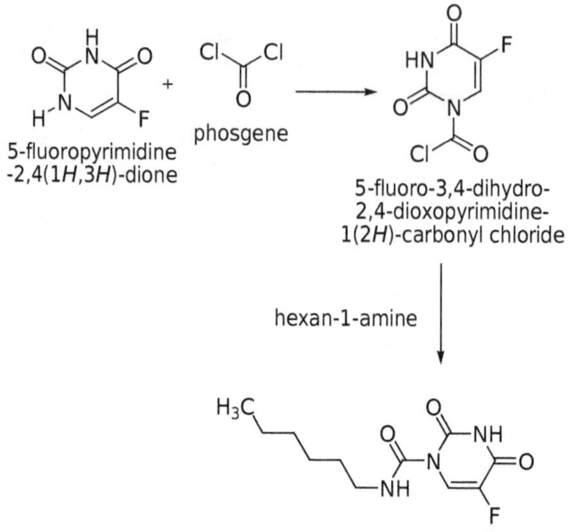

5-fluoropyrimidine-2,4(1*H*,3*H*)-dione + phosgene → 5-fluoro-3,4-dihydro-2,4-dioxopyrimidine-1(2*H*)-carbonyl chloride

↓ hexan-1-amine

Carmofur

CARPHENAZINE
Use: neuroleptic
Analysis:

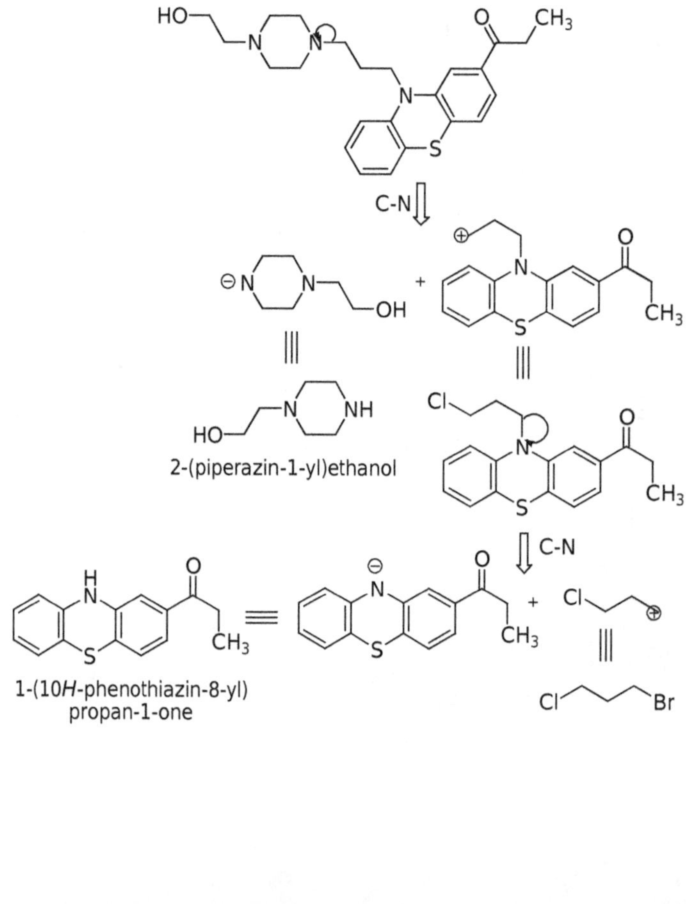

C-N ⇩

2-(piperazin-1-yl)ethanol

⇩ C-N

1-(10*H*-phenothiazin-8-yl)propan-1-one

Cl-CH₂CH₂CH₂-Br

Synthesis:

[Reaction: 1-(10H-phenothiazin-8-yl)propan-1-one + NaH / 1-bromo-3-chloropropane → N-(3-chloropropyl) phenothiazine propanone → (with 2-(piperazin-1-yl)ethanol) → **Carphenazine**]

CARTICAINE

Use: local anaesthetic

Analysis:

[Retrosynthetic analysis of carticaine:
- C-N disconnection → propan-1-amine (H₂N-CH₂-CH₂-CH₃) + methyl 3-(2-bromopropanamido)-4-methylthiophene-2-carboxylate
- C-N disconnection → 2-bromopropanoyl chloride + methyl 3-amino-4-methylthiophene-2-carboxylate]

Synthesis:

methyl 3-amino-4-methyl thiophene-2-carboxylate + 2-bromopropanoyl chloride → [intermediate] → **Carticaine**

CEFAZOLIN
Use: antibiotic
Analysis:

C-S ⇒ [cefazolin cation intermediate] + 5-methyl-1,3,4-thiadiazole-2-thiol

C-N ⇒ 2-(1H-tetrazol-1-yl) acetic acid + 7-amino cephalosporanic acid

Synthesis:

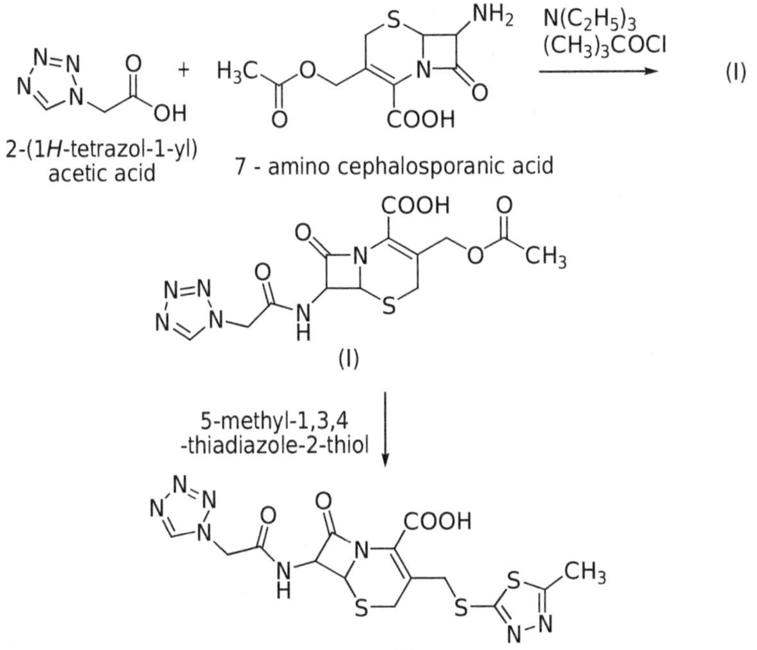

2-(1H-tetrazol-1-yl) acetic acid + 7-amino cephalosporanic acid → [N(C₂H₅)₃, (CH₃)₃COCl] → (I)

(I)

↓ 5-methyl-1,3,4-thiadiazole-2-thiol

Cefazolin

CEPHAPIRIN
Use: antibiotic
Analysis:

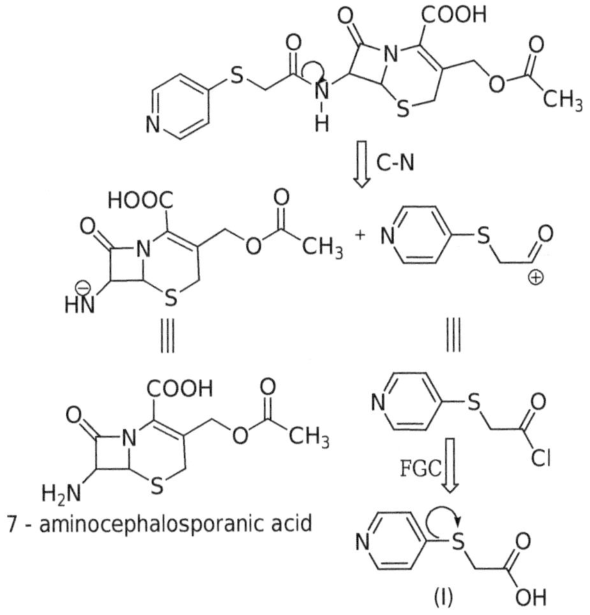

⇓ C–N

7-aminocephalosporanic acid   +   (pyridyl-S-CH₂-COCl)

⇑ FGC

(I) pyridyl-S-CH₂-COOH

Synthesis:

[Retrosynthetic scheme: compound (I) → C-S disconnection → 4-pyridyl cation + thioglycolate anion ≡ 4-chloropyridine + Thioglycolic acid]

4-chloropyridine + 2-mercaptoacetic acid →[NaOH] pyridyl-S-CH₂COOH →[PCl₅] 2-(pyridin-4-ylthio)acetyl chloride →[7-amino cephalosporanic acid] **Cephapirin**

CHLORAMPHENICOL

Use: antibiotic

Analysis:

[Retrosynthetic scheme: Chloramphenicol → C-N disconnection → dichloroacetyl cation + amino diol anion ≡ methyl 2,2-dichloro acetate + 2-amino-1-(4-nitrophenyl)propane-1,3-diol (I)]

Retrosynthetic Analysis and Synthesis of Drugs

Synthesis:

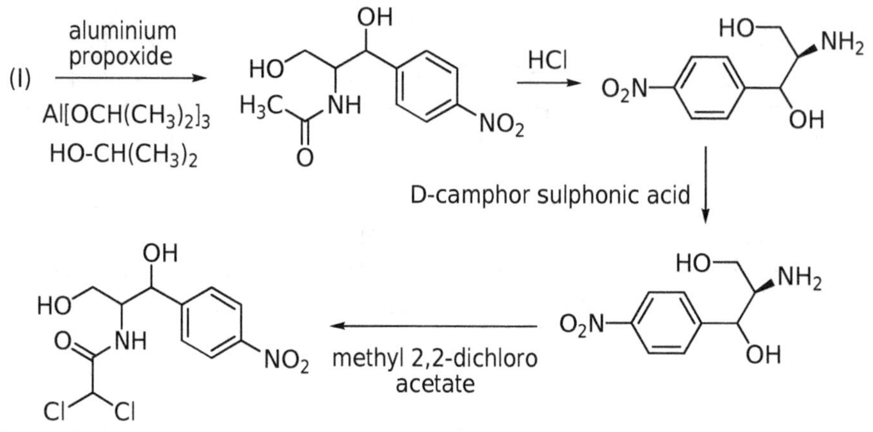

Chloramphenicol

CHLORCYCLIZINE

Use: antihistaminic

Analysis:

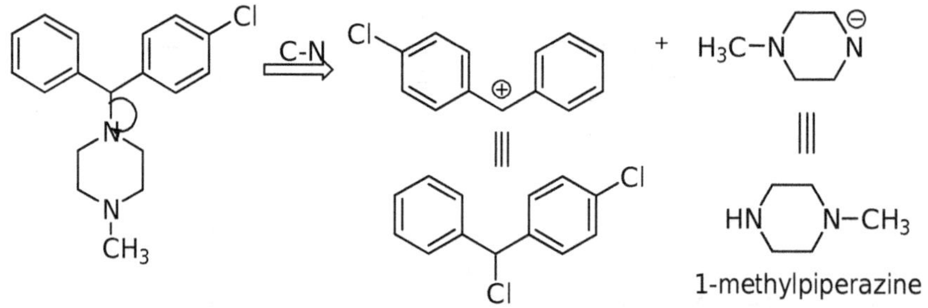

Synthesis:

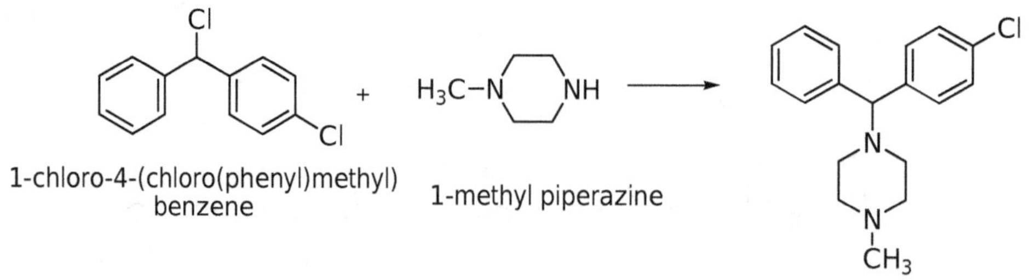

1-chloro-4-(chloro(phenyl)methyl) benzene + 1-methyl piperazine → Chlorcyclizine

CHLOROPHENESIN
Use: antifungal
Analysis:

[Retrosynthetic analysis: chlorophenesin is disconnected at C-O bond to give 4-chlorophenoxide anion and a carbocation from glycerol equivalent; synthons equivalent to 4-chlorophenol and 3-chloropropane-1,2-diol.]

Synthesis:

4-chlorophenol + 3-chloropropane-1,2-diol →(NaOH) Chlorophenesin

CHLOROPHENESIN CARBAMATE
Use: analgesic, muscle relaxant
Analysis:

[Retrosynthetic analysis: C-N disconnection gives chloroformate intermediate + NH₃; further C-O disconnection gives chlorophenesin alkoxide + phosgene (COCl₂).]

Synthesis:

[3-(4-chlorophenoxy)propane-1,2-diol] + COCl₂ → [chloroformate intermediate] →(NH₃)→ **Chlorophenesin Carbamate**

CHLOROPROCAINE

Use: local anaesthetic

Analysis:

Chloroprocaine ⇒(C-O) 4-amino-2-chlorobenzoyl cation + 2-(diethylamino)ethoxide

⇐(FGC) 4-amino-2-chlorobenzoyl chloride + 2-(diethylamino)ethanol

4-amino-2-chlorobenzoic acid

Synthesis:

4-amino-2-chlorobenzoic acid →(SOCl₂)→ 4-amino-2-chlorobenzoyl chloride →(2-(diethylamino)ethanol)→ **Chloroprocaine**

CHLOROPYRILENE
Use: antihistaminic
Analysis:

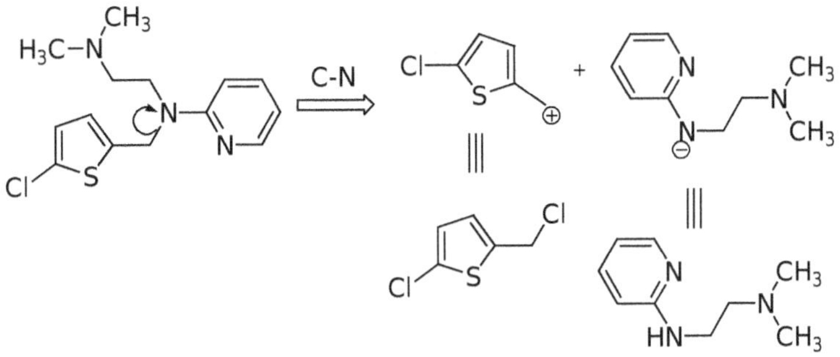

Synthesis:

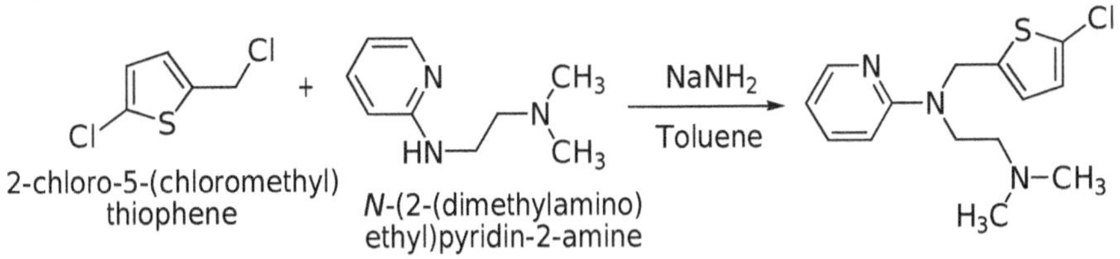

2-chloro-5-(chloromethyl)thiophene + N-(2-(dimethylamino)ethyl)pyridin-2-amine → (NaNH₂, Toluene) → **Chloropyrilene**

CHLOROQUINE
Use: antimalarial
Analysis:

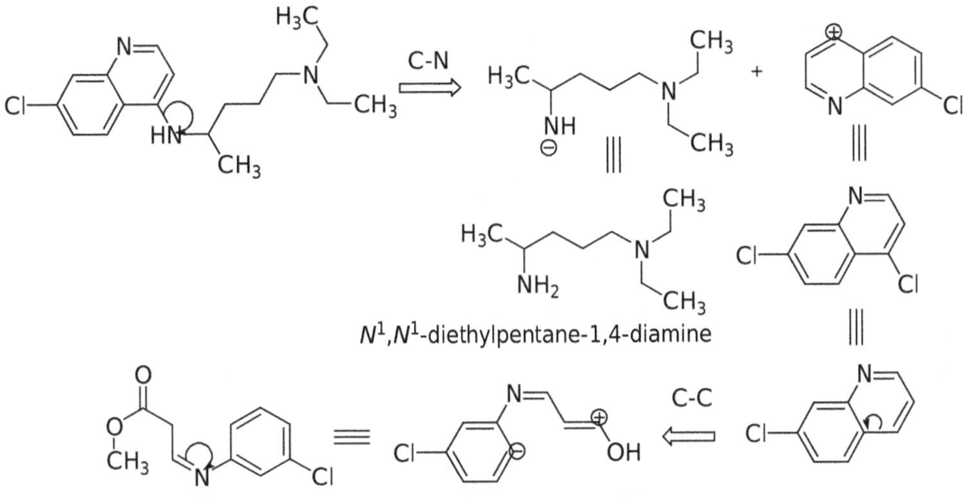

N^1,N^1-diethylpentane-1,4-diamine

(I)

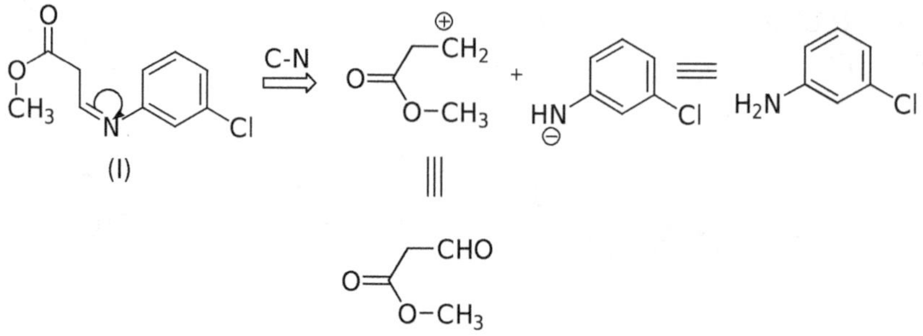

Synthesis:

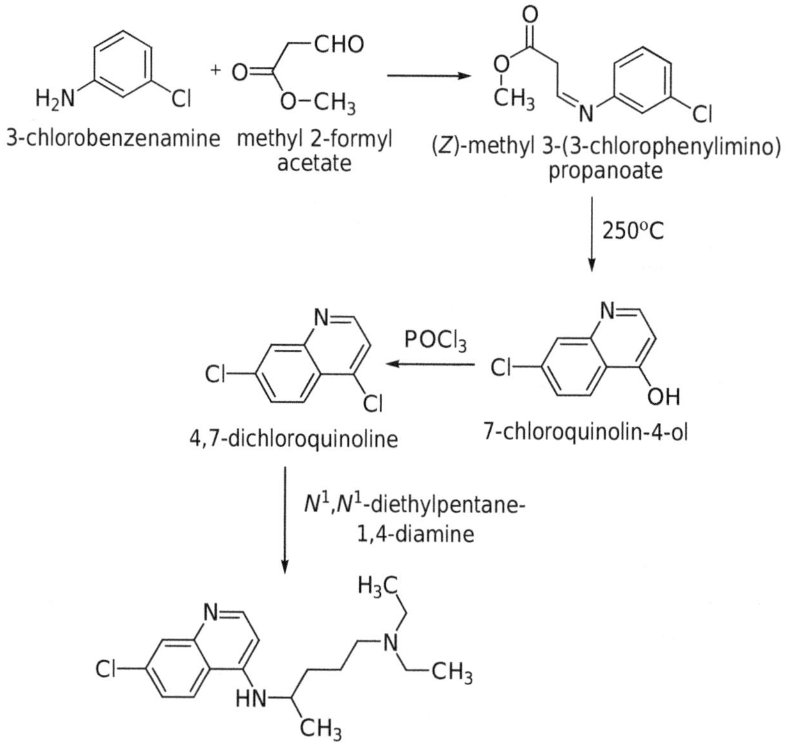

3-chlorobenzenamine + methyl 2-formyl acetate → (Z)-methyl 3-(3-chlorophenylimino)propanoate

250°C ↓

7-chloroquinolin-4-ol

POCl₃ → 4,7-dichloroquinoline

N^1,N^1-diethylpentane-1,4-diamine ↓

Chloroquine

CHLORZOXAZONE
Use: muscle relaxant
Analysis:

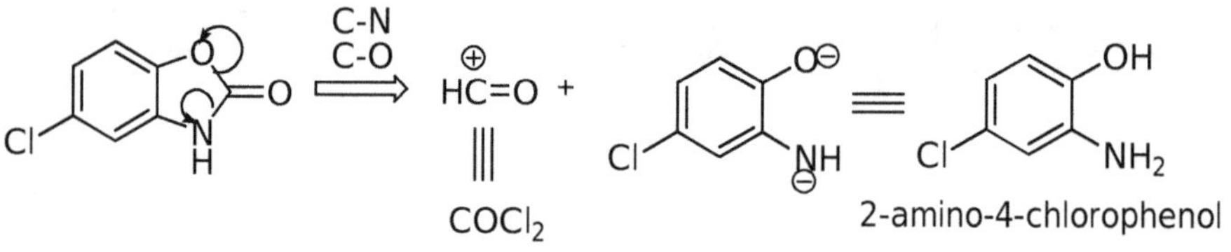

Chlorzoxazone ⇒ (C-N, C-O) HC=O⁺ + COCl₂ + chlorophenoxide-amide ≡ 2-amino-4-chlorophenol

Retrosynthetic Analysis and Synthesis of Drugs

Synthesis:

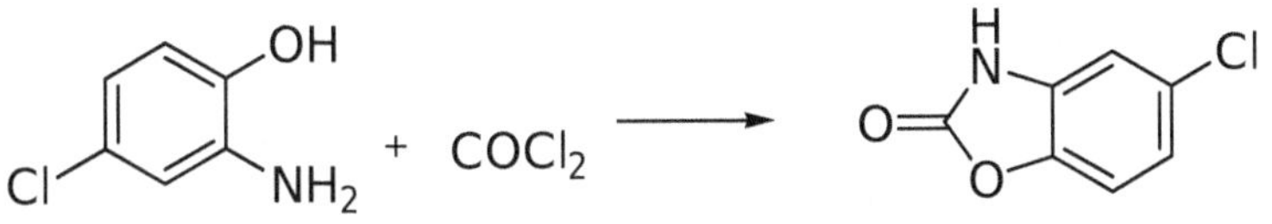

2-amino-4-chlorophenol + COCl₂ → Chlorzoxazone

CHLORPHENIRAMINE

Use: antihistaminic

Analysis:

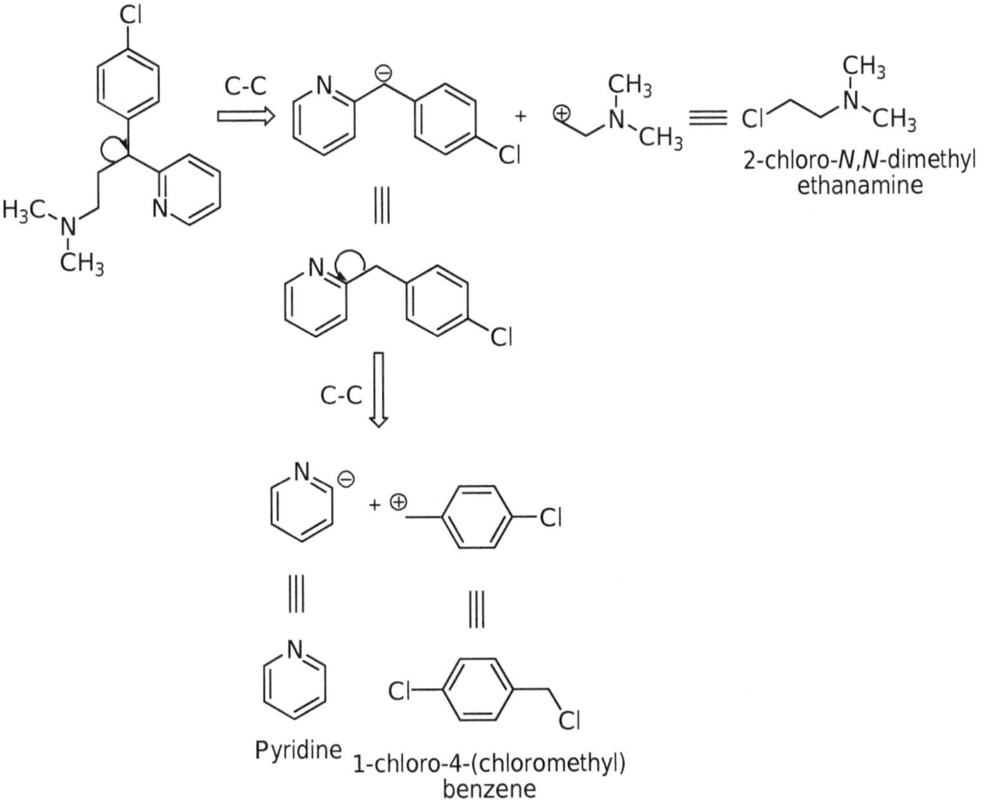

The target chlorpheniramine is disconnected (C-C) into a carbanion of 2-[(4-chlorophenyl)methyl]pyridine and the electrophile from 2-chloro-N,N-dimethyl ethanamine (Cl-CH₂CH₂-N(CH₃)₂).

The intermediate 2-[(4-chlorophenyl)methyl]pyridine is further disconnected (C-C) into pyridine carbanion and 4-chlorobenzyl cation, corresponding to pyridine and 1-chloro-4-(chloromethyl)benzene.

Synthesis:

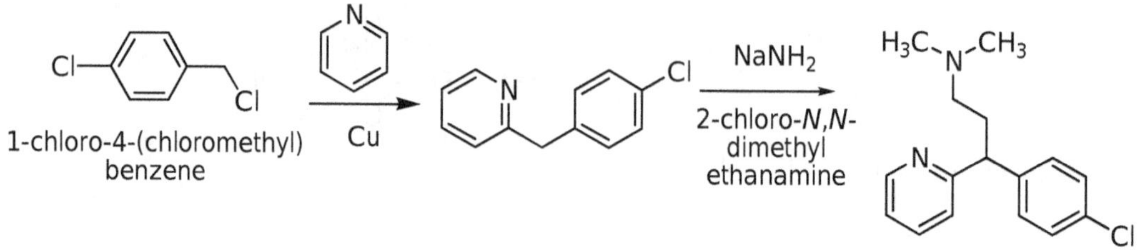

1-chloro-4-(chloromethyl)benzene + pyridine →(Cu) [2-(4-chlorobenzyl)pyridine] →(NaNH₂, 2-chloro-N,N-dimethyl ethanamine) **Chlorpheniramine**

CHLORPROPAMIDE

Use: antidiabetic

Analysis:

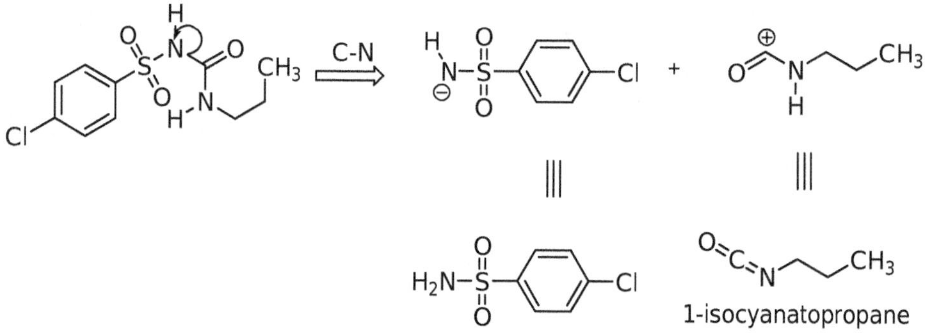

Chlorpropamide ⇒ (C-N disconnection) 4-chlorobenzenesulfonamide anion + protonated N-propyl formamide
≡ 4-chlorobenzenesulfonamide (H₂N-SO₂-C₆H₄-Cl) + 1-isocyanatopropane (O=C=N-CH₂CH₂CH₃)

Synthesis:

4-chlorobenzenesulfonamide + 1-isocyanatopropane →(N(C₂H₅)₃) **Chlorpropamide**

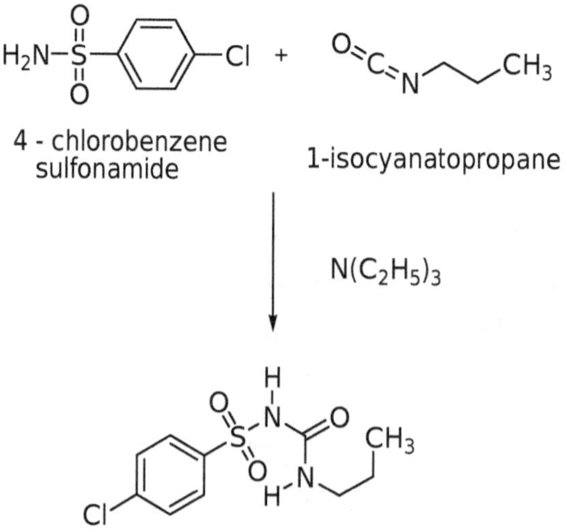

CIDOFOVIR

Use: antiviral

Analysis:

Synthesis:

CILOSTAZOLE

Use: platelet aggregation inhibitor

Analysis:

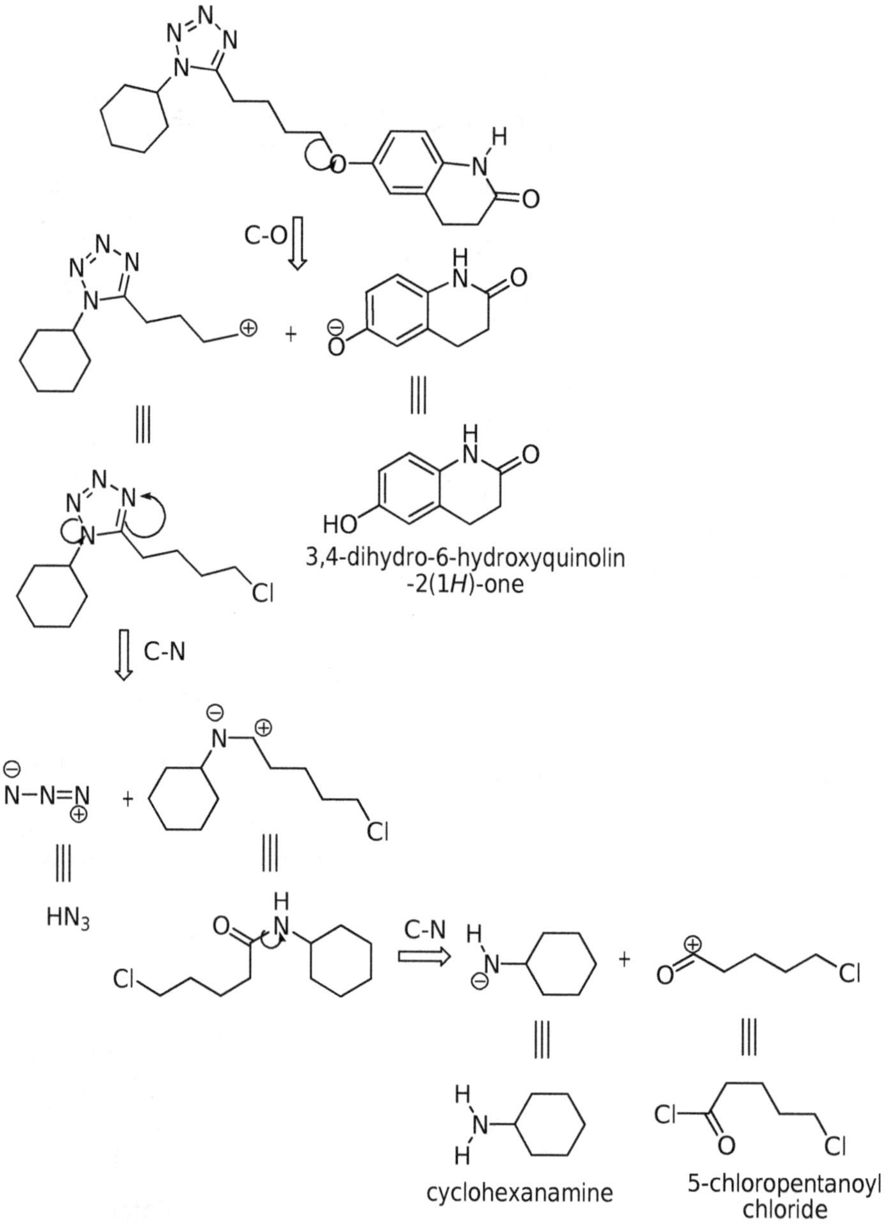
C-O
3,4-dihydro-6-hydroxyquinolin
-2(1H)-one
C-N
HN3
C-N
cyclohexanamine
5-chloropentanoyl
chloride

Retrosynthetic Analysis and Synthesis of Drugs

Synthesis:

cyclohexanamine + 5-chloropentanoyl chloride → 5-chloro-N-cyclohexylpentanamide

PCl_5 | NH_3 ↓

5-(4-chlorobutyl)-1-cyclohexyl-1H-tetrazole

3,4-dihydro-6-hydroxy quinolin-2(1H)-one →

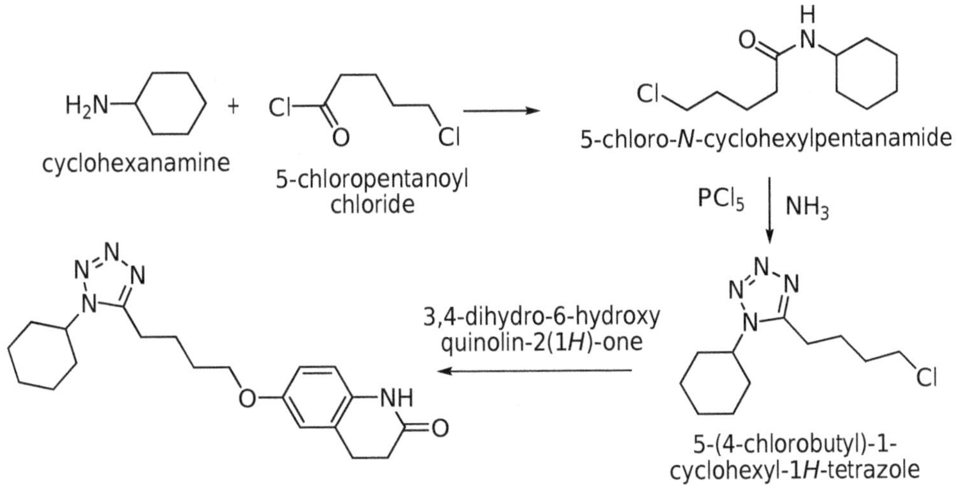

Cilostazole

CIMETIDINE

Use: H_2-receptor blocker

Analysis:

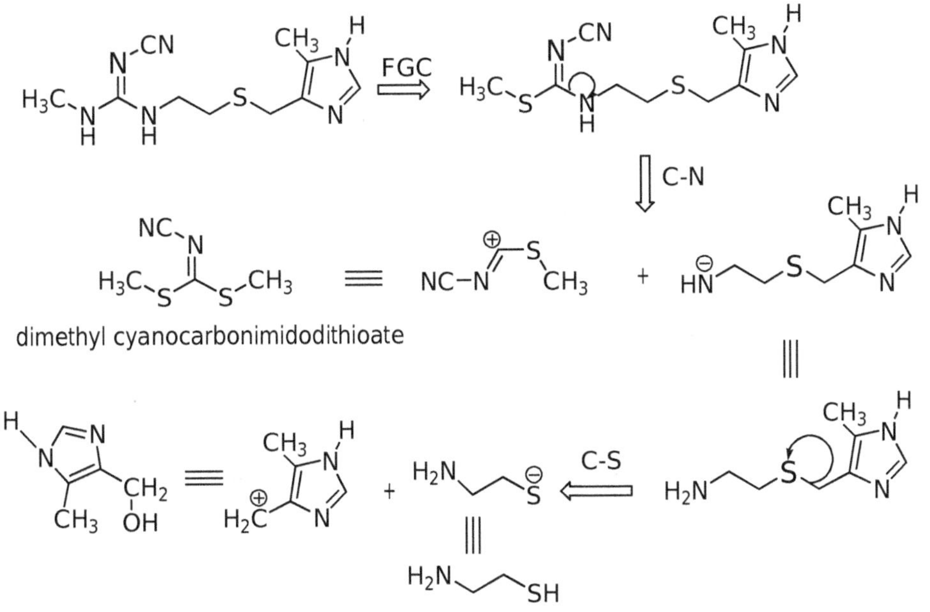

dimethyl cyanocarbonimidodithioate

Synthesis:

[Scheme: (5-methyl-1H-imidazol-4-yl)methanol + 2-aminoethanethiol, HCl → 2-((5-methyl-1H-imidazol-4-yl)methylthio)ethanamine; then dimethyl N-cyanocarbonimidodithioate; then CH₃NH₂ → **Cimetidine**]

CINEPAZATE

Use: vasodilator, antianginal

Analysis:

[Retrosynthetic analysis: ethyl 2-(4-(3-(3,4,5-trimethoxyphenyl)acryloyl)piperazin-1-yl)acetate ⇒ C–N disconnection → 3-(3,4,5-trimethoxyphenyl)acryloyl cation + ethyl 2-(piperazin-1-yl)acetate anion ⇒ 3-(3,4,5-trimethoxyphenyl)acryloyl chloride + ethyl 2-(piperazin-1-yl)acetate]

Synthesis:

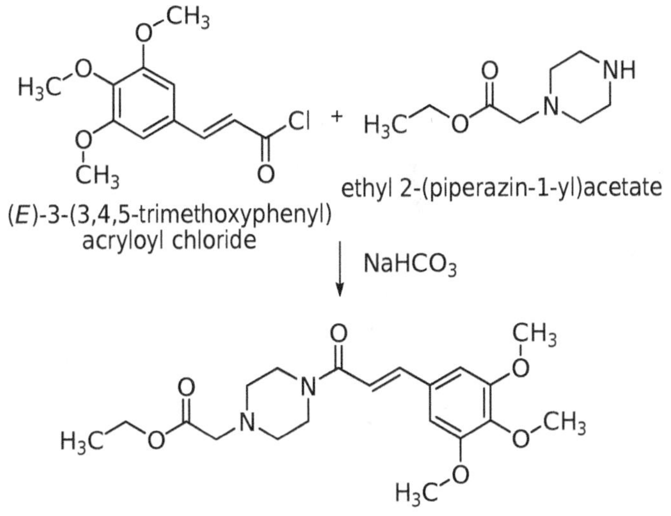

(E)-3-(3,4,5-trimethoxyphenyl) acryloyl chloride + ethyl 2-(piperazin-1-yl)acetate

↓ NaHCO₃

Cinepazate

CINNAMYLEPHEDRINE

Use: uterine antispasmodic

Analysis:

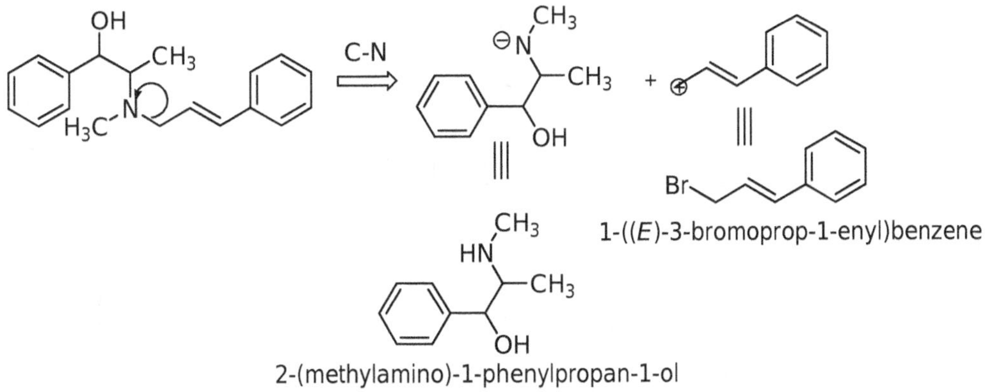

⇒ C-N

2-(methylamino)-1-phenylpropan-1-ol + 1-((E)-3-bromoprop-1-enyl)benzene

Synthesis:

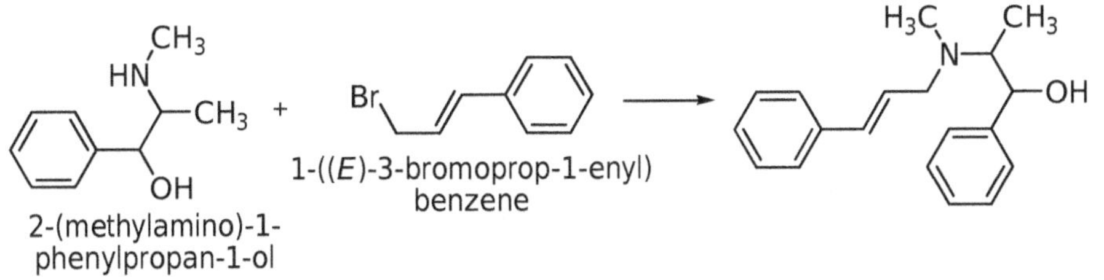

2-(methylamino)-1-phenylpropan-1-ol + 1-((E)-3-bromoprop-1-enyl) benzene ⟶ **Cinnamylephedrine**

CIPROFLOXACIN

Use: antibacterial

Analysis:

Synthesis:

[Scheme showing synthesis of Ciprofloxacin: 2,4-dichloro-5-fluorobenzoyl chloride + diethyl malonate with Mg(OC₂H₅)₂ → intermediate with OC₂H₅; then cyclopropylamine → enamine intermediate; then NaH cyclization → 7-chloro-6-fluoro-1-cyclopropyl-4-oxoquinoline-3-carboxylic acid; then piperazine → **Ciprofloxacin**]

CLOBAZAM
Use: minor tranquilizer
Analysis:

[Retrosynthetic analysis: Clobazam (N-methyl benzodiazepinedione with Cl and phenyl) ⟹ CH₃⁺ (from H₃C–Cl, chloromethane) + deprotonated benzodiazepinedione ≡ NH-benzodiazepinedione (I)]

(I)

Retrosynthetic Analysis and Synthesis of Drugs

Retrosynthetic Analysis and Synthesis of Drugs

Synthesis:

1,3-dichlorobenzene →(HNO₃, H₂SO₄)→ 2,4-dichloro-1-nitrobenzene →(Aniline)→ N-(5-chloro-2-nitrophenyl)benzenamine

→(ethyl 2-(chlorocarbonyl)acetate)→ ethyl 2-(N-(5-chloro-2-nitrophenyl)-N-phenylcarbamoyl)acetate

→(Zn, HCl)→ 8-chloro-1-phenyl-1H-benzo[b][1,4]diazepine-2,4(3H,5H)-dione

→(CH₃Cl, NaOCH₃)→ **Clobazam**

CLOFEXAMIDE
Use: psychoanaleptic
Analysis:

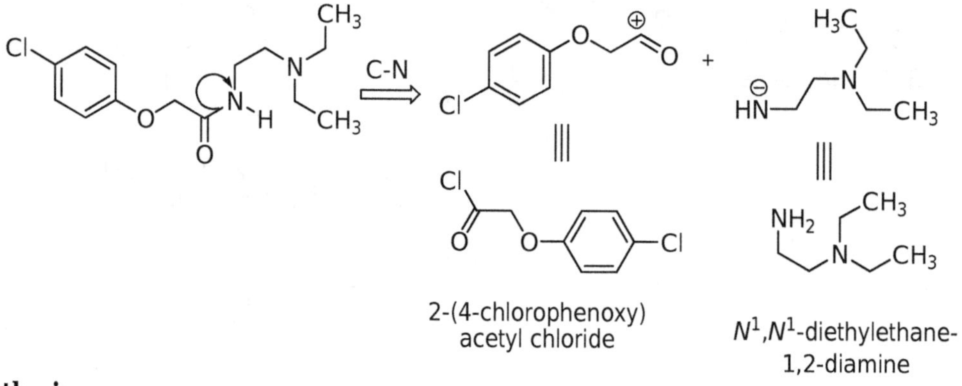

[Retrosynthetic scheme: Clofexamide ⟹ (C-N disconnection) 2-(4-chlorophenoxy)acetyl chloride + N^1,N^1-diethylethane-1,2-diamine]

Synthesis:

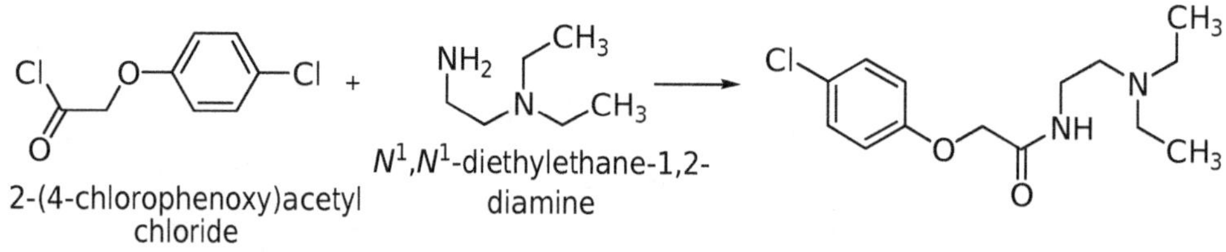

2-(4-chlorophenoxy)acetyl chloride + N^1,N^1-diethylethane-1,2-diamine → **Clofexamide**

CLONAZEPAM
Use: anticonvulsant
Analysis:

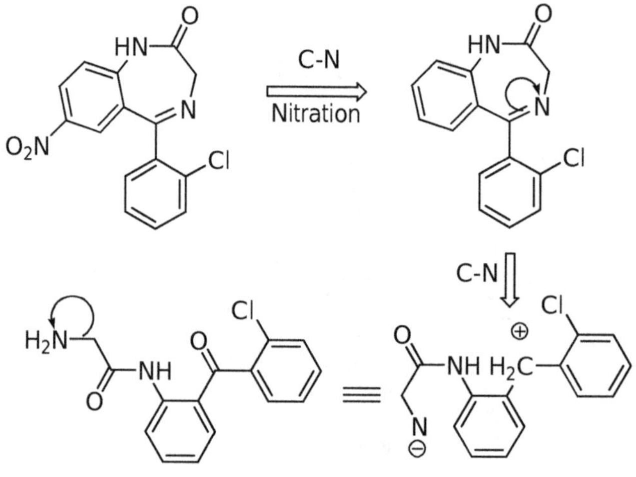

[Retrosynthetic scheme: Clonazepam ⟹ (C-N, Nitration) des-nitro benzodiazepine ⟹ (C-N) open-chain amide intermediate (I)]

(I)

Retrosynthetic Analysis and Synthesis of Drugs

Synthesis:

Clonazepam

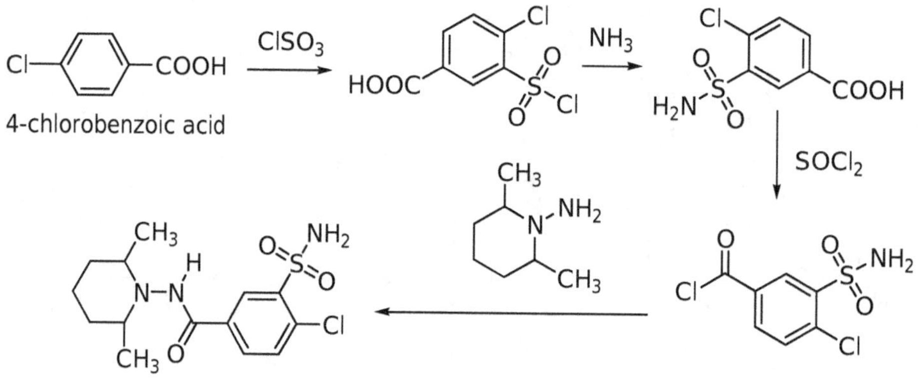

CLOPAMIDE
Use: diuretic
Analysis:

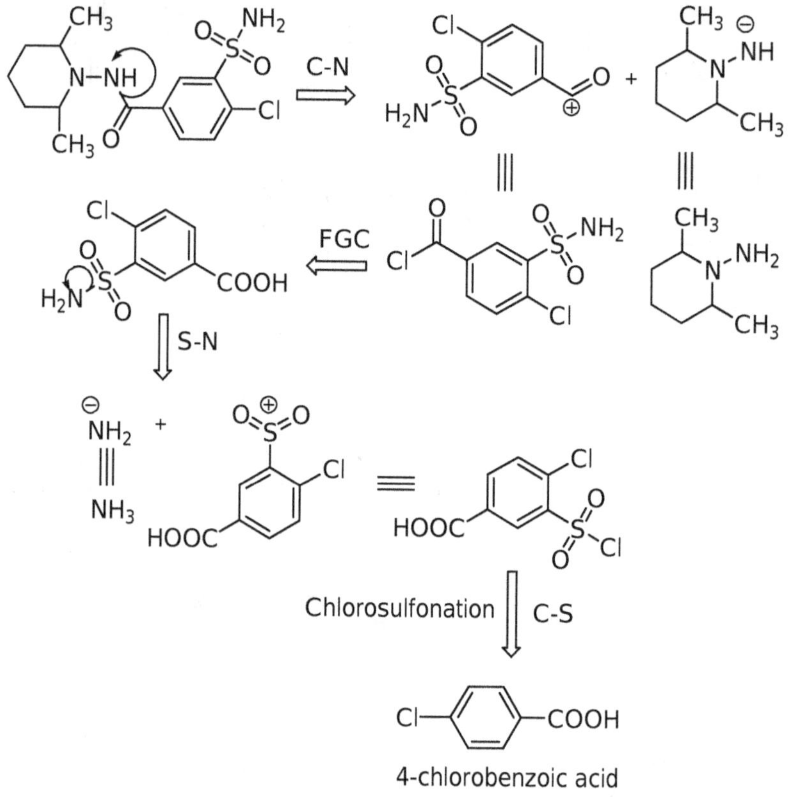

Synthesis:

CLOPERASTINE

Use: antitussive

Analysis:

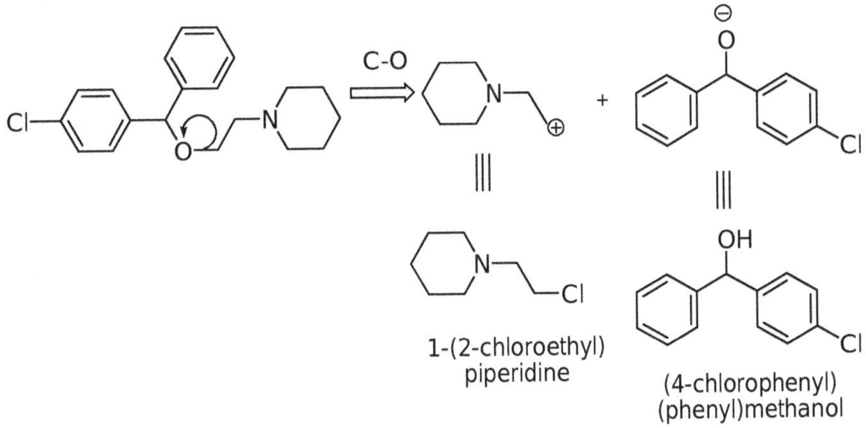

C-O
1-(2-chloroethyl)
piperidine
(4-chlorophenyl)
(phenyl)methanol

Synthesis:

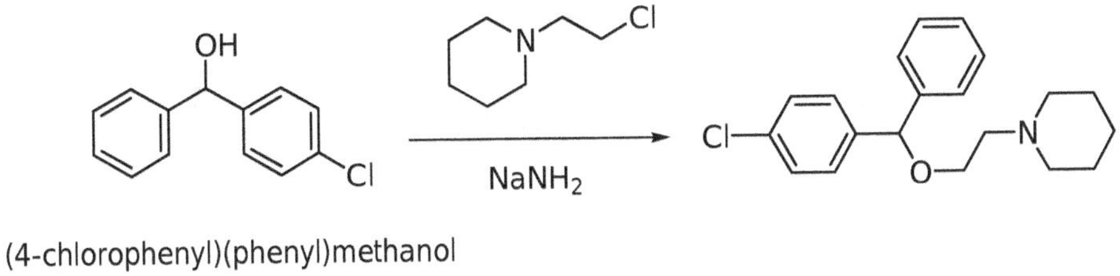

$NaNH_2$
(4-chlorophenyl)(phenyl)methanol

Cloperastine

CLOTRIMAZOLE

Use: antifungal

Analysis:

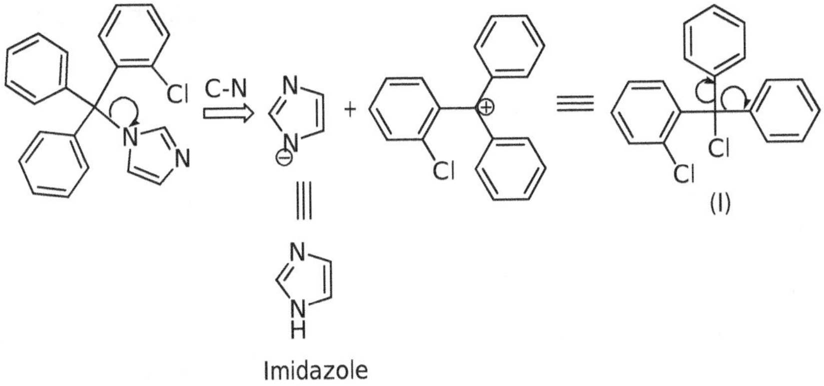

C-N
(I)
Imidazole

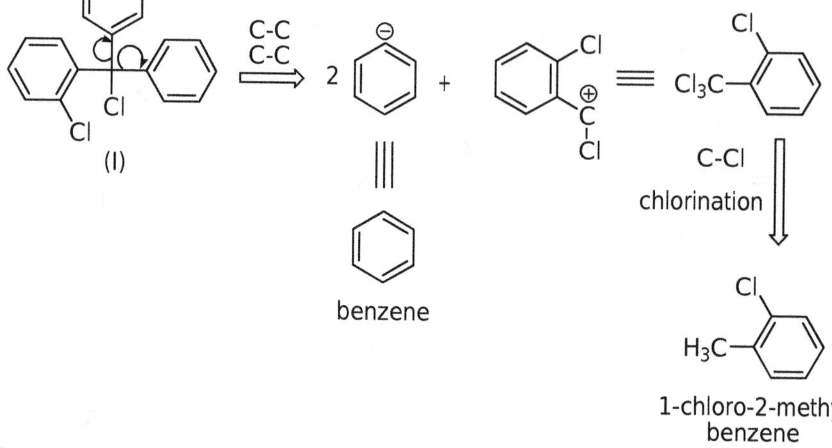

Retrosynthetic Analysis and Synthesis of Drugs

Synthesis:

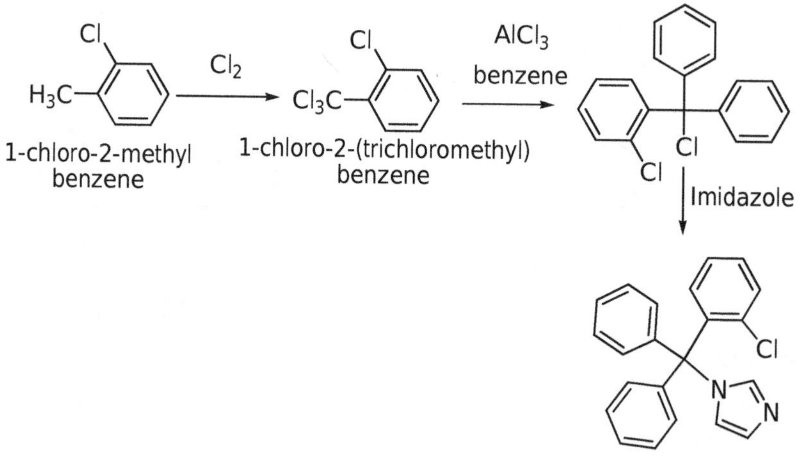

CLOTRIMAZOLE

CLOZAPINE
Use: neuroleptic
Analysis:

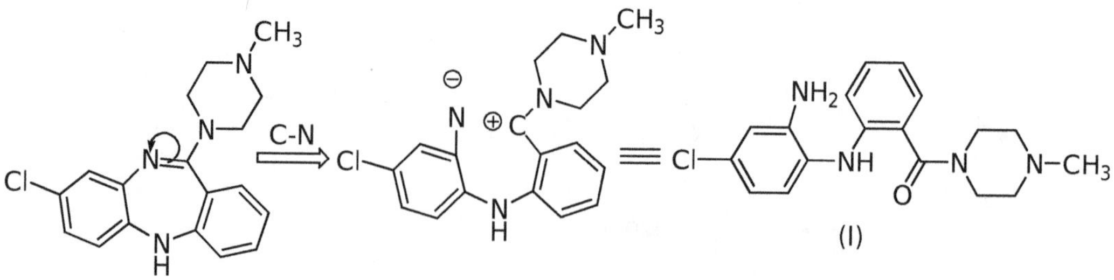

Retrosynthetic Analysis and Synthesis of Drugs

Synthesis:

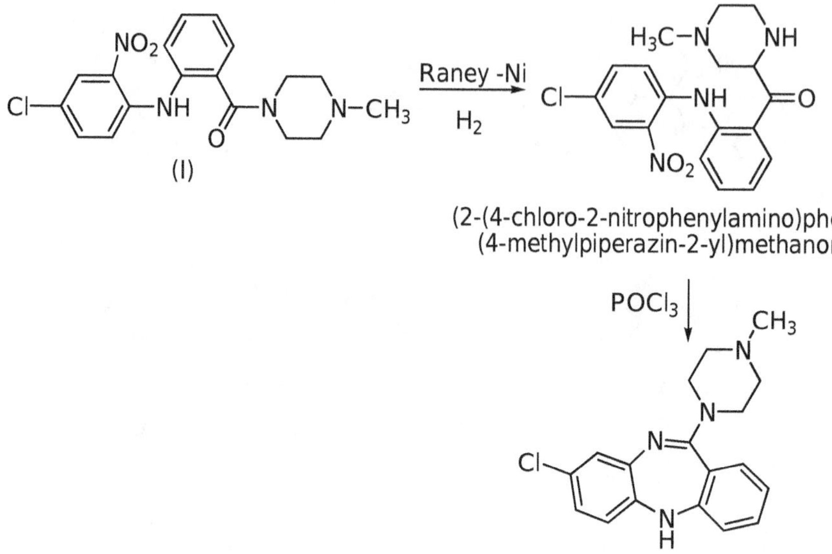
(I)
Raney -Ni
H_2
(2-(4-chloro-2-nitrophenylamino)phenyl)
(4-methylpiperazin-2-yl)methanone
$POCl_3$

Clozapine

CYCLIZINE

Use: antihistaminic

Analysis:

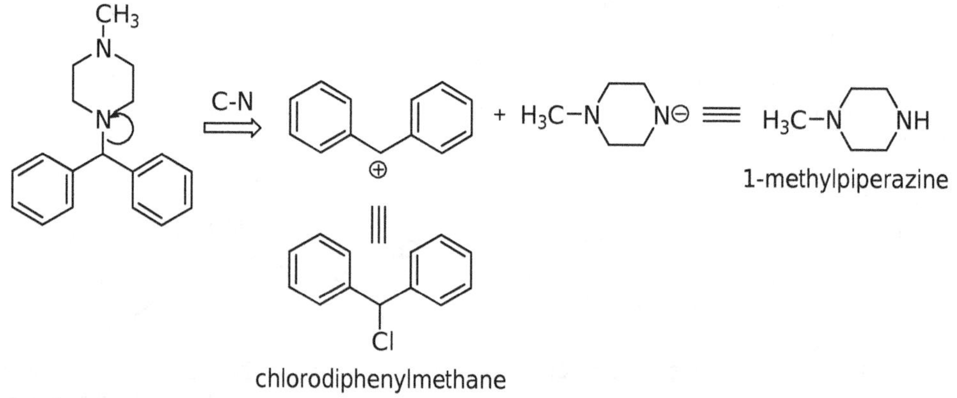
C-N
1-methylpiperazine
chlorodiphenylmethane

Synthesis:

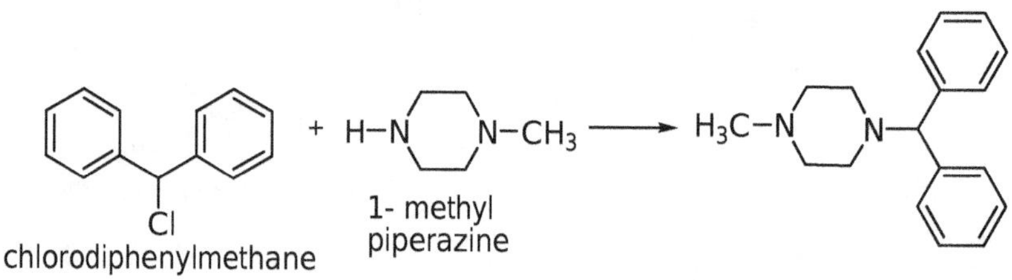
chlorodiphenylmethane
1- methyl
piperazine

Cyclizine

CYCLOMETHYLCAINE
Use: local anaesthetic
Analysis:

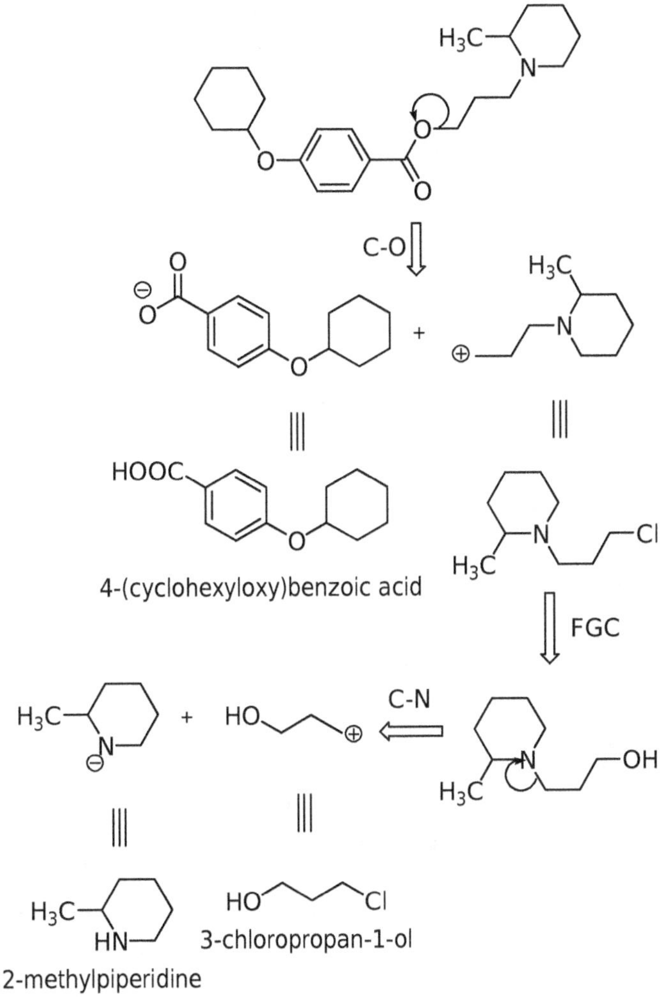

[Retrosynthetic scheme: Cyclomethylcaine disconnects at C-O to give 4-(cyclohexyloxy)benzoic acid and 1-(3-chloropropyl)-2-methylpiperidine. The latter, by FGC, comes from 3-(2-methylpiperidin-1-yl)propan-1-ol, which disconnects at C-N to 2-methylpiperidine and 3-chloropropan-1-ol.]

4-(cyclohexyloxy)benzoic acid

3-chloropropan-1-ol

2-methylpiperidine

Synthesis:

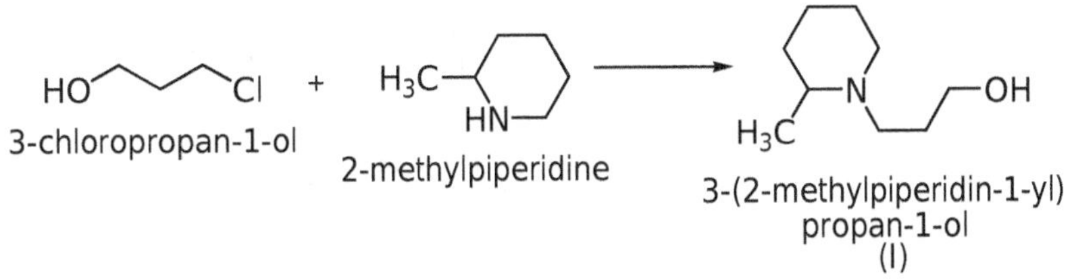

3-chloropropan-1-ol + 2-methylpiperidine → 3-(2-methylpiperidin-1-yl)propan-1-ol
(I)

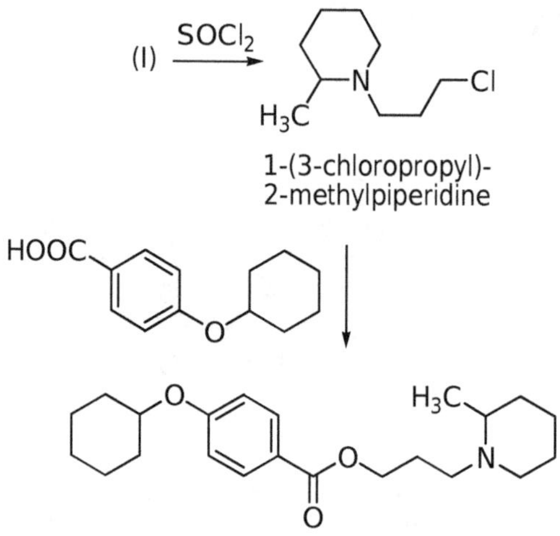

(I) →[SOCl$_2$] 1-(3-chloropropyl)-2-methylpiperidine

Cyclomethylcaine

CYCLOPHOSPHAMIDE

Use: antineoplastic

Analysis:

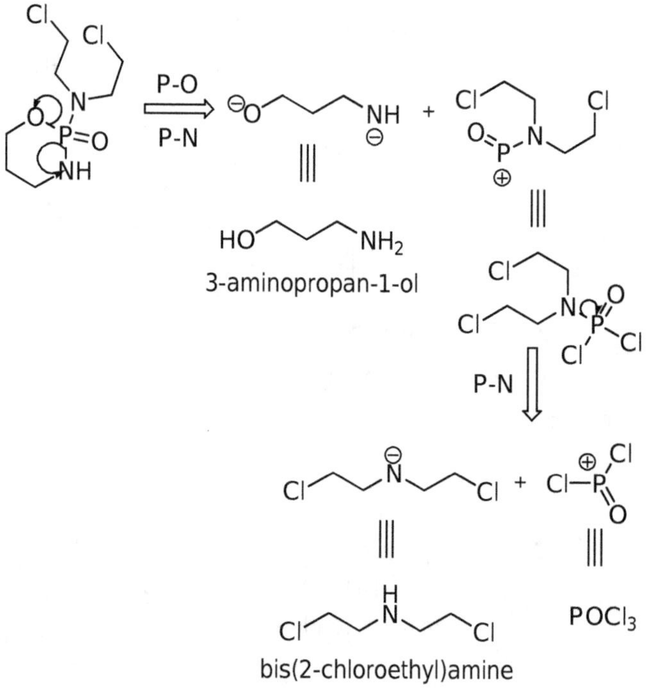

P-O, P-N ⇒ ⁻O~~~NH⁻ + bis(2-chloroethyl)phosphoramide cation

≡ 3-aminopropan-1-ol

≡ bis(2-chloroethyl)amine + POCl$_3$ derivative

⇓ P-N

bis(2-chloroethyl)amine + Cl–P⁺(Cl)=O (POCl$_3$)

Retrosynthetic Analysis and Synthesis of Drugs

Synthesis:

POCl₃ + bis(2-chloroethyl)amine → phosphoryl dichloride intermediate

Then with 3-aminopropanol, N(C₂H₅)₃ →

Cyclophosphamide

DAPSONE

Use: antileprotic

Analysis:

4-(4-aminophenylsulfonyl)benzenamine ⇒ (FGC) bis(4-nitrophenyl)sulfone

⇒ (S-O oxidation) bis(4-nitrophenyl)sulfide

⇒ (C-S, C-S) 2 O₂N—C₆H₄⁺ ≡ 2 O₂N—C₆H₄—Cl

Synthesis:

2 1-chloro-4-nitrobenzene —Na₂S→ bis(4-nitrophenyl)sulfane

—K₂Cr₂O₇ / H₂SO₄→ 1-(4-nitrophenylsulfonyl)-4-nitrobenzene

—SnCl₂ / HCl→ **Dapsone**

DIAZEPAM

Use: tranquilizer, hypnotic

Analysis:

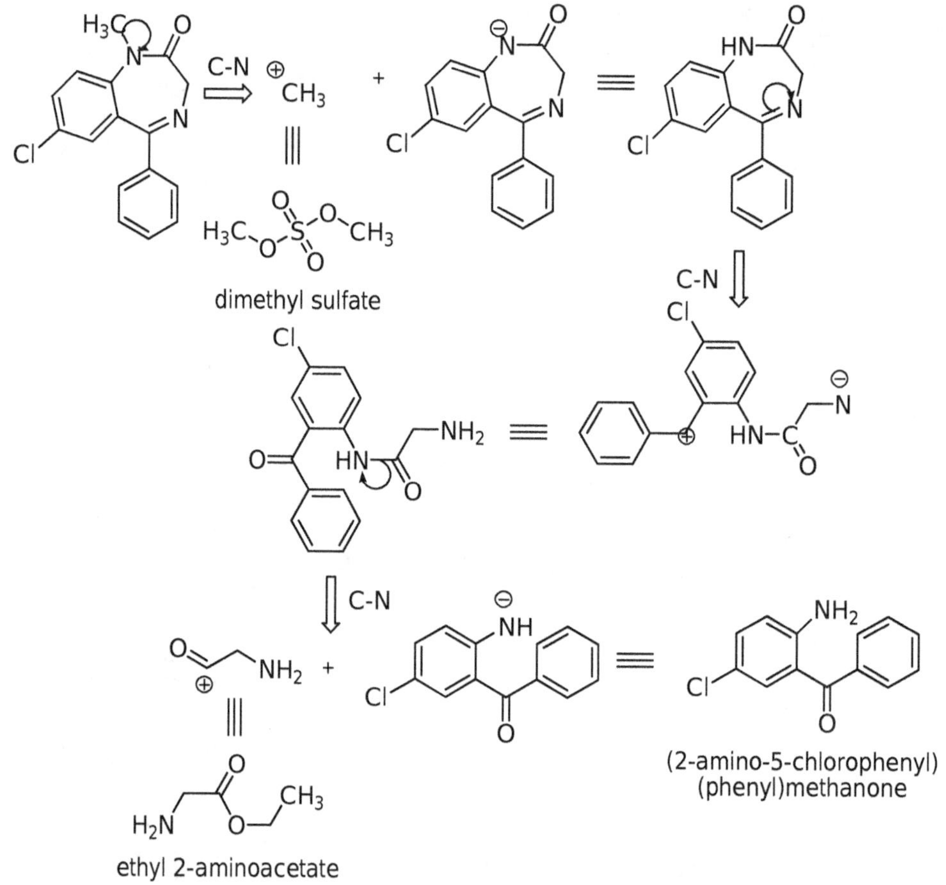

[Retrosynthetic analysis scheme showing diazepam disconnected via C-N bond to give the N-H benzodiazepinone and dimethyl sulfate (methylating agent); further C-N disconnection yields (2-amino-5-chlorophenyl)(phenyl)methanone and ethyl 2-aminoacetate (glycine ethyl ester).]

(2-amino-5-chlorophenyl)(phenyl)methanone

ethyl 2-aminoacetate

Synthesis:

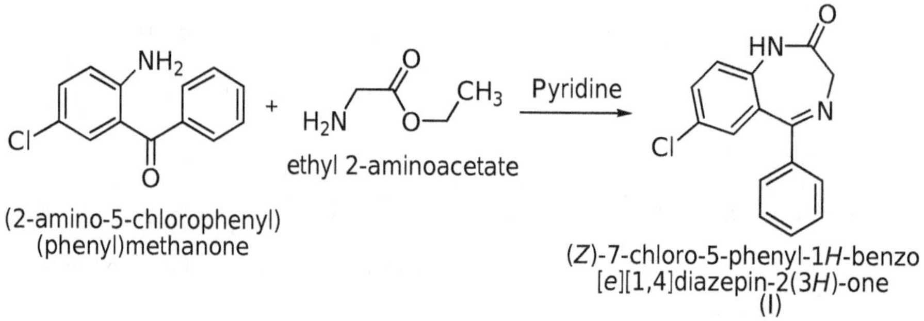

(2-amino-5-chlorophenyl)(phenyl)methanone + ethyl 2-aminoacetate →(Pyridine)→ (Z)-7-chloro-5-phenyl-1H-benzo[e][1,4]diazepin-2(3H)-one (I)

Retrosynthetic Analysis and Synthesis of Drugs

(I) →[dimethyl sulfate] **Diazepam**

DIBENZEPINE
Use: antidepressant
Analysis:

methyl 2-(methylamino)benzoate

Synthesis:

[Scheme: 1-bromo-2-nitrobenzene + methyl 2-(methylamino)benzoate →(K₂CO₃) coupled diarylamine →(H₂/Pd) methyl 2-(N-(2-aminophenyl)-N-methylamino)benzoate →(NaNH₂) dibenzodiazepinone →(ClCH₂CH₂N(CH₃)₂, NaNH₂) Dibenzepine]

Dibenzepine

DICHLORPHENAMIDE

Use: treatment of glaucoma

Analysis:

[Retrosynthetic scheme: dichlorphenamide ⇒ (S-N, S-N) NH₂⁻ / NH₃ + disulfonyl aromatic ≡ disulfonyl chloride ⇒(FGC) dichloro-hydroxy-disulfonyl chloride ⇐(C-S Chlorosulphonation) 2-chlorophenol]

Retrosynthetic Analysis and Synthesis of Drugs

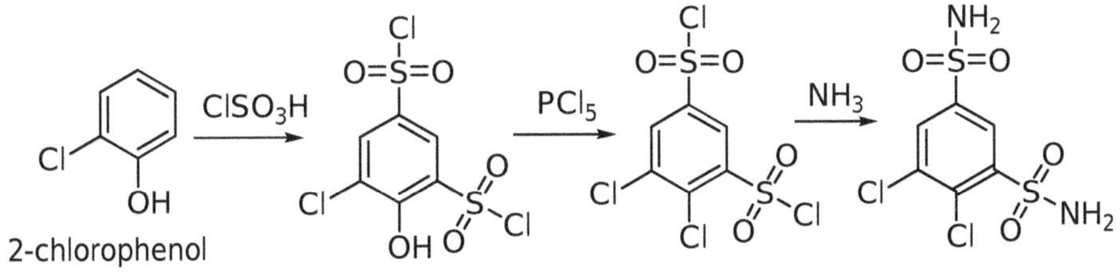

Synthesis:

2-chlorophenol → (ClSO$_3$H) → intermediate → (PCl$_5$) → intermediate → (NH$_3$) → **Dichlorphenamide**

DICYCLOVERINE

Use: antispasmodic

Analysis:

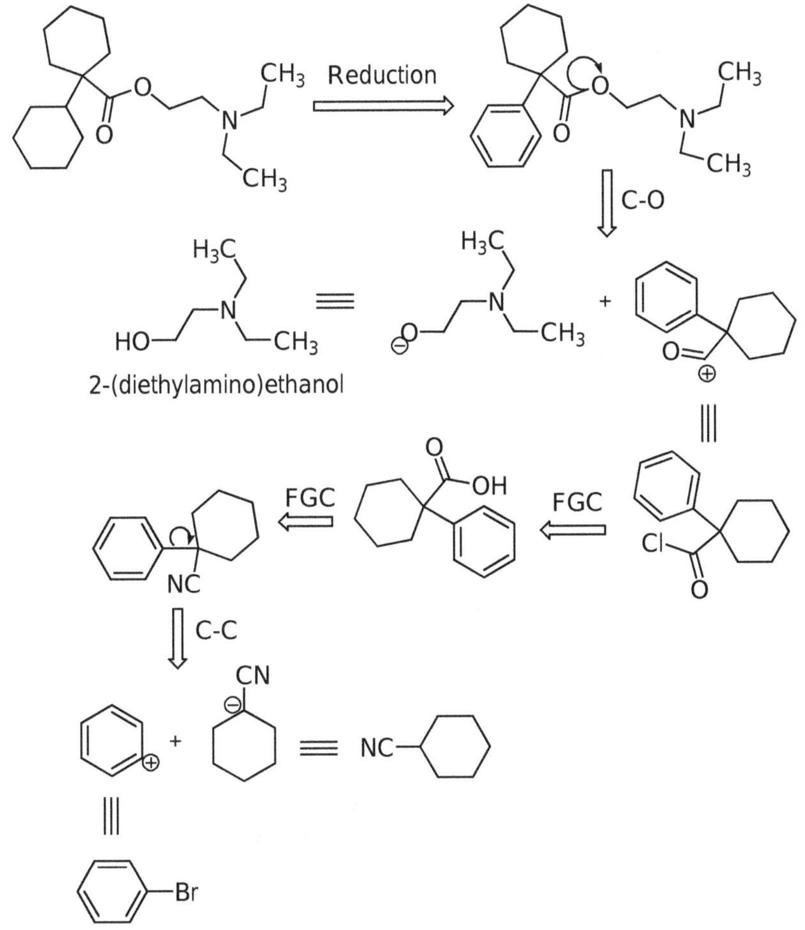

2-(diethylamino)ethanol

Synthesis:

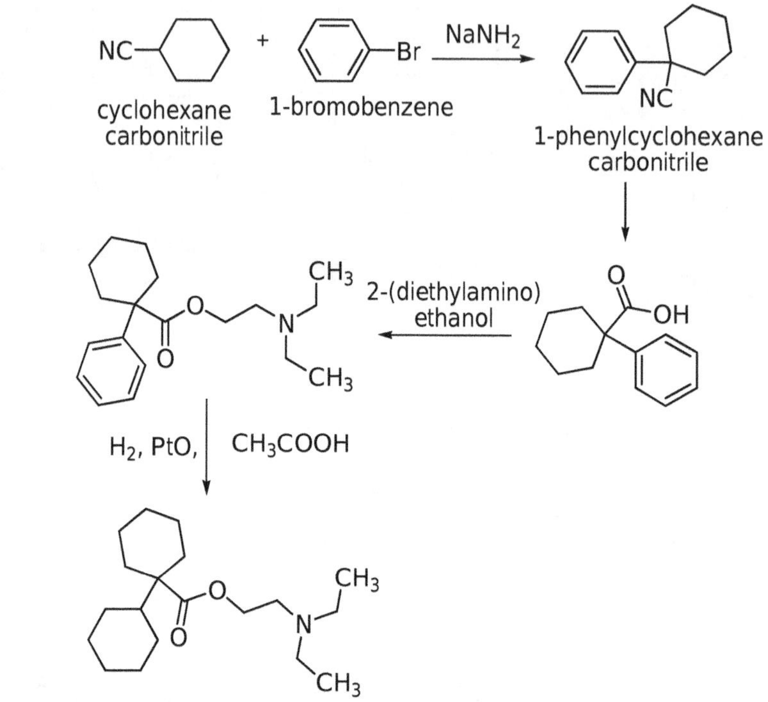

cyclohexane carbonitrile + 1-bromobenzene →(NaNH₂) 1-phenylcyclohexane carbonitrile → 1-phenylcyclohexane carboxylic acid →(2-(diethylamino)ethanol) ester →(H₂, PtO, CH₃COOH) **Dicycloverine**

DIETHYLCARBAMAZINE

Use: anthelmintic

Analysis:

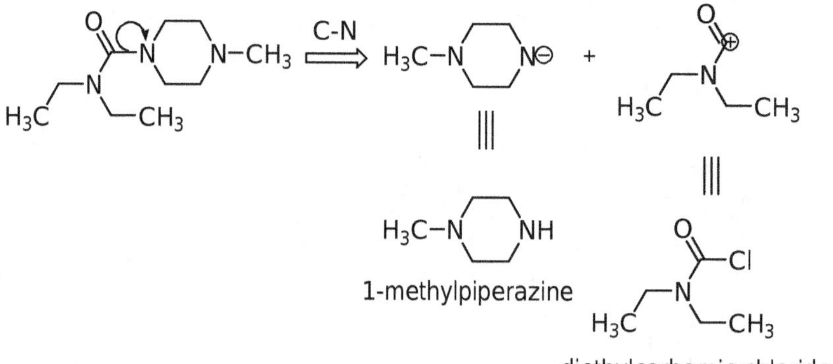

Diethylcarbamazine ⇒(C-N) 1-methylpiperazine + diethylcarbamic chloride

Synthesis:

1-methylpiperazine + diethylcarbamic chloride → N,N-diethyl-4-methylpiperazine-1-carboxamide

DILOXANIDE
Use: antiamobic
Analysis:

Diloxanide ⇒ 2,2-dichloroacetyl chloride + 4-(methylamino)phenol

Synthesis:

4-(methylamino)phenol + 2,2-dichloroacetyl chloride →(NaOH) **Diloxanide**

DILTIAZEM
Use: calcium channel blocker
Analysis:

(I)

Retrosynthetic Analysis and Synthesis of Drugs

Synthesis:

4-methoxybenzaldehyde + methyl 2-chloro acetate →(NaOCH₃) methyl 3-(4-methoxyphenyl)oxirane-2-carboxylate

↓ 2-nitrobenzenethiol

3-(2-nitrophenylthio)-2-hydroxy-3-(4-methoxyphenyl)propanoic acid

→(H₂, Pd) [2-aminophenylthio intermediate]

↓ Xylene

2,3-dihydro-3-hydroxy-2-(4-methoxyphenyl)benzo[*b*][1,4]thiazepin-4(5*H*)-one

→(Ac₂O, Pyridine) 2,3,4,5-tetrahydro-2-(4-methoxyphenyl)-4-oxobenzo[*b*][1,4]thiazepin-3-yl acetate

↓ 2-chloro-*N,N*-dimethylethanamine, NaH

Diltiazem

DIMETHOXANATE

Use: antitussive

Analysis:

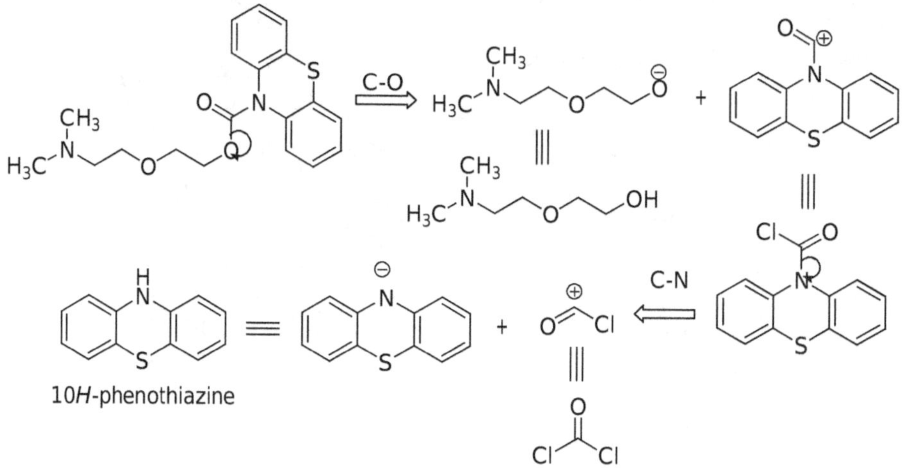

[Retrosynthetic analysis scheme showing dimethoxanate being disconnected at the C-O bond into 2-(2-(dimethylamino)ethoxy)ethanol and 10H-phenothiazine-10-carbonyl cation, then at the C-N bond into 10H-phenothiazine and phosgene (COCl₂).]

10H-phenothiazine

Synthesis:

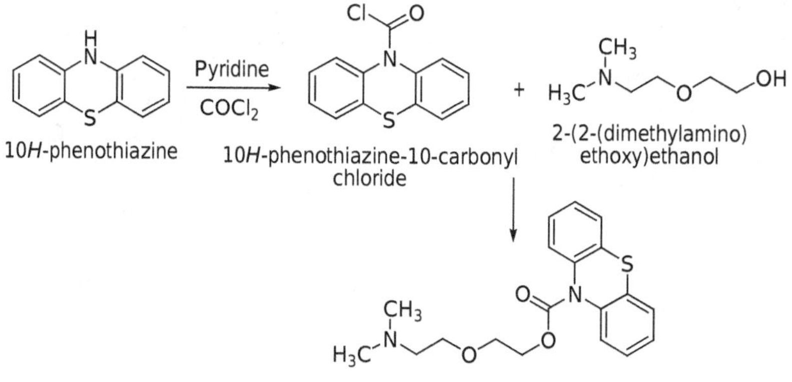

10H-phenothiazine → (Pyridine, COCl₂) → 10H-phenothiazine-10-carbonyl chloride + 2-(2-(dimethylamino)ethoxy)ethanol → **Dimethoxanate**

DIPERODON

Use: local anaesthetic

Analysis:

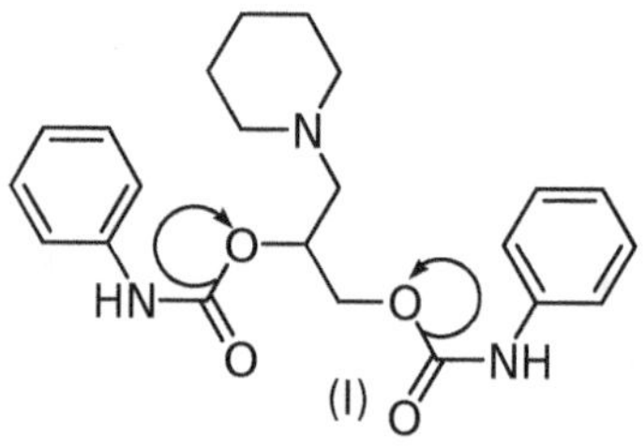

(I)

Retrosynthetic Analysis and Synthesis of Drugs

Synthesis:

(oxiran-2-yl)methanol → 3-(piperidin-1-yl)propane-1,2-diol → **Diperodon**

DIPHENOXYLATE

Use: antidiarrheal, antiperistaltic

Analysis:

Synthesis:

[Scheme: 4-bromo-2,2-diphenylbutanenitrile + ethyl 4-phenylpiperidine-4-carboxylate → Diphenoxylate]

DIPHENYLPYRALINE
Use: antihistaminic, antiallergic
Analysis:

[Retrosynthetic scheme: Diphenylpyraline ⇒ (C–O disconnection) 1-methylpiperidin-4-ol + bromodiphenylmethane]

Synthesis:

[Scheme: 1-methylpiperidin-4-ol + bromodiphenylmethane → Diphenylpyraline]

DIPIVEFRINE
Use: antiglaucoma
Analysis:

[Structure (I): dipivefrine]

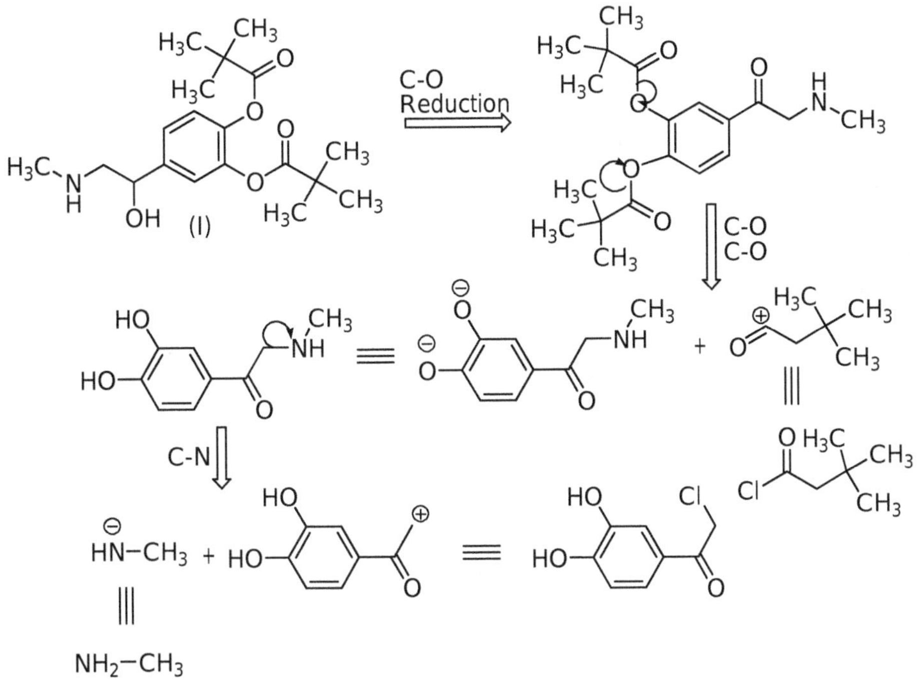

Retrosynthetic Analysis and Synthesis of Drugs

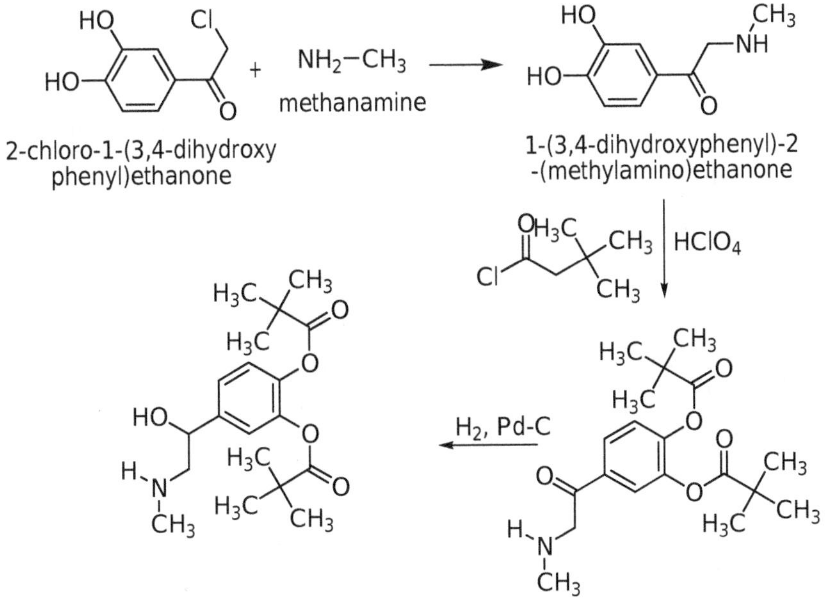

Synthesis:

2-chloro-1-(3,4-dihydroxy phenyl)ethanone + NH$_2$–CH$_3$ (methanamine) → 1-(3,4-dihydroxyphenyl)-2-(methylamino)ethanone

HClO$_4$, (CH$_3$)$_3$C-COCl → intermediate → H$_2$, Pd-C → **Dipivefrine**

DIPROPHYLLINE

Use: expectorant, bronchodilator

Analysis:

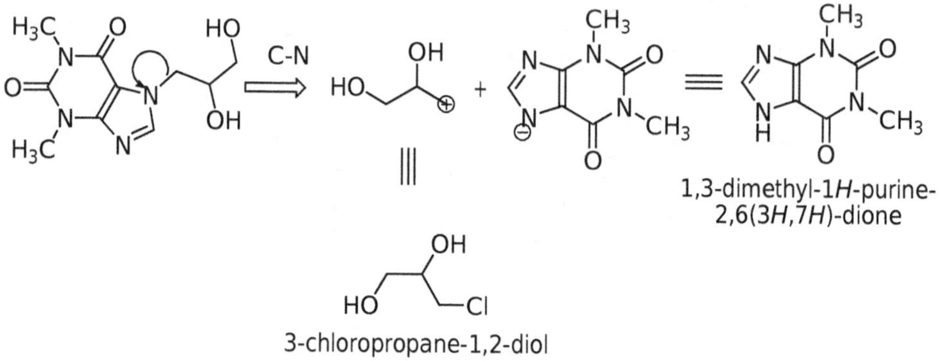

[Retrosynthetic scheme: Diprophylline ⇒ (via C-N disconnection) glycerol cation + 1,3-dimethyl-1H-purine-2,6(3H,7H)-dione anion ≡ 1,3-dimethyl-1H-purine-2,6(3H,7H)-dione; glycerol cation ≡ 3-chloropropane-1,2-diol]

Synthesis:

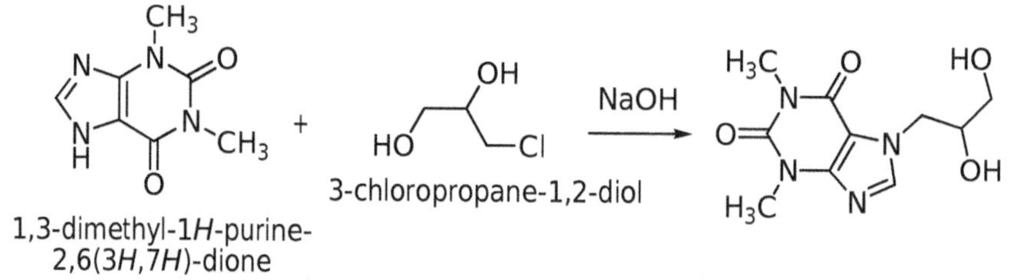

1,3-dimethyl-1H-purine-2,6(3H,7H)-dione + 3-chloropropane-1,2-diol $\xrightarrow{NaOH}$ **Diprophylline**

DISTIGMINE BROMIDE

Use: parasympathomimetic

Analysis:

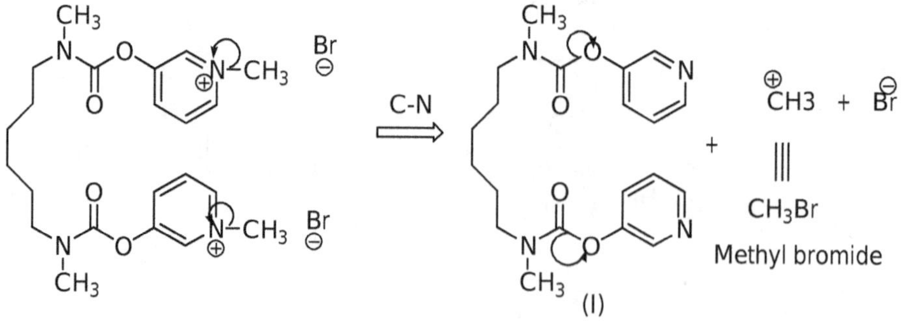

[Retrosynthetic scheme: Distigmine bromide ⇒ (via C-N disconnection) intermediate (I) + $\overset{\oplus}{CH_3}$ + $\overset{\ominus}{Br}$ ≡ CH₃Br (Methyl bromide)]

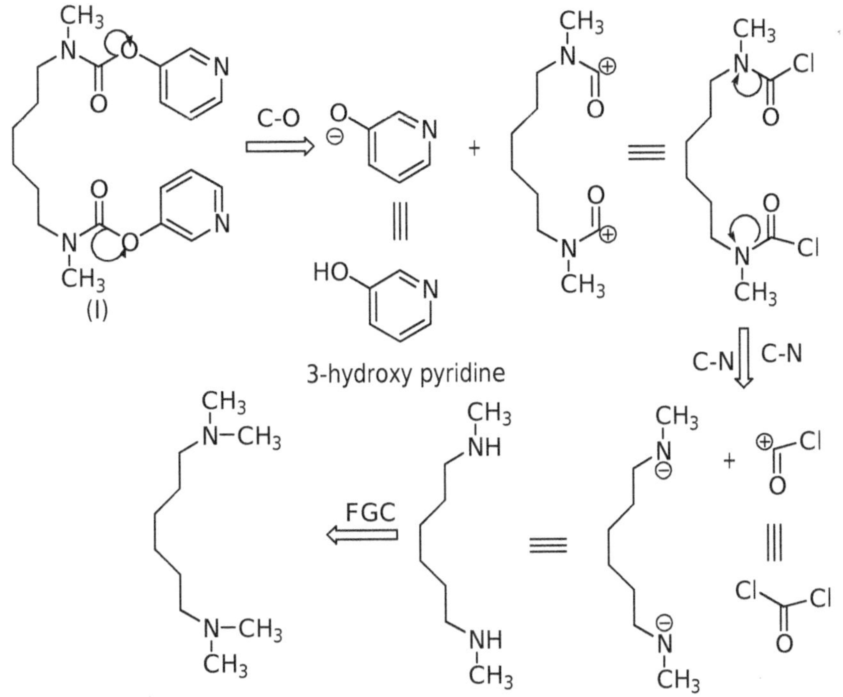

Synthesis:

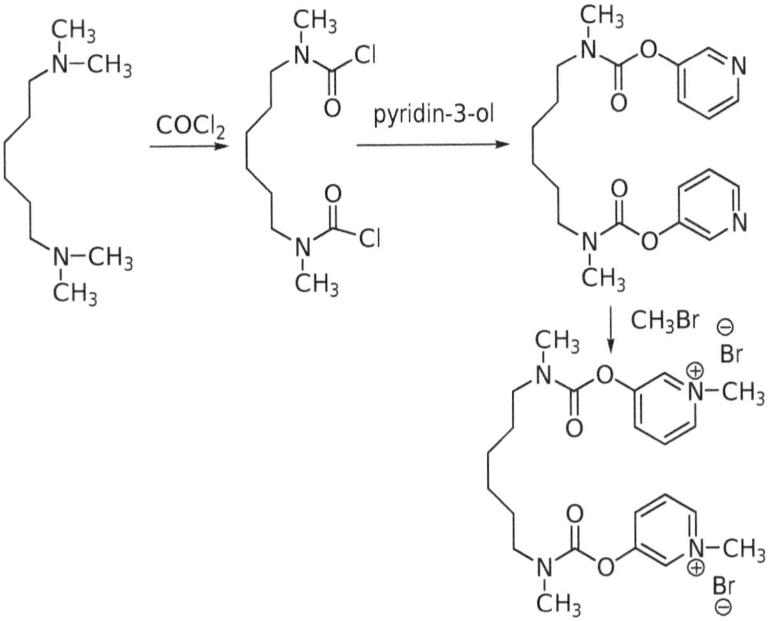

Distigmine Bromide

DIXYRAZINE
Use: neuroleptic, antihistaminic
Analysis:

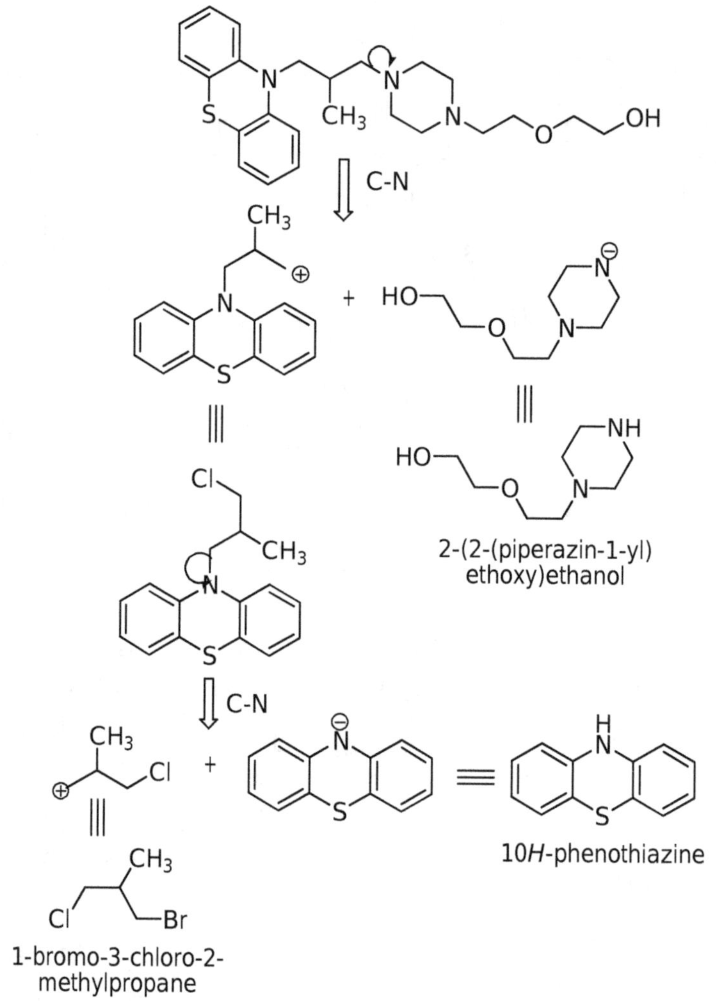

2-(2-(piperazin-1-yl)ethoxy)ethanol

10H-phenothiazine

1-bromo-3-chloro-2-methylpropane

Synthesis:

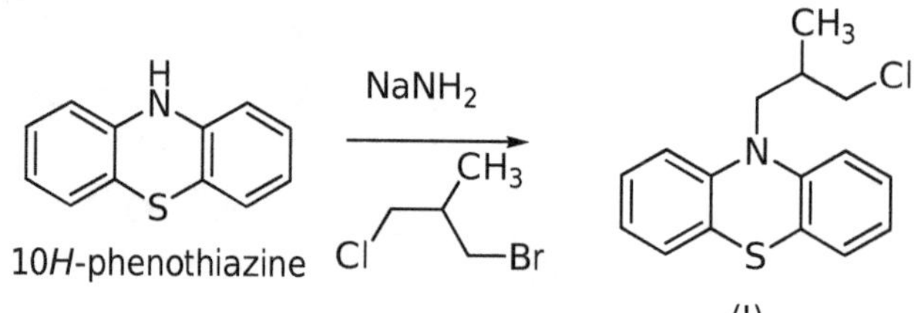

10H-phenothiazine + 1-bromo-3-chloro-2-methylpropane →(NaNH₂)→ (I)

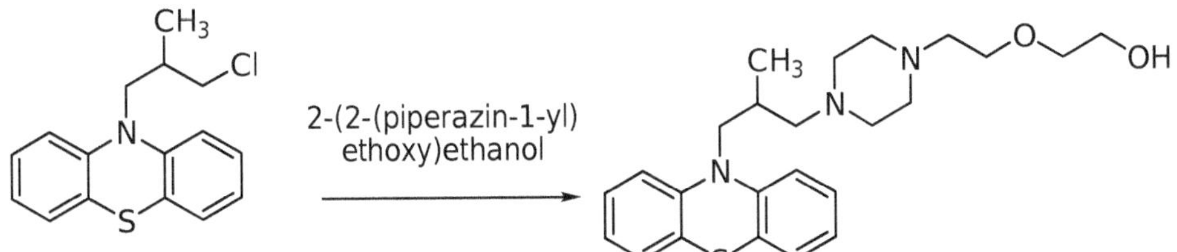

Retrosynthetic Analysis and Synthesis of Drugs

Dixyrazine

10-(3-chloro-2-methylpropyl)-10H-phenothiazine (I) + 2-(2-(piperazin-1-yl)ethoxy)ethanol → Dixyrazine

DOFETILIDE

Use: antiarrythmic agent

Analysis:

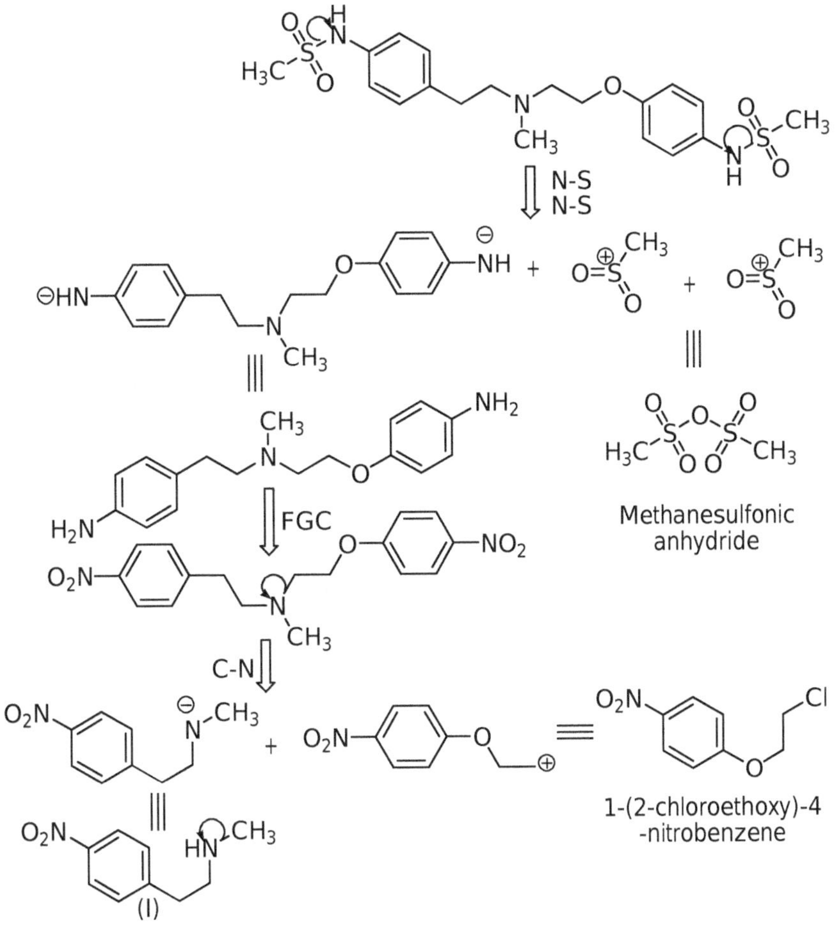

[Retrosynthetic scheme showing disconnections: N–S, N–S bonds giving bis-aniline intermediate plus methanesulfonic anhydride; FGC to bis-nitro intermediate; C–N disconnection giving 4-nitrophenethyl(methyl)amine (I) and 1-(2-chloroethoxy)-4-nitrobenzene]

1-(2-chloroethoxy)-4-nitrobenzene

Methanesulfonic anhydride

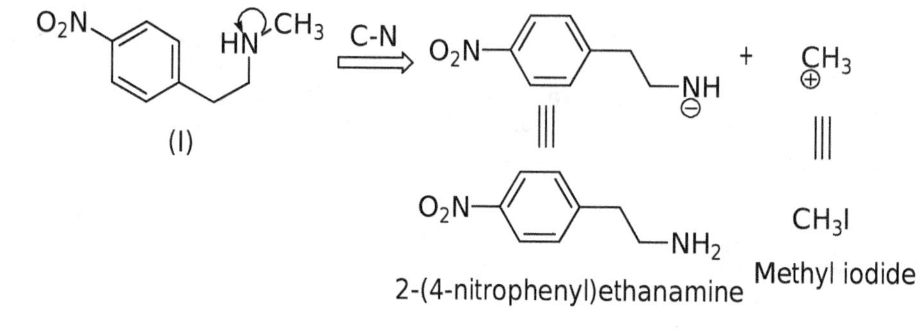

Retrosynthetic Analysis and Synthesis of Drugs

(I) ⟹ [C-N] 2-(4-nitrophenyl)ethanamine + Methyl iodide (CH₃I)

Synthesis:

2-(4-nitrophenyl)ethanamine $\xrightarrow{\text{CH}_3\text{I, NaOH, H}_2\text{O, CH}_3\text{OH}}$ N-methyl-2-(4-nitrophenyl)ethanamine

↓ (with 1-(2-chloroethoxy)-4-nitrobenzene)

[tertiary amine intermediate with two 4-nitrophenyl groups]

$\xrightarrow{\text{H}_2, \text{Raney Ni, } \text{H}_3\text{COH} \ ; \ (\text{CH}_3\text{SO}_2)_2\text{O}}$

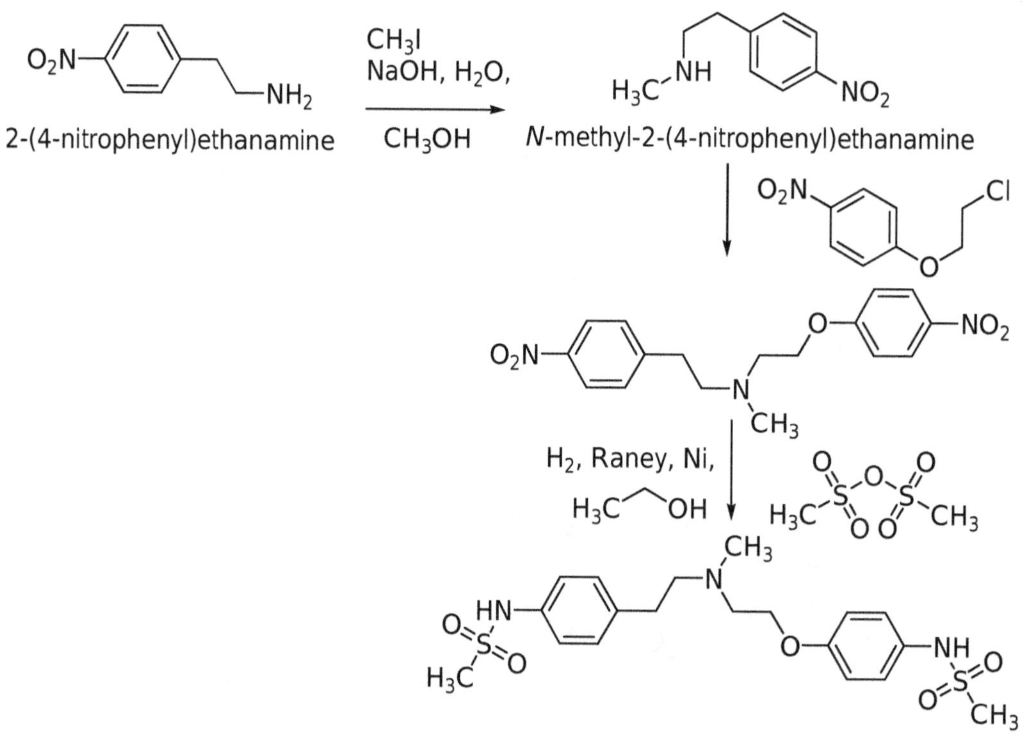

Dofetilide

DOPEXAMINE

Use: cardiotonic

Analysis:

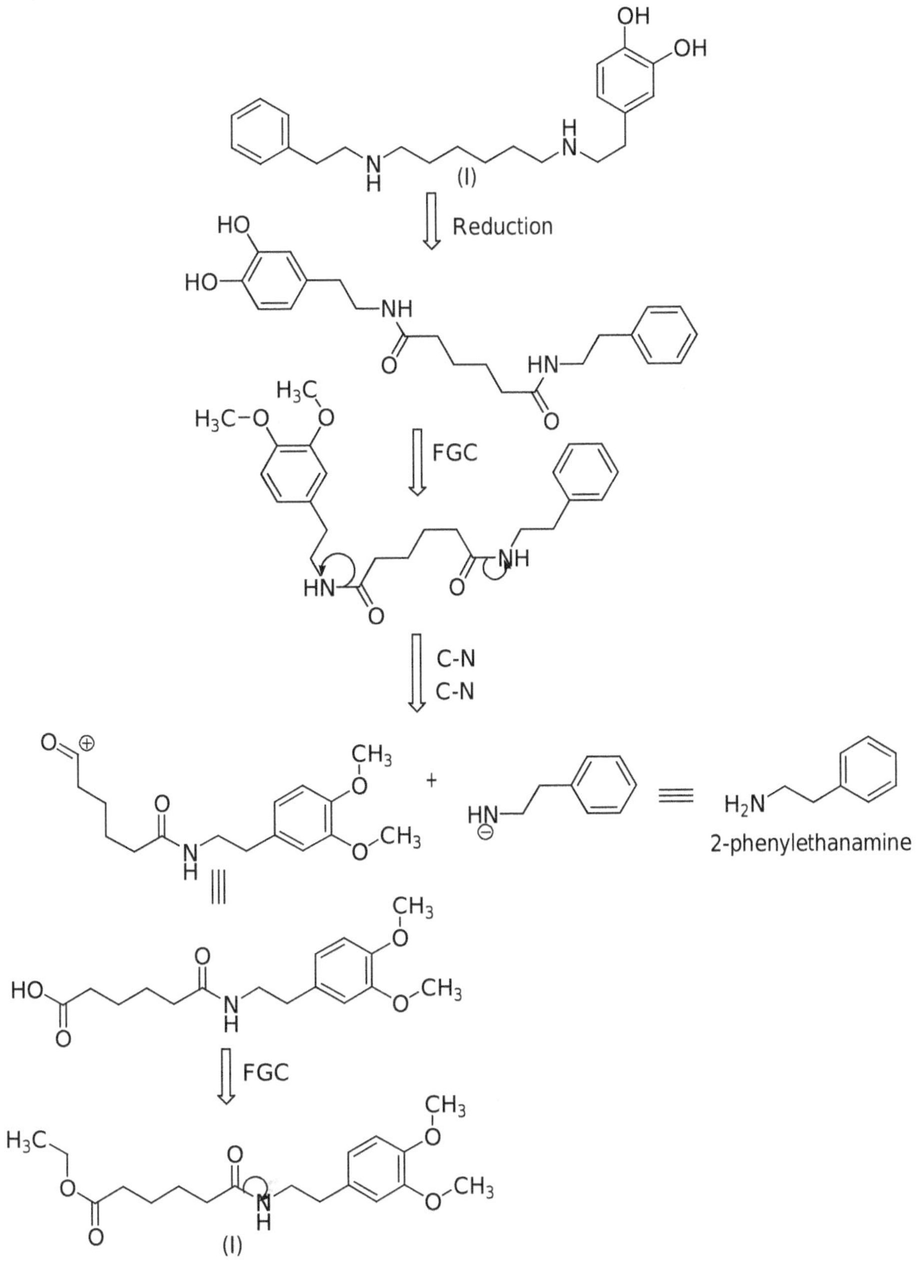

[Retrosynthetic scheme showing dopexamine (I) undergoing Reduction to a bis-amide intermediate, then FGC to a dimethoxy bis-amide, then C-N / C-N disconnection to give an acyl cation-amide with 3,4-dimethoxyphenethylamide and 2-phenylethanamine, then the carboxylic acid intermediate, then FGC to the ethyl ester (I).]

2-phenylethanamine

Synthesis:

5-(ethoxycarbonyl)pentanoic acid → (SOCl₂) → ethyl 5-(chlorocarbonyl)pentanoate

↓ 2-(3,4-dimethoxyphenyl)ethanamine

ethyl 5-(3,4-dimethoxyphenethylcarbamoyl)pentanoate
(I)

Retrosynthetic Analysis and Synthesis of Drugs

5-(3,4-dimethoxyphenethylcarbamoyl) pentanoic acid

N^1-(3,4-dimethoxyphenethyl)-N^6-phenethyladipamide

Dopexamine

DROPROPIZINE
Use: antitussive
Analysis:

1-phenylpiperazine   (oxiran-2-yl)methanol

Synthesis:

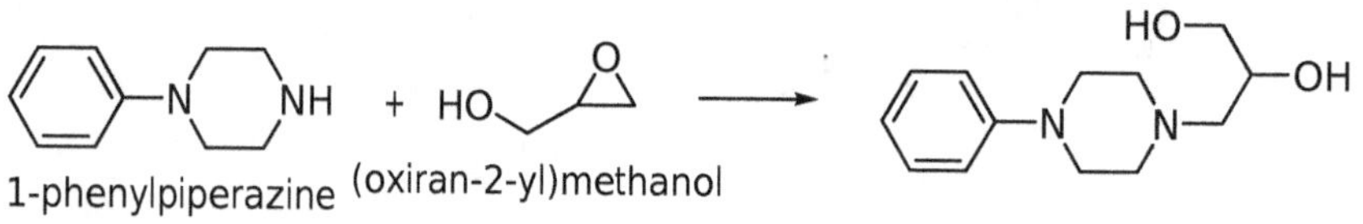

1-phenylpiperazine + (oxiran-2-yl)methanol ⟶ **Dropropizine**

EBASTINE

Use: antihistaminic

Analysis:

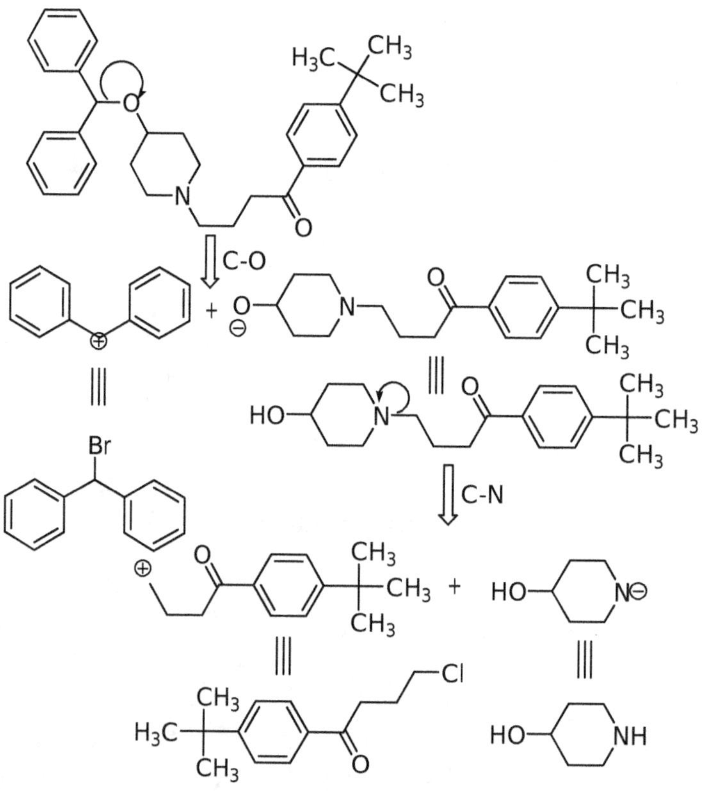

1-(4-*tert*-butylphenyl)-4-chlorobutan-1-one

Synthesis:

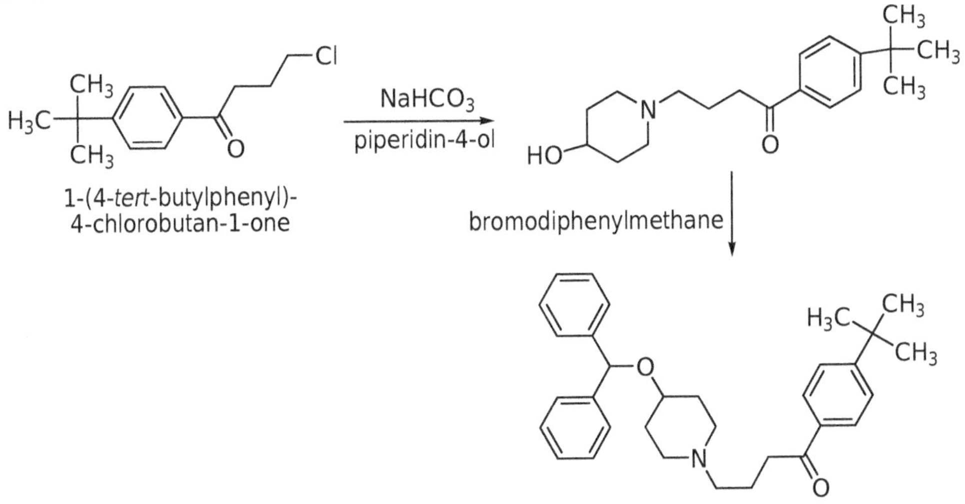

1-(4-*tert*-butylphenyl)-4-chlorobutan-1-one → (NaHCO₃, piperidin-4-ol) → intermediate → (bromodiphenylmethane) → **Ebastine**

ECONAZOLE

Use: antifungal

Analysis:

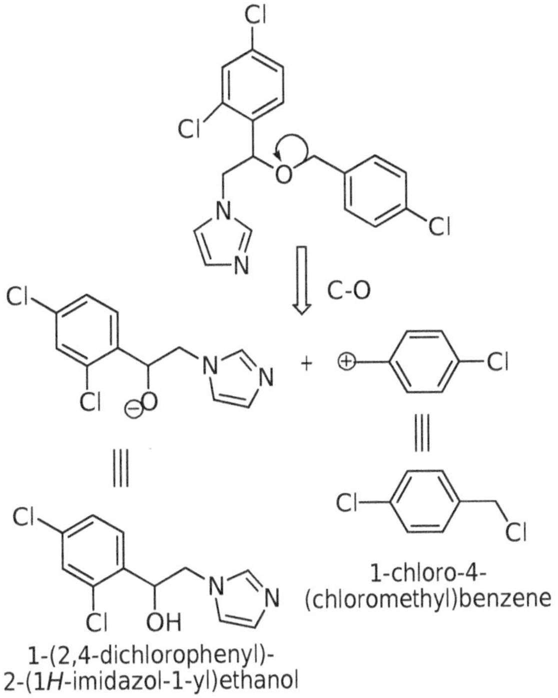

Retrosynthetic disconnection (C–O) of econazole gives:

- 1-(2,4-dichlorophenyl)-2-(1H-imidazol-1-yl)ethanol
- 1-chloro-4-(chloromethyl)benzene

Synthesis:

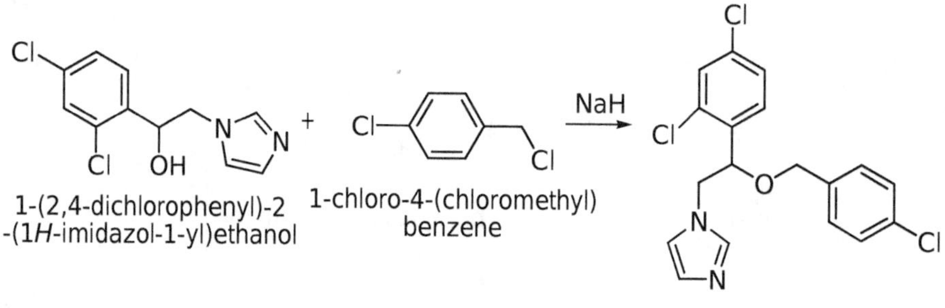

1-(2,4-dichlorophenyl)-2-(1H-imidazol-1-yl)ethanol + 1-chloro-4-(chloromethyl)benzene —NaH→ **Econazole**

EDROPHONIUM CHLORIDE

Use: cholinergic

Analysis:

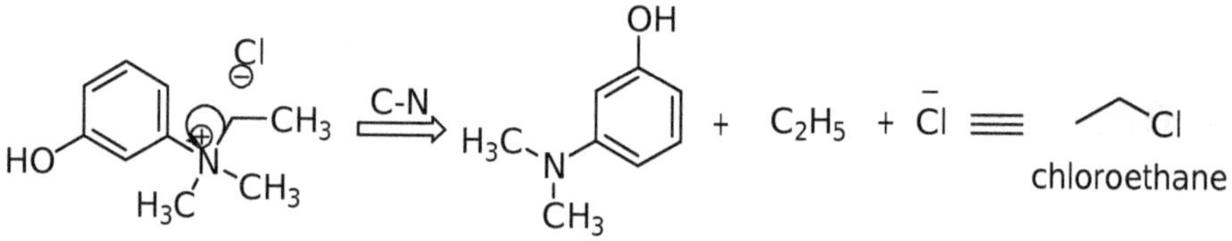

[structure of edrophonium] ⟹ (C-N) 3-(methylamino)phenol derivative + C_2H_5 + Cl^- ≡ chloroethane (CH_3CH_2Cl)

Synthesis:

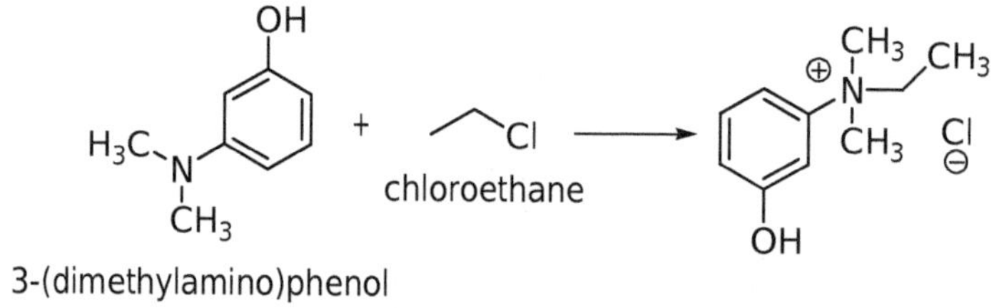

3-(dimethylamino)phenol + chloroethane ⟶ **Edrophonium Chloride**

EMEDASTINE

Use: antihistaminic

Analysis:

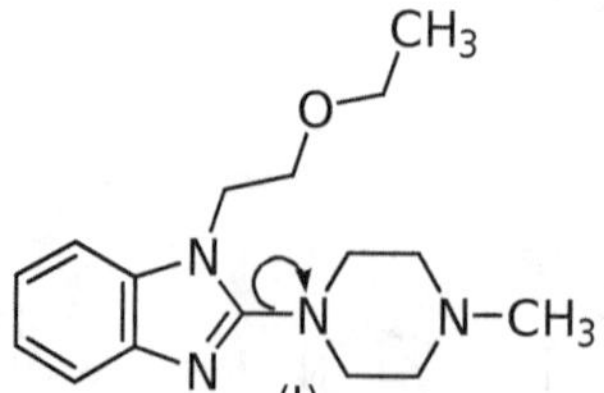

[structure (I)]

Retrosynthetic Analysis and Synthesis of Drugs

Synthesis:

2-chloro-1H-benzo[d]imidazole + 1-chloro-2-ethoxyethane →(Na₂CO₃, KI)→ 2-chloro-1-(2-ethoxyethyl)-1H-benzo[d]imidazole

→(1-methylpiperazine)→ **Emedastine**

ENTACAPONE
Use: antiparkinsonian
Analysis:

2-cyano-*N*,*N*-diethyl acetamide

4-hydroxy-3-methoxybenzaldehyde

Synthesis:

4-hydroxy-3-methoxybenzaldehyde → 4-hydroxy-3-methoxy-5-nitrobenzaldehyde → 3,4-dihydroxy-5-nitro benzaldehyde → **Entacapone**

Reagents: CH₃COOH / HNO₃; Conc. HBr; C₂H₅OH, 2-cyano-N,N-diethylacetamide, piperidine (H–N), CH₃COOH

EPINEPHRINE

Use: sympathomimetic

Analysis:

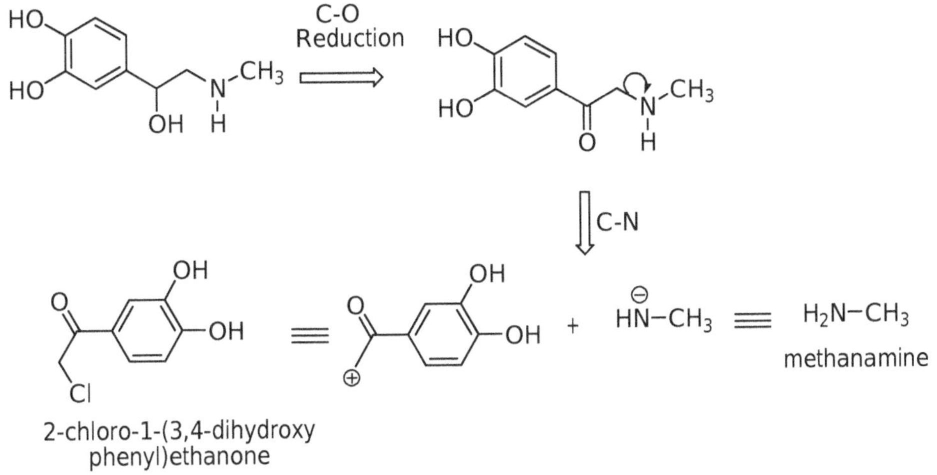

[Retrosynthetic scheme: Epinephrine → (C-O Reduction) → 1-(3,4-dihydroxyphenyl)-2-(methylamino)ethanone → (C-N) → 2-chloro-1-(3,4-dihydroxyphenyl)ethanone + methanamine (H_2N-CH_3)]

Synthesis :

[2-chloro-1-(3,4-dihydroxyphenyl)ethanone + H_3C-NH_2 (methanamine) → 1-(3,4-dihydroxyphenyl)-2-(methylamino)ethanone → (H_2, Raney-Ni) → **Epinephrine**]

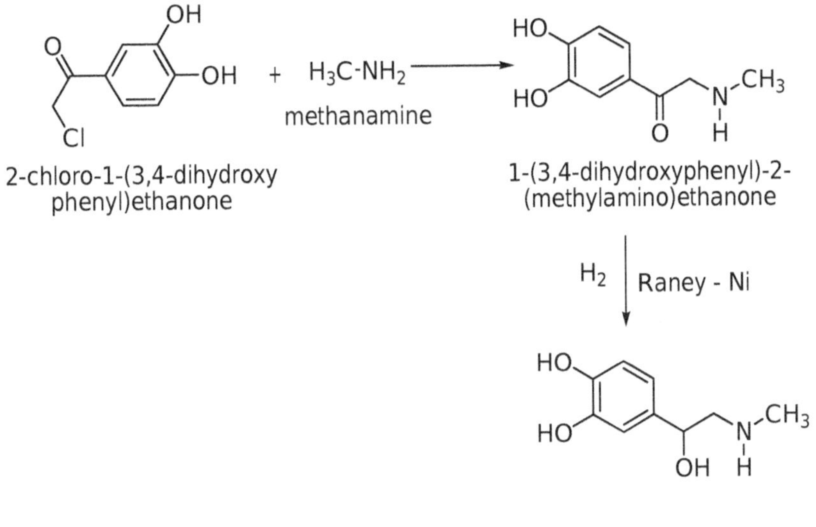

EPITIZIDE

Use: antihypertensive, diuretic

Analysis:

[Retrosynthetic scheme: Epitizide disconnects via C-N, C-N bonds to give HC(+)-S-CH2-CF3 (≡ 2,2-dimethoxyethyl trifluoroethyl sulfane) and 4-amino-6-chloro-1,3-benzenedisulfonamide dianion (≡ 4-amino-6-chlorobenzene-1,3-disulfonamide). The sulfane further disconnects via C-S bond to 2,2-dimethoxyethanethiolate anion and CF3-CH2(+) cation (≡ 1,1,1-trifluoro-2-iodoethane).]

2,2-dimethoxyethanethiol   1,1,1-trifluoro-2-iodoethane

Synthesis:

$$\text{2,2-dimethoxyethanethiol} + \text{1,1,1-trifluoro-2-iodoethane} \xrightarrow{\text{NaOCH}_3, \text{CH}_3\text{OH}} \text{(2,2,2-trifluoroethyl)(2,2-dimethoxyethyl)sulfane}$$

[Then reaction with 4-amino-6-chlorobenzene-1,3-disulfonamide yields]

Epitizide

ESMOLOL

Use: antiarrythmic, β-blocker

Analysis:

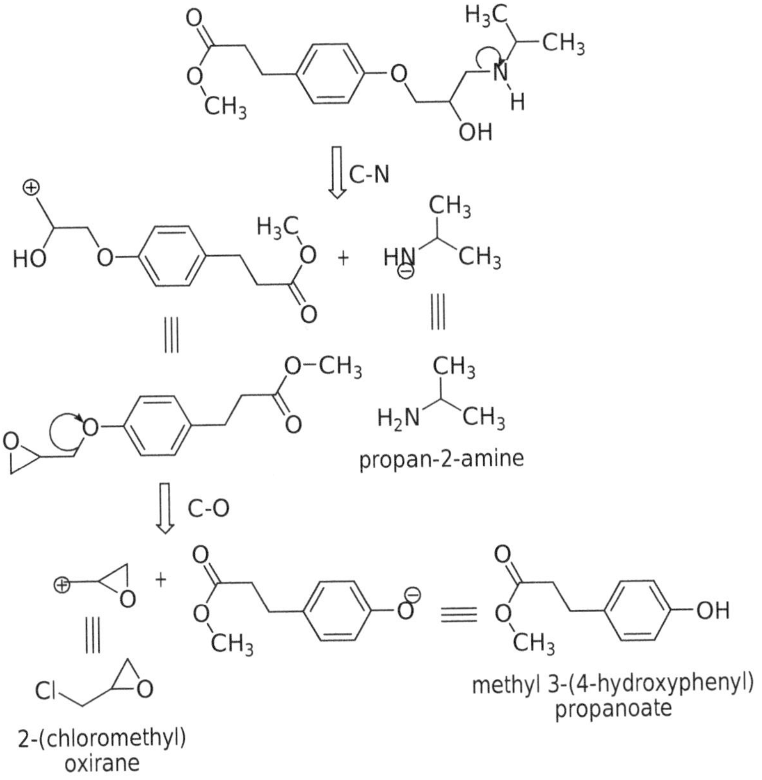

propan-2-amine

2-(chloromethyl) oxirane

methyl 3-(4-hydroxyphenyl) propanoate

Synthesis:

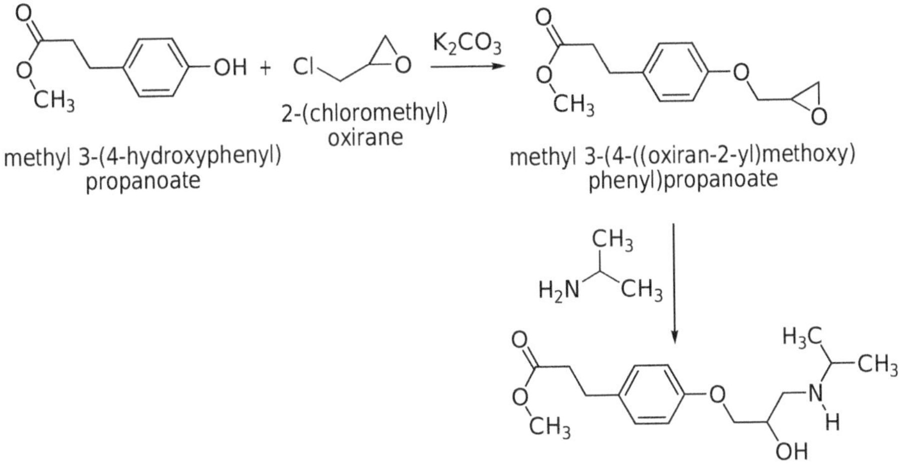

methyl 3-(4-hydroxyphenyl) propanoate + 2-(chloromethyl) oxirane →[K_2CO_3] methyl 3-(4-((oxiran-2-yl)methoxy) phenyl)propanoate

→ **Esmolol**

ETHAMBUTOL

Use: tuberculostatic

Analysis:

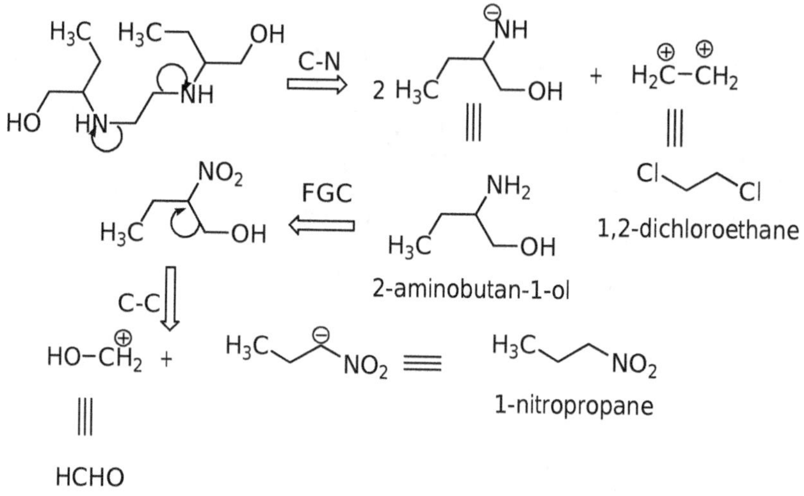

Synthesis:

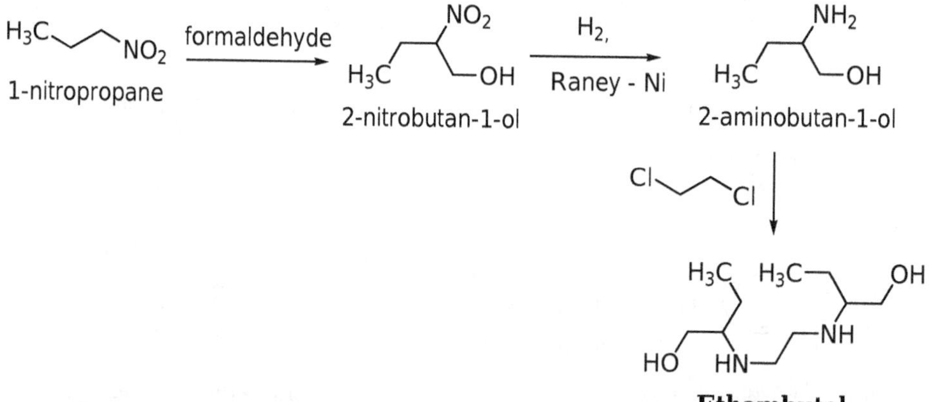

ETHOTOIN

Use: antiepileptic

Analysis:

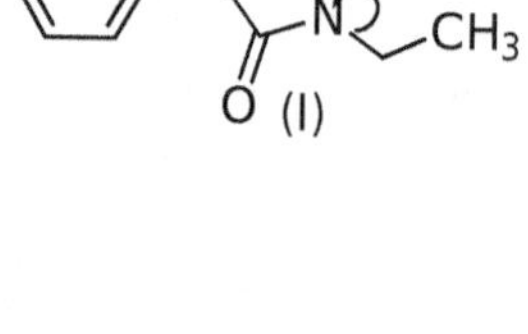

Retrosynthetic Analysis and Synthesis of Drugs

Synthesis:

Ethotoin

ETOFIBRATE

Use: antihyperlipidemic

Analysis:

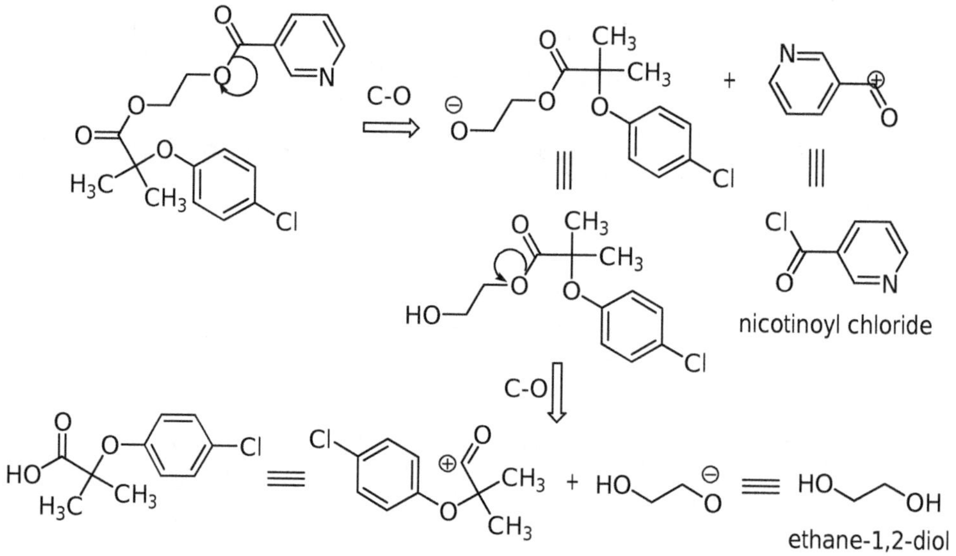
C-O
C-O
nicotinoyl chloride
ethane-1,2-diol

Synthesis:

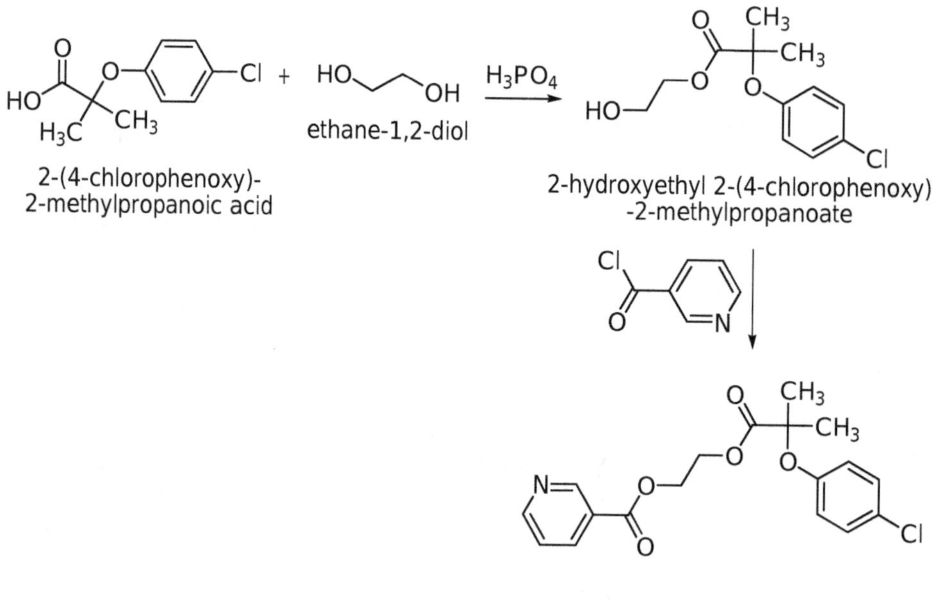
H3PO4
ethane-1,2-diol
2-(4-chlorophenoxy)-
2-methylpropanoic acid
2-hydroxyethyl 2-(4-chlorophenoxy)
-2-methylpropanoate

Etofibrate

ETOFYLLINE

Use: bronchodilator, cardiotonic

Analysis:

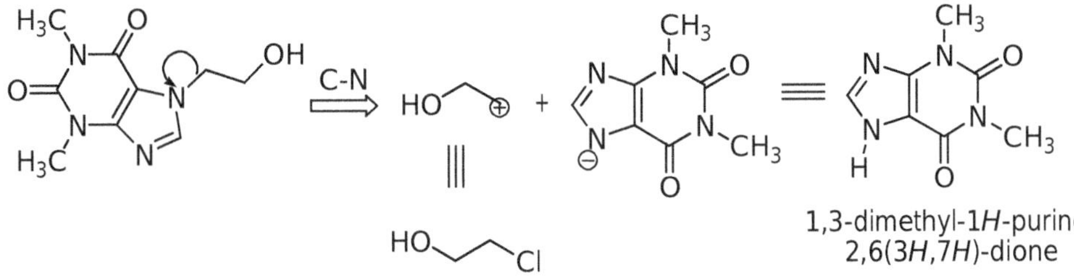

Synthesis:

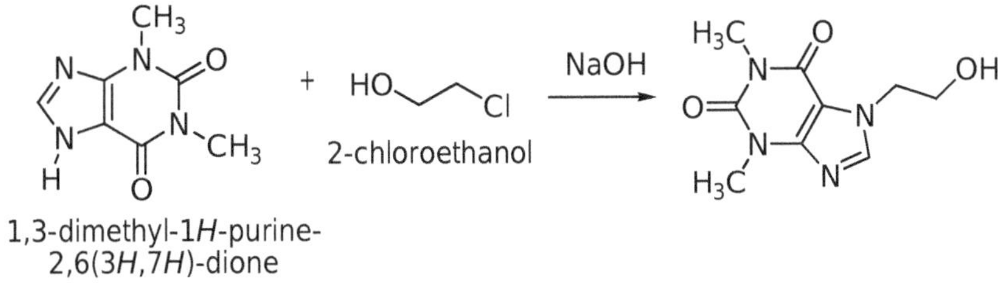

1,3-dimethyl-1H-purine-2,6(3H,7H)-dione + 2-chloroethanol →(NaOH) Etofylline

EXALAMIDE

Use: antifungal

Analysis:

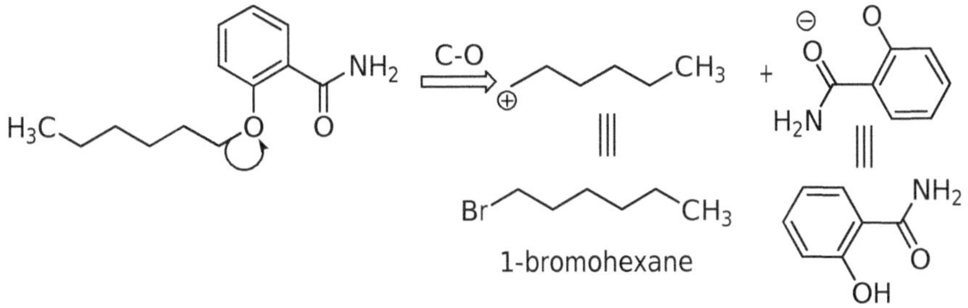

Synthesis:

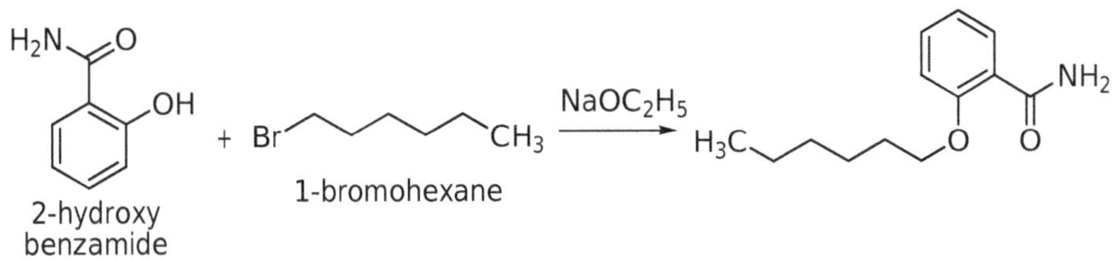

2-hydroxy benzamide + 1-bromohexane →(NaOC$_2$H$_5$) Exalamide

FEBUPROL
Use: choleritic
Analysis:

[Retrosynthetic analysis: Febuprol disconnects (C-O) into 2-(hydroxymethyl)-2-phenoxy cation + butan-1-ol (or butoxide); the epoxide 2-(phenoxymethyl)oxirane is equivalent. Further C-O disconnection gives 2-(chloromethyl)oxirane and phenol.]

2-(chloromethyl)oxirane   Phenol

Synthesis:

phenol + 2-(chloromethyl)oxirane $\xrightarrow{KOH}$ 2-(phenoxymethyl)oxirane

$\xrightarrow{n\text{-butanol}}$ **Febuprol**

FENALCOMINE
Use: cardiac stimulant
Analysis:

[Retrosynthetic step: Fenalcomine ⇒ (I) via C-O Reduction of the corresponding aryl ketone]

(I)

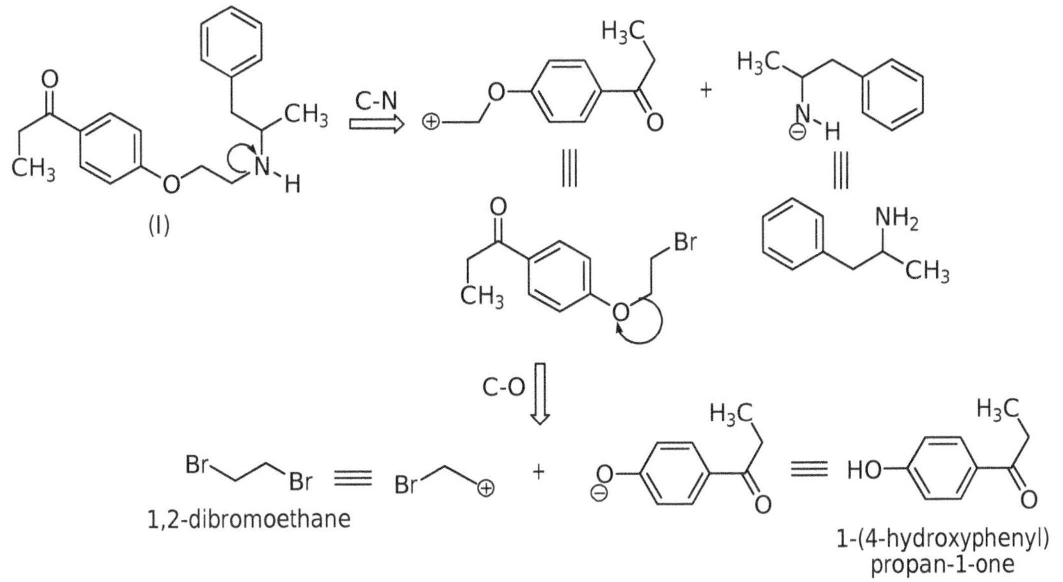

Synthesis:

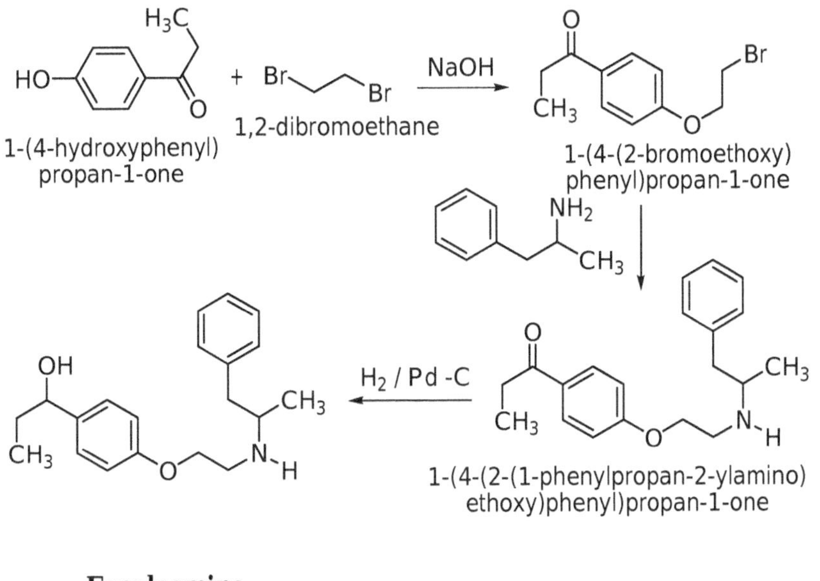

Fenalcomine

FENBUFEN
Use: anti-inflammatory, analgesic
Analysis:

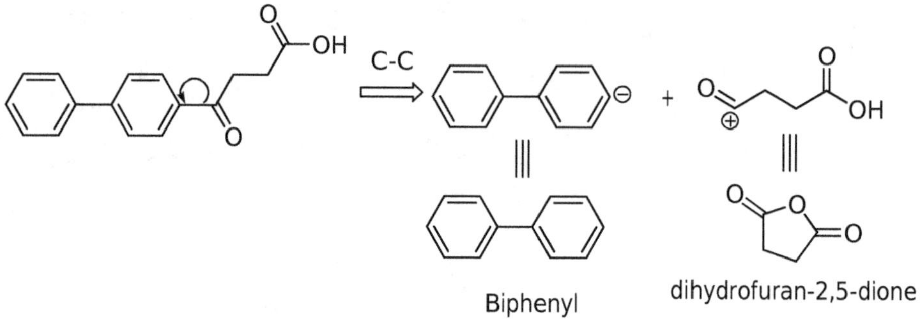

Biphenyl dihydrofuran-2,5-dione

Synthesis:

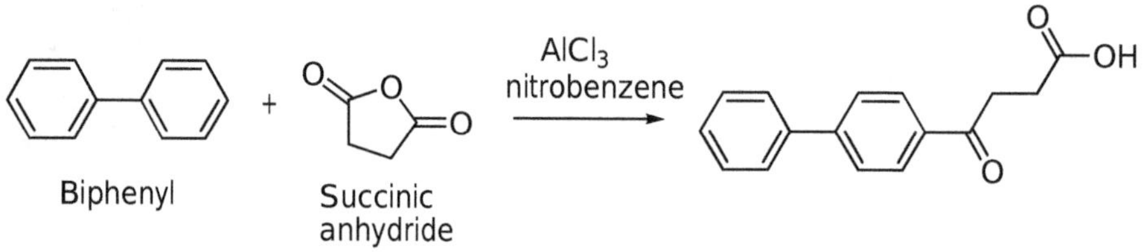

Biphenyl + Succinic anhydride → (AlCl₃, nitrobenzene) → Fenbufen

FENETHYLLINE
Use: CNS stimulant, psychotic
Analysis:

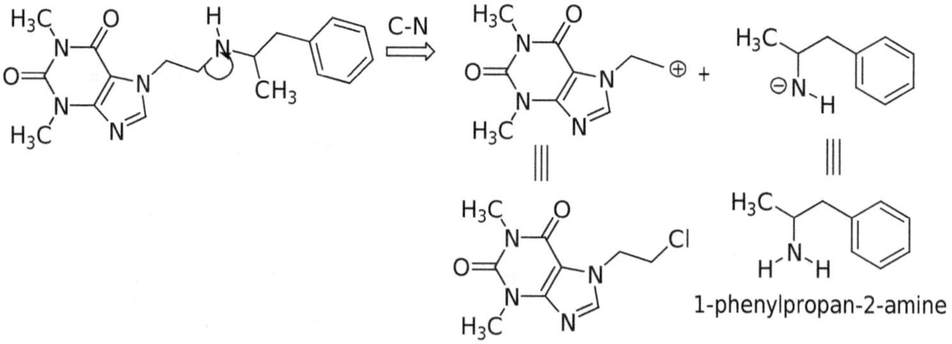

1-phenylpropan-2-amine

Synthesis:

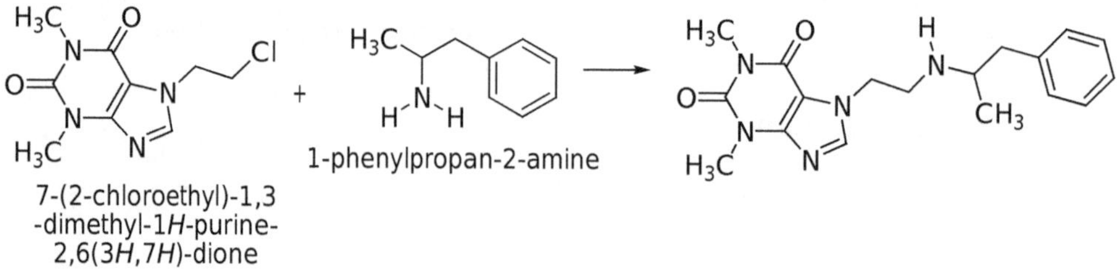

7-(2-chloroethyl)-1,3-dimethyl-1H-purine-2,6(3H,7H)-dione + 1-phenylpropan-2-amine → Fenethylline

FENOFIBRATE

Use: cholesterol depressant

Analysis:

Synthesis:

[Scheme: 4-chlorobenzoyl chloride + anisole → (with AlCl₃) (4-chlorophenyl)(4-methoxyphenyl)methanone → (HBr) (4-chlorophenyl)(4-hydroxyphenyl)methanone → (with 2-chloro-2-methylpropanoic acid / ClC(CH₃)₂COOH) intermediate acid → (with isopropanol, HOCH(CH₃)₂) **Fenofibrate**]

FENOPROFEN

Use: antirheumatic

Analysis:

[Retrosynthetic scheme: 2-(3-phenoxyphenyl)propanoic acid ⟹ (FGC) nitrile (CH₃-CH(CN)-C₆H₄-O-C₆H₅) ⟹ (C–C disconnection) 1-(1-bromoethyl)-3-phenoxybenzene (I) ≡ cation (3-phenoxyphenyl-CH(+)-CH₃) + ⁻C≡N ≡ NaCN]

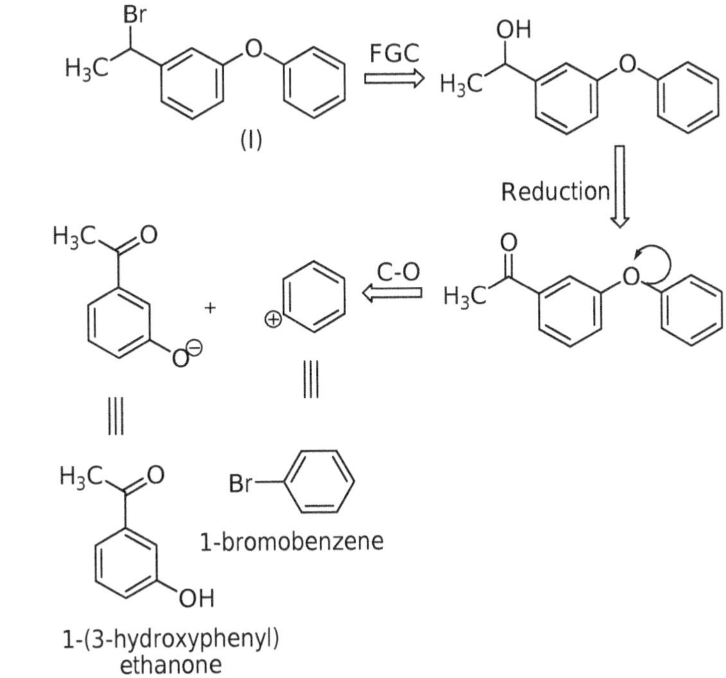

Retrosynthetic Analysis and Synthesis of Drugs

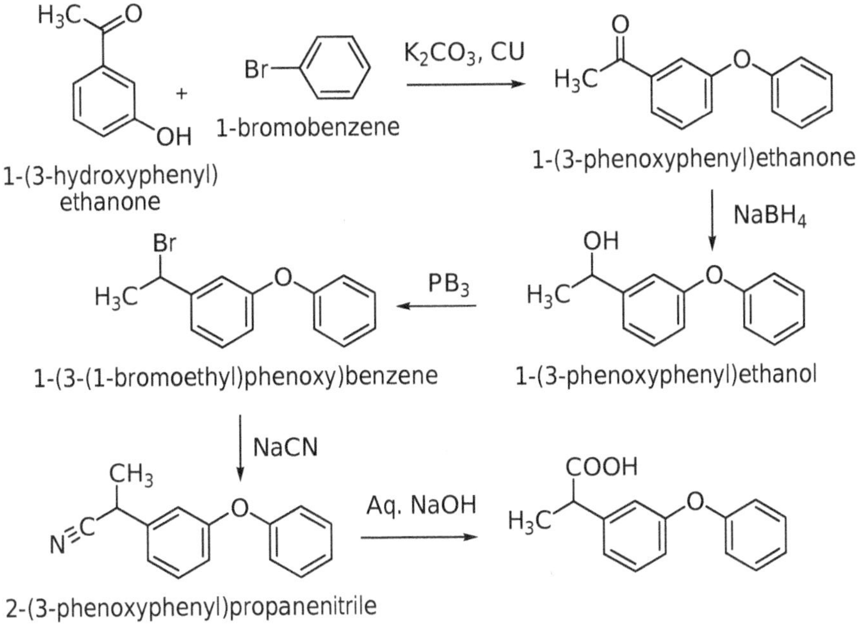

Retrosynthesis:

The target molecule (I), 1-bromo-1-(3-phenoxyphenyl)ethane, undergoes Functional Group Conversion (FGC) to give 1-(3-phenoxyphenyl)ethanol, which on reduction disconnection gives 1-(3-phenoxyphenyl)ethanone. C–O disconnection gives 3-acetylphenoxide ion and phenyl cation, equivalent to 1-(3-hydroxyphenyl)ethanone and 1-bromobenzene (bromobenzene).

Synthesis:

1-(3-hydroxyphenyl)ethanone + 1-bromobenzene → (K₂CO₃, Cu) → 1-(3-phenoxyphenyl)ethanone

1-(3-phenoxyphenyl)ethanone → (NaBH₄) → 1-(3-phenoxyphenyl)ethanol

1-(3-phenoxyphenyl)ethanol → (PBr₃) → 1-(3-(1-bromoethyl)phenoxy)benzene

1-(3-(1-bromoethyl)phenoxy)benzene → (NaCN) → 2-(3-phenoxyphenyl)propanenitrile

2-(3-phenoxyphenyl)propanenitrile → (Aq. NaOH) → **Fenoprofen**

FENOVERINE
Use: antispasmodic
Analysis:

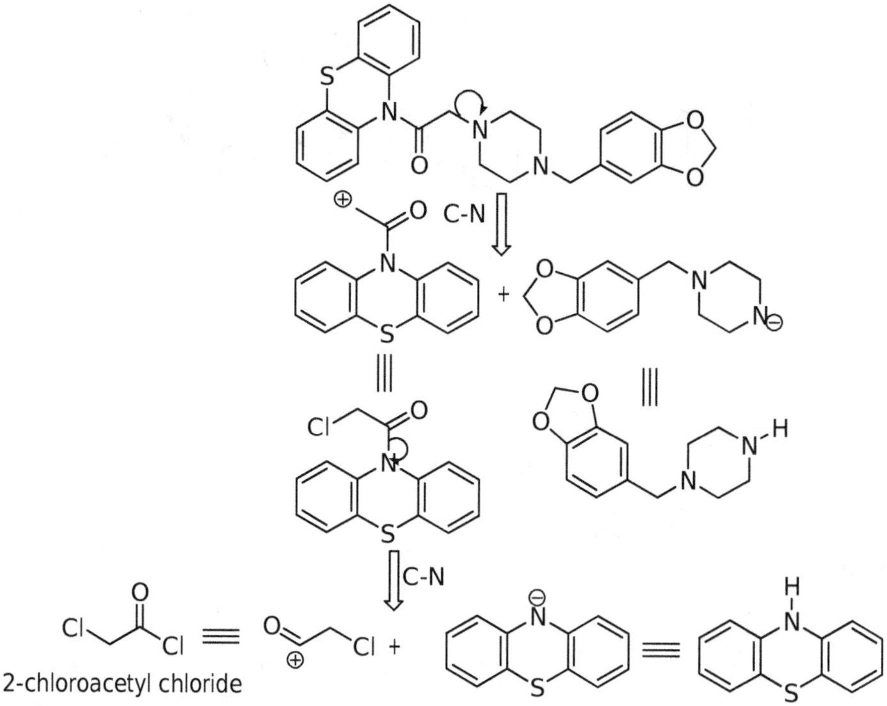

Synthesis:

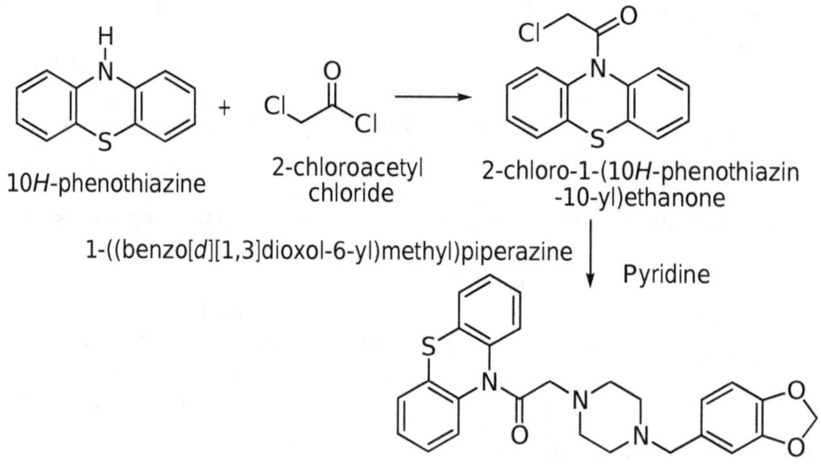

10H-phenothiazine + 2-chloroacetyl chloride → 2-chloro-1-(10H-phenothiazin-10-yl)ethanone

1-((benzo[*d*][1,3]dioxol-6-yl)methyl)piperazine, Pyridine

Fenoverine

FENTANYL
Use: analgesic
Analysis:

Retrosynthetic Analysis and Synthesis of Drugs

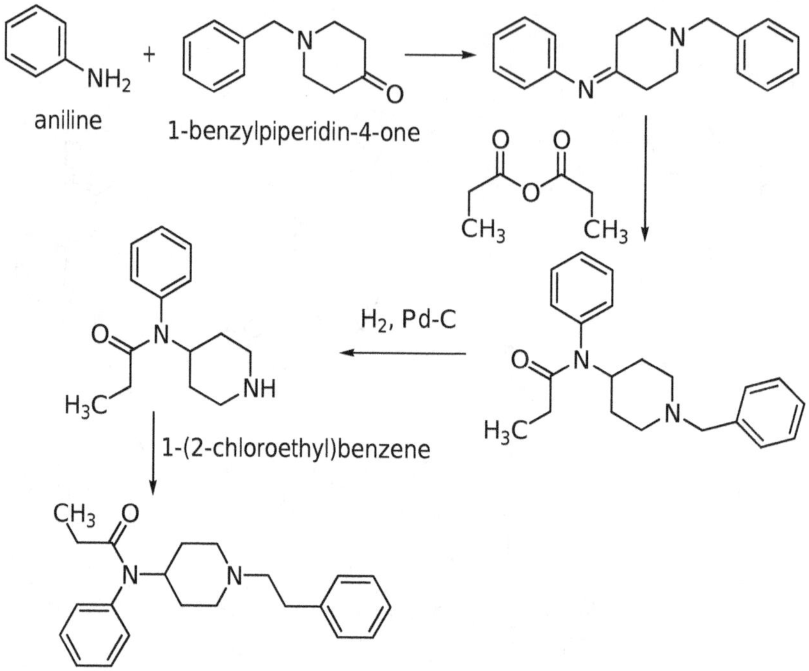

Synthesis:

[Scheme: aniline + 1-benzylpiperidin-4-one → imine intermediate; then propionic anhydride → N-phenyl-N-(1-benzylpiperidin-4-yl)propanamide; H₂, Pd-C → N-phenyl-N-(piperidin-4-yl)propanamide; 1-(2-chloroethyl)benzene → **Fentanyl**]

FLOREDIL
Use: coronary vasodilator
Analysis:

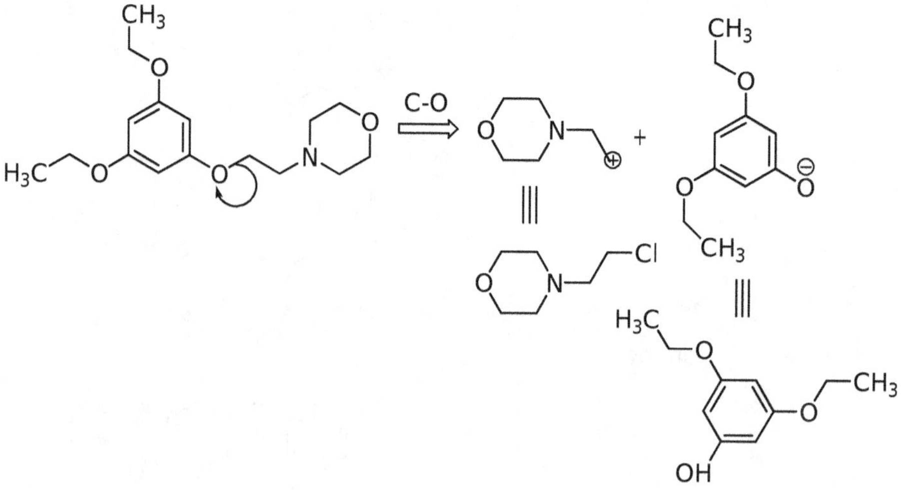

[Retrosynthetic scheme: 3,5-diethoxyphenyl 2-morpholinoethyl ether ⇒ C–O disconnection giving morpholinyl-CH₂⁺ (≡ 4-(2-chloroethyl)morpholine) + 3,5-diethoxyphenoxide (≡ 3,5-diethoxyphenol)]

Retrosynthetic Analysis and Synthesis of Drugs

4-(2-chloroethyl)morpholine + 3,5-diethoxyphenol $\xrightarrow{NaOC_2H_5}$ **Floredil**

FLUANISONE

Use: neuroleptic

Analysis:

Fluanisone $\xRightarrow{C-N}$ 1-(2-methoxyphenyl)piperazine anion + 4-fluorophenyl butyl cation

≡ 1-(2-methoxyphenyl)piperazine + 4-chloro-1-(4-fluorophenyl)butan-1-one

Synthesis:

1-(2-methoxyphenyl)piperazine + 4-chloro-1-(4-fluorophenyl)butan-1-one → **Fluanisone**

FLUCOXACILLIN

Use: antibiotic

Analysis:

Synthesis:

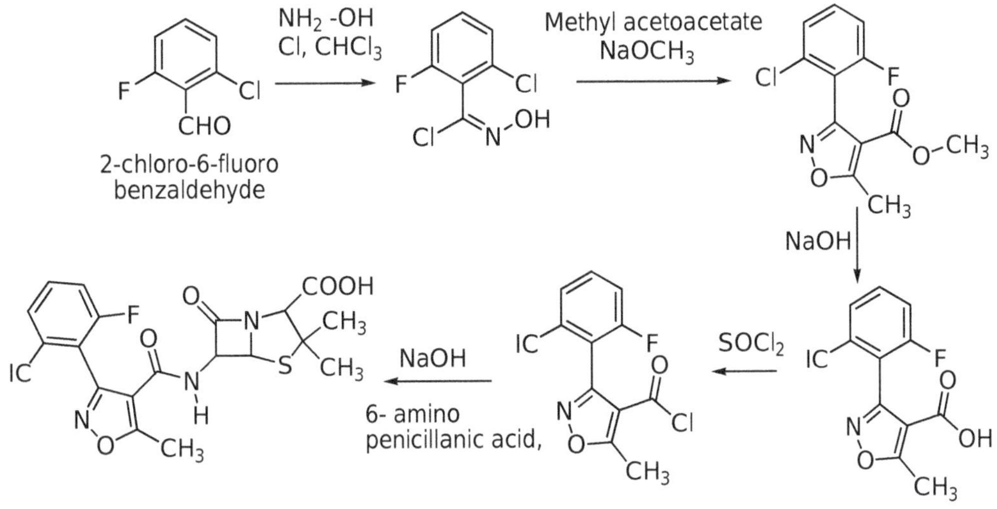
NH_2 -OH
Cl, $CHCl_3$
Methyl acetoacetate
$NaOCH_3$
2-chloro-6-fluoro benzaldehyde
NaOH
$SOCl_2$
NaOH
6- amino penicillanic acid,

Flucoxacillin

FLUFENAMIC ACID

Use: anti-inflammatory, antirheumatic

Analysis:

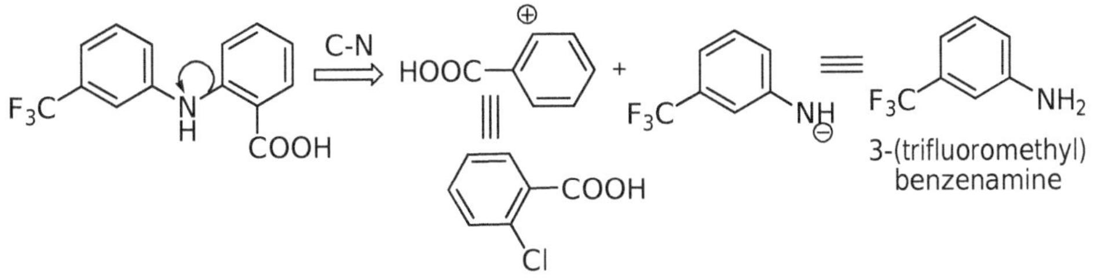
C-N
3-(trifluoromethyl) benzenamine

Synthesis:

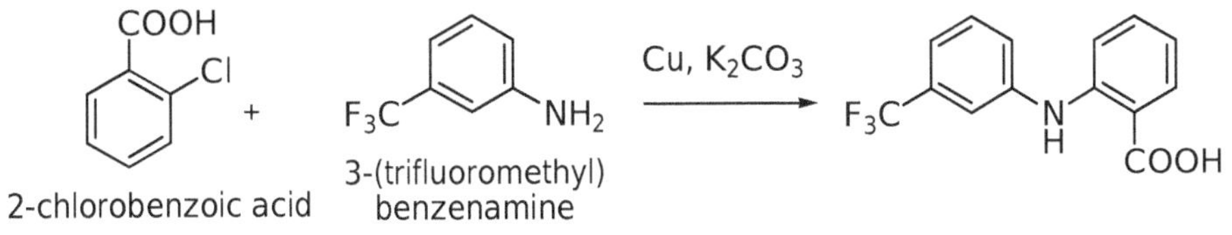
Cu, K_2CO_3
2-chlorobenzoic acid
3-(trifluoromethyl) benzenamine

Flufenamic acid

FLUNARIZINE
Use: vasodilator
Analysis:

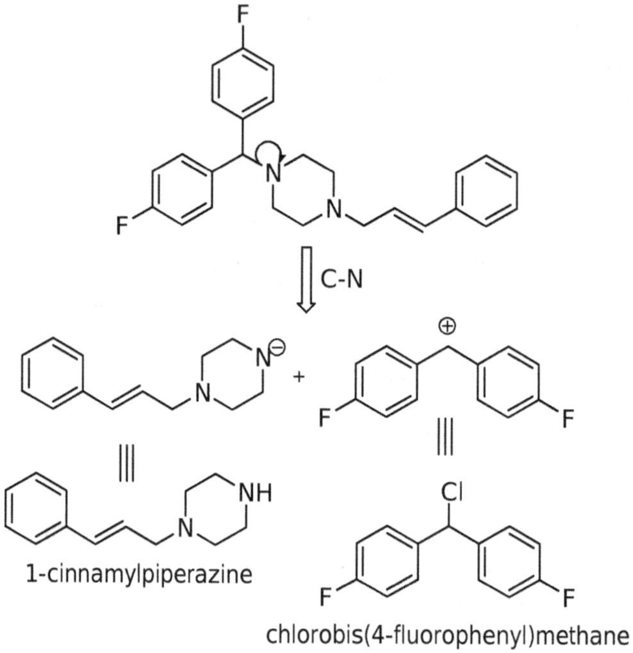

[Retrosynthetic analysis: Flunarizine is disconnected at the C–N bond to give the cinnamylpiperazine anion and the bis(4-fluorophenyl)methyl cation, corresponding synthons being 1-cinnamylpiperazine and chlorobis(4-fluorophenyl)methane.]

Synthesis:

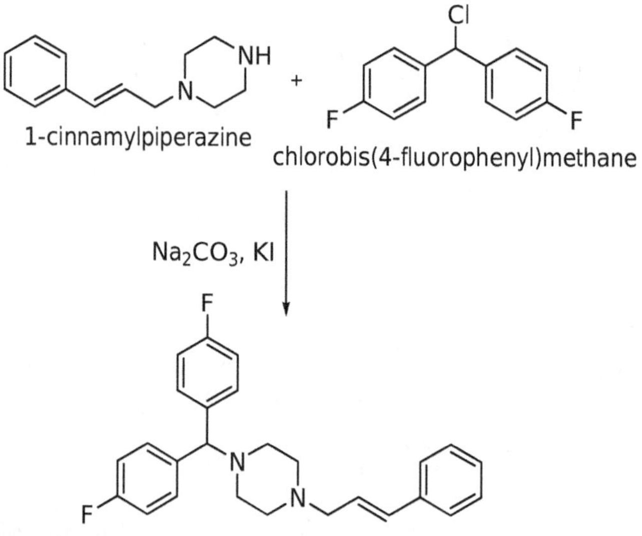

1-cinnamylpiperazine + chlorobis(4-fluorophenyl)methane

$\xrightarrow{Na_2CO_3,\ KI}$

Flunarizine

FLUOXETINE

Use: antidepressant

Analysis:

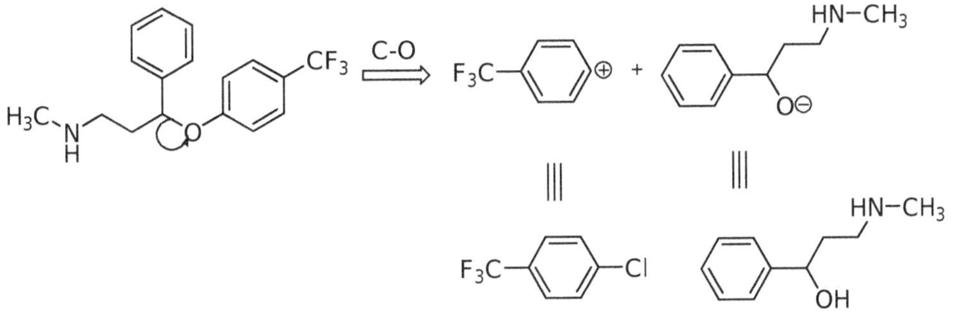

[Retrosynthetic scheme: Fluoxetine ⇒ C-O disconnection giving F₃C-C₆H₄⁺ cation + alkoxide of 3-(methylamino)-1-phenylpropan-1-ol; equivalents: 1-chloro-4-(trifluoromethyl)benzene and 3-(methylamino)-1-phenylpropan-1-ol]

Synthesis:

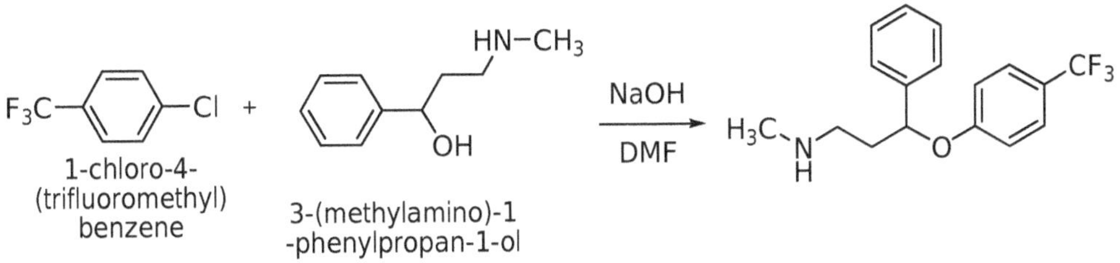

1-chloro-4-(trifluoromethyl)benzene + 3-(methylamino)-1-phenylpropan-1-ol → (NaOH, DMF) → **Fluoxetine**

FLUTAMIDE

Use: antineoplastic

Analysis:

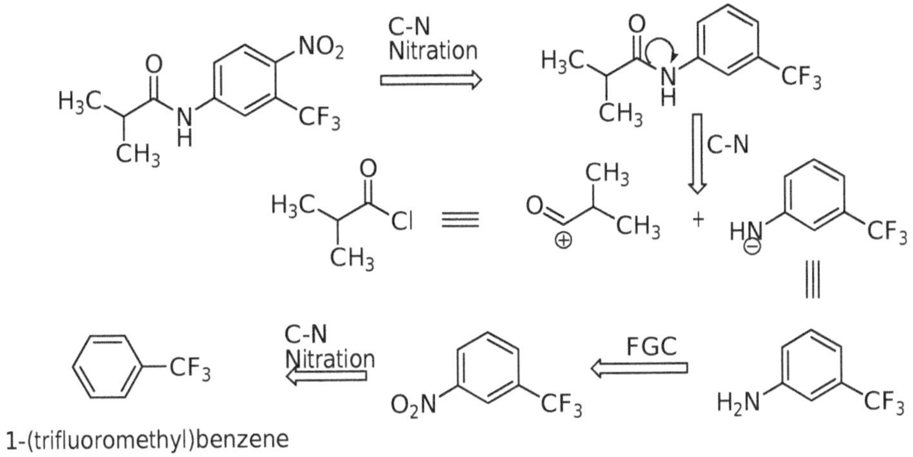

[Retrosynthetic scheme: Flutamide ⇒ (C-N, Nitration) → isobutyramide of 3-(trifluoromethyl)aniline ⇒ (C-N) → isobutyryl chloride (≡ acylium cation) + 3-(trifluoromethyl)aniline ⇐ (FGC) 3-nitro(trifluoromethyl)benzene ⇐ (C-N, Nitration) 1-(trifluoromethyl)benzene]

Synthesis:

1-(trifluoromethyl)benzene →(HNO₃/H₂SO₄)→ 1-(trifluoromethyl)-3-nitrobenzene →(H₂, Pd-C)→ 3-(trifluoromethyl)benzenamine →(isobutyryl chloride, Pyridine)→ N-(3-(trifluoromethyl)phenyl)isobutyramide →(HNO₃)→ N-(4-nitro-3-(trifluoromethyl)phenyl)isobutyramide

FUROSEMIDE

Use: diuretic

Analysis:

Furosemide ⇒ (C–N) (furan-2-yl)methanamine + 4-chloro-5-sulfamoyl-2-chlorobenzoic acid cation

(furan-2-yl)methanamine: H_2N-CH_2-furan

⇒ 2,4-dichloro-5-sulfamoylbenzoic acid ⇒ (C–N) 2,4-dichloro-5-(chlorosulfonyl)benzoic acid + NH_3 (NH_2^-)

⇐ (C–S, Chlorosulfonation) 2,4-dichlorobenzoic acid

Synthesis:

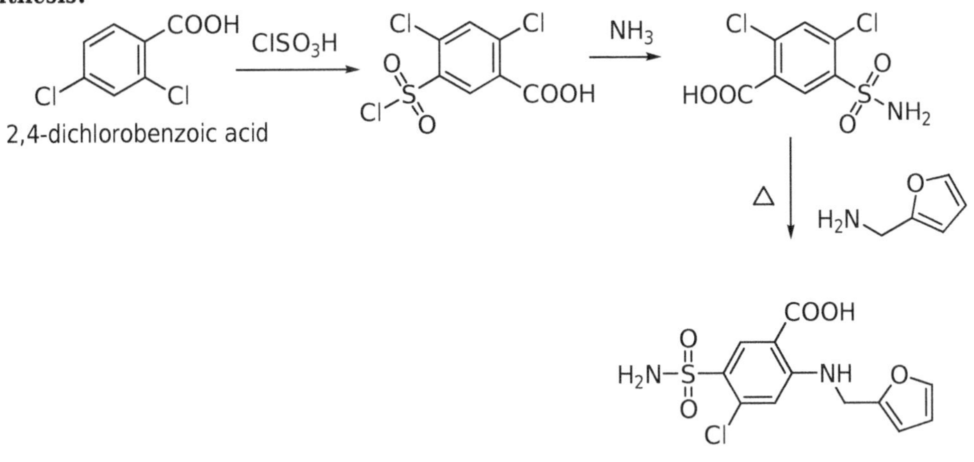
COOH
Cl
Cl
2,4-dichlorobenzoic acid
ClSO3H
NH3
HOOC
NH2
H2N
COOH
NH

Furosemide

GABEXATE

Use: protease inhibitor

Analysis:

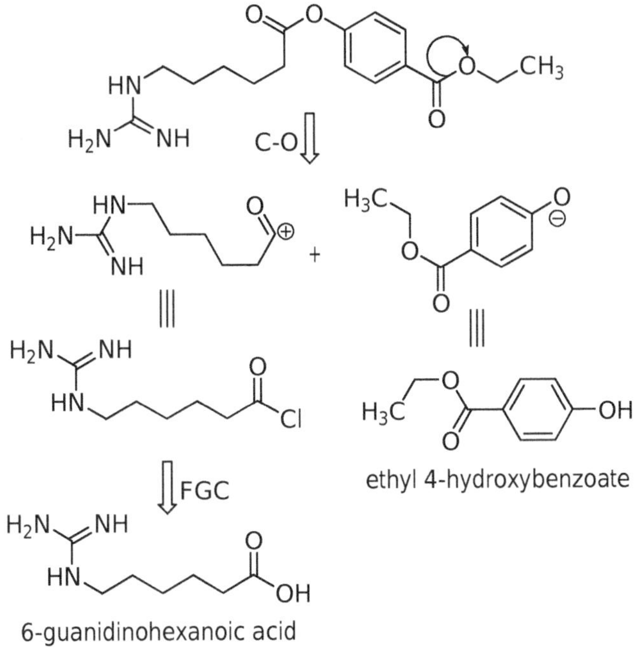
C-O
FGC
ethyl 4-hydroxybenzoate
6-guanidinohexanoic acid

Synthesis:

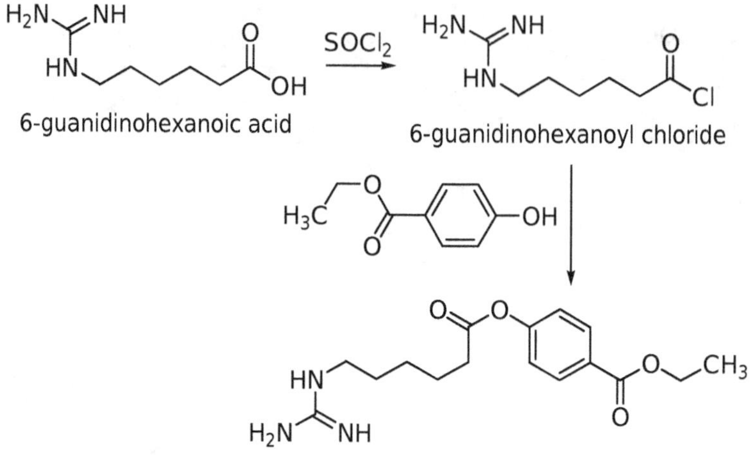

6-guanidinohexanoic acid → (SOCl₂) → 6-guanidinohexanoyl chloride

Gabexate

GALLOPAMIL
Use: coronary vasodilator
Analysis:

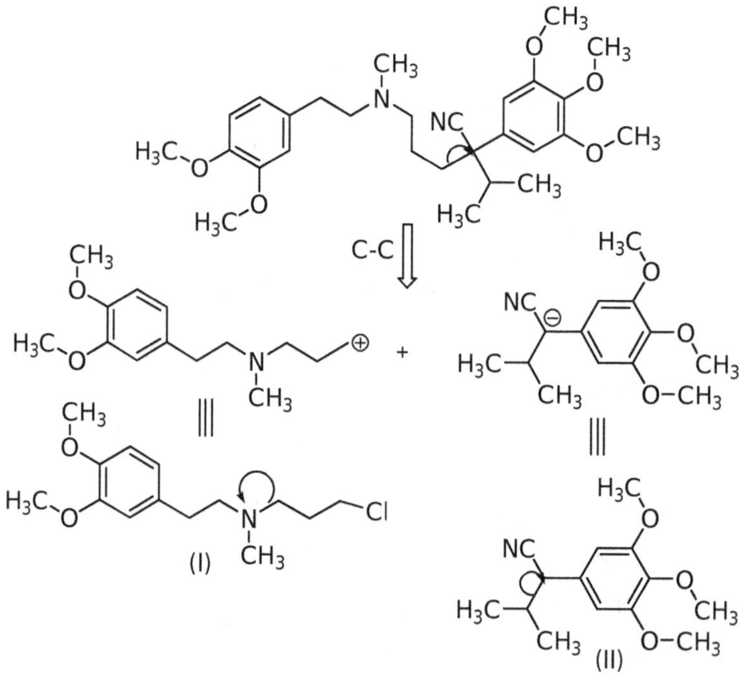

Retrosynthetic Analysis and Synthesis of Drugs

Synthesis:

(I) + (II) →[NaNH₂] **Gallopamil**

GEFARNATE

Use: antispasmodic

Analysis:

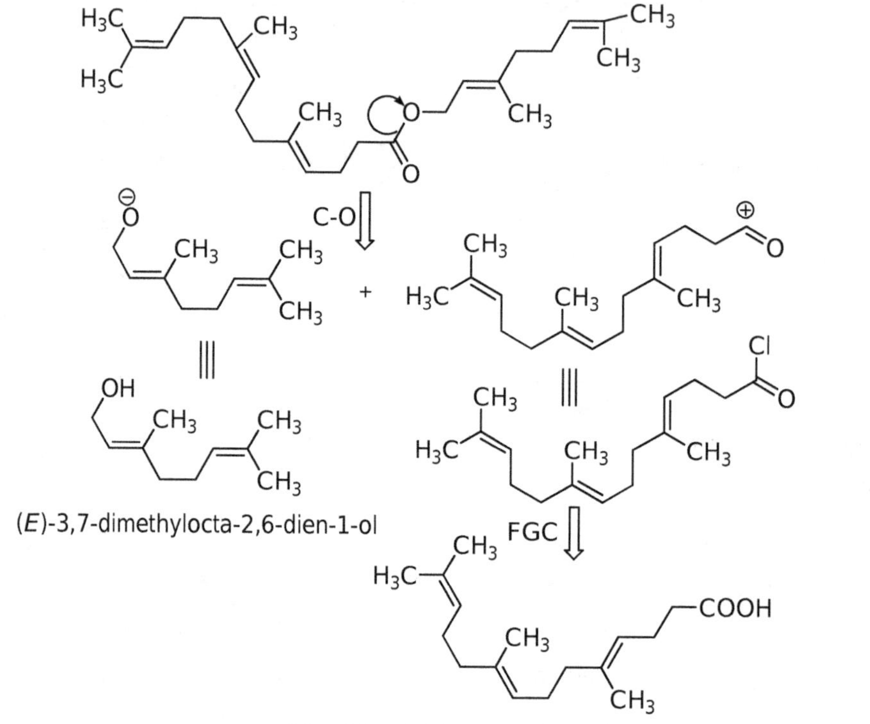

(E)-3,7-dimethylocta-2,6-dien-1-ol

(4E,8E)-5,9,13-trimethyltetradeca-4,8,12-trienoic acid

Synthesis:

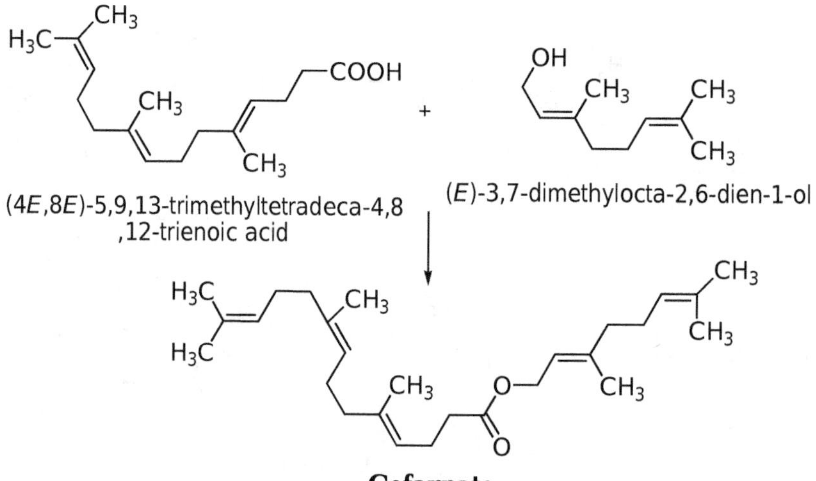

(4E,8E)-5,9,13-trimethyltetradeca-4,8,12-trienoic acid

(E)-3,7-dimethylocta-2,6-dien-1-ol

Gefarnate

GLIBENCLAMIDE

Use: antidiabetic

Analysis:

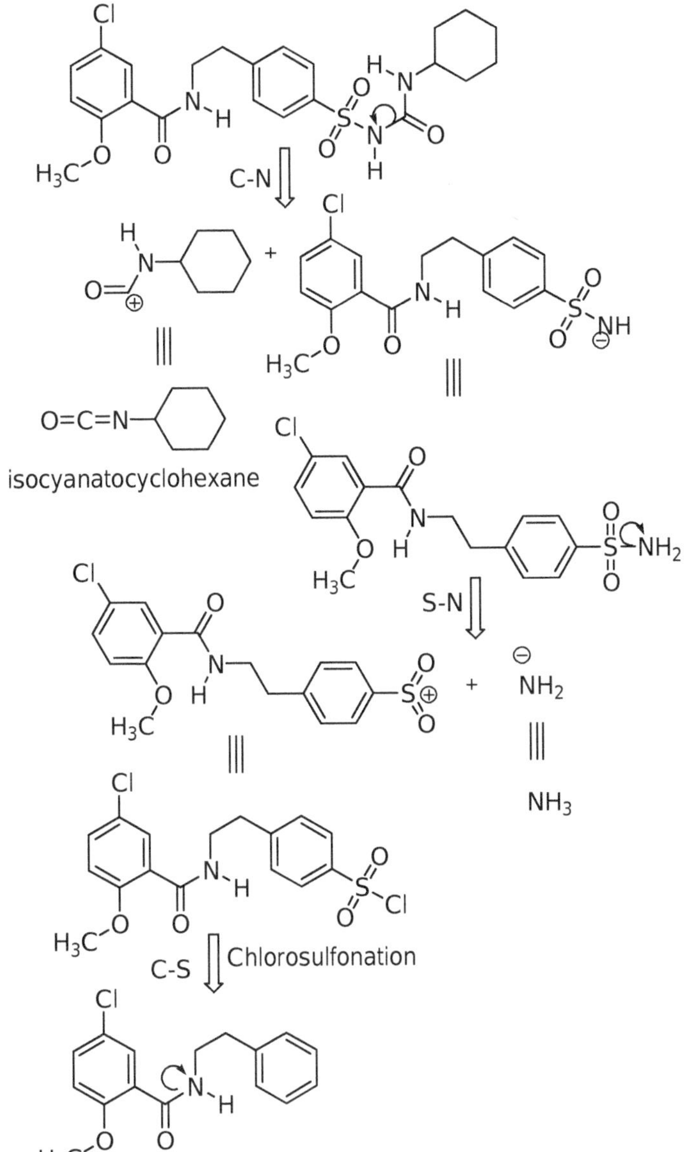

Retrosynthetic Analysis and Synthesis of Drugs

[Retrosynthetic scheme showing compound (I) disconnected at C-N bond to give acylium cation from 5-chloro-2-methoxybenzoyl and 2-phenylethanamine; FGC back to 5-chloro-2-methoxybenzoic acid]

Synthesis:

5-chloro-2-methoxybenzoic acid —SOCl₂→ 5-chloro-2-methoxybenzoyl chloride —2-phenylethanamine→ amide intermediate —ClSO₃H, NH₃→ sulfonamide intermediate —isocyanato cyclohexane→ **Glibenclamide**

GLIMEPIRIDE

Use: antidiabetic

Analysis:

[Structure of Glimepiride (I)]

Retrosynthetic Analysis and Synthesis of Drugs

137

Synthesis:

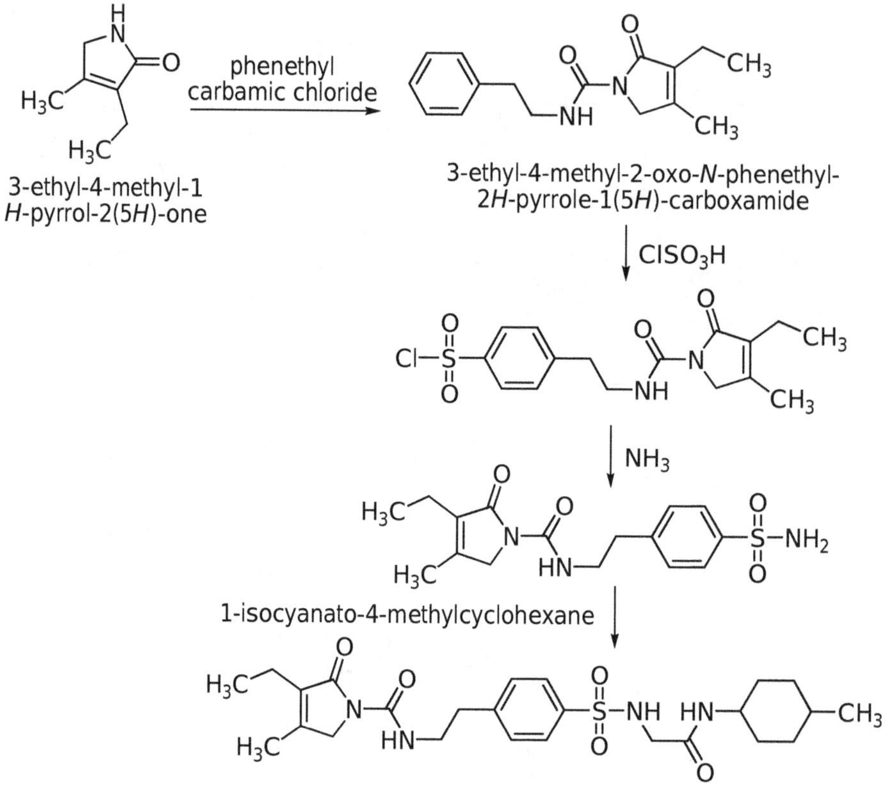

3-ethyl-4-methyl-1H-pyrrol-2(5H)-one + phenethyl carbamic chloride → 3-ethyl-4-methyl-2-oxo-N-phenethyl-2H-pyrrole-1(5H)-carboxamide

↓ ClSO$_3$H

(4-chlorosulfonyl intermediate)

↓ NH$_3$

(sulfonamide intermediate)

↓ 1-isocyanato-4-methylcyclohexane

Glimepiride

GLIPIZIDE

Use: antidiabetic

Analysis:

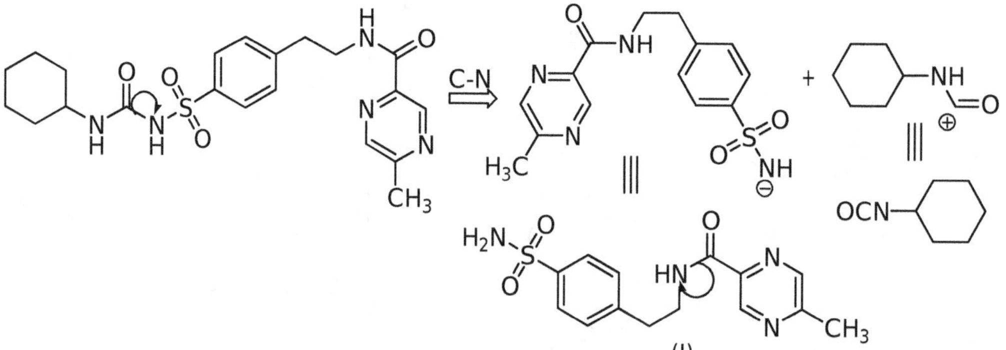

(I)

Retrosynthetic Analysis and Synthesis of Drugs

Synthesis:

5-methylpyrazine-2-carboxylic acid →(SOCl₂)→ 5-methylpyrazine-2-carbonyl chloride

↓ 4-(2-ethyl amino)-benzenesulfonamide

[N-(2-(4-sulfamoylphenyl)ethyl)-5-methylpyrazine-2-carboxamide]

↓ Cyclohexyl isocyanate | NaOH

Glipizide

GLYBUZOLE

Use: antidiabetic

Analysis:

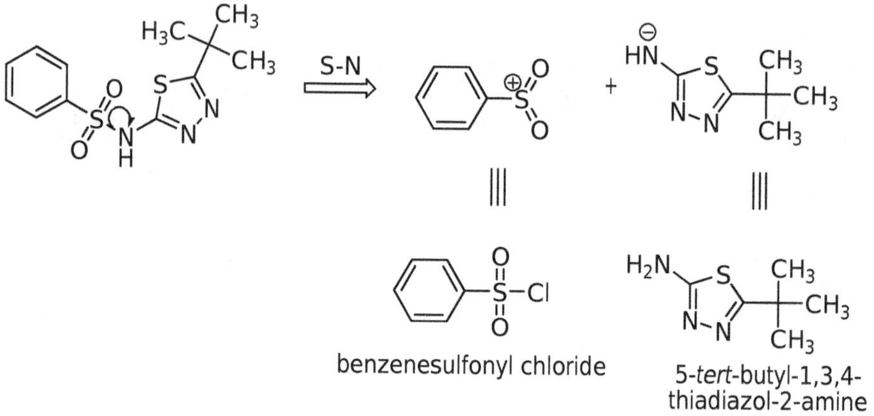

[Retrosynthetic scheme: Glybuzole ⇒ (S–N disconnection) benzenesulfonyl cation + 5-*tert*-butyl-1,3,4-thiadiazol-2-aminide ≡ benzenesulfonyl chloride + 5-*tert*-butyl-1,3,4-thiadiazol-2-amine]

Synthesis:

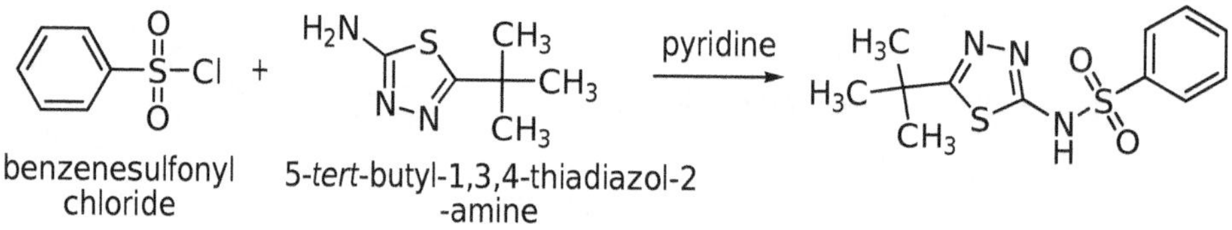

benzenesulfonyl chloride + 5-*tert*-butyl-1,3,4-thiadiazol-2-amine →(pyridine) **Glybuzole**

GUAIFENESIN

Use: muscle relaxant, expectorant

Analysis:

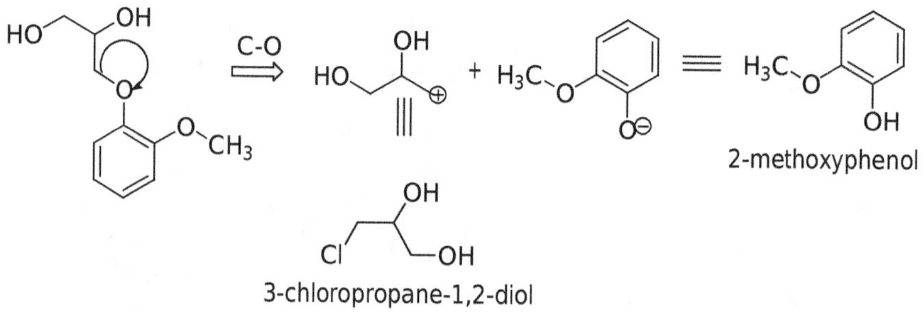

[Retrosynthetic scheme: Guaifenesin ⇒ (C–O disconnection) glycidol cation + 2-methoxyphenoxide ≡ 2-methoxyphenol + 3-chloropropane-1,2-diol]

Synthesis:

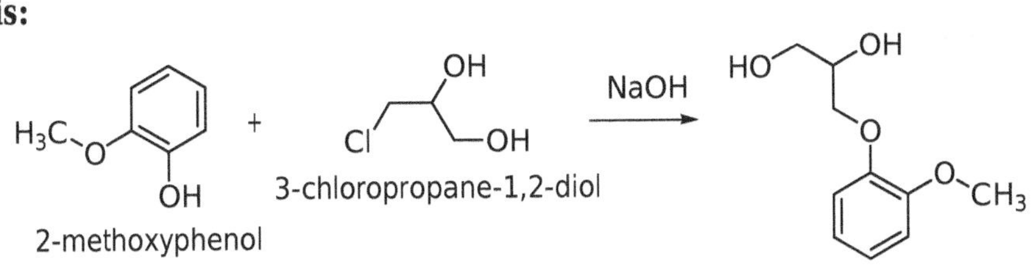

2-methoxyphenol + 3-chloropropane-1,2-diol →[NaOH] Guaifenesin

HISTAPYRRODINE

Use: antihistaminic

Analysis:

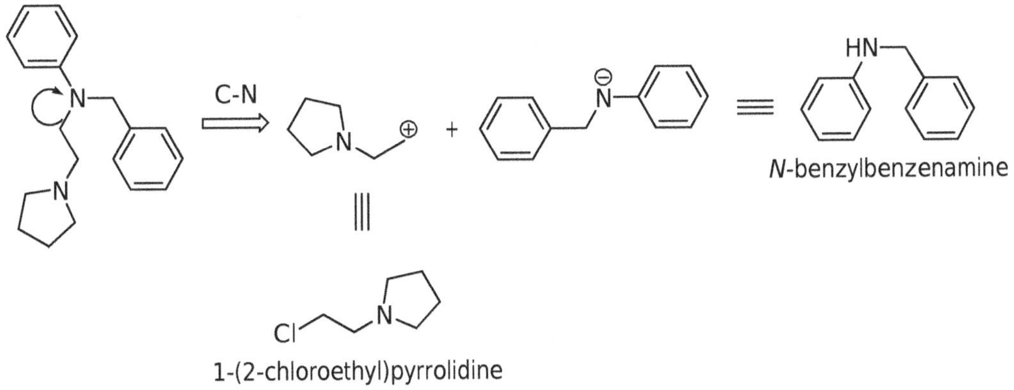

Histapyrrodine ⇒ (C-N) pyrrolidine-CH₂⁺ cation + N-benzyl-phenyl anion ≡ N-benzylbenzenamine

≡ 1-(2-chloroethyl)pyrrolidine

Synthesis:

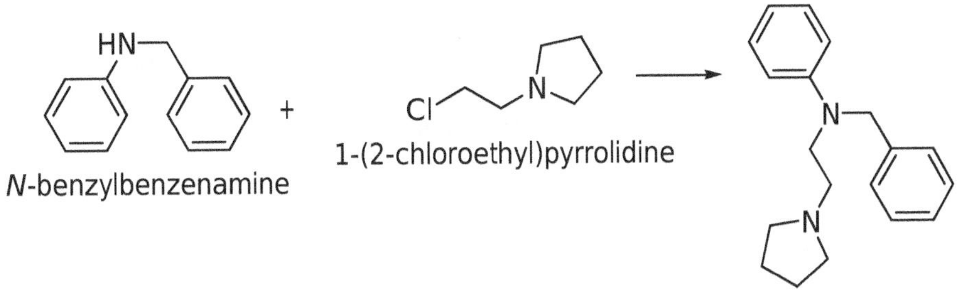

N-benzylbenzenamine + 1-(2-chloroethyl)pyrrolidine → **Histapyrrodine**

HOMOFENAZINE
Use: neuroleptic
Analysis:

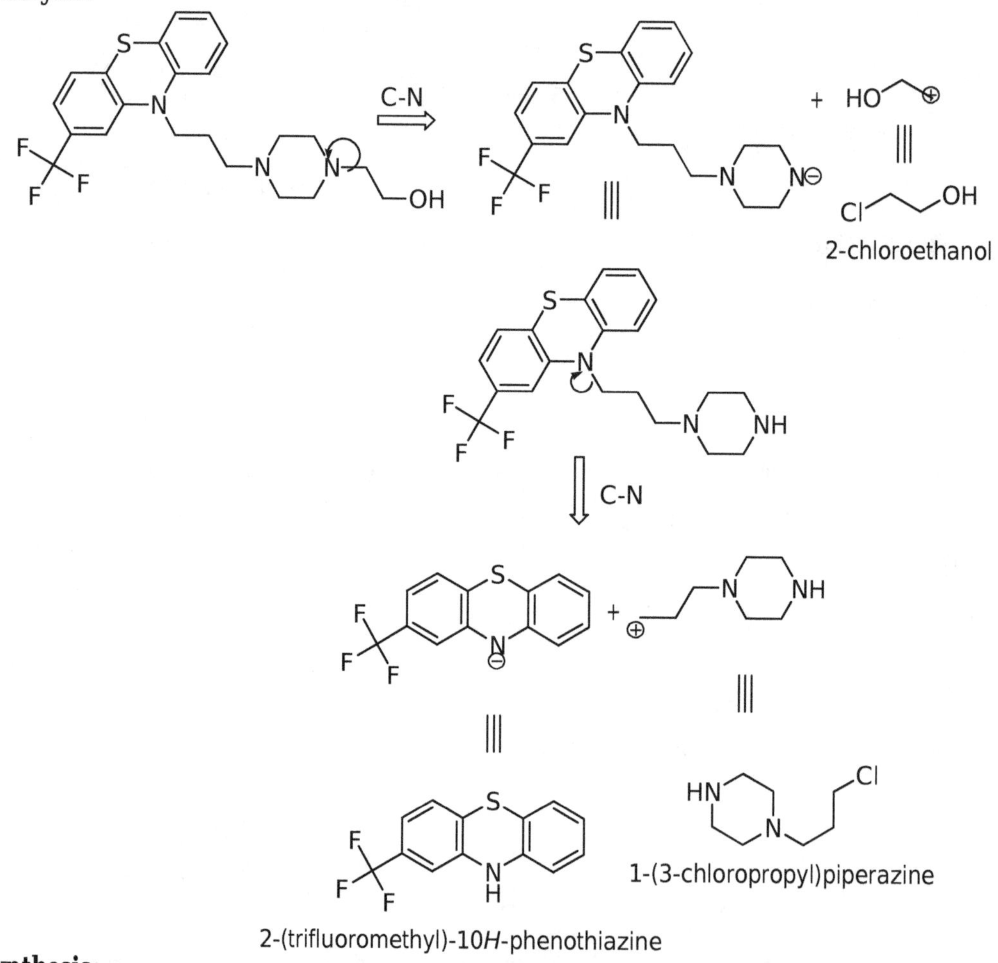

[Retrosynthetic analysis: Homofenazine → 2-(trifluoromethyl)-10-(3-(piperazin-1-yl)propyl)-10H-phenothiazine + 2-chloroethanol (via C-N disconnection)

Further disconnection (C-N): → 2-(trifluoromethyl)-10H-phenothiazine + 1-(3-chloropropyl)piperazine]

Synthesis:

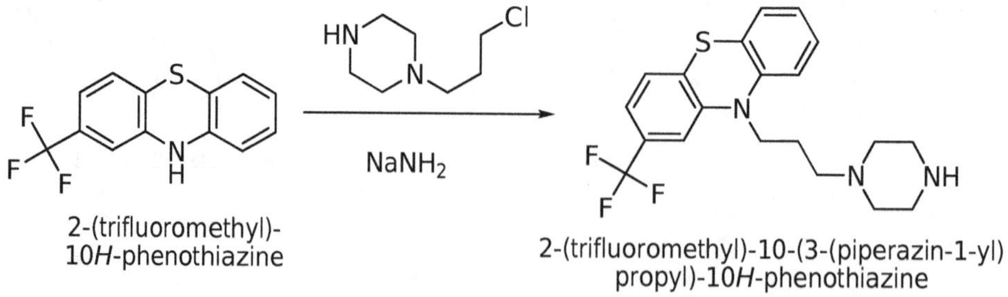

2-(trifluoromethyl)-10H-phenothiazine + 1-(3-chloropropyl)piperazine, NaNH₂ → 2-(trifluoromethyl)-10-(3-(piperazin-1-yl)propyl)-10H-phenothiazine (I)

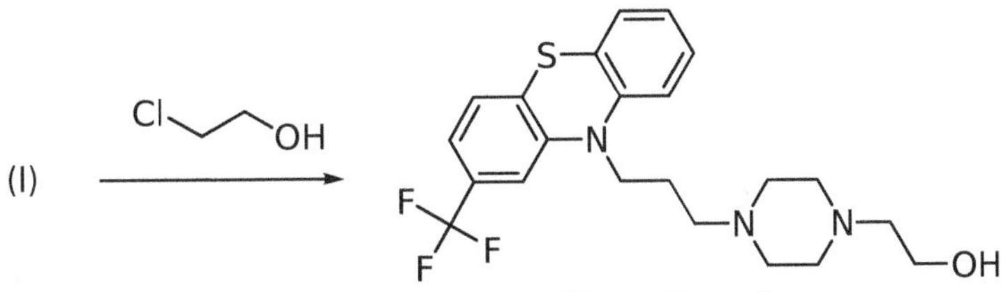

(I) + ClCH₂CH₂OH → **Homofenazine**

HYDROXYZINE

Use: tranquilizer

Analysis:

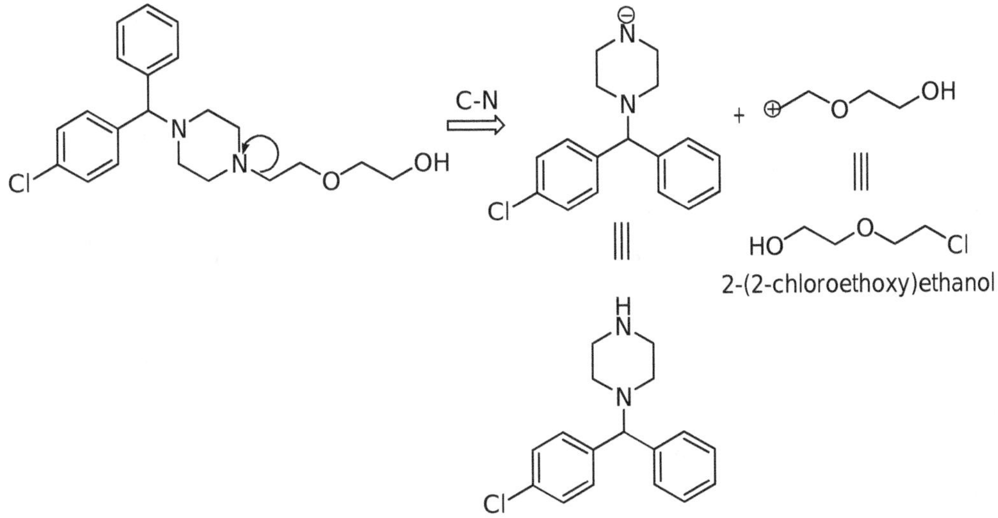

Hydroxyzine ⇒ (C-N disconnection) 1-((4-chlorophenyl)(phenyl)methyl)piperazine + ⁺CH₂OCH₂CH₂OH

≡ 2-(2-chloroethoxy)ethanol

Synthesis:

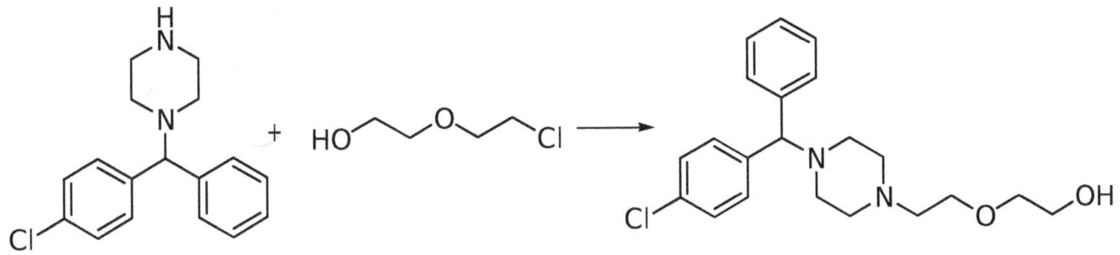

1-((4-chlorophenyl)(phenyl)methyl)piperazine + HOCH₂CH₂OCH₂CH₂Cl → **Hydroxyzine**

IBOPAMINE
Use: cardiotonic
Analysis:

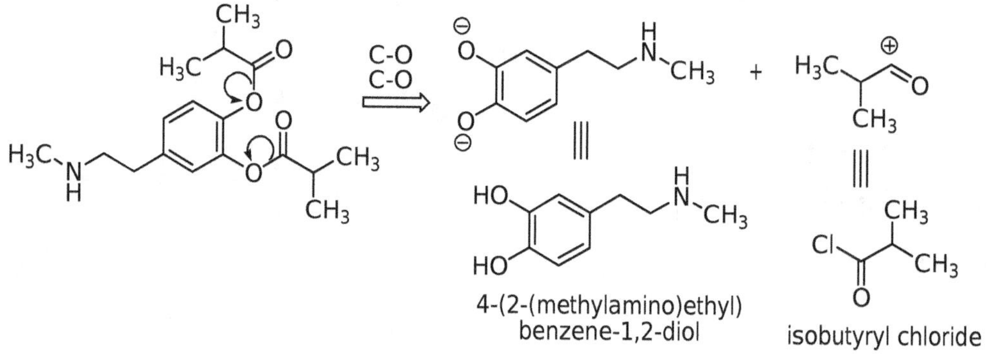

Synthesis:

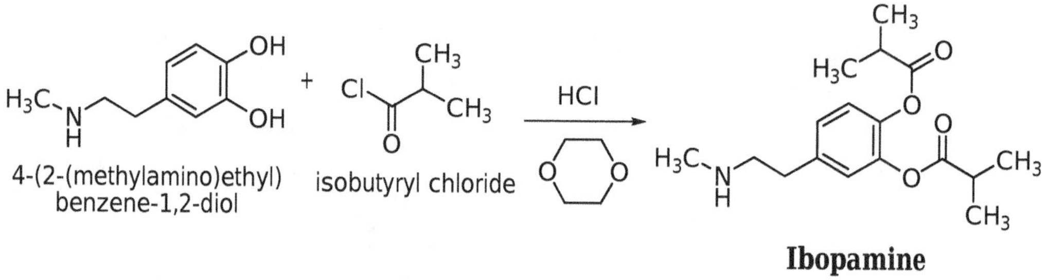

IBUPROFEN
Use: anti-inflammatory, analgesic
Analysis:

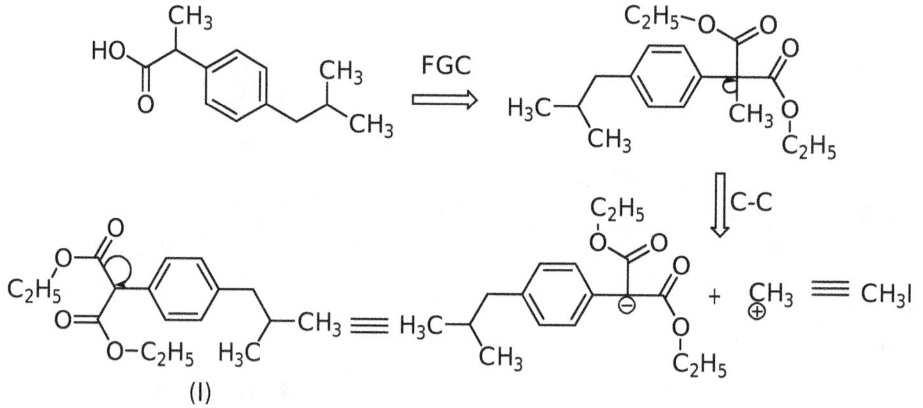

Retrosynthetic Analysis and Synthesis of Drugs

Synthesis:

IMIPRAMINE
Use: antidepressant
Analysis:

10,11-dihydro-5-H-dibenz[b,f] azepine

Synthesis:

10,11-dihydro-5-H-dibenz[b,f] azepine + 3-chloro-N,N-dimethyl propan-1-amine $\xrightarrow{NaNH_2}$ **Imipramine**

INDECAINIDE
Use: cardiac depressant
Analysis:

9H-fluorene-9-carbonitrile

3-chloro-N-isopropylpropan-1-amine

Synthesis:

9H-fluorene-9-carbonitrile + 3-chloro-N-isopropylpropan-1-amine →[NaNH₂] 9-(3-(isopropylamino)propyl)-9H-fluorene-9-carbonitrile →[H₂SO₄] **Indecainide**

ISOAMINILE
Use: antitussive
Analysis:

Retrosynthetic analysis:

Isoaminile ⇒(C-C) 1-chloro-N,N-dimethylpropan-2-amine + (phenyl-substituted nitrile carbanion)

⇒(C-C) 2-phenylacetonitrile + 2-chloropropane

Synthesis:

[Scheme: 2-phenylacetonitrile + 2-chloropropane, NaNH₂ → 3-methyl-2-phenylbutanenitrile; then NaNH₂ / 1-chloro-N,N-dimethyl-2-propanamine → **Isoaminile**]

ISOCONAZOLE
Use: antifungal
Analysis:

[Retrosynthetic scheme: Isoconazole → (C–O disconnection) 2,6-dichlorobenzyl alkoxide + 1-(2,4-dichlorophenyl)-2-(1H-imidazol-1-yl)ethyl cation; equivalents: 2,6-dichlorobenzyl alcohol and 1-chloro-1-(2,4-dichlorophenyl)-2-(imidazol-1-yl)ethane; FGC → 1-(2,4-dichlorophenyl)-2-(imidazol-1-yl)ethanol; Reduction → 1-(2,4-dichlorophenyl)-2-(imidazol-1-yl)ethanone; C–N disconnection → 1H-imidazole + 2-bromo-1-(2,4-dichlorophenyl)ethanone; C-Br Bromination ⇒ 1-(2,4-dichlorophenyl)ethanone]

1H-imidazole

1-(2,4-dichlorophenyl)ethanone

Retrosynthetic Analysis and Synthesis of Drugs

Synthesis:

1-(2,4-dichlorophenyl)ethanone → (Br₂, CH₃OH) → 2-bromo-1-(2,4-dichlorophenyl)ethanone (I)

(I) + imidazole / CH₃OH → 1-(2,4-dichlorophenyl)-2-(1H-imidazol-1-yl)ethanone → NaBH₄ / CH₃OH → 1-(2,4-dichlorophenyl)-2-(1H-imidazol-1-yl)ethanol

+ (2,6-dichlorophenyl)methanol → **Isoconazole**

ISOETARINE

Use: bronchodilator

Analysis:

4-(1-hydroxy-2-(isopropylamino)butyl)benzene-1,2-diol ⇒ (Reduction) ⇒ 1-(3,4-dihydroxyphenyl)-2-(isopropylamino)butan-1-one

⇓ FGC

(I)

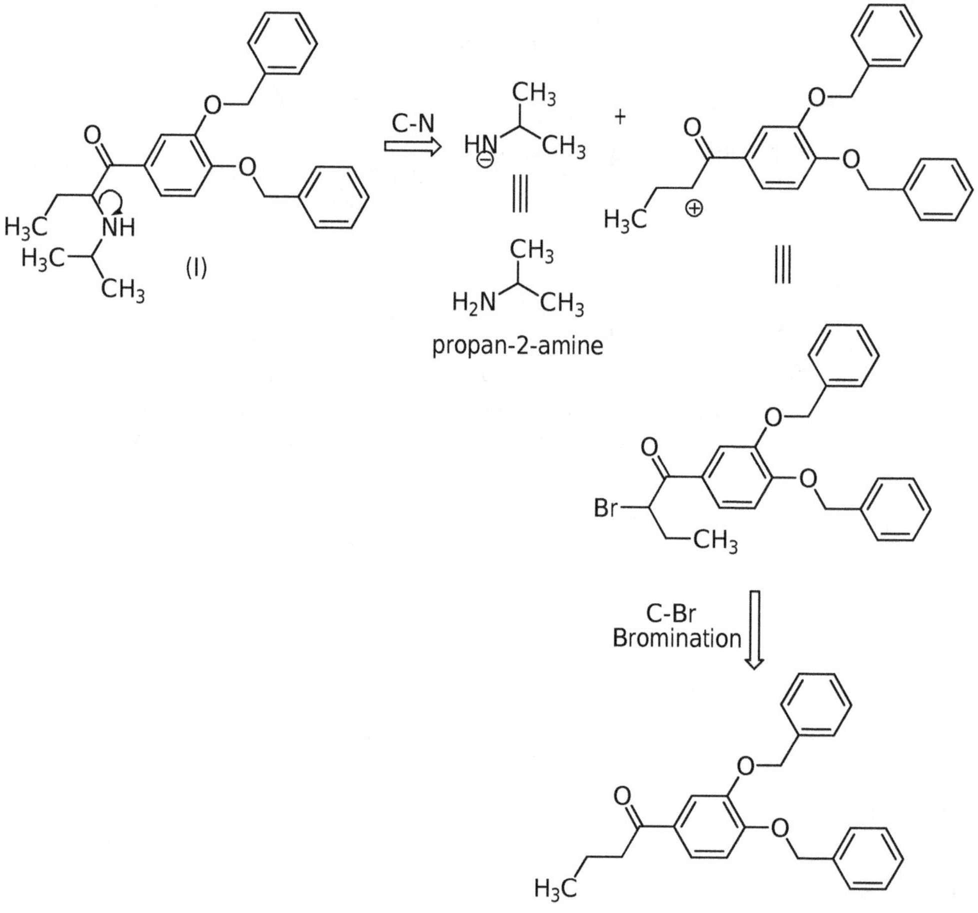

Retrosynthetic Analysis and Synthesis of Drugs

propan-2-amine

1-(3,4-bis(benzyloxy)phenyl)butan-1-one

Synthesis:

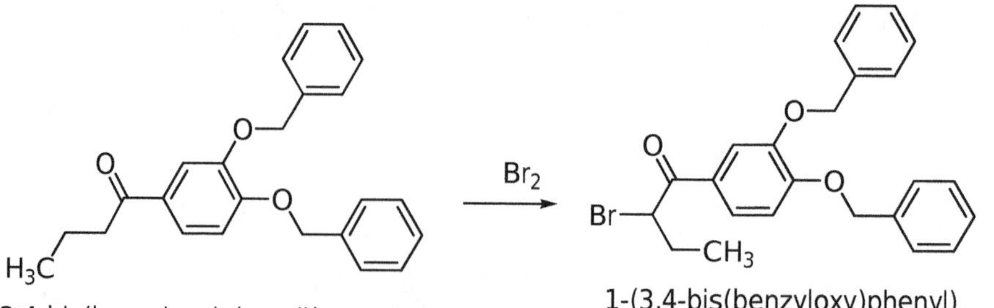

1-(3,4-bis(benzyloxy)phenyl)butan-1-one $\xrightarrow{Br_2}$ 1-(3,4-bis(benzyloxy)phenyl)-2-bromobutan-1-one (I)

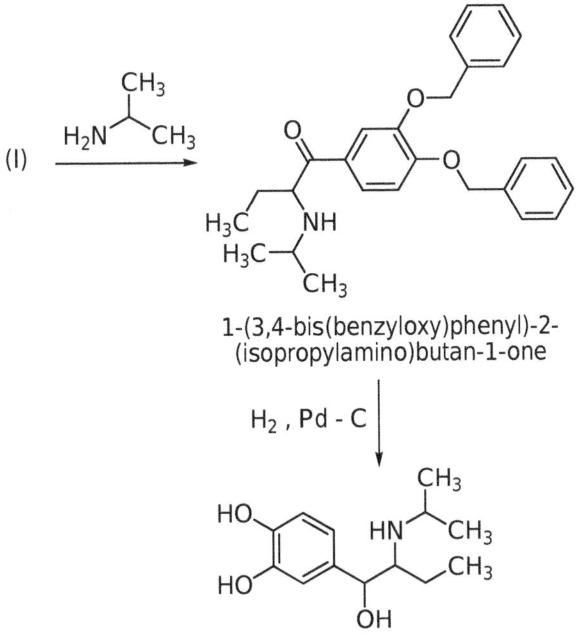

(I) $\xrightarrow{\text{H}_2\text{N-CH(CH}_3)_2}$ 1-(3,4-bis(benzyloxy)phenyl)-2-(isopropylamino)butan-1-one

$\xrightarrow{\text{H}_2, \text{Pd-C}}$

Isoetarine

ISONIAZID

Use: tuberculostatic

Analysis:

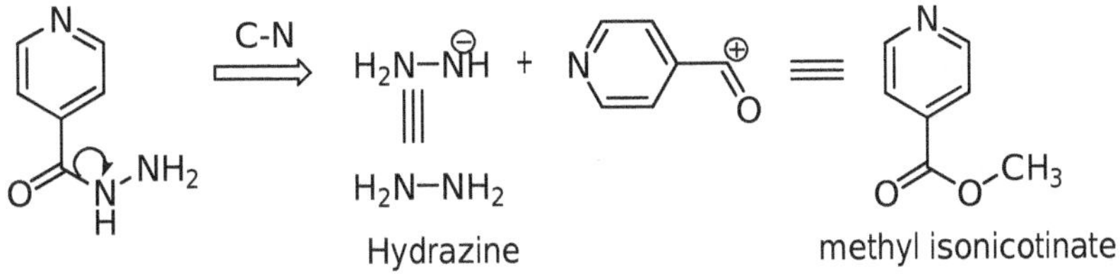

Isoniazid $\xRightarrow{\text{C-N}}$ H$_2$N–NH$_2$ (Hydrazine) + methyl isonicotinate cation ≡ methyl isonicotinate

Synthesis:

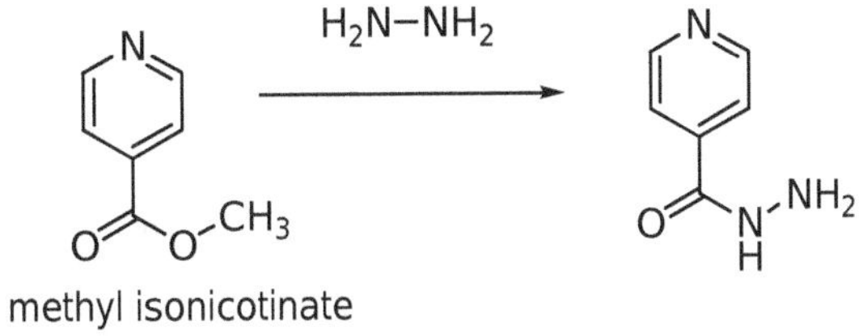

methyl isonicotinate $\xrightarrow{\text{H}_2\text{N-NH}_2}$ **Isoniazid**

LACTOPHENIN

Use: analgesic, antipyretic

Analysis:

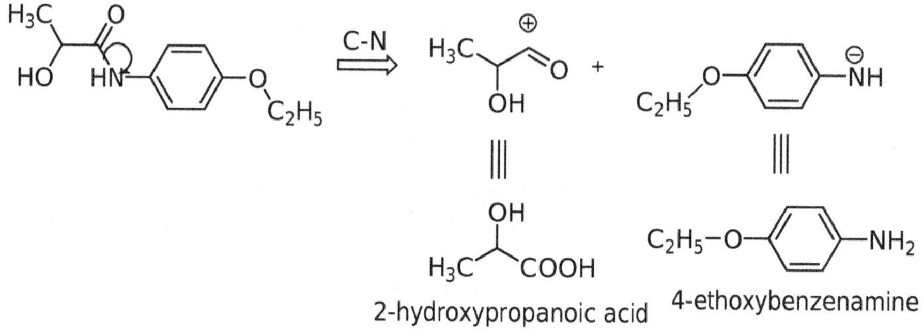

[Retrosynthetic scheme: Lactophenin structure (H₃C-CH(OH)-C(=O)-NH-C₆H₄-O-C₂H₅) disconnected at C-N bond to give H₃C-CH(OH)-CO⁺ (≡ 2-hydroxypropanoic acid, H₃C-CH(OH)-COOH) and ⁻HN-C₆H₄-O-C₂H₅ (≡ 4-ethoxybenzenamine, C₂H₅-O-C₆H₄-NH₂)]

Synthesis:

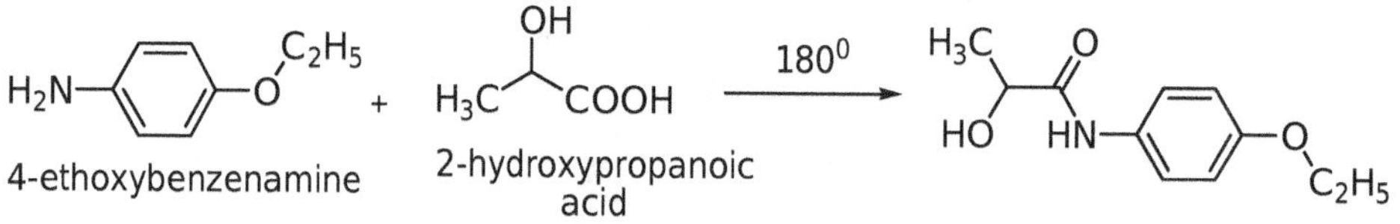

$$\text{H}_2\text{N-C}_6\text{H}_4\text{-O-C}_2\text{H}_5 \; + \; \text{H}_3\text{C-CH(OH)-COOH} \xrightarrow{180°} \text{Lactophenin}$$

4-ethoxybenzenamine + 2-hydroxypropanoic acid → Lactophenin

LETROZOLE

Use: antineoplastic

Analysis:

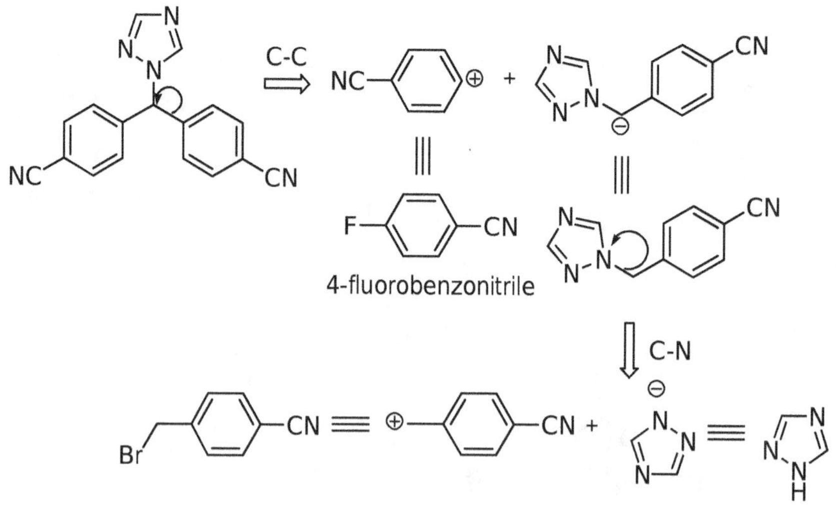

[Retrosynthetic scheme: Letrozole (bis(4-cyanophenyl)methyl-1,2,4-triazole) disconnected at C-C bond to give NC-C₆H₄⁺ (≡ 4-fluorobenzonitrile, F-C₆H₄-CN) and triazole-CH⁻-C₆H₄-CN (≡ triazole-CH=C₆H₄-CN).

Further C-N disconnection gives Br-CH₂-C₆H₄-CN and ⁺CH-C₆H₄-CN plus triazole anion (≡ 1H-1,2,4-triazole)]

Retrosynthetic Analysis and Synthesis of Drugs

Synthesis:

4-(bromomethyl)benzonitrile + 1H-1,2,4-triazole →(CH₂Cl₂) 4-((1H-1,2,4-triazol-1-yl)methyl)benzonitrile

↓ 2. DMF, 0° C, F—C₆H₄—CN

Letrozole

LEVAMISOLE

Use: anthelmintic

Analysis:

2,3,5,6-tetrahydro-6-phenyl imidazo[2,1-b]thiazole

⇒(C-N) thiazolidine intermediate ≡ N-acetyl hydroxy intermediate

⇓ FGC

(I) ≡ iminium intermediate + CH₃C(O)⁺ ⇐(C-N) N-acetyl ketone intermediate

≡ acetic anhydride (H₃C-C(O)-O-C(O)-CH₃)

Synthesis:

Levamisole

LEVOBUNOLOL

Use: β-blocker

Analysis:

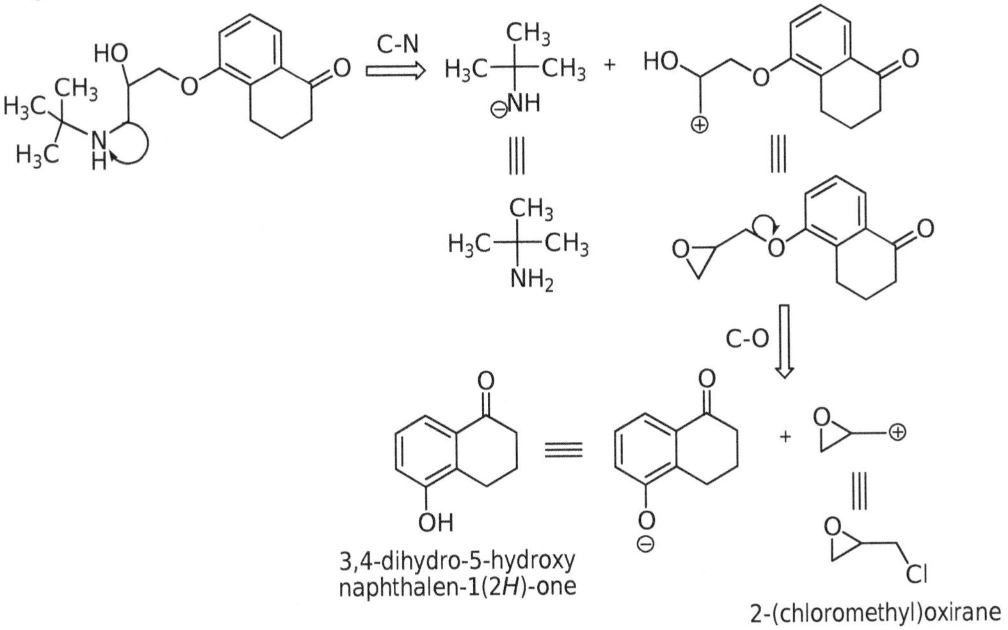

(retrosynthetic scheme: Levobunolol ⇒ via C–N disconnection to 2-methylpropan-2-amine (tert-butylamine) + epoxide intermediate; the epoxide intermediate ⇒ via C–O disconnection to 3,4-dihydro-5-hydroxynaphthalen-1(2H)-one + 2-(chloromethyl)oxirane)

3,4-dihydro-5-hydroxy naphthalen-1(2H)-one

2-(chloromethyl)oxirane

Synthesis:

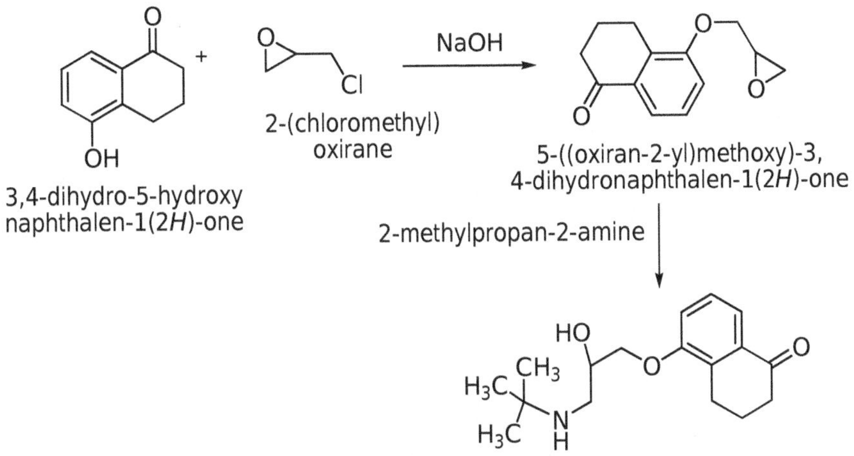

3,4-dihydro-5-hydroxy naphthalen-1(2H)-one + 2-(chloromethyl)oxirane —NaOH→ 5-((oxiran-2-yl)methoxy)-3,4-dihydronaphthalen-1(2H)-one

↓ 2-methylpropan-2-amine

Levobunolol

LEVODOPA
Use: antiparkinsonian
Analysis:

2-amino-3-(3,4-dihydroxyphenyl)propanoic acid ⟹ (C-O hydroxylation) 2-amino-3-(4-hydroxyphenyl)propanoic acid

Synthesis:

2-amino-3-(4-hydroxyphenyl)propanoic acid → (enzymatic hydroxylation) **Levodopa**

LIDOFLAZINE
Use: coronary vasodilator
Analysis:

C-N disconnection ⟹ acylium cation of N-(2,6-dimethylphenyl)amide + piperazinyl-4,4-bis(4-fluorophenyl)butane

≡ 2-chloroacetyl chloride + 2,6-dimethylaniline (via acyl chloride + amine)

≡ 1-[4,4-bis(4-fluorophenyl)butyl]piperazine (piperazine NH)

Synthesis:

[Scheme: 2-chloroacetyl chloride + 2,6-dimethyl benzenamine → chloroacetamide intermediate; then with 1-(4,4-bis(4-fluorophenyl)butyl)piperazine → **Lidoflazine**]

LOBENZARIT

Use: anti-iflammatory

Analysis:

[Retrosynthetic scheme: Lobenzarit ⇒ C–N disconnection → 4-chlorobenzoic acid cation (≡ 2,4-dichlorobenzoic acid) + 2-aminobenzoate anion (≡ 2-aminobenzoic acid)]

Synthesis:

2-aminobenzoic acid + 2,4-dichlorobenzoic acid $\xrightarrow{K_2CO_3,\ Cu, I_2}$ **Lobenzarit**

LOMIFYLLINE

Use: vasodilator

Analysis:

[Retrosynthetic scheme: lomifylline → C-N disconnection → pentan-2-one cation + theophylline anion; the electrophile equivalent is 6-bromohexan-2-one, and the anion equivalent is theophylline]

Synthesis:

6-bromohexan-2-one + theophylline → **Lomifylline**

LOMUSTINE

Use: antineoplastic

Analysis:

[Retrosynthetic scheme: lomustine → N-N disconnection → NO⁺ (from NaNO₂) + N-(2-chloroethyl)-N'-cyclohexylurea → FGC → N-(2-hydroxyethyl)-N'-cyclohexylurea → C-N disconnection → isocyanatocyclohexane + 2-aminoethanol (H₂N-CH₂-CH₂-OH)]

Synthesis:

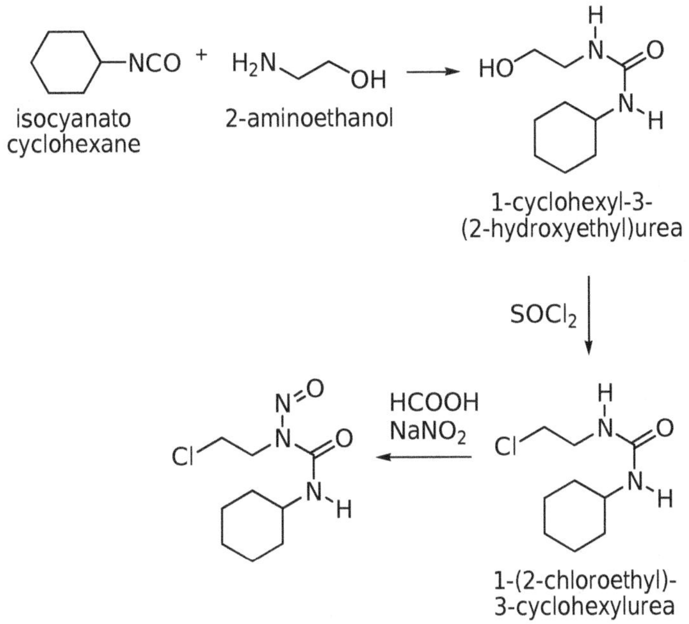

[Scheme: isocyanatocyclohexane + 2-aminoethanol → 1-cyclohexyl-3-(2-hydroxyethyl)urea → (SOCl₂) → 1-(2-chloroethyl)-3-cyclohexylurea → (HCOOH, NaNO₂) → **Lomustine**]

LONIDAMINE

Use: antineoplastic

Analysis:

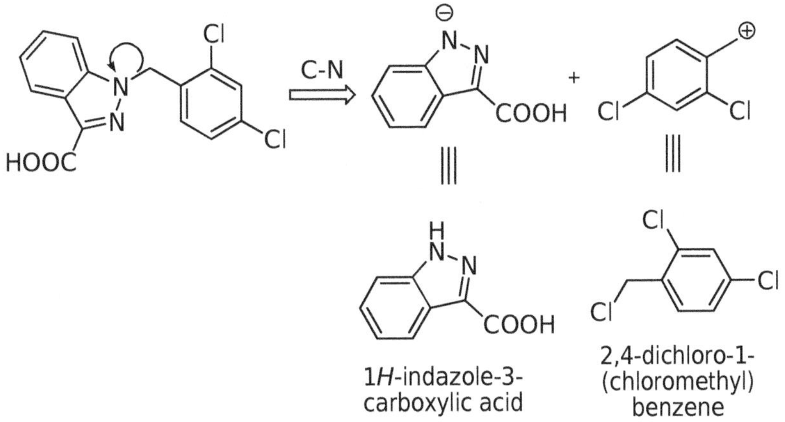

[Retrosynthetic scheme: Lonidamine ⟹ C–N disconnection → 1H-indazole-3-carboxylic acid anion + 2,4-dichlorobenzyl cation, from 1H-indazole-3-carboxylic acid and 2,4-dichloro-1-(chloromethyl)benzene]

Synthesis:

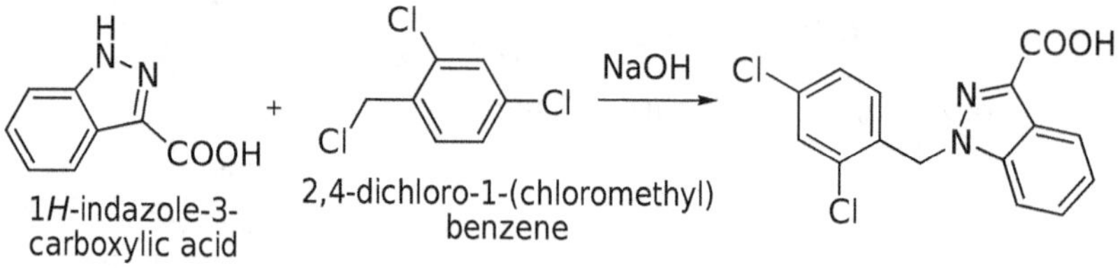

1H-indazole-3-carboxylic acid + 2,4-dichloro-1-(chloromethyl)benzene →(NaOH) **Lonidamine**

LOPRAMINE

Use: antidepressant

Analysis:

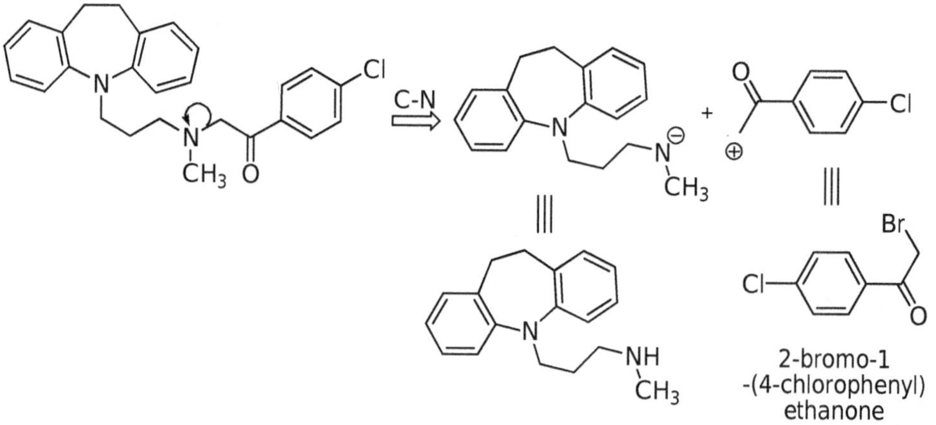

[C-N disconnection of lopramine yields a dibenzazepine-propyl-methylamine fragment and a 4-chlorobenzoyl cation, equivalent to the secondary amine and 2-bromo-1-(4-chlorophenyl)ethanone.]

Synthesis:

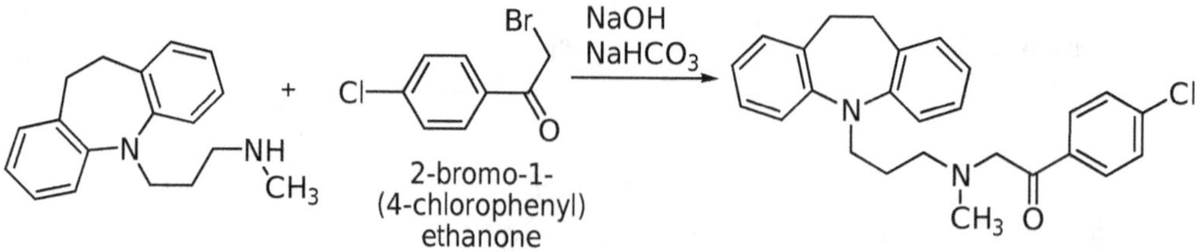

Dibenzazepine-propyl-N-methylamine + 2-bromo-1-(4-chlorophenyl)ethanone →(NaOH, NaHCO$_3$) **Lopramine**

LOSARTAN

Use: antihypertensive

Analysis:

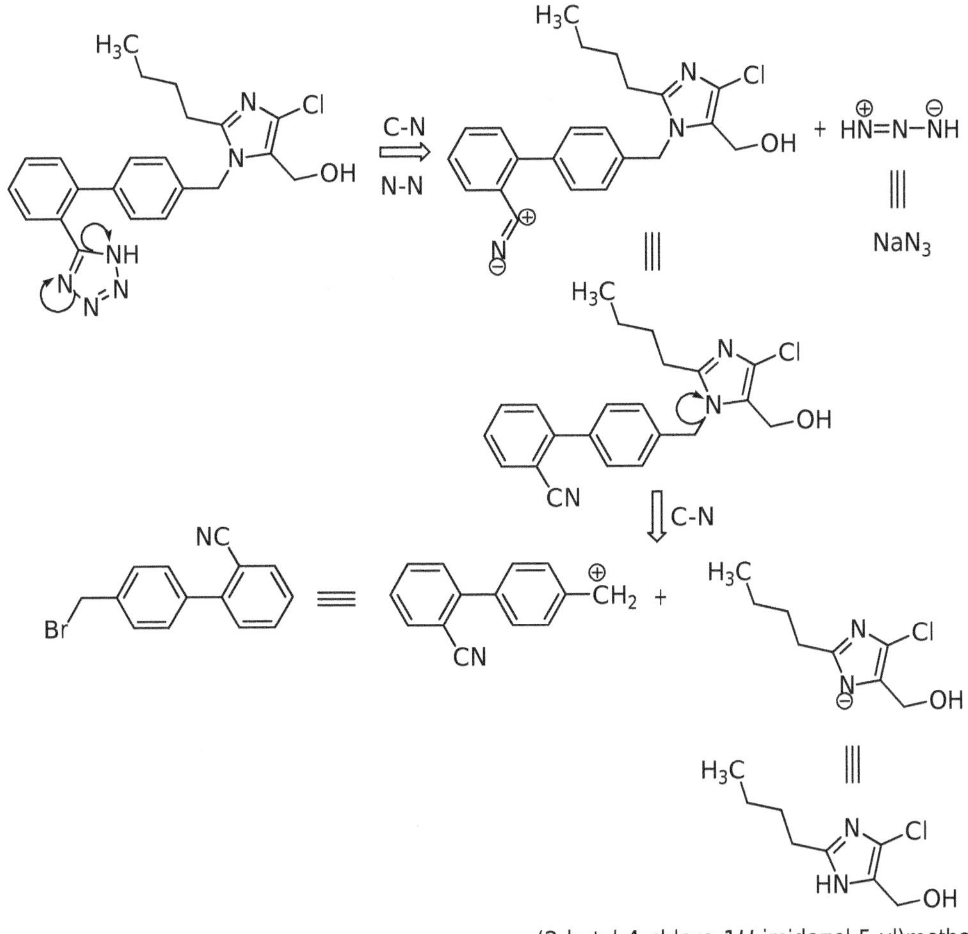

(2-butyl-4-chloro-1*H*-imidazol-5-yl)methanol

Synthesis:

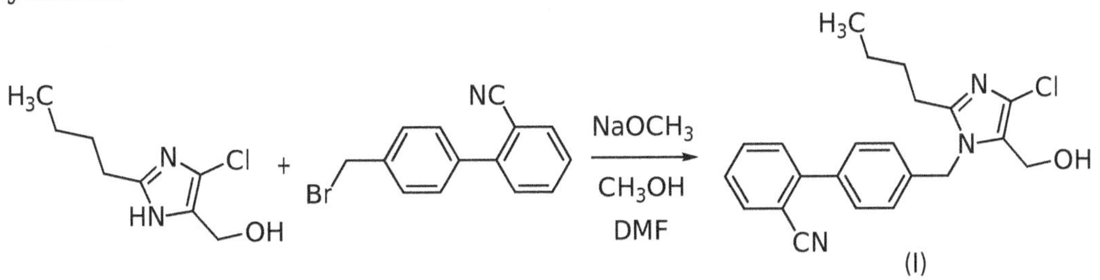

(I)

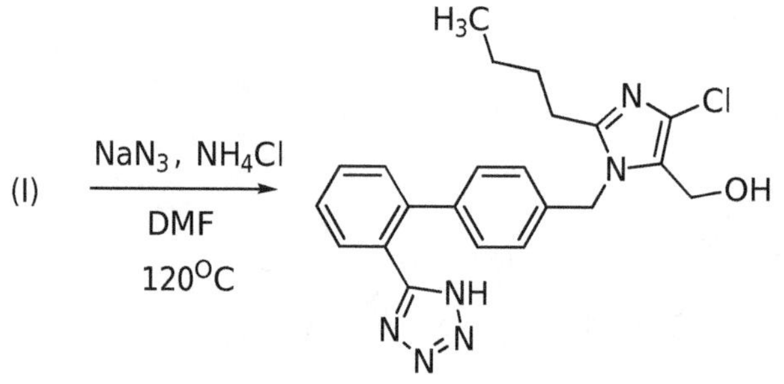

(I) →[NaN₃, NH₄Cl][DMF, 120°C] **Losartan**

MABUPROFEN
Use: topical anti-inflammatory
Analysis:

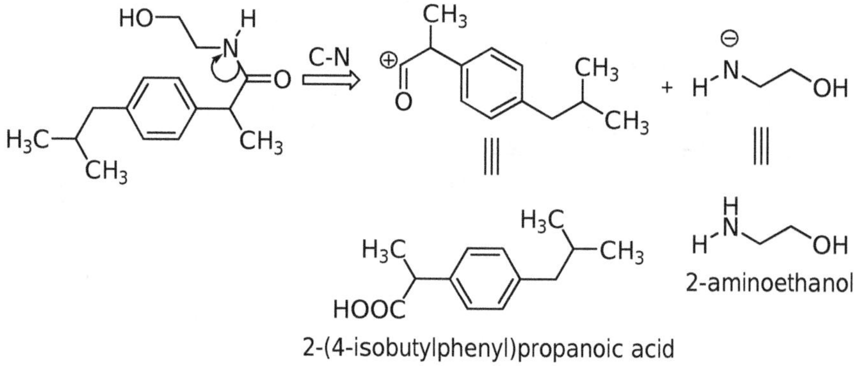

The amide bond in mabuprofen is disconnected (C-N) into an acylium cation from 2-(4-isobutylphenyl)propanoic acid and 2-aminoethanol.

Synthesis:

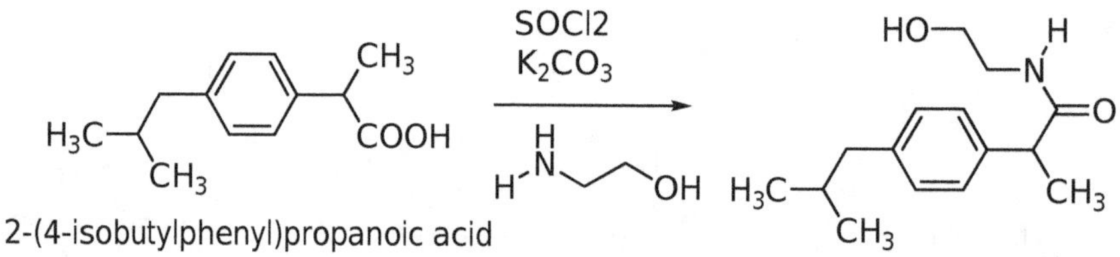

2-(4-isobutylphenyl)propanoic acid + H₂N-CH₂CH₂-OH →[SOCl₂, K₂CO₃] **Mabuprofen**

MANIDIPINE

Use: antihypertensive

Analysis:

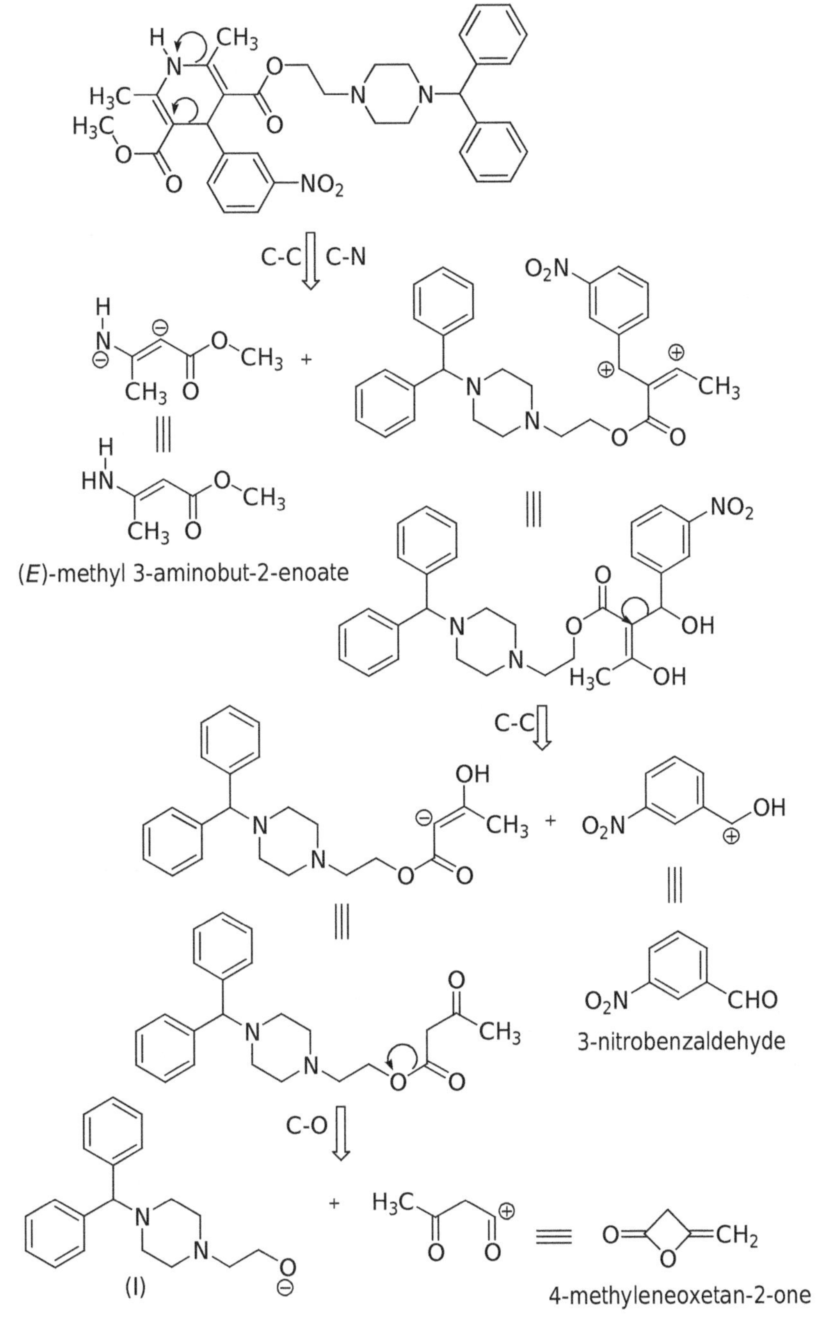
C-C
C-N
(E)-methyl 3-aminobut-2-enoate
C-C
3-nitrobenzaldehyde
C-O
(I)
4-methyleneoxetan-2-one

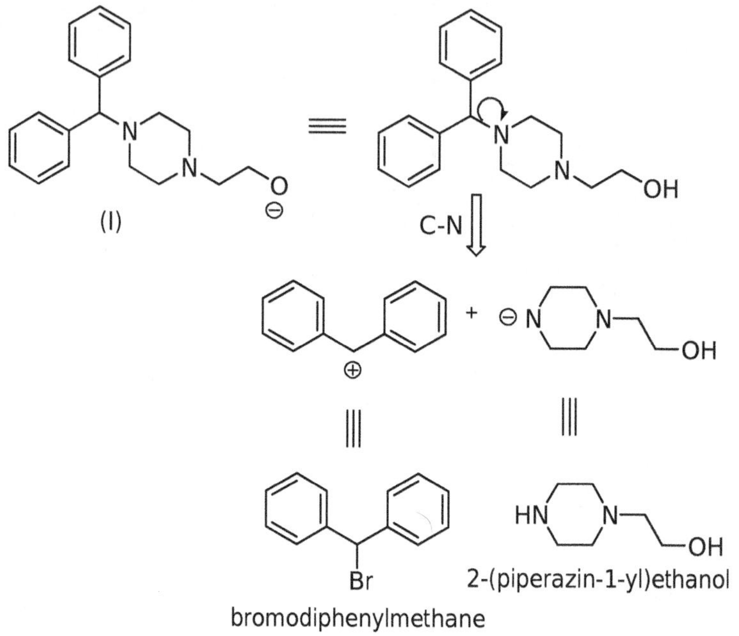

Retrosynthetic Analysis and Synthesis of Drugs

Synthesis:

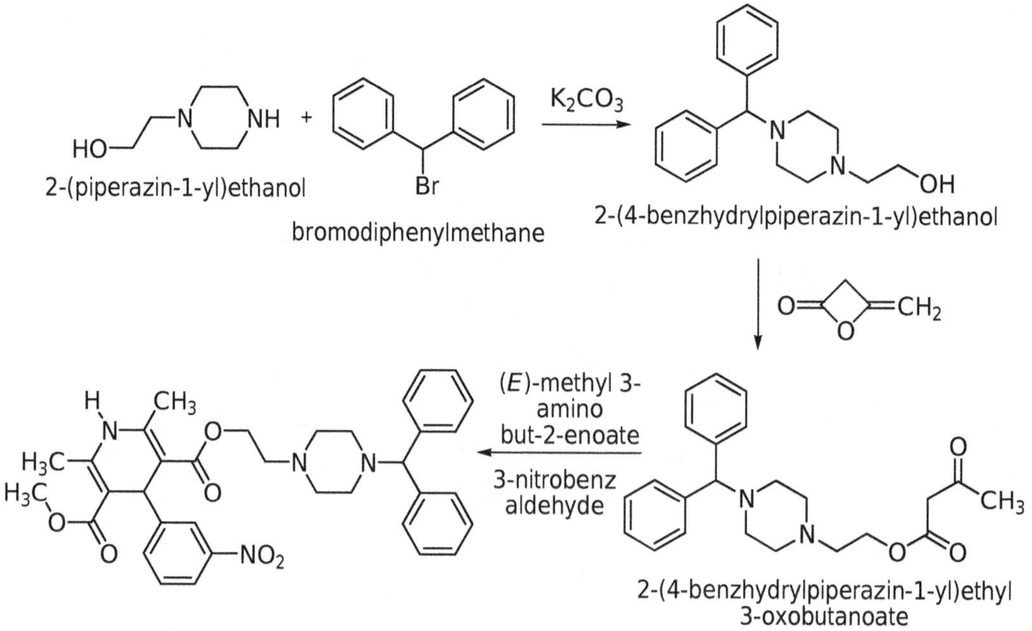

Manidipine

MEBENDAZOLE

Use: anthelmintic

Analysis:

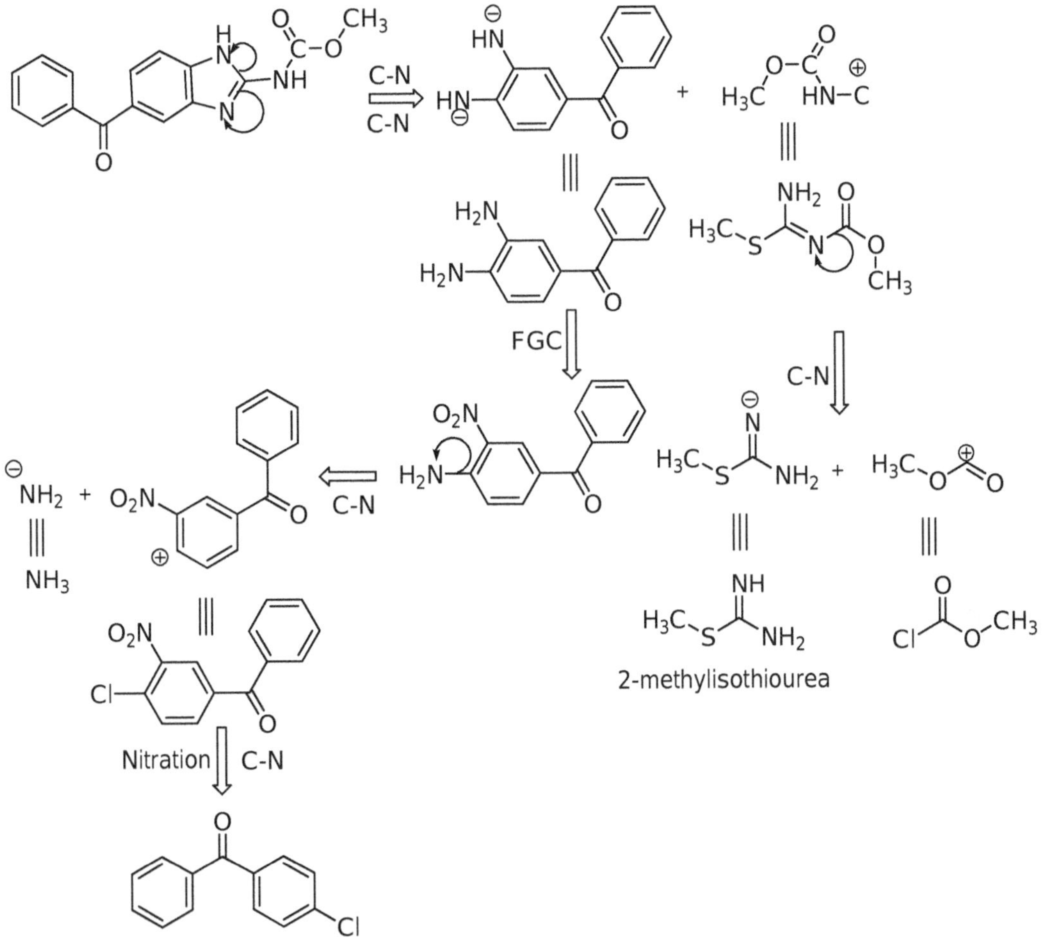

Synthesis:

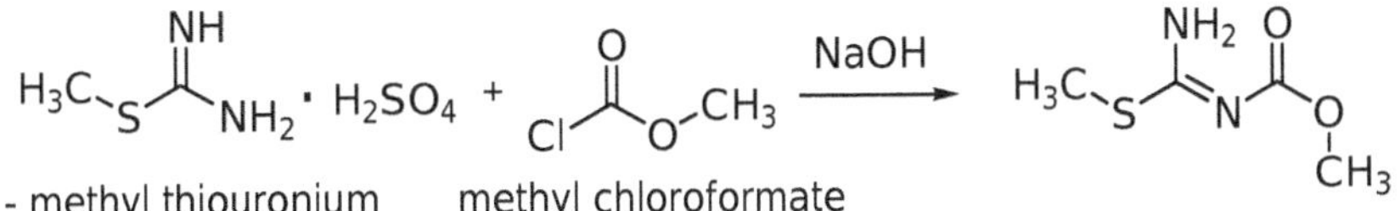

S - methyl thiouronium sulphate + methyl chloroformate → (I)

2-methylisothiourea

(4-chlorophenyl)(phenyl)methanone

MECLOFENOXATE
Use: neuroenergetic
Analysis:

Retrosynthesis gives 2-(4-chlorophenoxy)acetic acid and chloro-*N*,*N*-dimethyl methanamine.

Synthesis:

2-(4-chlorophenoxy)acetic acid + chloro-*N*,*N*-dimethyl methanamine → **Meclofenoxate**

MECLOQUALONE

Use: hypnotic, sedative

Analysis:

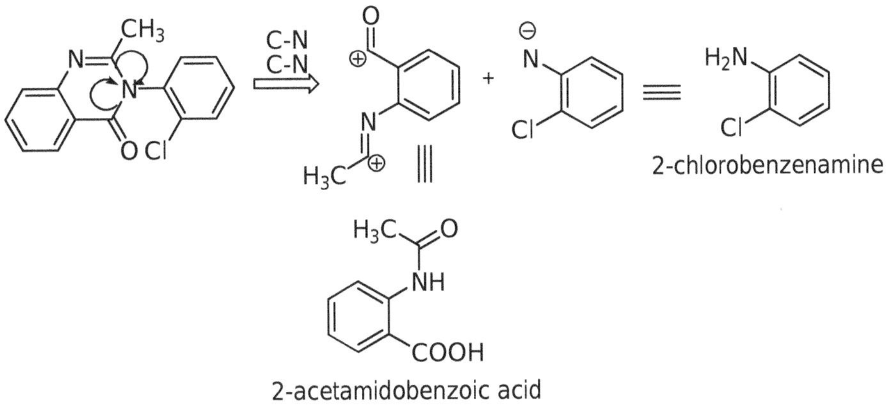

[Retrosynthetic scheme: Mecloqualone ⟹ (C-N, C-N disconnections) acylium cation + 2-chlorobenzenamine anion ≡ 2-chlorobenzenamine (H₂N-C₆H₄-Cl); and 2-acetamidobenzoic acid]

Synthesis:

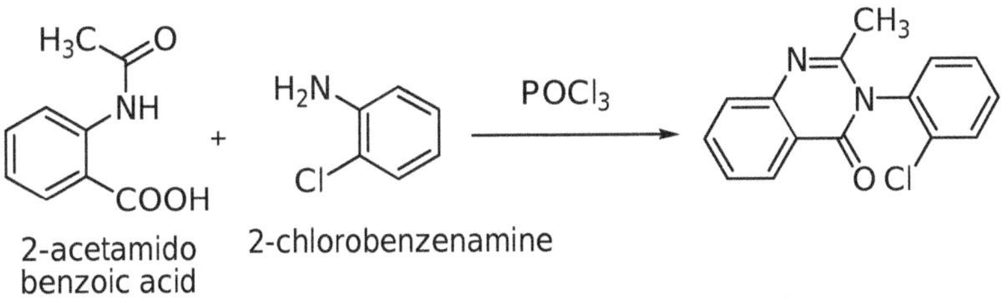

2-acetamidobenzoic acid + 2-chlorobenzenamine $\xrightarrow{POCl_3}$ **Mecloqualone**

MEDIBAZINE

Use: coronary vasodilator

Analysis:

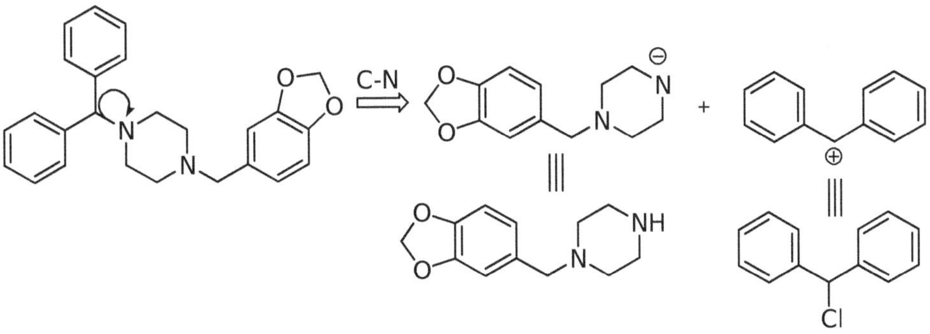

[Retrosynthetic scheme: Medibazine ⟹ (C-N disconnection) piperonyl-piperazine anion ≡ piperonyl-piperazine (NH) + benzhydryl cation ≡ benzhydryl chloride]

Synthesis:

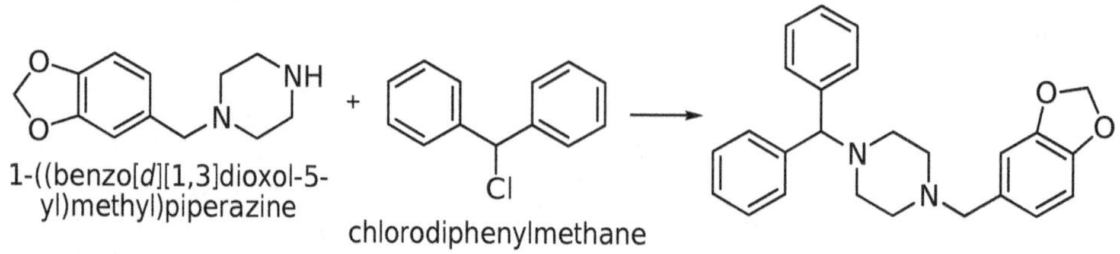

1-((benzo[*d*][1,3]dioxol-5-yl)methyl)piperazine + chlorodiphenylmethane → **Medibazine**

MEDIFOXAMINE

Use: antidepressant

Analysis:

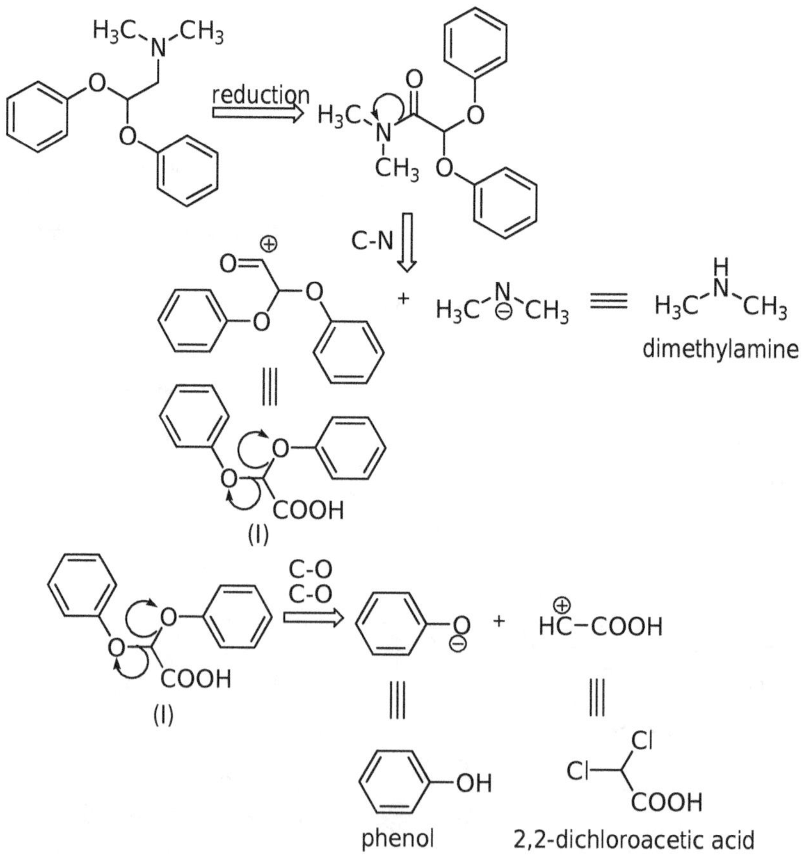

(reduction) ⇒ ... (C-N) ⇒ ... + H₃C–N(⊖)–CH₃ ≡ dimethylamine

(I)

(C-O, C-O) ⇒ phenoxide + HC(⊕)–COOH

≡ phenol + 2,2-dichloroacetic acid

Synthesis:

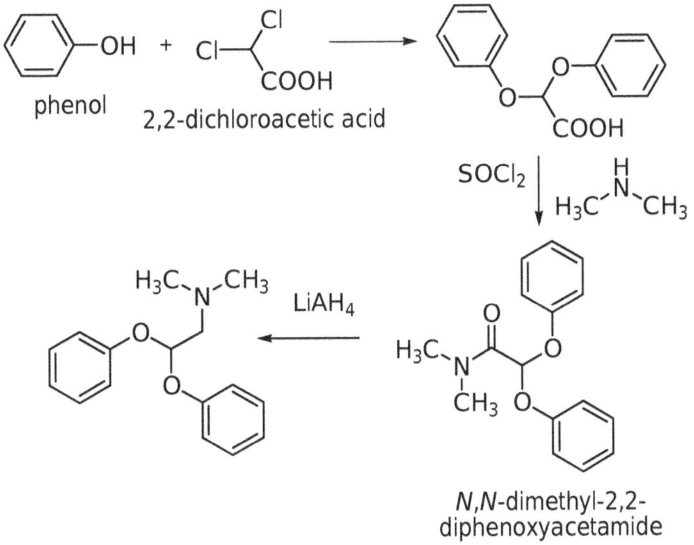

phenol + 2,2-dichloroacetic acid → diphenoxyacetic acid

SOCl₂ | HN(CH₃)₂

→ N,N-dimethyl-2,2-diphenoxyacetamide

LiAlH₄ → **Medifoxamine**

MEDRYLAMINE

Use: topical antihistaminic

Analysis:

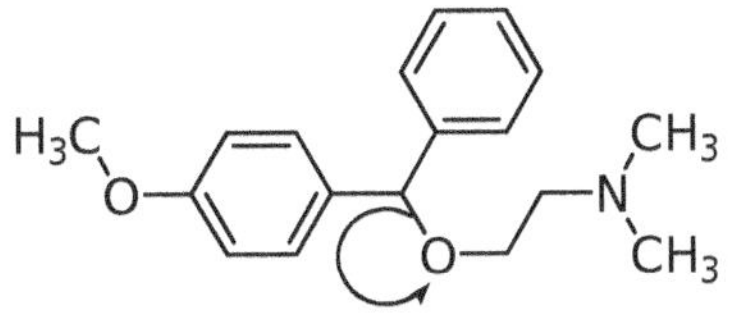

(I) ⟹ C-O disconnection → benzhydryl cation (phenyl, 4-methoxyphenyl) + ⁻O-CH₂CH₂-N(CH₃)₂

≡ 1-(chloro(phenyl)methyl)-4-methoxybenzene

≡ 2-(dimethylamino)ethanol

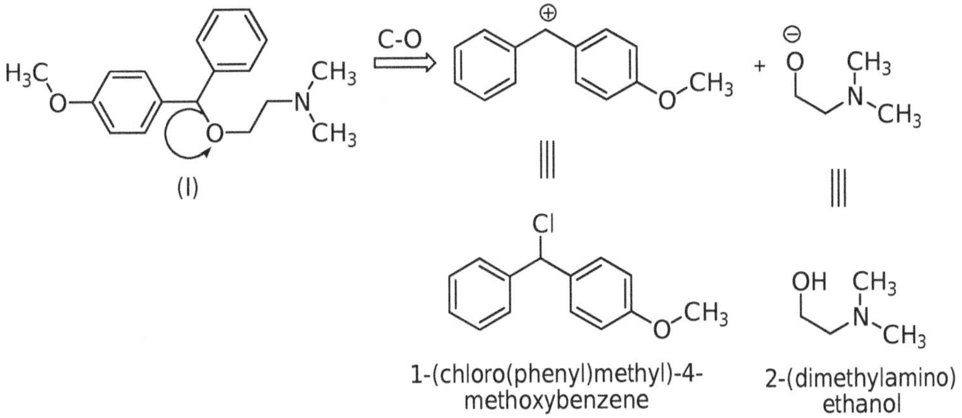

Synthesis:

4-methoxybenzhydryl chloride + 2-(dimethylamino)ethanol →[NaOH] **Medrylamine**

MEFANAMIC ACID

Use: anti-inflammatory, antirheumatic

Analysis:

Mefenamic acid ⇒[C-N] benzoic acid cation + 2,3-dimethylaniline anion

≡ 2-bromobenzoic acid + 2,3-dimethyl benzenamine

Synthesis:

2-bromobenzoic acid + 2,3-dimethyl benzenamine →[Copper acetate] **Mefanamic acid**

MEFEXAMIDE
Use: psychoanaleptic, CNS stimulant
Analysis:

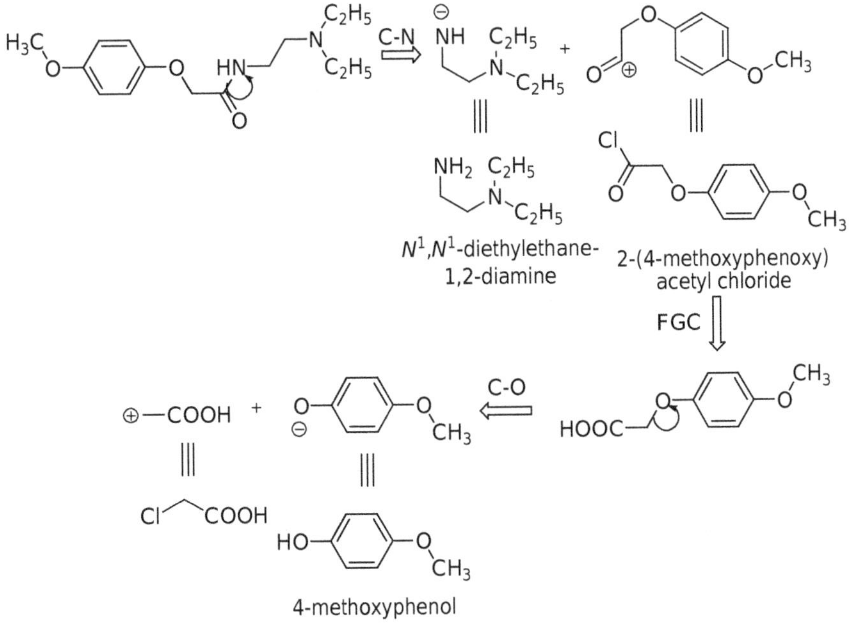

Disconnection C-N gives N^1,N^1-diethylethane-1,2-diamine and 2-(4-methoxyphenoxy)acetyl chloride (via FGC from 2-(4-methoxyphenoxy)acetic acid).

C-O disconnection gives chloroacetic acid (⊕-COOH synthon) and 4-methoxyphenol (⊖-O synthon).

Synthesis:

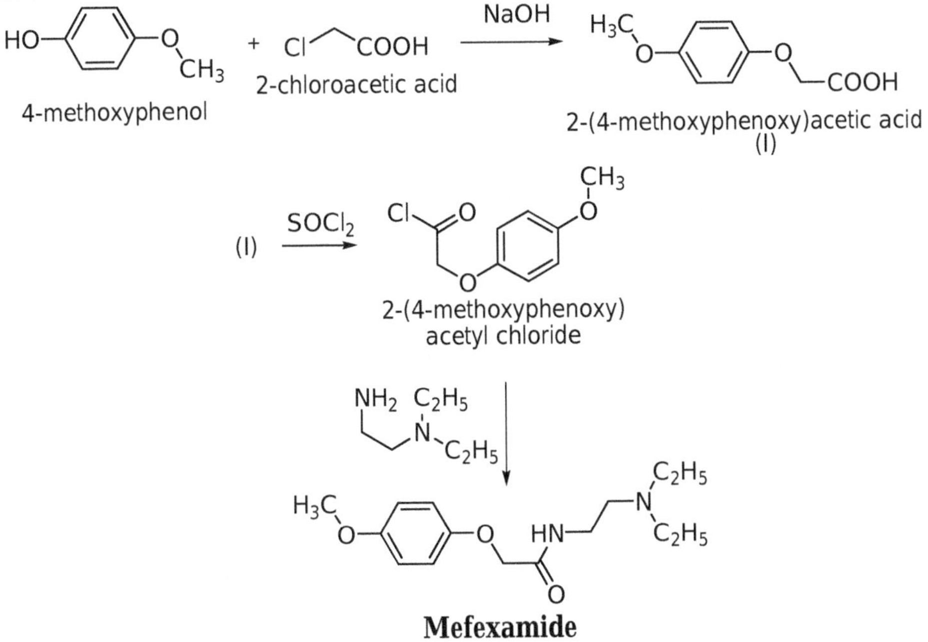

4-methoxyphenol + 2-chloroacetic acid $\xrightarrow{\text{NaOH}}$ 2-(4-methoxyphenoxy)acetic acid (I)

(I) $\xrightarrow{\text{SOCl}_2}$ 2-(4-methoxyphenoxy)acetyl chloride

+ N^1,N^1-diethylethane-1,2-diamine → **Mefexamide**

MEPACRINE
Use: antimalarial
Analysis:

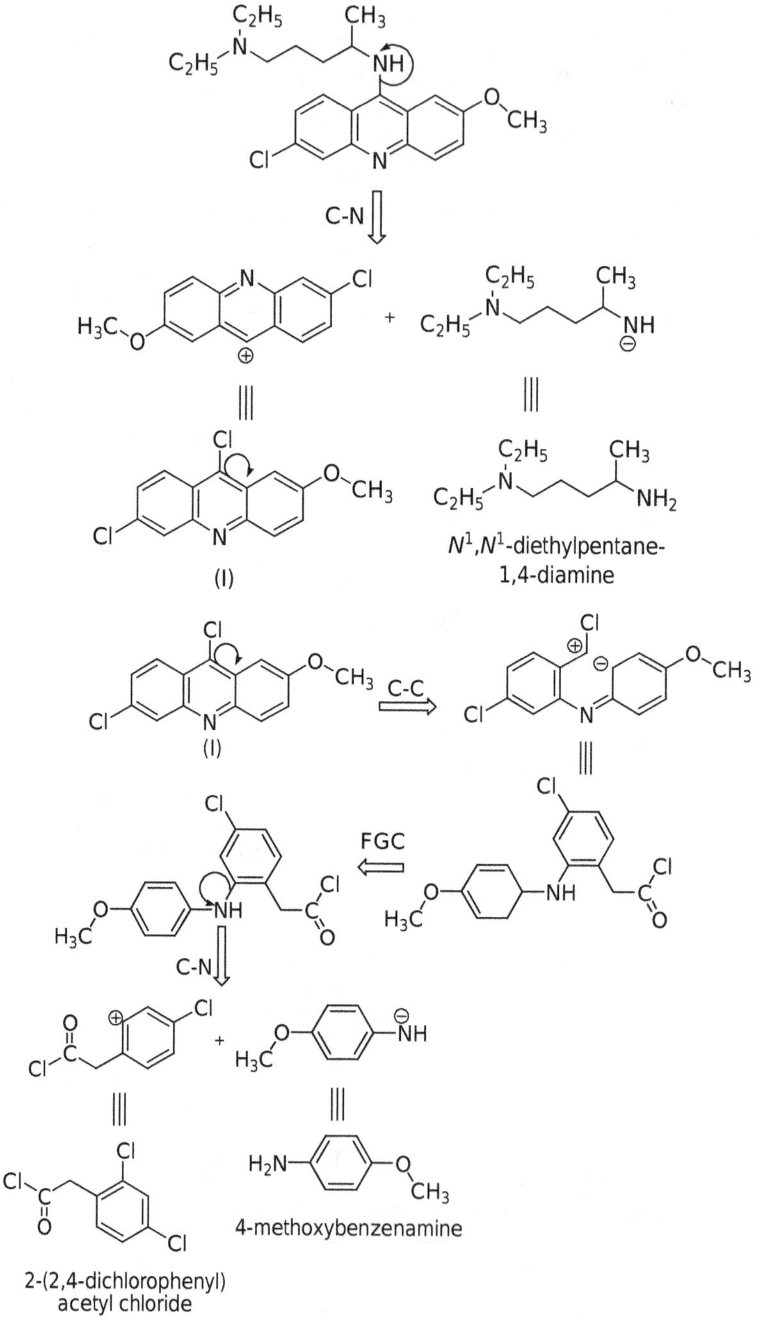

[Retrosynthetic scheme]

Intermediate (I): 6,9-dichloro-2-methoxyacridine

N^1,N^1-diethylpentane-1,4-diamine

2-(2,4-dichlorophenyl)acetyl chloride

4-methoxybenzenamine

Synthesis:

[Scheme: 2-(2,4-dichlorophenyl)acetyl chloride + 4-methoxycyclohexa-2,4-dienamine → intermediate (HOOC-substituted diphenylamine) → POCl₃ → 6,9-dichloro-2-methoxyacridine → N^1,N^1-diethylpentane-1,4-diamine → Mepacrine]

MEPHENESIN

Use: muscle relaxant

Analysis:

[Retrosynthetic scheme: Mephenesin ⟹ o-cresol (phenoxide) + 3-chloropropane-1,2-diol]

Synthesis:

o-cresol + 3-chloropropane-1,2-diol $\xrightarrow{\text{NaOH}}$ **Mephenesin**

MEPROBAMATE
Use: tranquilizer
Analysis:

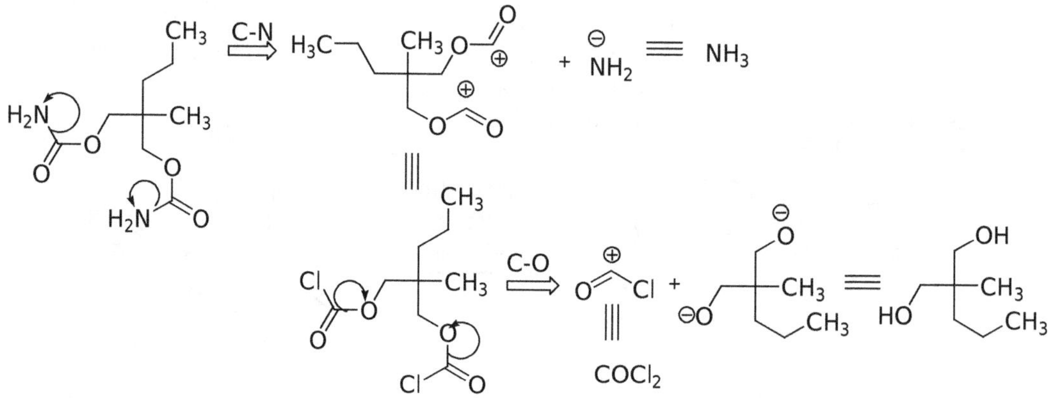

Synthesis:

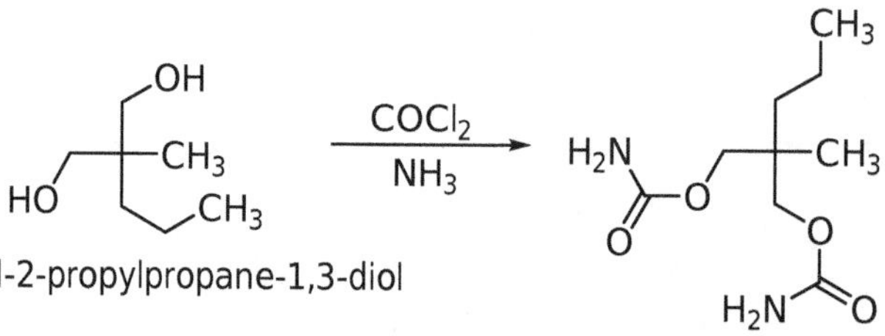

2-methyl-2-propylpropane-1,3-diol $\xrightarrow{\text{COCl}_2, \text{NH}_3}$ **Meprobamate**

MEPRYLCAINE
Use: local anaesthetic
Analysis:

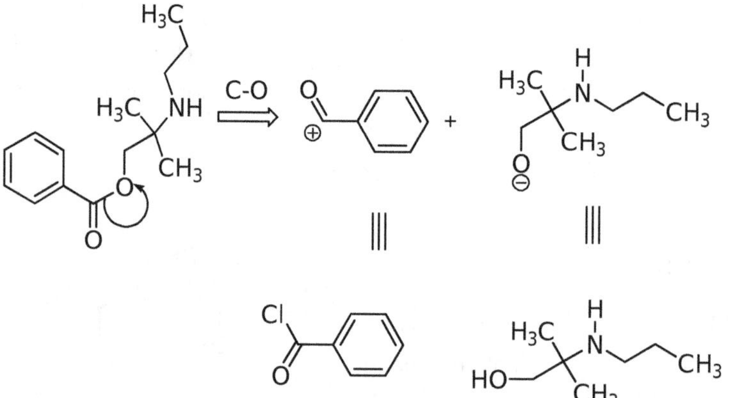

benzoyl chloride

2-methyl-2-(propylamino)propan-1-ol

Synthesis:

benzoyl chloride + 2-methyl-2-(propylamino)propan-1-ol → (NaOH, H₂O) → **Meprylcaine**

MESALAZINE
Use: treatment of gastrointestinal disorder

Analysis:

5-amino-2-hydroxy benzoic acid ⇒ (FGC) ⇒ 2-hydroxy-5-nitrobenzoic acid ⇒ (C-N Nitration) ⇒ 2-hydroxybenzoic acid

Synthesis:

2-hydroxy benzoic acid → (HNO₃) → 2-hydroxy-5-nitrobenzoic acid → (Zn, HCl) → **Mesalazine**

METAHEXAMIDE
Use: antidiabetic

Analysis:

[Retrosynthetic scheme showing metahexamide ⇒ (FGC) ⇒ acetamido intermediate ⇒ (C-N) ⇒ intermediate (I) + cyclohexanamine (H₂N-cyclohexyl)]

Synthesis:

[Scheme: 3-acetylamino-4-methylbenzene-sulfonamide + ethyl chloroformate → (K₂CO₃, acetone) → intermediate → (DMF, cyclohexylamine H₂N-C₆H₁₁) → **Metahexamide**]

METFORMIN

Use: antidiabetic

Analysis:

[Retrosynthetic scheme: Metformin ⇒ dimethylamine + cyanoguanidine]

Synthesis:

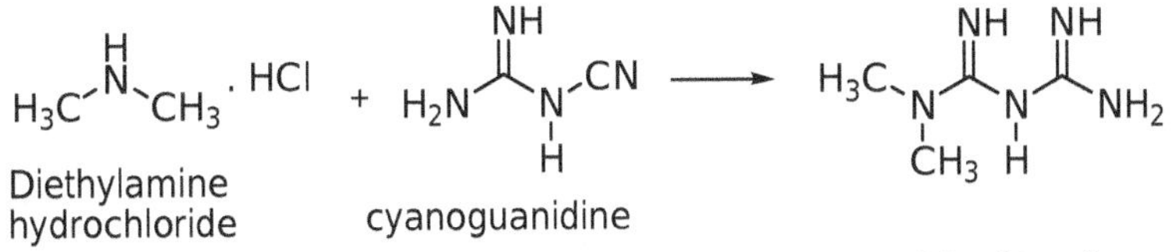

Diethylamine hydrochloride + cyanoguanidine → **Metformin**

METHDILAZINE

Use: antihistaminic

Analysis:

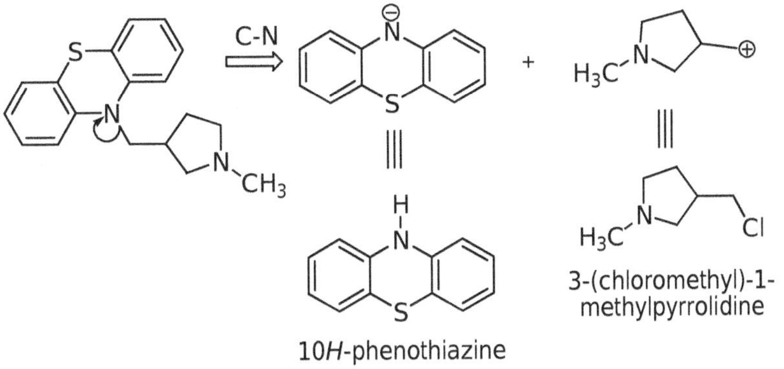

Methdilazine ⇒ (C–N) 10H-phenothiazine + 3-(chloromethyl)-1-methylpyrrolidine

Synthesis:

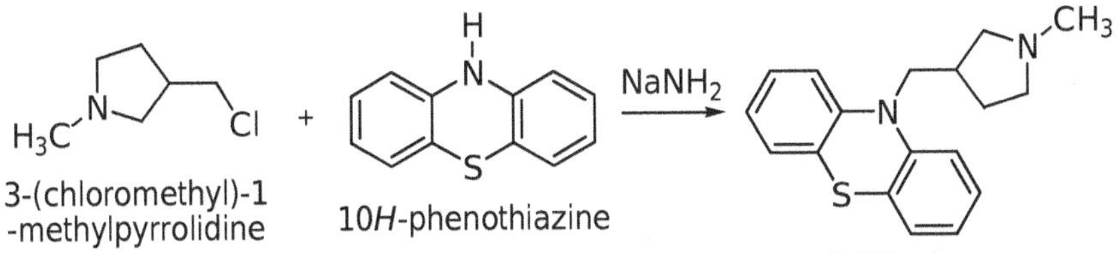

3-(chloromethyl)-1-methylpyrrolidine + 10H-phenothiazine $\xrightarrow{NaNH_2}$ **Methdilazine**

METHICILLIN

Use: antibiotic

Analysis:

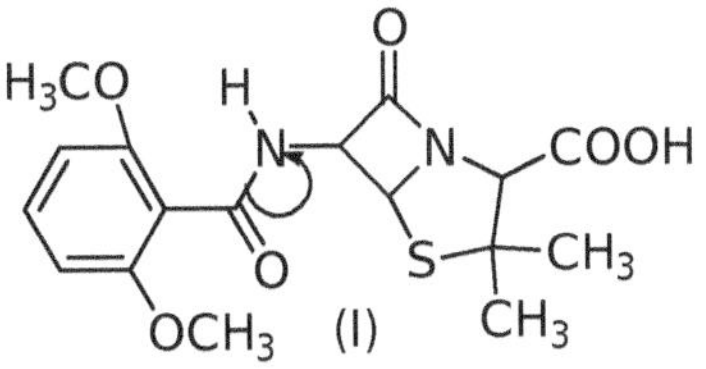

(I)

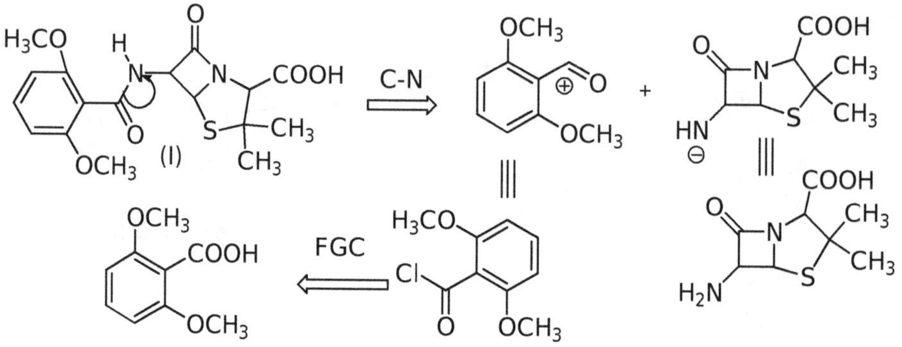

Synthesis (Methicillin):

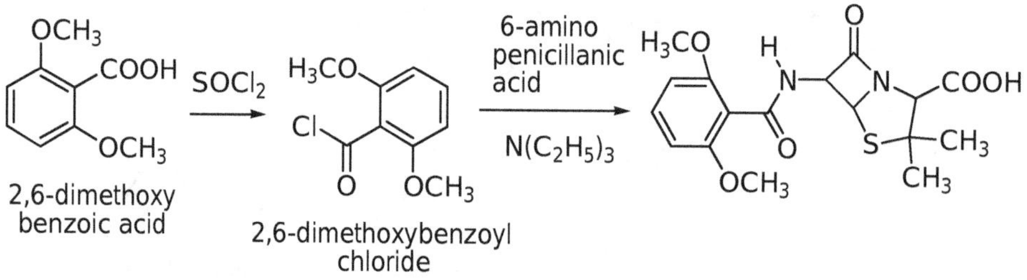

2,6-dimethoxy benzoic acid → (SOCl₂) → 2,6-dimethoxybenzoyl chloride → (6-aminopenicillanic acid, N(C₂H₅)₃) → **Methicillin**

METHIXENE

Use: antiparkinsonian, antispasmodic

Analysis:

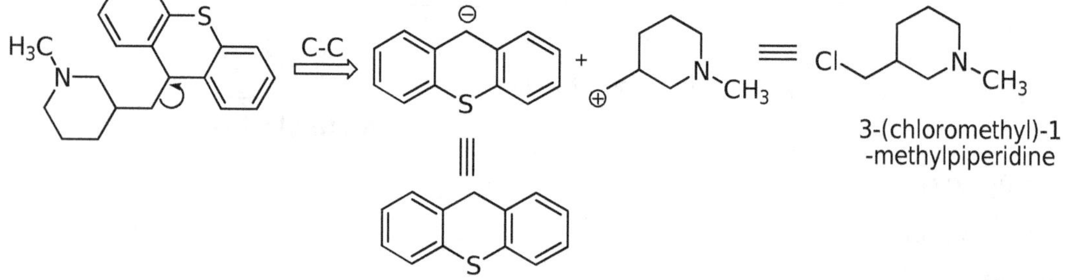

Methixene ⇒ (C-C) thioxanthene cation + 3-(piperidinyl) carbanion ≡ 9H-thioxanthene + 3-(chloromethyl)-1-methylpiperidine

Synthesis:

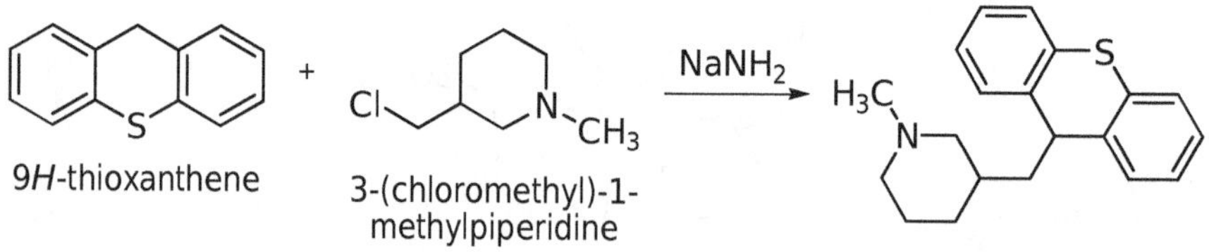

9H-thioxanthene + 3-(chloromethyl)-1-methylpiperidine → (NaNH₂) → **Methixene**

METHOCARBAMOL

Use: muscle relaxant

Analysis:

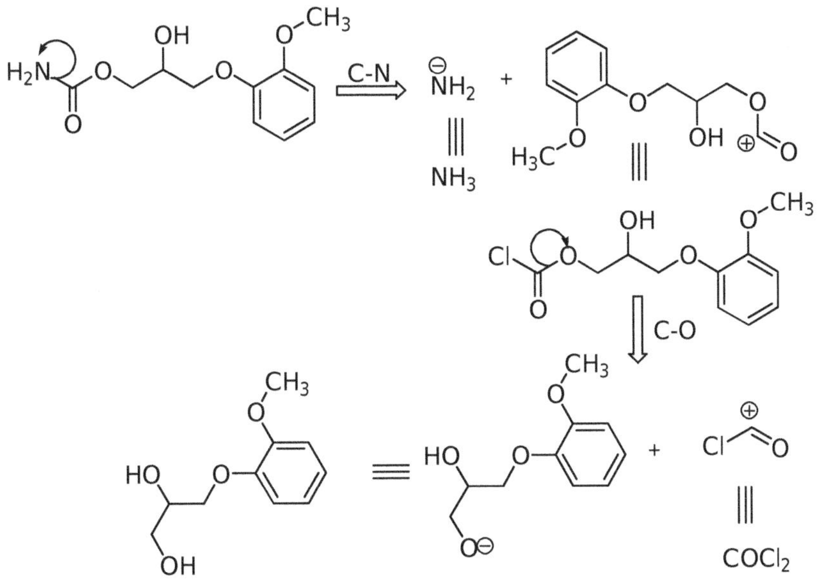

[Retrosynthetic analysis scheme showing methocarbamol disconnected via C-N bond to NH₃ and chloroformate intermediate, then via C-O to 3-(2-methoxyphenoxy)propane-1,2-diol and COCl₂]

3-(2-methoxyphenoxy)propane-1,2-diol

Synthesis:

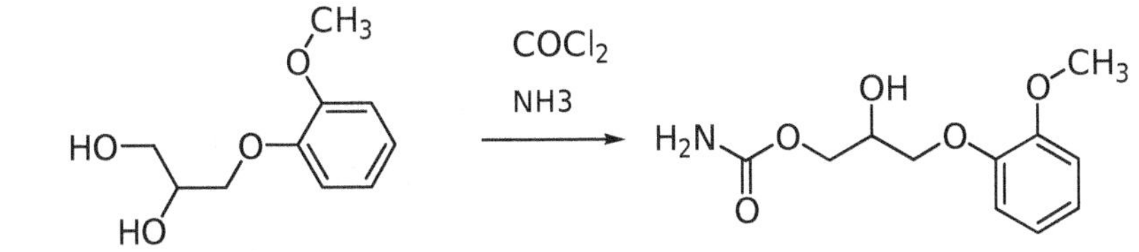

3-(2-methoxyphenoxy)propane-1,2-diol $\xrightarrow{\text{COCl}_2,\ \text{NH}_3}$ **Methocarbamol**

METHYLDOPA

Use: antihypertensive

Analysis:

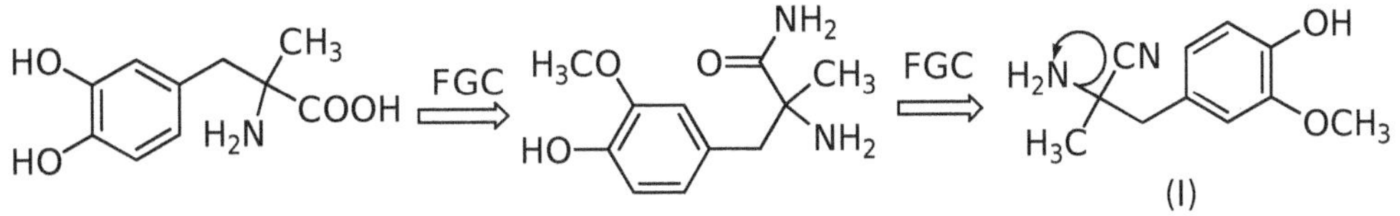

[Retrosynthetic scheme: methyldopa ⟹ (FGC) methylated amide intermediate ⟹ (FGC) aminonitrile (I)]

Retrosynthetic Analysis and Synthesis of Drugs

[Retrosynthetic scheme showing disconnection of compound (I) to 1-(4-hydroxy-3-methoxyphenyl)propan-2-one via C-N and C-CN disconnections and FGC (functional group conversions).]

Synthesis:

1-(4-hydroxy-3-methoxyphenyl)propan-2-one →[HCN, NH₃]→ 2-chloro-3-(4-hydroxy-3-methoxyphenyl)-2-methylpropanenitrile →[CONH₂, HCl]→ 2-(4-hydroxy-3-methoxybenzyl)-2-aminopropanamide →[HBr]→ **Methyldopa**

METHYLPERONE

Use: neuroleptic
Analysis:

[Retrosynthetic scheme: methylperone ⇒ 4-methylpiperidine anion + acyl cation equivalent; C-N disconnection gives 4-methylpiperidine and 4-chloro-1-(4-fluorophenyl)butan-1-one]

Synthesis:

4-methylpiperidine + 4-chloro-1-(4-fluorophenyl)butan-1-one —KI→ **Methylperone**

METHYLPHENIDATE

Use: psychotonic
Analysis:

[Retrosynthetic scheme: methylphenidate ⇒ (via reduction) pyridine analog ⇒ (C-O) methoxide + acyl cation; via FGC to carboxylic acid and acid chloride; then to α-phenyl-α-(2-pyridyl)acetonitrile; C-C disconnection to 2-chloropyridine (≡ pyridinium cation) + 2-phenylacetonitrile anion (≡ 2-phenylacetonitrile)]

Synthesis:

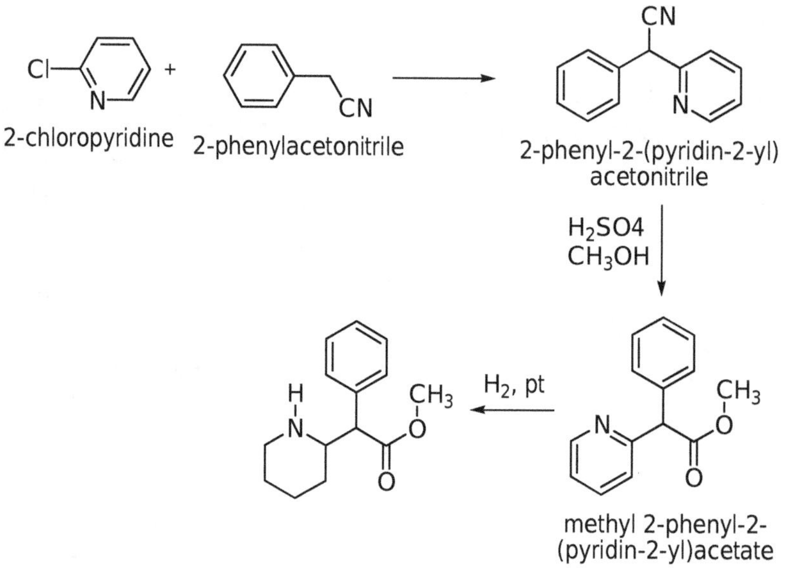
2-chloropyridine
2-phenylacetonitrile
2-phenyl-2-(pyridin-2-yl)
acetonitrile
H2SO4
CH3OH
H2, pt
methyl 2-phenyl-2-
(pyridin-2-yl)acetate

Methylphenidate

METOCLOPRAMIDE

Use: antiemetic

Analysis:

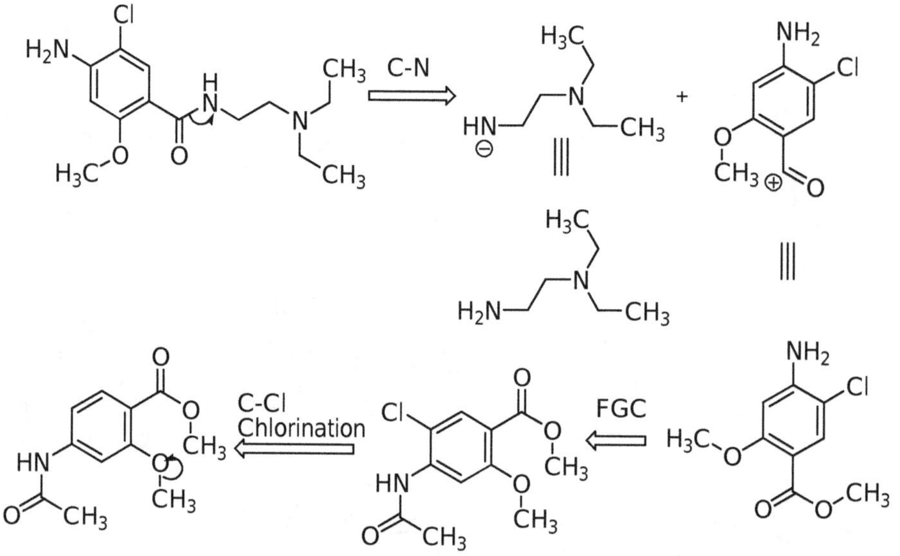
C-N
C-Cl
Chlorination
FGC

(I)

Retrosynthetic Analysis and Synthesis of Drugs

Synthesis:

4-amino-2-hydroxybenzoic acid + CH₃OH (methanol) → methyl 4-amino-2-hydroxybenzoate

Then acetic anhydride (H₃C-CO-O-CO-CH₃) → methyl 4-acetamido-2-hydroxybenzoate

Then dimethyl sulfate (H₃C-O-SO₂-O-CH₃) → (I)

Retrosynthetic Analysis and Synthesis of Drugs

(I) →[Cl₂, CH₃COOH] **methyl 4-acetamido-5-chloro-2-methoxybenzoate**

↓ N,N-diethylethylenediamine, Aluminium isopropylate, HCl

Metoclopramide

METOPIMIZINE
Use: antiemetic
Analysis:

Synthesis:

[Synthesis scheme: 2-(methylsulfonyl)-10H-phenothiazine + Br(CH₂)₃Cl with NaNH₂ → N-(3-chloropropyl) intermediate; then with isonipecotamide and Na₂CO₃ → **Metopimizine**]

2-(methylsulfonyl)-10H-phenothiazine

Metopimizine

METRONIDAZOLE

Use: chemotherapeutic

Analysis:

[Retrosynthetic analysis: Metronidazole ⇒ C–N disconnection to HOCH₂⁺ (≡ 2-chloroethanol) + 2-methyl-5-nitroimidazole anion; then C–N nitration disconnection ⇒ 2-methyl-1H-imidazole]

2-chloroethanol

2-methyl-1H-imidazole

Synthesis:

2-methyl-1H-imidazole —HNO₃→ 2-methyl-5-nitro-1H-imidazole —ClCH₂CH₂OH→ **Metronidazole**

MICONAZOLE

Use: antifungal

Analysis:

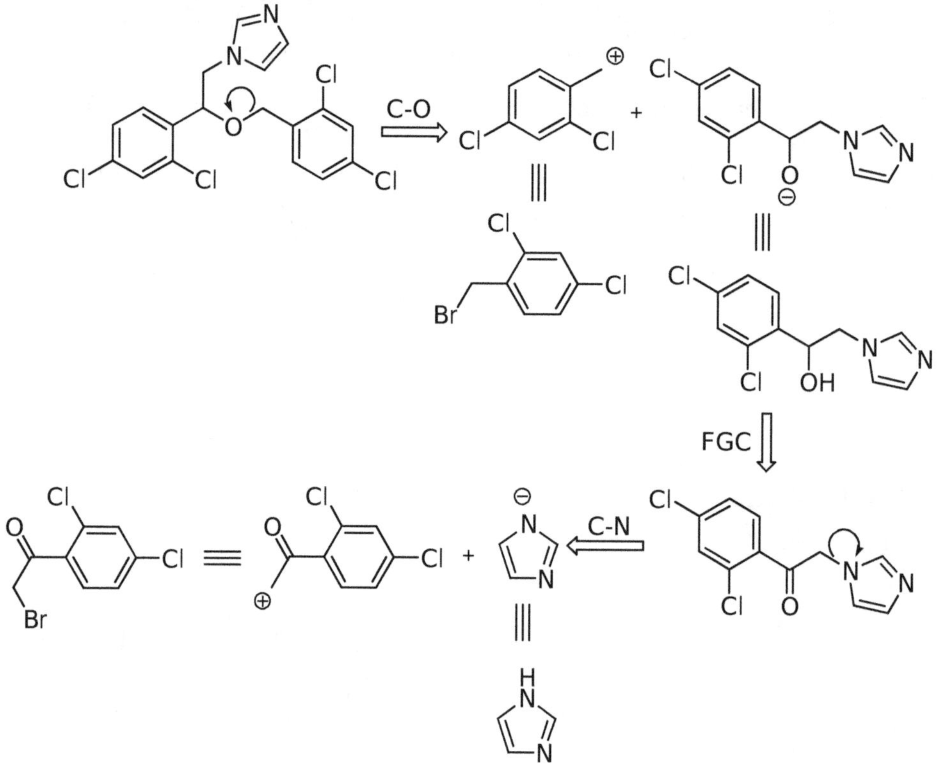

Synthesis:

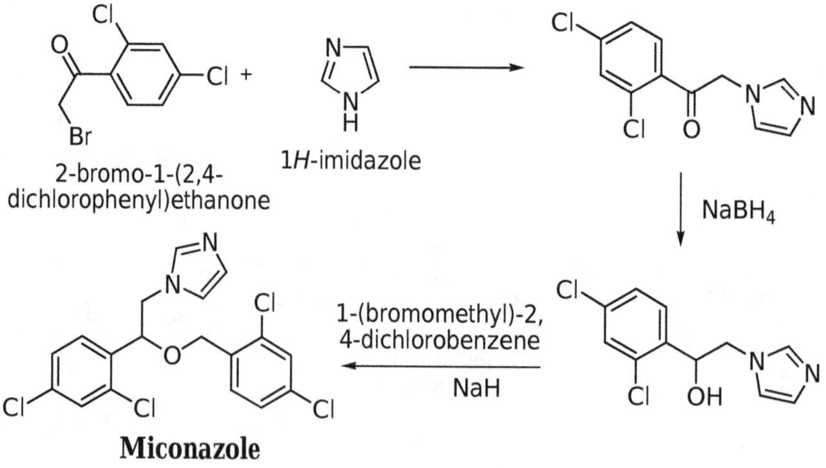

2-bromo-1-(2,4-dichlorophenyl)ethanone + 1*H*-imidazole → (2,4-dichlorophenyl imidazolyl ethanone)

NaBH₄ ↓

→ alcohol intermediate

1-(bromomethyl)-2,4-dichlorobenzene / NaH →

Miconazole

MIDAZOLAM
Use: hypnotic
Analysis:

Synthesis:

[Scheme: (2-amino-5-chlorophenyl)(2-fluorophenyl)methanone + ethyl 2-aminoacetate → (Pyridine) → (E)-7-chloro-5-(2-fluorophenyl)-1H-benzo[e][1,4]diazepin-2(3H)-one → (KOC(CH₃)₃, O₂N–CH₃) → nitro intermediate → (H₂, Raney-Ni; then (H₃C-CO)₂O) → acetamide intermediate → (Polyphosphoric acid) → dihydro imidazobenzodiazepine → (MnO₂) → **Midazolam**]

Reagents and intermediates shown:
- (2-amino-5-chlorophenyl)(2-fluorophenyl)methanone
- ethyl 2-aminoacetate
- Pyridine
- (E)-7-chloro-5-(2-fluorophenyl)-1H-benzo[e][1,4]diazepin-2(3H)-one
- $KOC(CH_3)_3$ | O_2N-CH_3
- $H_3C-CO-O-CO-CH_3$ (acetic anhydride)
- H_2, Raney-Ni
- Polyphosphoric acid
- MnO_2

Midazolam

MINAPRINE
Use: antidepressant
Analysis:

(I)

Synthesis:

2-morpholino ethanamine + 3-chloro-4-methyl-6-phenylpyridazine → (Cu/butanol, Δ) **Minaprine**

MIRTAZAPINE
Use: antidepressant
Analysis:

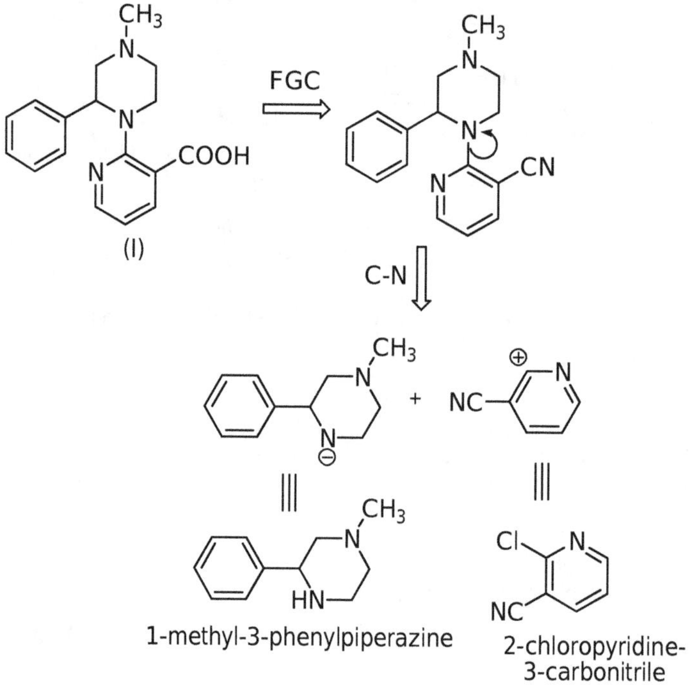

Retrosynthetic Analysis and Synthesis of Drugs

(I)

FGC ⇒

C-N ⇒

1-methyl-3-phenylpiperazine + 2-chloropyridine-3-carbonitrile

Synthesis:

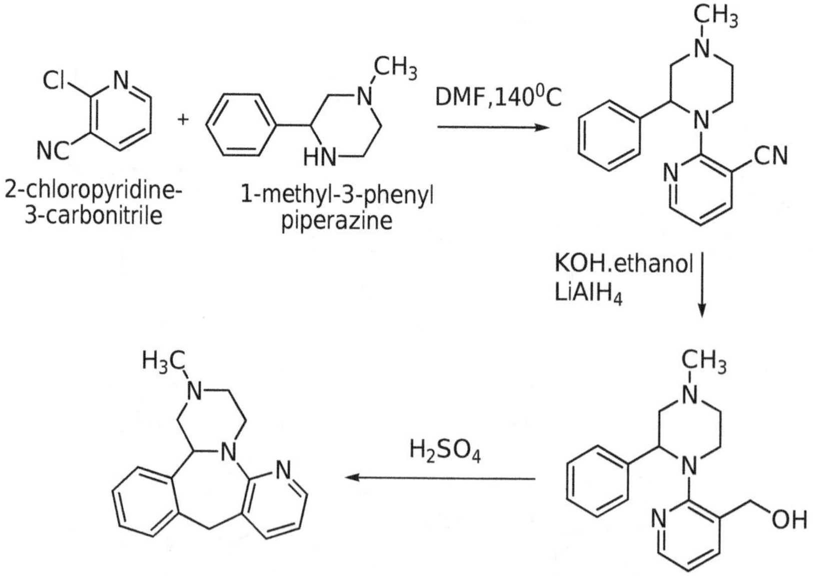

2-chloropyridine-3-carbonitrile + 1-methyl-3-phenyl piperazine →(DMF, 140°C)→ [intermediate with CN]

↓ KOH.ethanol / LiAlH₄

[intermediate with CH₂OH]

←(H₂SO₄)—

Mirtazapine

MOCLOBEMIDE
Use: antidepressant
Analysis:

[Retrosynthetic scheme: 4-chlorobenzamide with morpholinoethyl group disconnects (C-N) to 4-chlorobenzoyl cation and morpholinoethyl amide anion, corresponding to 4-chlorobenzoyl chloride and 2-morpholinoethanamine]

Synthesis:

4-chlorobenzoyl chloride + 2-morpholinoethanamine —pyridine→ **Moclobemide**

MOFEBUTAZONE
Use: anti-inflammatory, antirheumatic
Analysis:

[Retrosynthetic scheme: pyrazolidinedione disconnects (C-N, C-N) to phenylhydrazine anion and dicarbonyl cation, corresponding to 1-phenylhydrazine and diethyl 2-butylmalonate]

Retrosynthetic Analysis and Synthesis of Drugs

Synthesis:

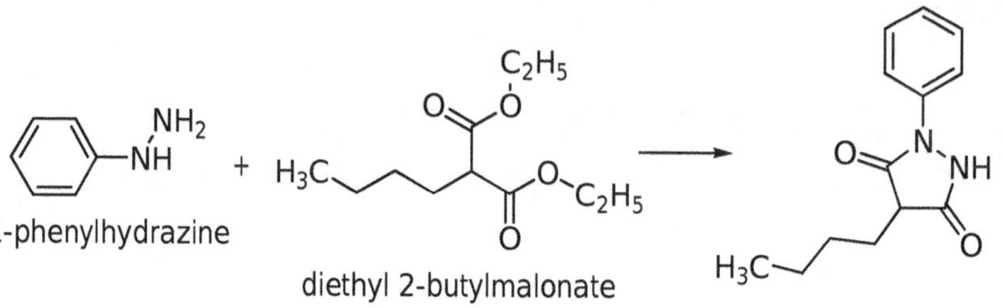

1-phenylhydrazine + diethyl 2-butylmalonate → **Mofebutazone**

MOROXYDINE

Use: antiviral

Analysis:

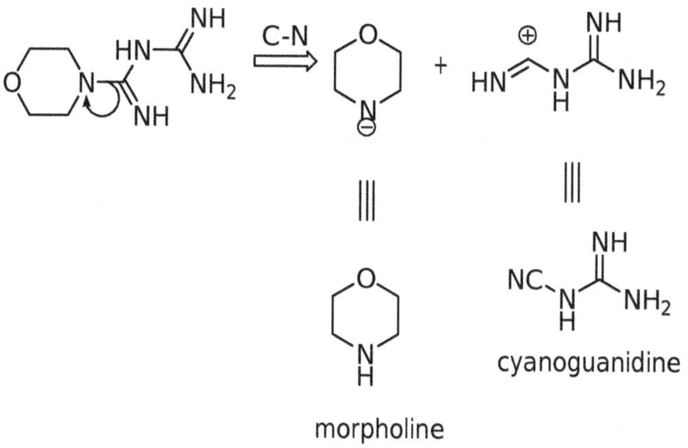

morpholine + cyanoguanidine

Synthesis:

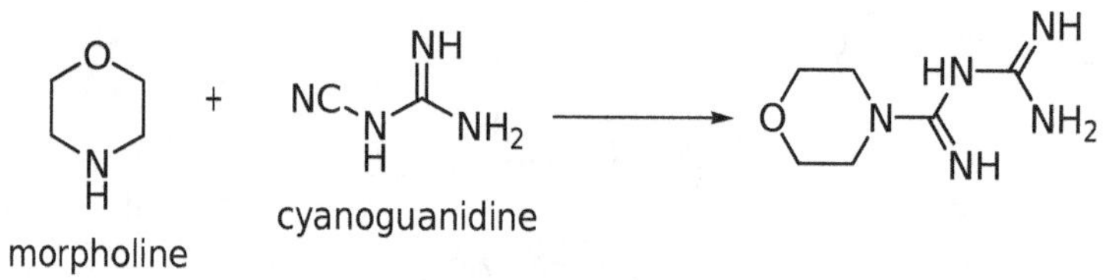

morpholine + cyanoguanidine → **Moroxydine**

NABUMETONE

Use: anti-inflammatory

Analysis:

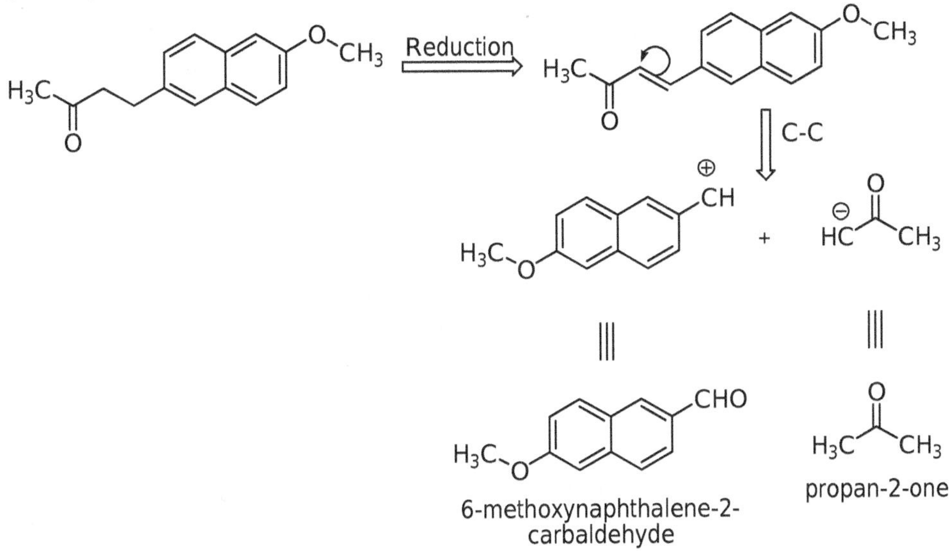

Synthesis:

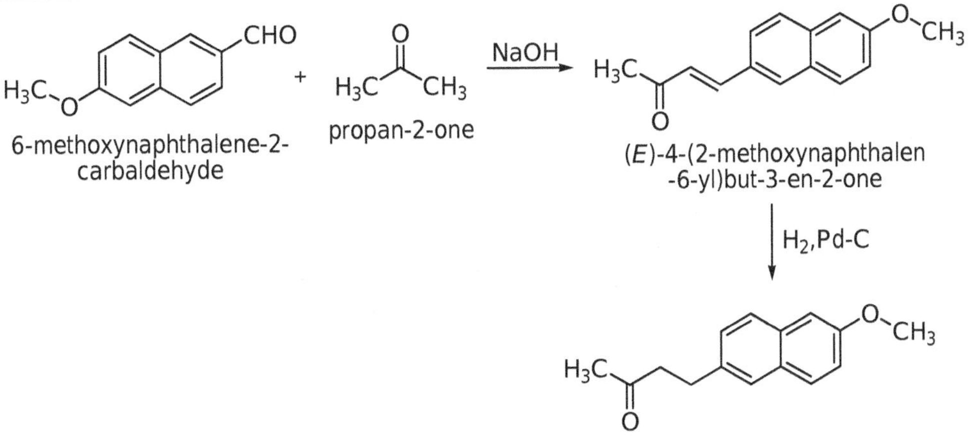

Nabumetone

NAFCILLIN
Use: antibiotic
Analysis:

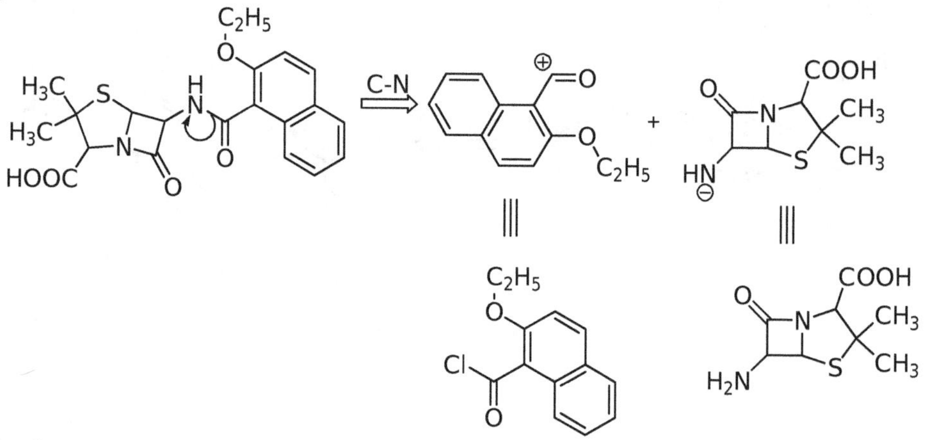

[Retrosynthetic analysis showing nafcillin disconnected at the C–N amide bond to give an acylium cation of 2-ethoxynaphthalene-1-carbonyl and the amine anion of 6-aminopenicillanic acid, corresponding to 2-ethoxynaphthalene-1-carbonyl chloride and 6-aminopenicillanic acid.]

Synthesis:

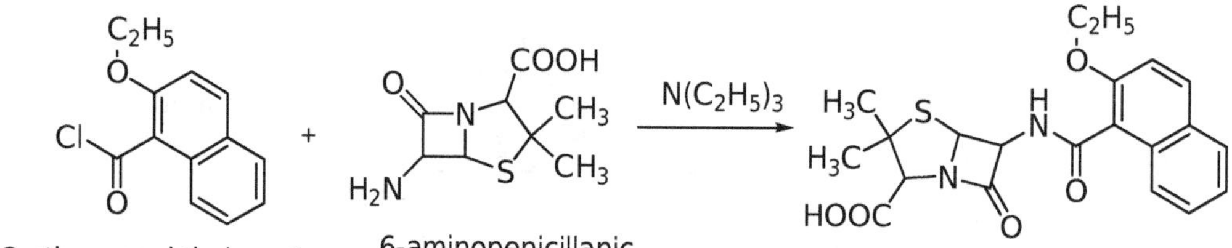

2-ethoxynaphthalene-1-carbonyl chloride + 6-aminopenicillanic acid $\xrightarrow{N(C_2H_5)_3}$ **Nafcillin**

NAFTIFINE
Use: antifungal
Analysis:

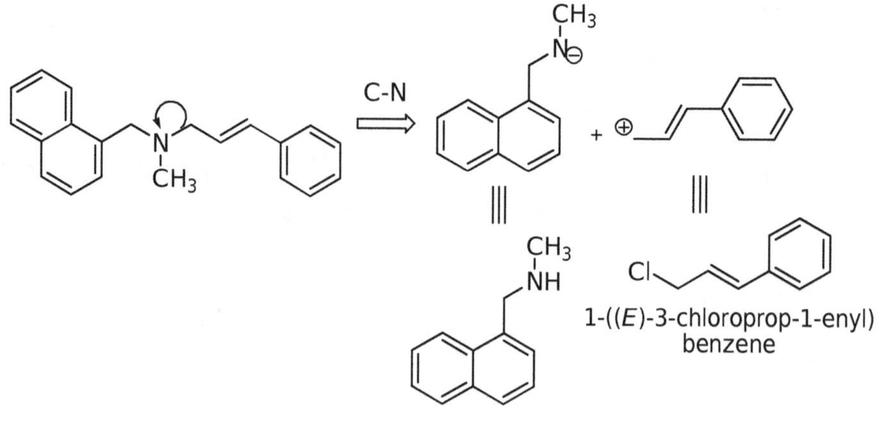

[Retrosynthetic analysis showing naftifine disconnected at the C–N bond to give N-methyl-1-naphthalenemethylamine anion and cinnamyl cation, corresponding to N-methyl-1-(naphthalen-1-yl)methanamine and 1-((E)-3-chloroprop-1-enyl)benzene.]

Synthesis:

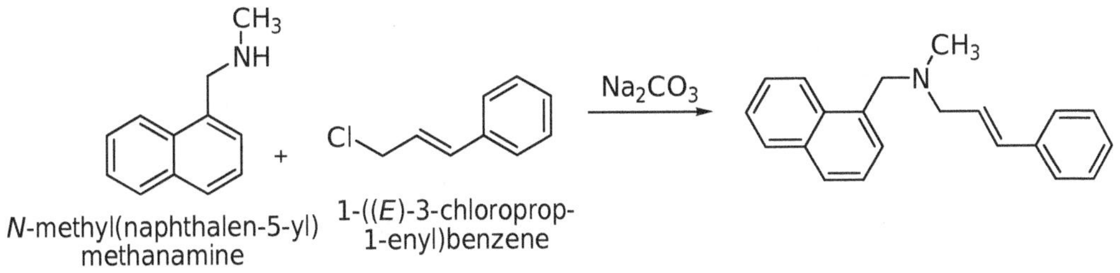

N-methyl(naphthalen-5-yl)methanamine + 1-((E)-3-chloroprop-1-enyl)benzene → (Na₂CO₃) **Naftifine**

NAFTOPIDIL

Use: antihypertensive

Analysis:

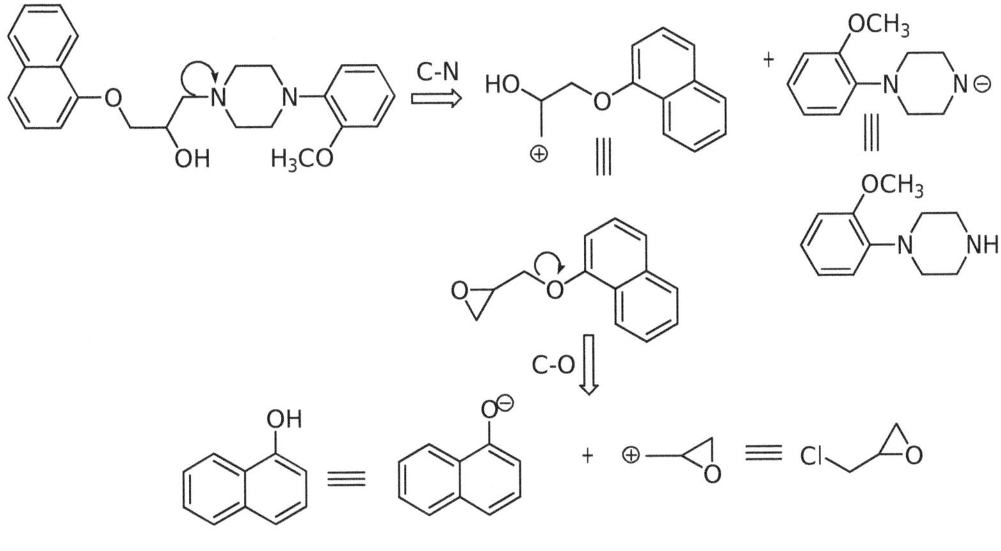

C-N retrosynthesis and C-O retrosynthesis shown, giving naphthalen-1-ol + chloromethyl oxirane, and 1-(2-methoxyphenyl)piperazine.

Synthesis:

naphthalen-1-ol + 2-(chloromethyl)oxirane → (NaOH) 2-((naphthalen-5-yloxy)methyl)oxirane

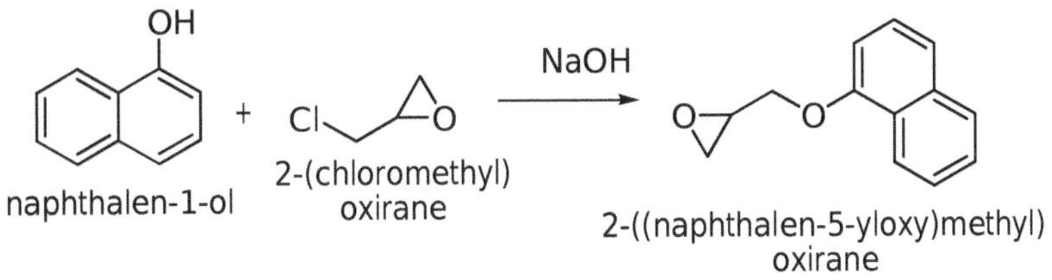

(I)

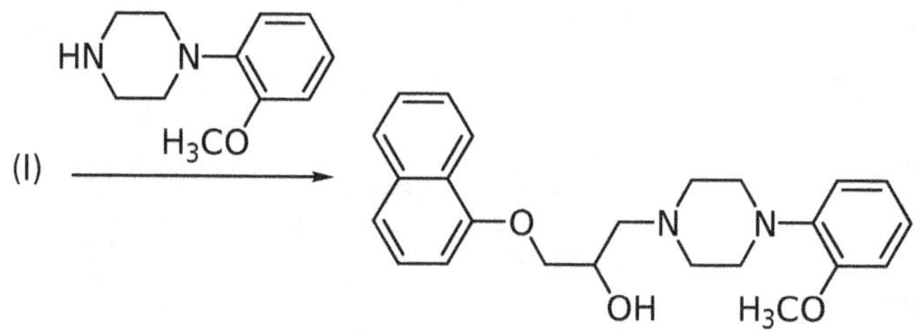

Naftopidil (structure shown from (I) + piperazine derivative)

NEVIRAPINE
Use: anti-HIV
Analysis:

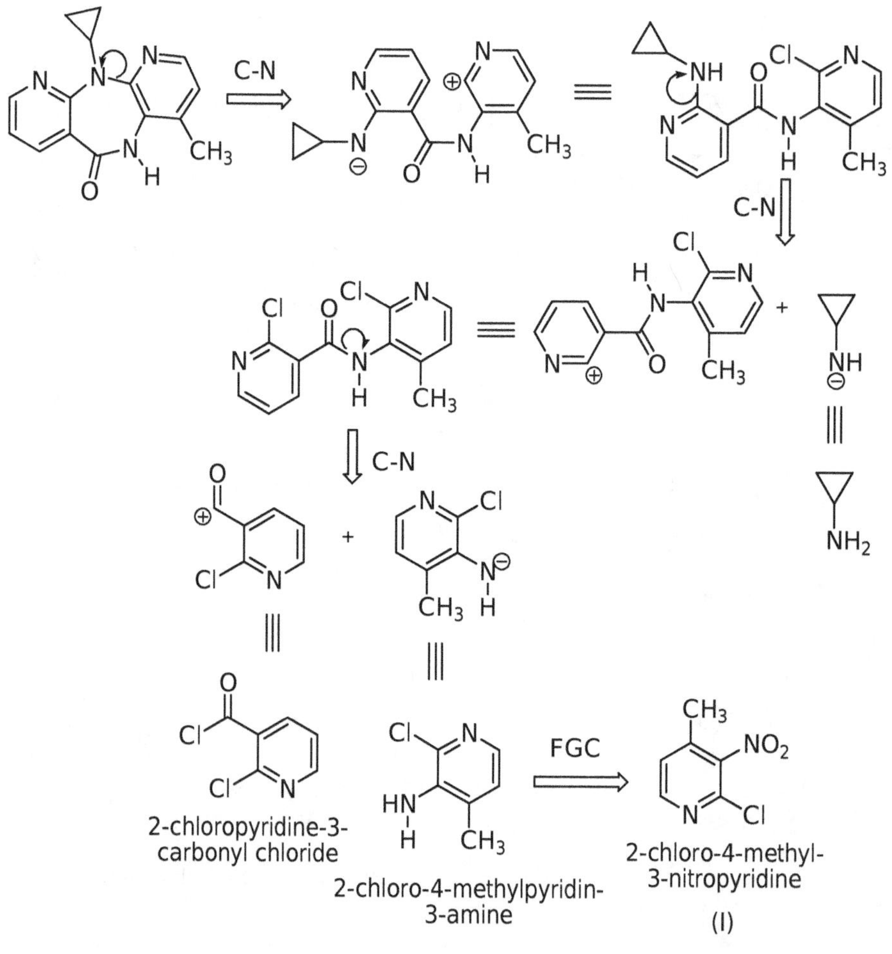

[Retrosynthetic scheme leading to:]

- 2-chloropyridine-3-carbonyl chloride
- 2-chloro-4-methylpyridin-3-amine
- cyclopropylamine

$$\xrightarrow{FGC}$$ 2-chloro-4-methyl-3-nitropyridine (I)

Retrosynthetic Analysis and Synthesis of Drugs

[Scheme: 2-chloro-4-methyl-3-nitropyridine (I) ⇒ (FGC) 4-methyl-3-nitropyridin-2-ol]

Synthesis:

4-methyl-3-nitropyridin-2-ol →(POCl₃, PCl₅)→ 2-chloro-4-methyl-3-nitropyridine →(H₃C-COOH, SnCl₂)→ 2-chloro-4-methyl pyridin-3-amine →(2-chloropyridine-3-carbonyl chloride, pyridine)→ [bis-pyridyl amide intermediate] →(H₂N-cyclopropyl, 2-Xylene)→ [cyclopropylamino intermediate] →(DMF, NaH)→ **Nevirapine**

NICERITROL

Use: cholesterol depressant

Analysis:

[Retrosynthetic scheme: niceritrol (tetra-nicotinoyl ester of pentaerythritol) ⇒ (C-O) pentaerythritol tetra-alkoxide + nicotinoyl cation; corresponding to pentaerythritol (HOCH₂)₄C and nicotinoyl chloride]

Synthesis:

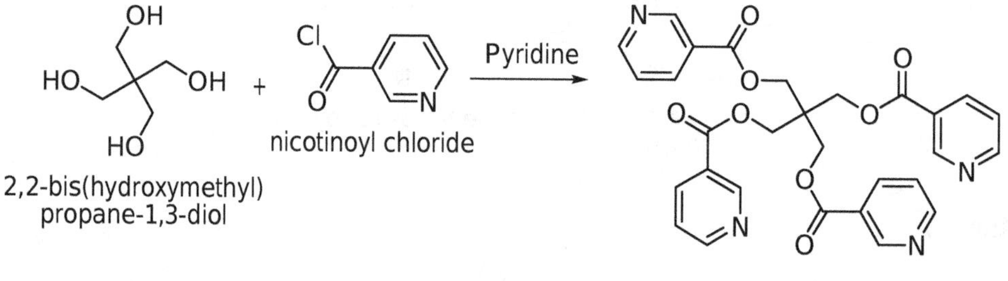

2,2-bis(hydroxymethyl)propane-1,3-diol + nicotinoyl chloride $\xrightarrow{\text{Pyridine}}$ **Niceritrol**

NICLOSAMIDE

Use: anthelmintic

Analysis:

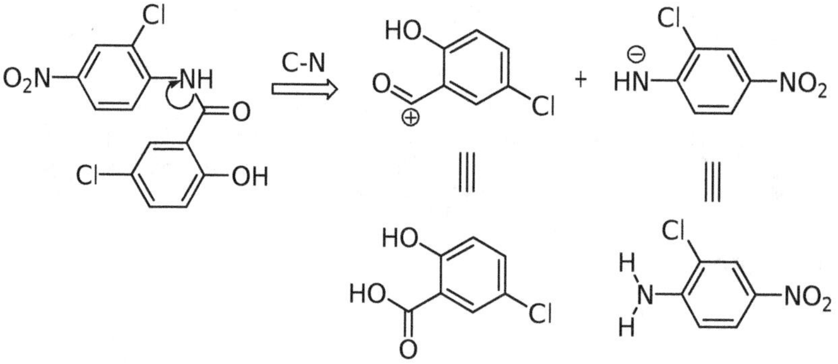

Niclosamide $\xRightarrow{\text{C-N}}$ acylium cation of 5-chloro-2-hydroxybenzoic acid + amide anion of 2-chloro-4-nitroaniline

≡ 5-chloro-2-hydroxybenzoic acid

≡ 2-chloro-4-nitroaniline

Synthesis:

5-chloro-2-hydroxy benzoic acid + 2-chloro-4-nitro benzenamine $\xrightarrow{\text{PCl}_3}$ **Niclosamide**

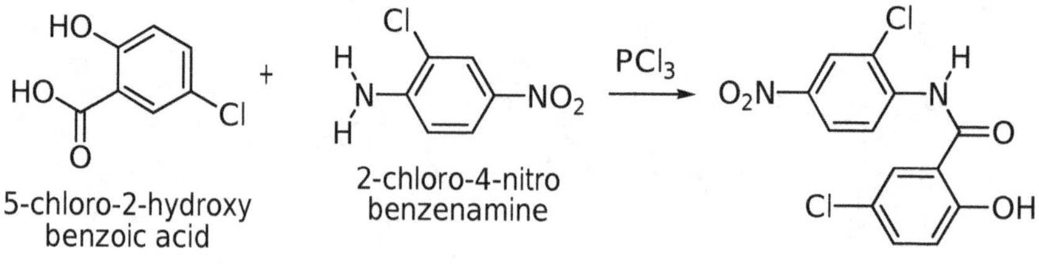

NICOTAFURYL
Use: antirheumatic
Analysis:

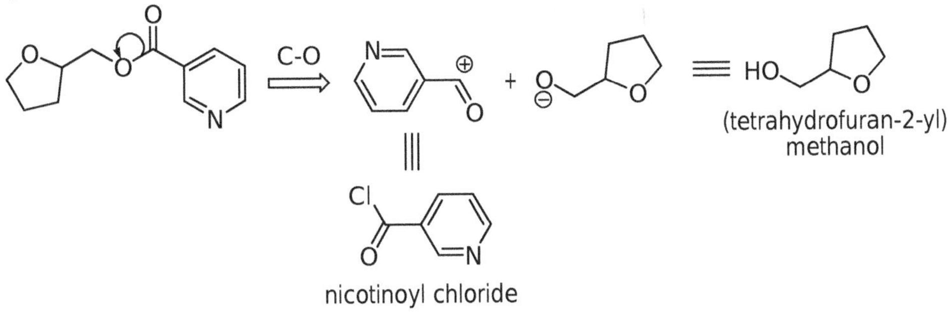

The target ester is disconnected at the C–O bond to give the nicotinoyl cation (equivalent to nicotinoyl chloride) and the alkoxide from (tetrahydrofuran-2-yl)methanol.

Synthesis:

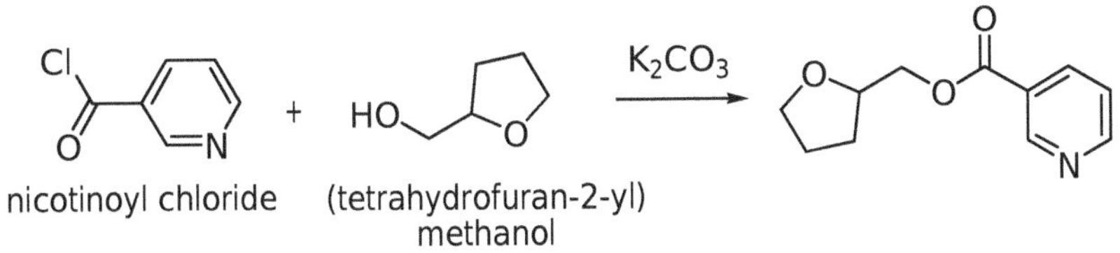

nicotinoyl chloride + (tetrahydrofuran-2-yl)methanol $\xrightarrow{K_2CO_3}$ **Nicotafuryl**

NICOTINAMIDE
Use: antipellagra agent
Analysis:

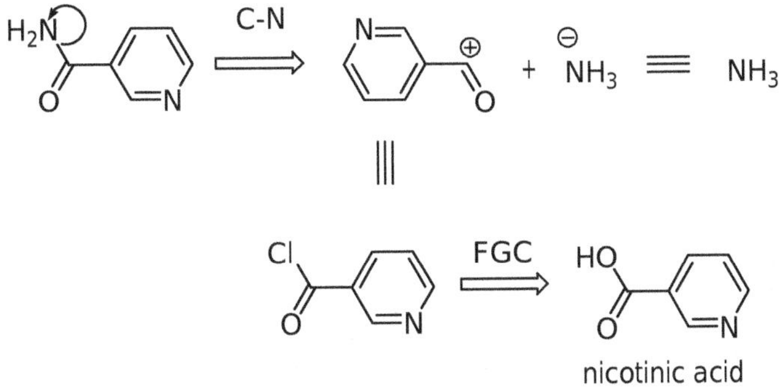

The amide is disconnected at the C–N bond to give the nicotinoyl cation and ammonia; the acyl cation equivalent is nicotinoyl chloride, obtained by FGC from nicotinic acid.

Synthesis:

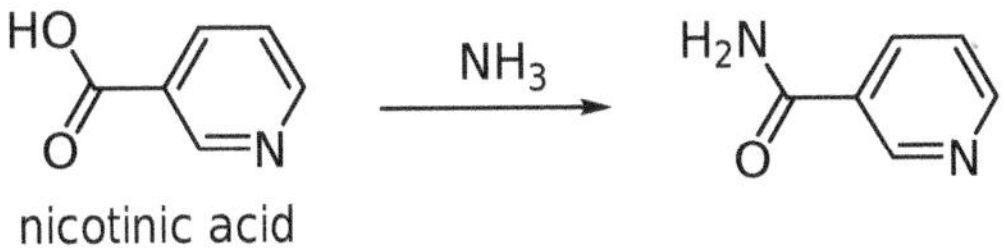

nicotinic acid $\xrightarrow{NH_3}$ **Nicotinamide**

NIFENALOL

Use: antiarrhythmic, antianginal

Analysis:

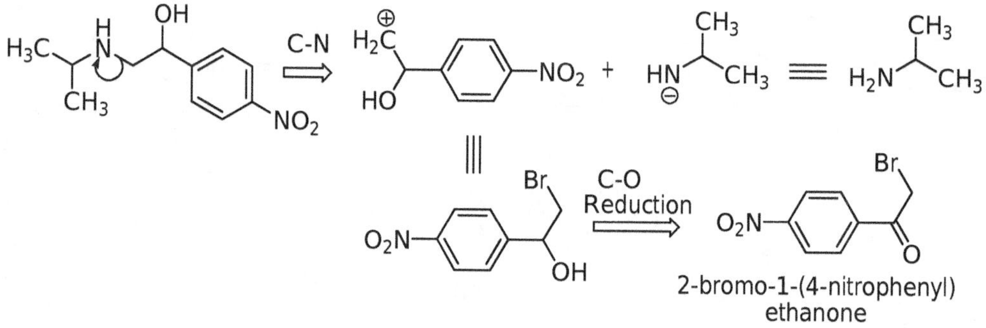

[Retrosynthetic scheme: Nifenalol ⇒ (C-N disconnection) α-hydroxy cation of 1-(4-nitrophenyl)ethanol + isopropylamine anion ≡ isopropylamine; the cation ≡ 2-bromo-1-(4-nitrophenyl)ethanol ⇒ (C-O reduction) 2-bromo-1-(4-nitrophenyl)ethanone]

Synthesis:

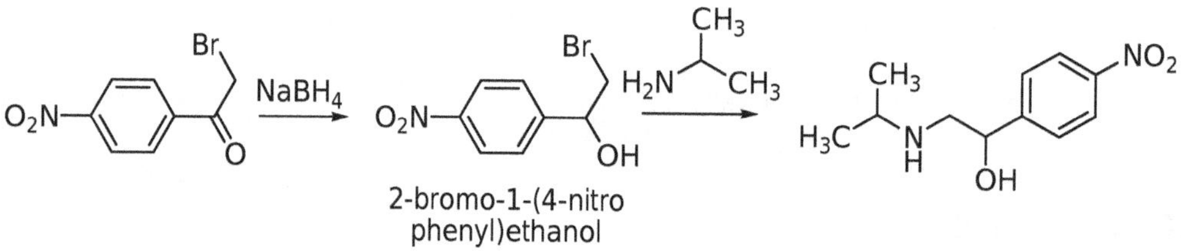

2-bromo-1-(4-nitrophenyl)ethanone $\xrightarrow{NaBH_4}$ 2-bromo-1-(4-nitrophenyl)ethanol $\xrightarrow{(CH_3)_2CHNH_2}$ **Nifenalol**

NIFLUMIC ACID

Use: anti-inflammatory, antirheumatic

Analysis:

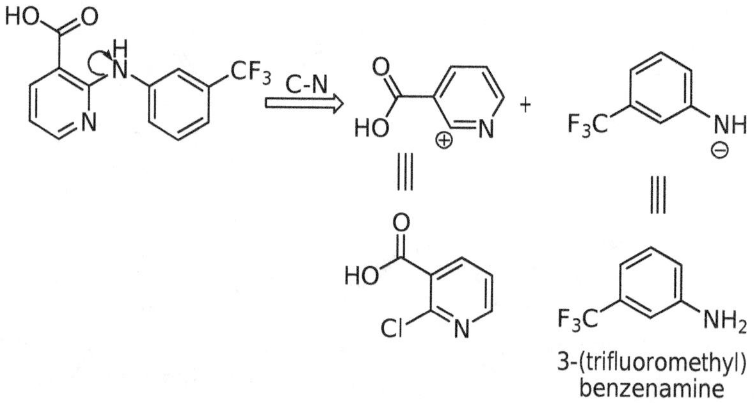

[Retrosynthetic scheme: Niflumic acid ⇒ (C-N disconnection) 2-carboxypyridinium cation + 3-(trifluoromethyl)aniline anion; cation ≡ 2-chloronicotinic acid; anion ≡ 3-(trifluoromethyl)benzenamine]

Synthesis:

[Scheme: 2-chloropyridine-3-carboxylic acid + 3-(trifluoromethyl)benzenamine → Niflumic acid]

NIKETHAMIDE

Use: respiratory analeptic

Analysis:

[Retrosynthetic scheme: Nikethamide ⟹ (C-N disconnection) nicotinoyl cation + diethylamide anion ≡ diethylamine; also ≡ nicotinoyl chloride ⟹ (FGC) nicotinic acid]

Synthesis:

[Scheme: nicotinic acid + diethylamine, POCl$_3$ → Nikethamide]

NIMESULIDE

Use: anti-inflammatory

Analysis:

[Retrosynthetic scheme: Nimesulide ⟹ (C-N, Nitration) intermediate (I)]

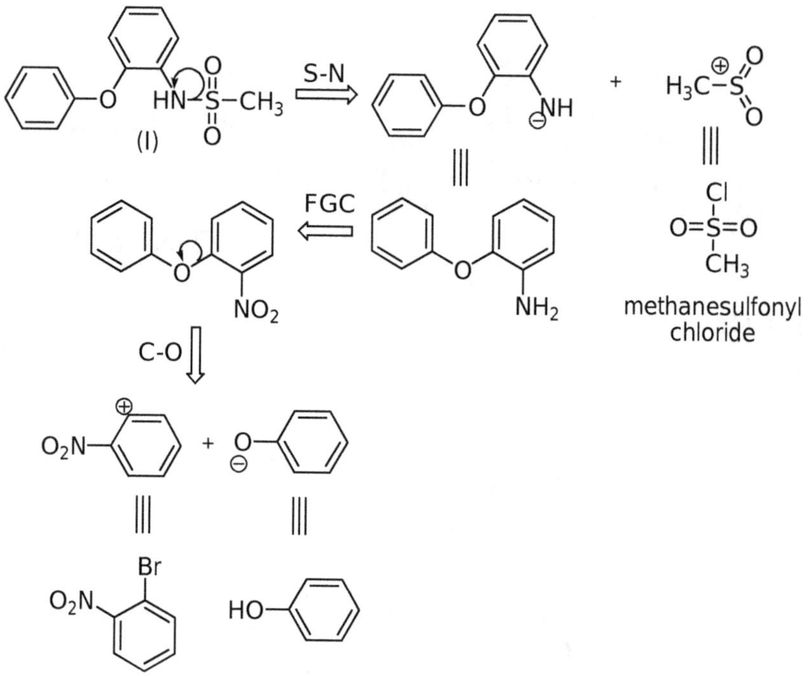

Synthesis:

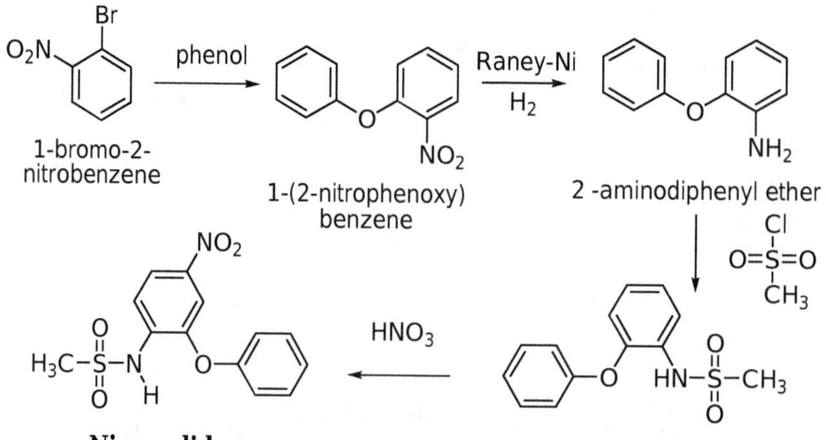

Nimesulide

NIRIDAZOLE

Use: antischistosomal
Analysis:

[Retrosynthetic scheme: 5-nitrothiazol-2-yl imidazolidinone ⇒ (C-N) ring-opened urea cation ⇒ 2-amino-5-nitrothiazole + 2-chloroethyl isocyanate intermediate ⇒ (C-N) 2-amino-5-nitrothiazole + 2-chloroethyl isocyanate ⇒ (C-N, Nitration) thiazol-2-amine]

Synthesis:

[Scheme: thiazol-2-amine + HNO₃ → 2-amino-5-nitrothiazole; + Cl-CH₂CH₂-NCO → 1-(2-chloroethyl)-3-(5-nitrothiazol-2-yl)urea; Δ → **Niridazole**]

NITRAZEPAM

Use: hypnotic, anticonvulsant
Analysis:

[Structure (I): 7-nitro-5-phenyl-1,3-dihydro-2H-1,4-benzodiazepin-2-one]

Synthesis:

(2-aminophenyl)(phenyl)methanone + ethyl 2-aminoacetate →(Pyridine) (Z)-5-phenyl-1H-benzo[e][1,4]diazepin-2(3H)-one →(HNO_3, H_2SO_4) **Nitrazepam**

NITREFAZOLE
Use: alcohol deterrent
Analysis:

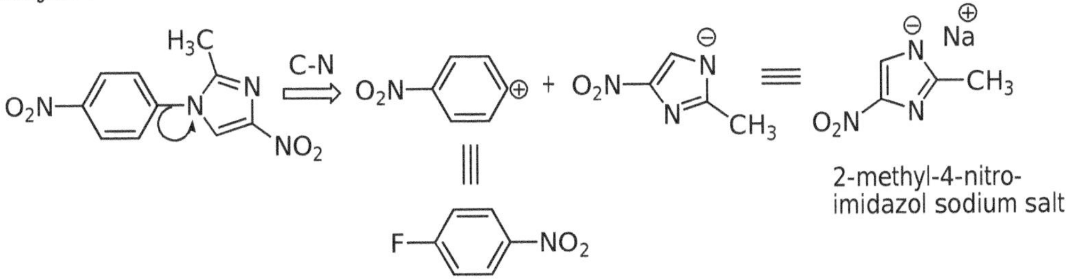

[Retrosynthetic scheme: Nitrefazole ⟹ (C-N disconnection) 4-nitrophenyl cation + 2-methyl-4-nitroimidazole anion ≡ 2-methyl-4-nitro-imidazol sodium salt; the cation equivalent is 1-fluoro-4-nitrobenzene]

Synthesis:

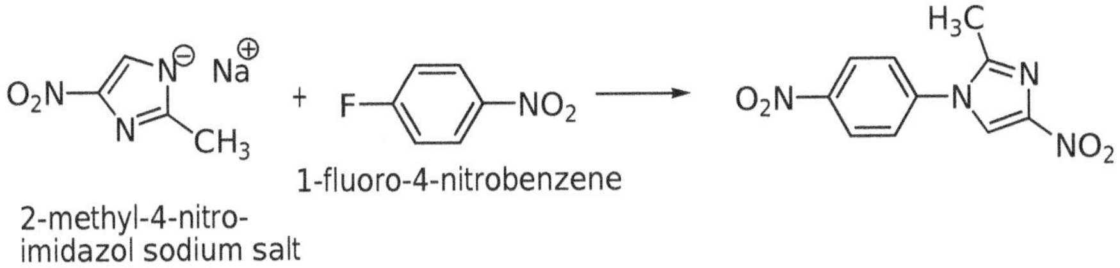

2-methyl-4-nitro-imidazol sodium salt + 1-fluoro-4-nitrobenzene ⟶ Nitrefazole

NITROFURANTOIN
Use: chemotherapeutic for urinary tract infection
Analysis:

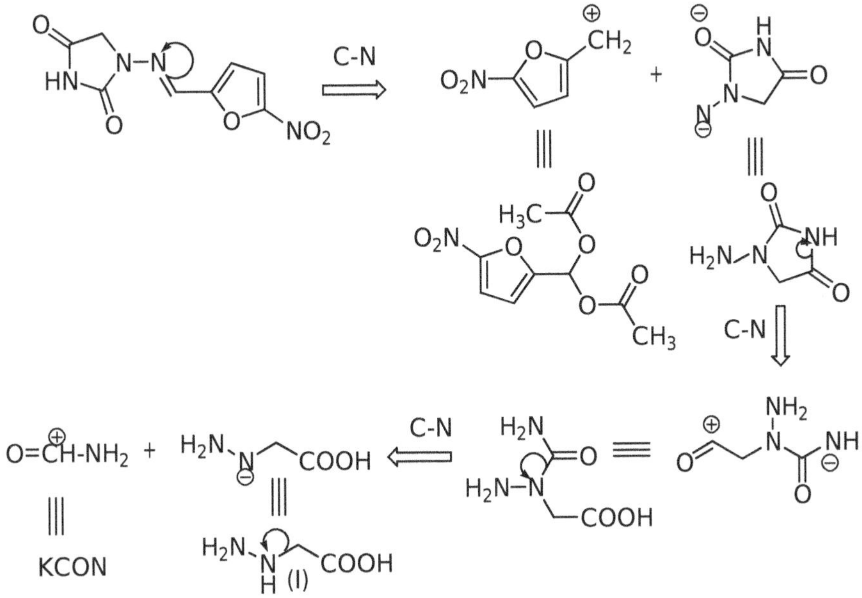

[Retrosynthetic scheme: Nitrofurantoin ⟹ (C-N) 5-nitrofurfuryl cation + 1-aminohydantoin anion; cation equivalent is 5-nitrofurfural diacetate (H_3C-CO-O-CH(furan-NO_2)-O-CO-CH_3); the hydantoin fragment derives via C-N disconnection from semicarbazide + glyoxylic acid type synthon ⟹ H_2N-NH-CO-NH$_2$ + H_2N-N(-COOH)- ⟸ (C-N) O=$\overset{+}{C}$H-NH$_2$ (≡ KCON) + H_2N-NH-CH$_2$-COOH (I)]

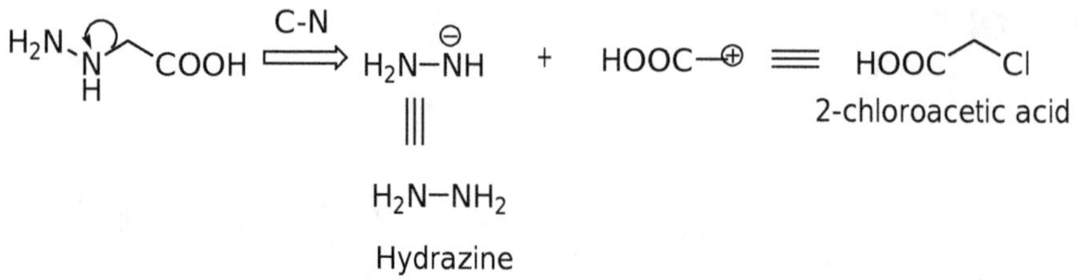

Retrosynthetic Analysis and Synthesis of Drugs

$$H_2N-NH-CH_2-COOH \xrightarrow{C-N} H_2N-NH^{\ominus} + HOOC-CH_2^{\oplus} \equiv HOOC-CH_2-Cl$$

2-chloroacetic acid

H_2N-NH_2
Hydrazine

Synthesis:

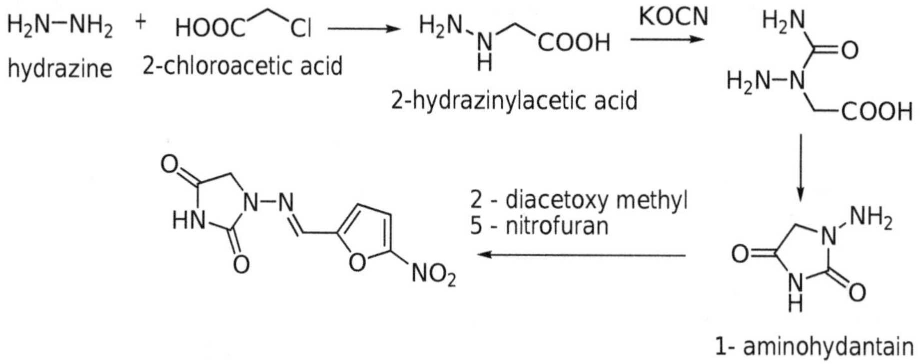

H_2N-NH_2 (hydrazine) + $HOOC-CH_2-Cl$ (2-chloroacetic acid) ⟶ $H_2N-NH-CH_2-COOH$ (2-hydrazinylacetic acid) $\xrightarrow{KOCN}$ $H_2N-CO-NH-NH-CH_2-COOH$ ⟶ 1-aminohydantoin ⟶ (with 2-diacetoxy methyl 5-nitrofuran) **Nitrofurantoin**

NOMIFENSINE

Use: antidepressant

Analysis:

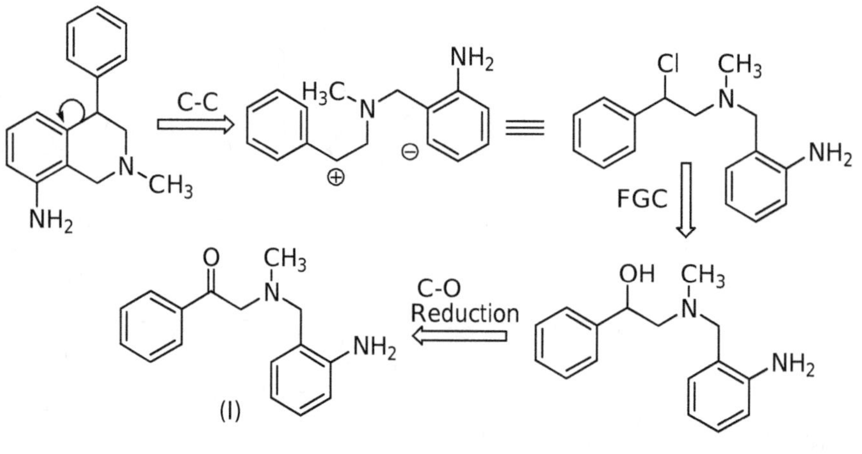

Nomifensine $\xRightarrow{C-C}$ [phenyl cation + aminobenzyl-N-methylamine anion] ≡ [2-chloro-2-phenylethyl-N-methyl-N-(2-aminobenzyl)amine] $\Uparrow$ FGC

(I) phenacyl-N-methyl-N-(2-aminobenzyl)amine $\xLeftarrow{C-O\ Reduction}$ 2-hydroxy-2-phenylethyl-N-methyl-N-(2-aminobenzyl)amine

Retrosynthetic Analysis and Synthesis of Drugs

Synthesis:

Nomifensine

NORFLOXACIN
Use: antibiotic
Analysis:

Synthesis:

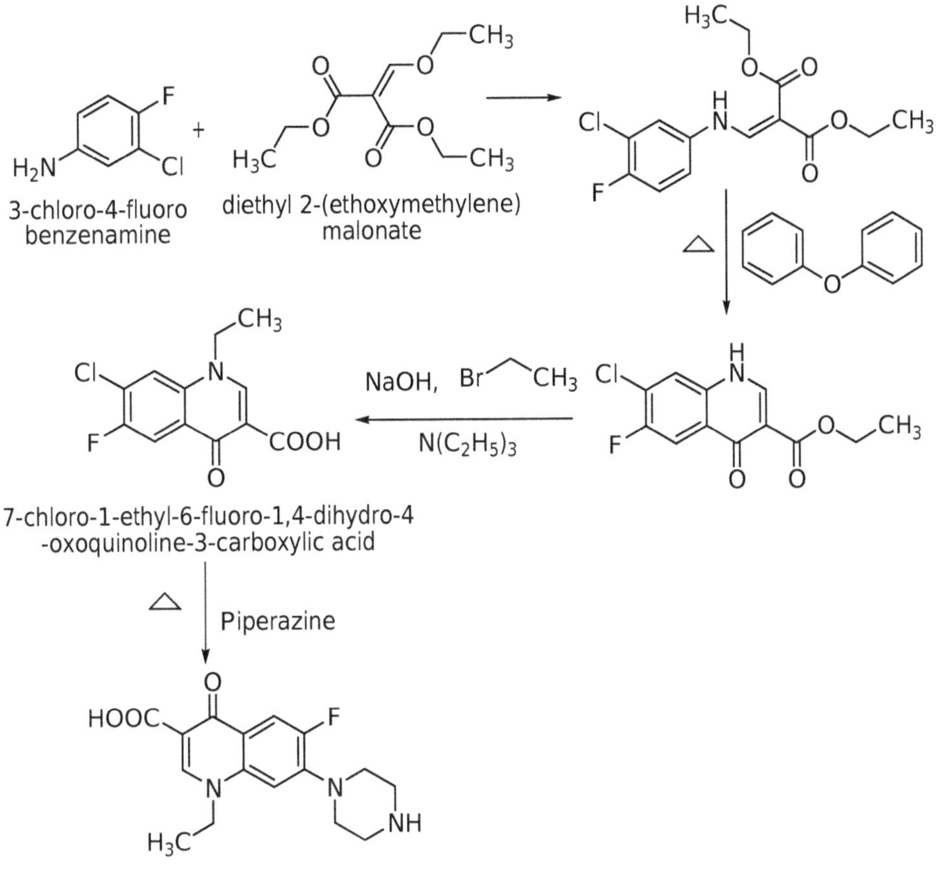
3-chloro-4-fluoro benzenamine
diethyl 2-(ethoxymethylene) malonate
NaOH, Br CH3
N(C2H5)3
7-chloro-1-ethyl-6-fluoro-1,4-dihydro-4 -oxoquinoline-3-carboxylic acid
Piperazine

Norfloxacin

NOTRIPTYLINE

Use: antidepressant

Analysis:

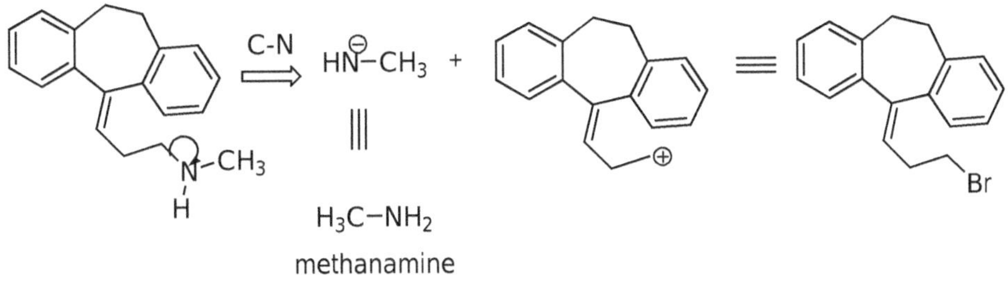
C-N
H3C−NH2
methanamine

Synthesis:

[Structure: dibenzosuberene with 3-bromopropylidene side chain] + H₃C—NH₂ (methanamine) ⟶ **Notriptyline**

OCTOPAMAINE

Use: sympathomimetic

Analysis:

HO–C₆H₄–CH(OH)–CH₂–NH₂ ⇒(C–O Reduction)⇒ HO–C₆H₄–CO–CH₂–NH₂ ⇒(C–C)⇒ HO–C₆H₄⁻ + ⁺CO–CH₂–NH₂

≡ phenol (HO–C₆H₅)

≡ H₂N–CH₂–CO–Cl ⇓ FGC

H₂N–CH₂–COOH ⇐FGC⇐ NC–CH₂–NH₂ (2-aminoacetonitrile)

Synthesis:

phenol (C₆H₅–OH) + NC–CH₂–NH₂ (2-aminoacetonitrile) —HCl, AlCl₃→ HO–C₆H₄–CO–CH₂–NH₂ (2-amino-1-(4-hydroxyphenyl)ethanone) —H₂ Raney-Ni→ HO–C₆H₄–CH(OH)–CH₂–NH₂

Octopamaine

OMOCONAZOLE
Use: antimycotic
Analysis:

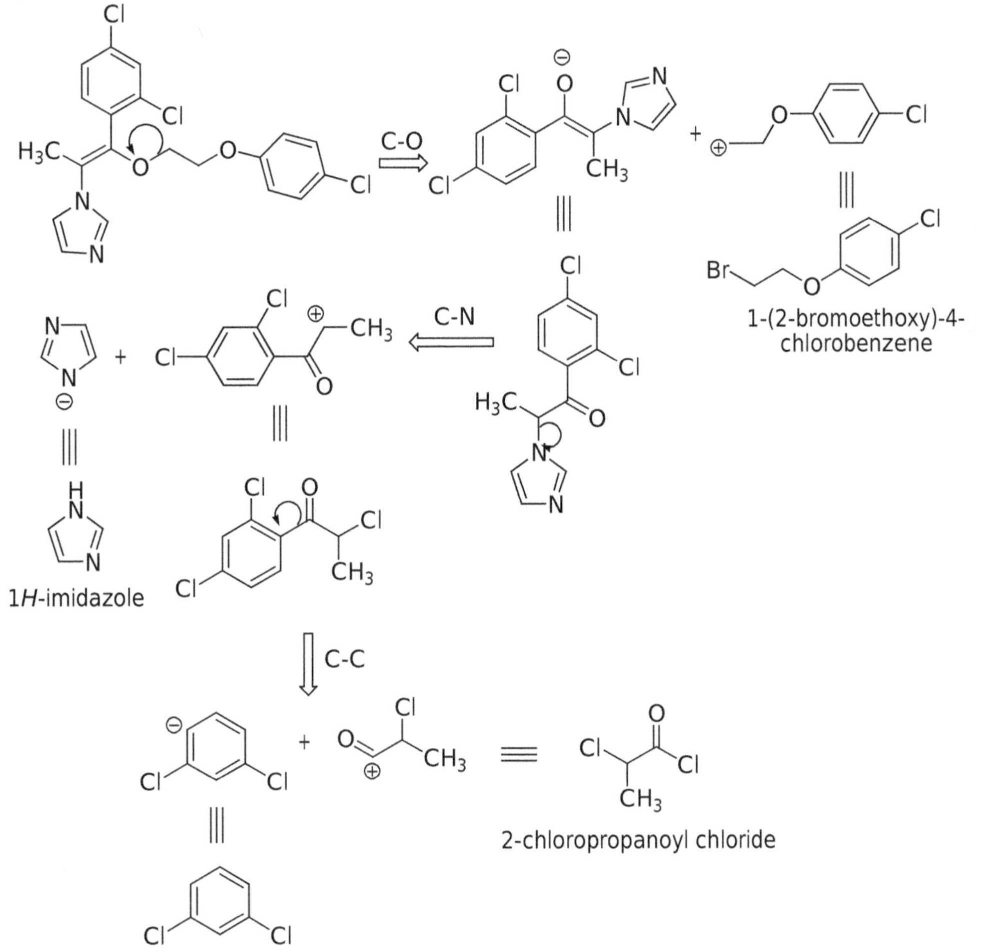

[Retrosynthetic analysis scheme showing disconnection of omoconazole: C-O disconnection gives an enolate intermediate plus 1-(2-bromoethoxy)-4-chlorobenzene; C-N disconnection gives 1H-imidazole plus 2-chloro-1-(2,4-dichlorophenyl)propan-1-one cation; C-C disconnection gives 1,3-dichlorobenzene plus 2-chloropropanoyl chloride.]

Synthesis:

1,3-dichlorobenzene + 2-chloropropanoyl chloride → 2-chloro-1-(2,4-dichlorophenyl)propan-1-one → (with 1H-imidazole) → (I)

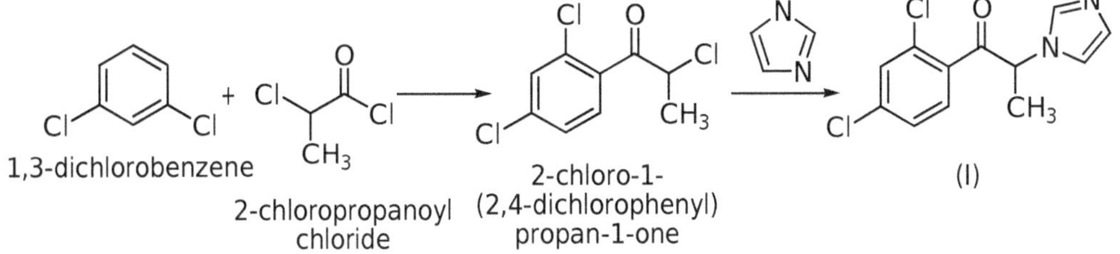

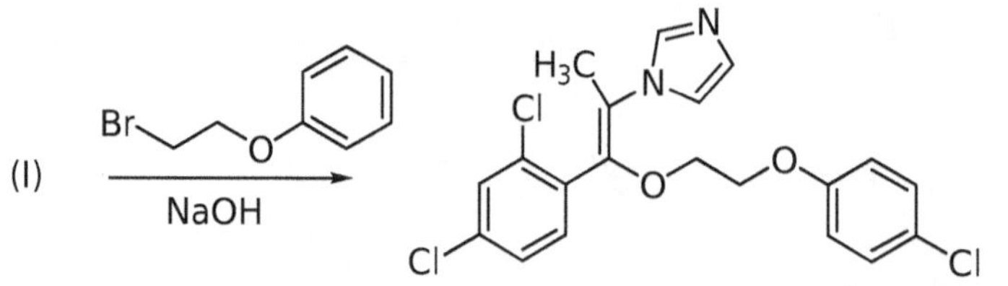

(I) + Br-CH₂CH₂-O-C₆H₅ —NaOH→ **Omoconazole**

OPIPRAMOL
Use: antidepressant
Analysis:

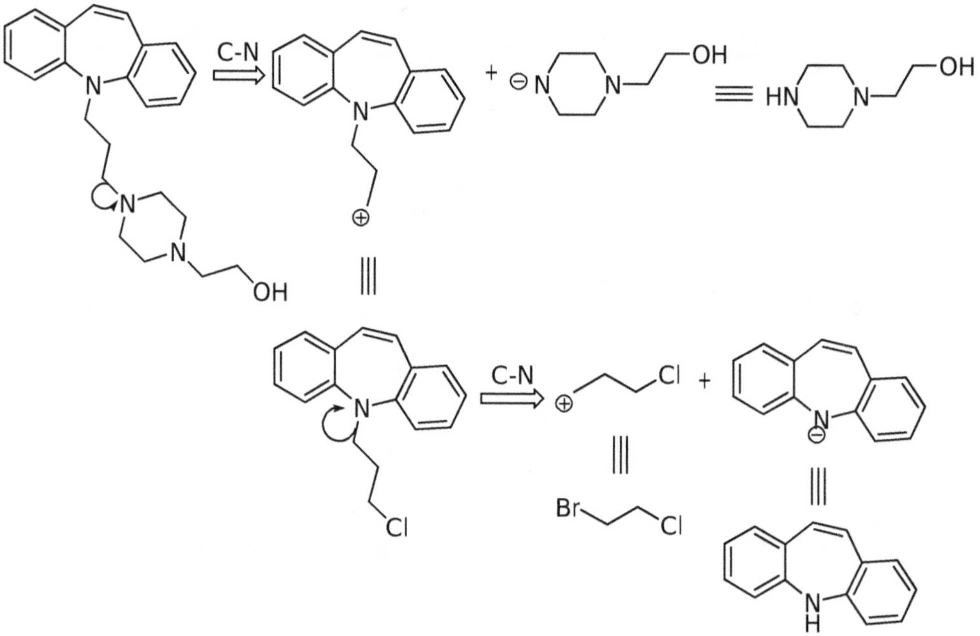

[Retrosynthetic analysis showing disconnection of opipramol into iminodibenzyl-propyl cation and 1-(2-hydroxyethyl)piperazine anion, equivalent to HN-piperazine-CH₂CH₂OH; further disconnection of the iminodibenzyl-propyl chloride into iminodibenzyl anion and 2-chloroethyl cation (equivalent to Br-CH₂CH₂-Cl and iminodibenzyl NH).]

Synthesis:

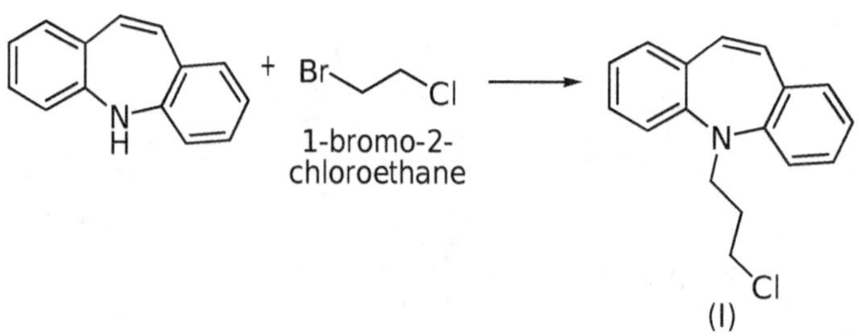

Iminodibenzyl (NH) + Br-CH₂CH₂-Cl (1-bromo-2-chloroethane) ⟶ N-(2-chloroethyl)iminodibenzyl (I)

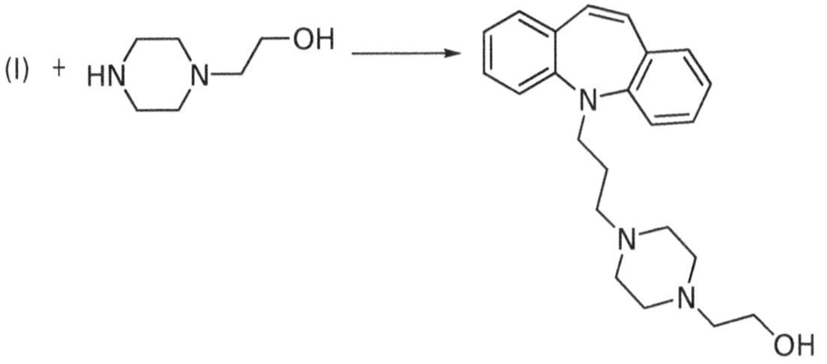

(I) + HN‹piperazine›N-CH₂CH₂-OH ⟶ **Opipramol**

ORPHENADRINE
Use: antiparkinsonian, muscle relaxant
Analysis:

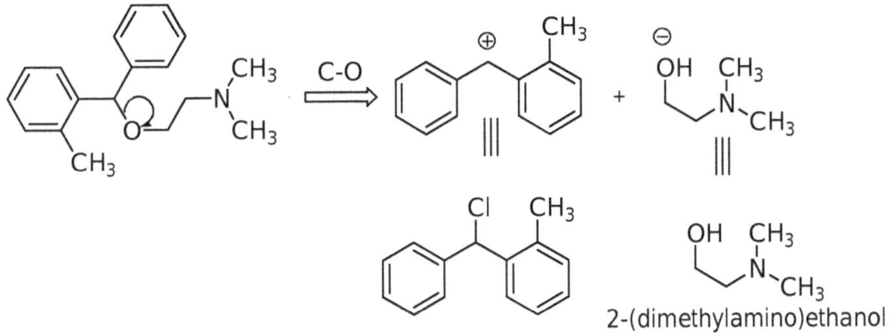

[Retrosynthetic disconnection at C–O bond yielding a benzhydryl cation (from 2-methylbenzhydryl chloride) and 2-(dimethylamino)ethanol as the alkoxide]

2-(dimethylamino)ethanol

Synthesis:

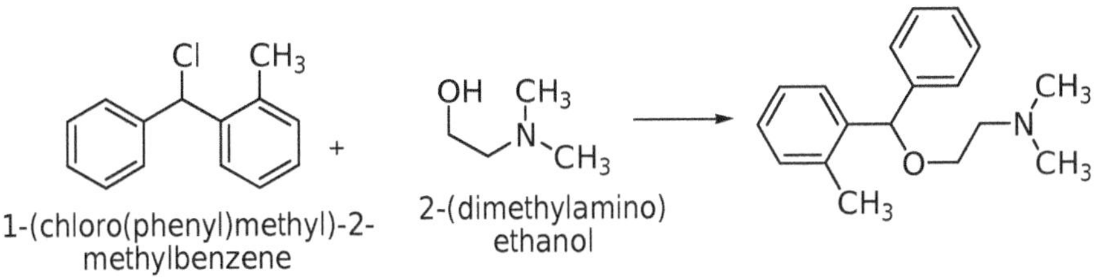

1-(chloro(phenyl)methyl)-2-methylbenzene + 2-(dimethylamino)ethanol ⟶ **Orphenadrine**

OXACEPROL
Use: antirheumatic
Analysis:

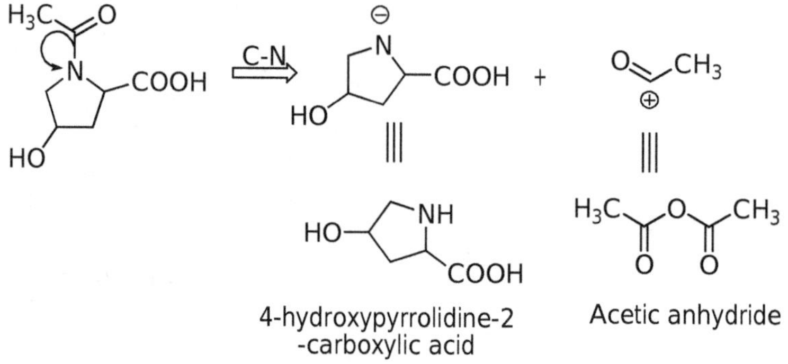

[Retrosynthetic scheme: N-acetyl-4-hydroxypyrrolidine-2-carboxylic acid (Oxaceprol) ⇒ (C-N disconnection) acetyl cation + pyrrolidine nitrogen anion ≡ 4-hydroxypyrrolidine-2-carboxylic acid + Acetic anhydride]

Synthesis:

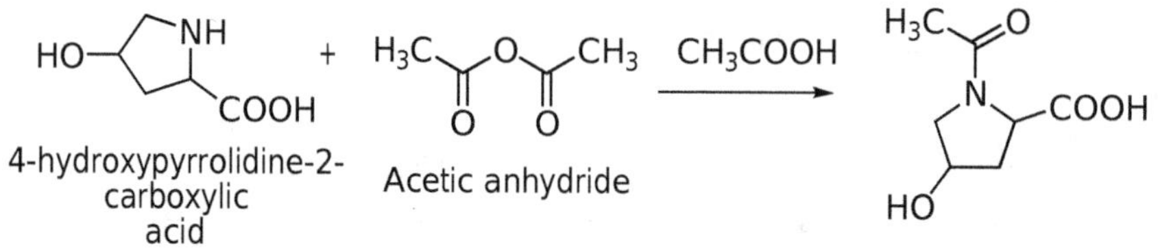

4-hydroxypyrrolidine-2-carboxylic acid + Acetic anhydride $\xrightarrow{CH_3COOH}$ **Oxaceprol**

OXATOMIDE
Use: antiallergic
Analysis:

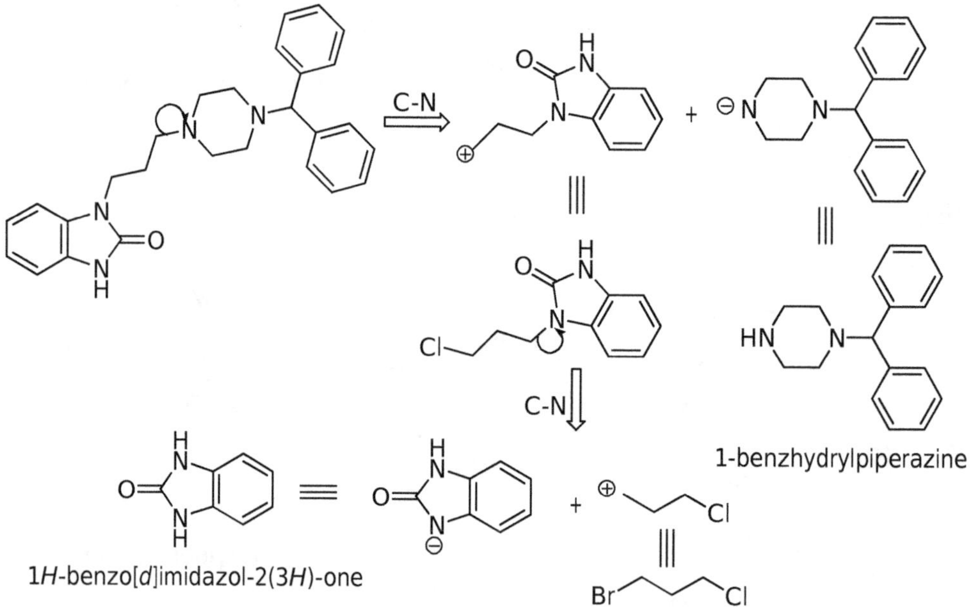

[Retrosynthetic scheme: Oxatomide ⇒ (C-N) 1-(3-chloropropyl)-benzimidazol-2(3H)-one cation equivalent + 1-benzhydrylpiperazine anion; further C-N disconnection to 1H-benzo[d]imidazol-2(3H)-one + 1-bromo-3-chloropropane]

1-benzhydrylpiperazine

1H-benzo[d]imidazol-2(3H)-one

Retrosynthetic Analysis and Synthesis of Drugs

Synthesis:

1H-benzo[d]imidazol-2(3H)-one + 1-bromo-3-chloropropane ⟶ [N-(3-chloropropyl)benzimidazolone]

↓ 1-benzhydrylpiperazine

Oxatomide

OXELADIN

Use: antitussive

Analysis:

[Retrosynthetic scheme: Oxeladin ⇒ (C-N disconnection) oxocarbenium intermediate + diethylamine; ⇒ (C-O disconnection) 2-ethyl-2-phenylbutanoic acid (I) + bis(2-chloroethyl) ether]

- 2-ethyl-2-phenylbutanoic acid (I)
- diethylamine
- Cl-CH₂CH₂-O-CH₂CH₂-Cl

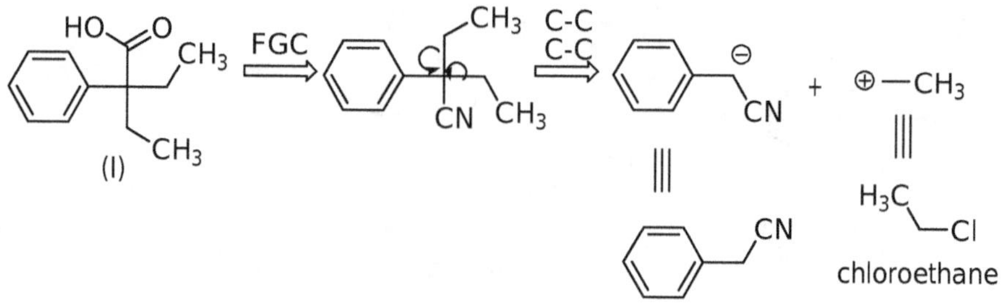
HO
O
CH3
(I)
CH3
FGC
CH3
CN
CH3
C-C
C-C
CN
+
⊕—CH3
CN
H3C
Cl
chloroethane

Synthesis:

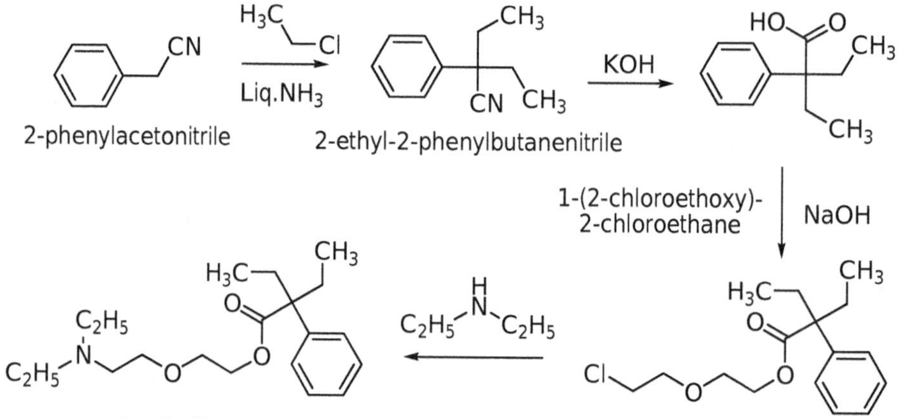
CN
2-phenylacetonitrile
H3C
Cl
Liq.NH3
CH3
CN
CH3
2-ethyl-2-phenylbutanenitrile
KOH
HO
O
CH3
CH3
1-(2-chloroethoxy)-
2-chloroethane
NaOH
H3C
CH3
O
Cl
O
O
H
N
C2H5
C2H5
C2H5
N
C2H5
O
O
H3C
CH3
O

Oxeladin

OXOMEMAZINE

Use: antiallergic

Analysis:

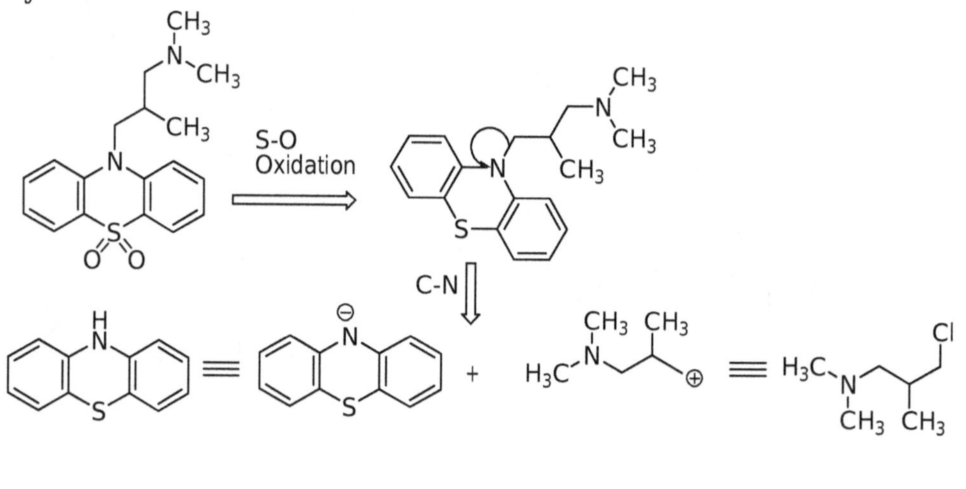
CH3
N
CH3
CH3
N
S
O
O
S-O
Oxidation
CH3
N
CH3
N
CH3
S
C-N
H
N
S
N
S
+
CH3
CH3
H3C
N
Cl
H3C
N
CH3
CH3

Synthesis:

[Scheme: 10H-phenothiazine + 3-chloro-N,N,2-trimethylpropan-1-amine → (NaNH₂) → N,N,2-trimethyl-3-(10H-phenothiazin-10-yl)propan-1-amine → (H₂O₂, CH₃COOH) → **Oxomemazine**]

OXYBUPROCAINE

Use: local anaesthetic

Analysis:

[Retrosynthetic scheme showing oxybuprocaine → FGC → nitro ester intermediate → C-O disconnection → acid chloride (I) + 2-(diethylamino)ethanol]

Retrosynthetic Analysis and Synthesis of Drugs

Synthesis:

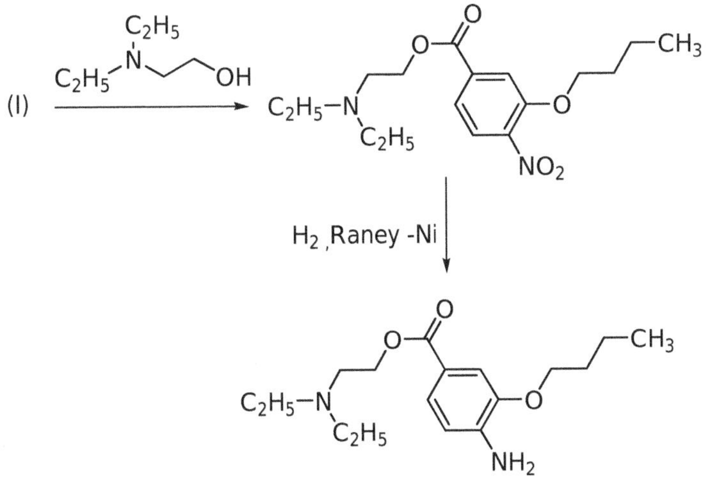

Retrosynthetic Analysis and Synthesis of Drugs

Oxybuprocaine

OXYPENDYL

Use: antiemetic

Analysis:

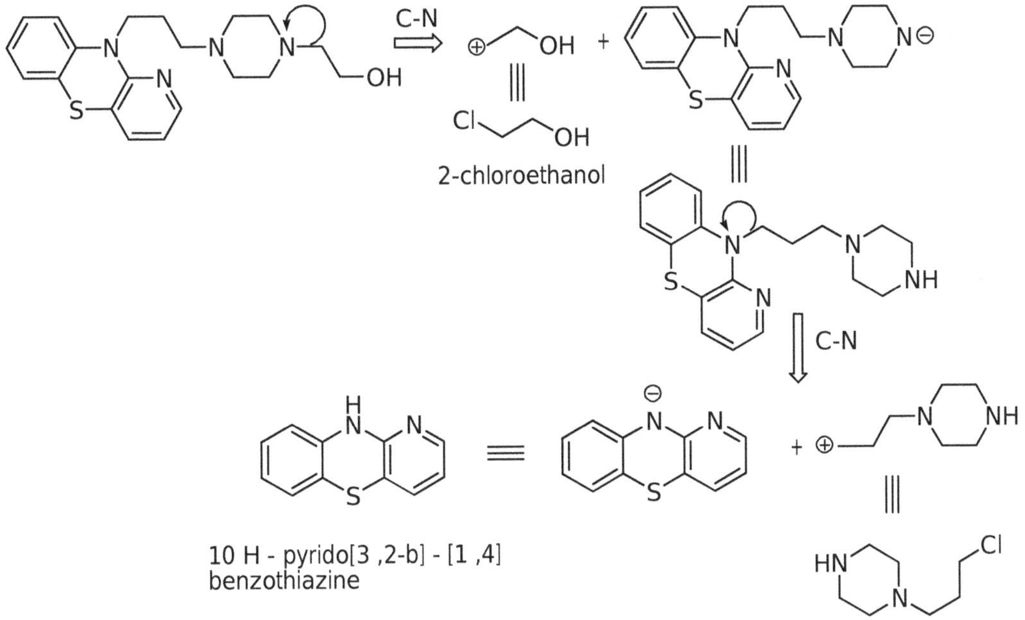

10 H - pyrido[3,2-b] - [1,4] benzothiazine

2-chloroethanol

Synthesis:

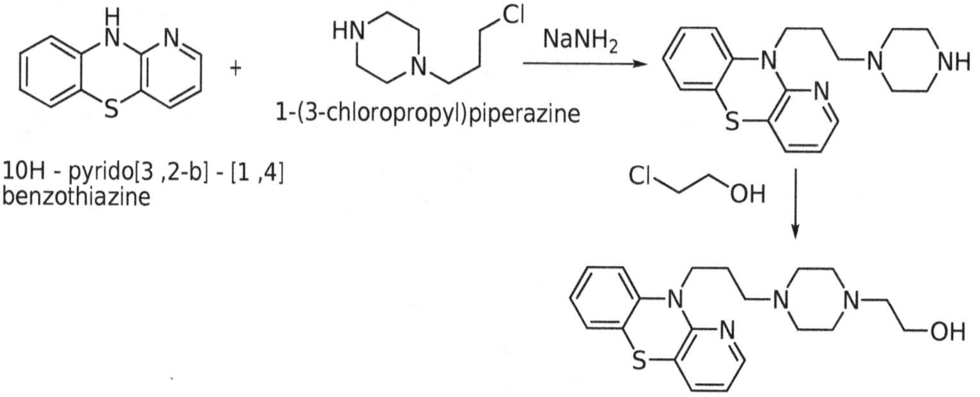

[10H-pyrido[3,2-b]-[1,4]benzothiazine] + [1-(3-chloropropyl)piperazine] → (NaNH₂) → intermediate → (with 2-chloroethanol) → **Oxypendyl**

PARACETAMOL

Use: analgesic, antipyretic

Analysis:

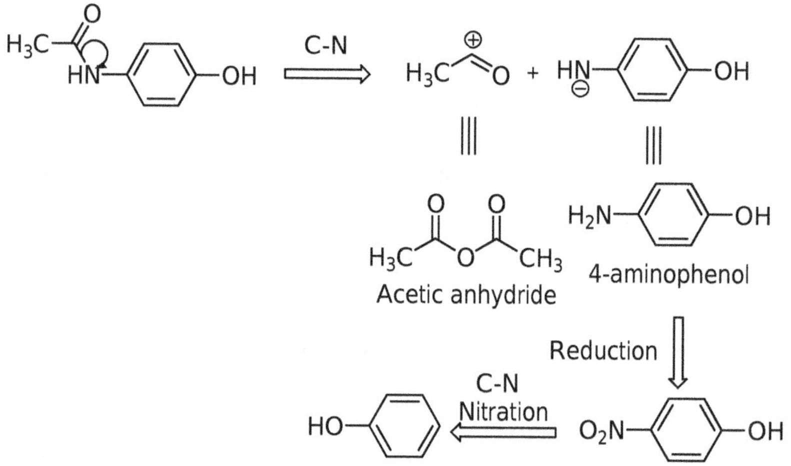

Paracetamol ⇒ (C-N) acetyl cation + 4-aminophenol anion
≡ Acetic anhydride + 4-aminophenol
⇓ Reduction
4-nitrophenol ⇐ (C-N Nitration) phenol

Synthesis:

phenol → (HNO₃) → 4-nitrophenol → (H₂, Raney-Ni) → 4-aminophenol (I)

(I) → (Acetic anhydride) → **Paracetamol**

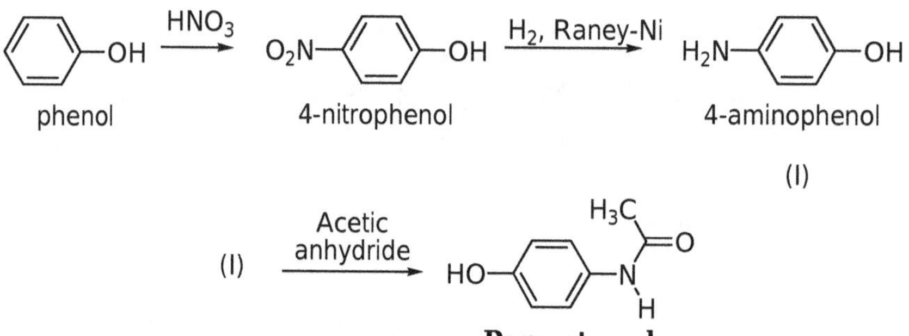

PARETHOXYCAINE

Use: local anaesthetic

Analysis:

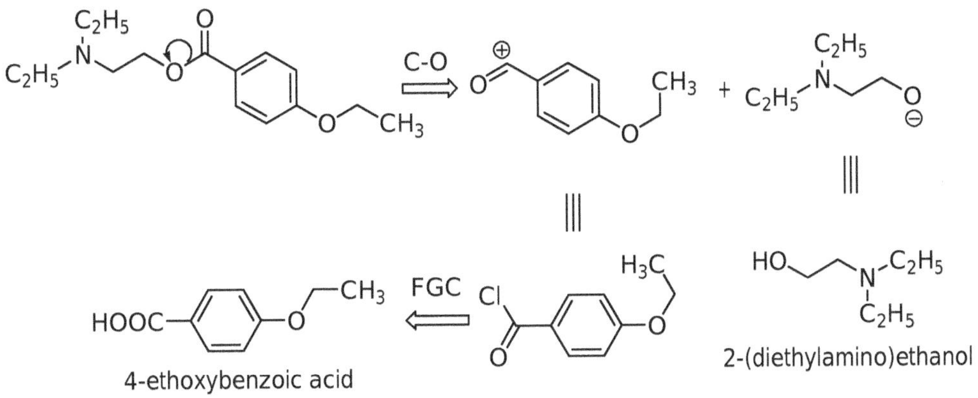

[Retrosynthetic analysis showing parethoxycaine disconnecting at the C-O bond of the ester to give an acylium cation of 4-ethoxybenzoyl and 2-(diethylamino)ethoxide, which correspond to 4-ethoxybenzoyl chloride (via FGC from 4-ethoxybenzoic acid) and 2-(diethylamino)ethanol.]

4-ethoxybenzoic acid

2-(diethylamino)ethanol

Synthesis:

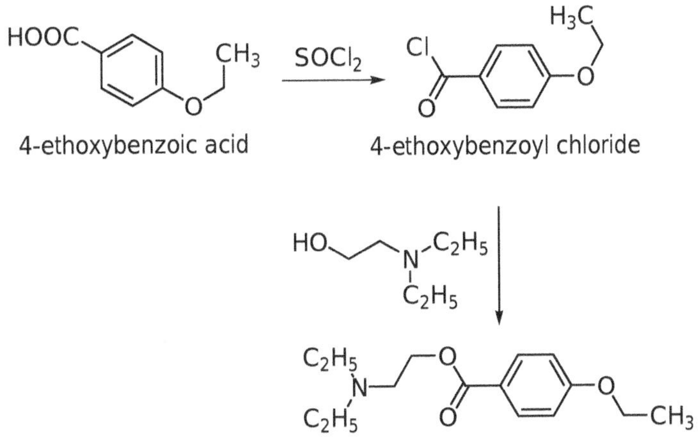

4-ethoxybenzoic acid $\xrightarrow{SOCl_2}$ 4-ethoxybenzoyl chloride

$\xrightarrow{HOCH_2CH_2N(C_2H_5)_2}$

Parethoxycaine

PARGYLINE
Use: antihypertensive, MAO inhibitor
Analysis:

[Retrosynthetic analysis: Pargyline (N-benzyl-N-methyl-propargylamine) ⇒ C–N disconnection gives propargyl cation (≡ 3-bromoprop-1-yne, HC≡C–CH$_2$Br) + N-methylbenzylamine anion (≡ N-methyl(phenyl)methanamine, PhCH$_2$–NH–CH$_3$).]

Synthesis:

N-methyl(phenyl)methanamine + 3-bromoprop-1-yne (Br–CH$_2$–C≡CH) $\xrightarrow{Na_2CO_3}$ **Pargyline**

PARSALMIDE
Use: anti-inflammatory
Analysis:

[Retrosynthesis of parsalmide: 5-amino-2-(prop-2-ynyloxy)-N-butylbenzamide ⇒ FGC ⇒ 5-acetamido-2-(prop-2-ynyloxy)-N-butylbenzamide ⇒ C–O disconnection gives propargyl cation (≡ HC≡C–CH$_2$Br, 3-bromoprop-1-yne) + phenoxide (≡ 5-acetamido-2-hydroxy-N-butylbenzamide (I)).]

Retrosynthetic Analysis and Synthesis of Drugs

(I)

5-acetamido-2-acetoxybenzoic acid

Synthesis:

5-acetamido-2-acetoxy benzoic acid $\xrightarrow{SOCl_2}$ 2-(chlorocarbonyl)-4-acetamido phenyl acetate

$\xrightarrow{\text{butan-1-amine} \mid NaOH}$ 5-acetamido-N-butyl-2-hydroxybenzamide

$\xrightarrow[H_2O]{\text{3-bromoprop-1-yne} \; H_2SO_4}$ **Parsalmide**

PENBUTOLOL

Use: β-blocker

Analysis:

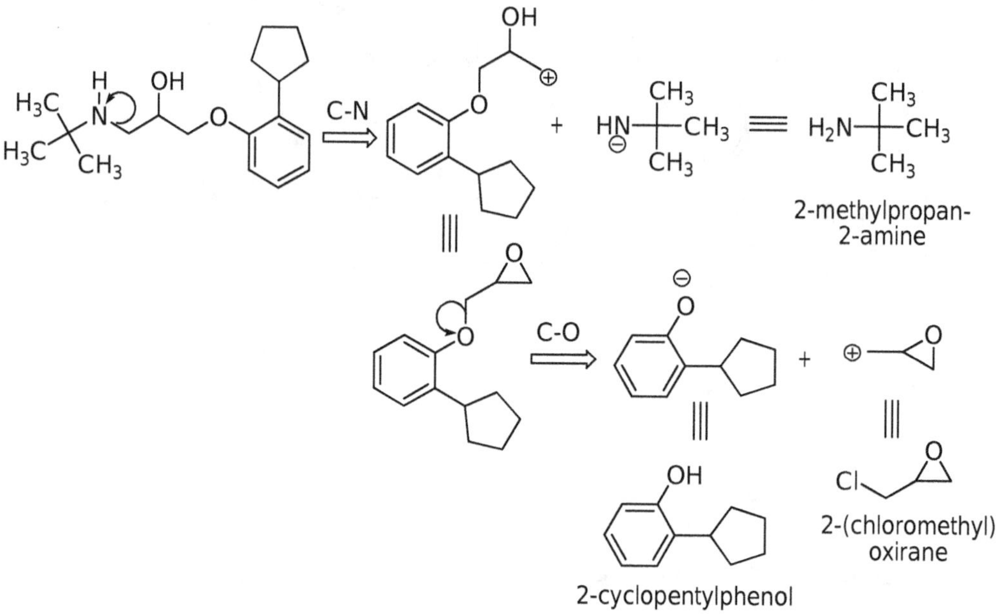

Synthesis:

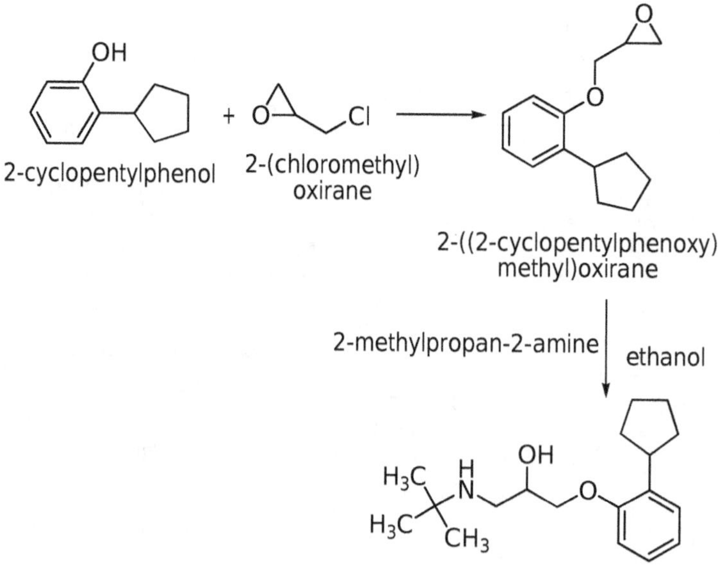

2-cyclopentylphenol + 2-(chloromethyl)oxirane → 2-((2-cyclopentylphenoxy)methyl)oxirane

2-methylpropan-2-amine / ethanol ↓

Penbutolol

PENTAPIPERIDE
Use: antispasmodic
Analysis:

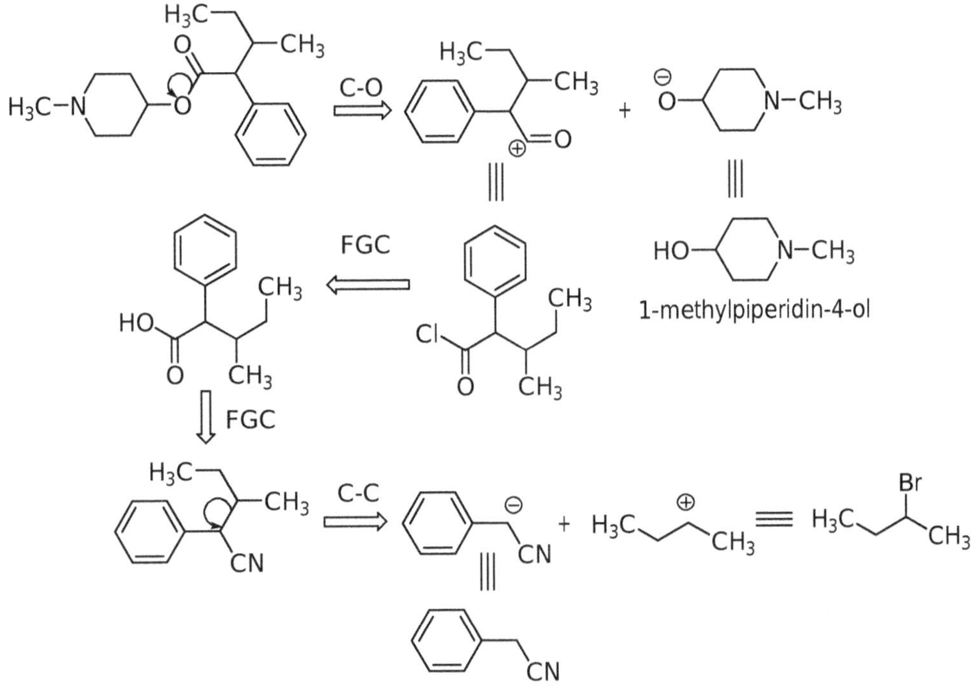

[Retrosynthetic scheme: Pentapiperide ⇒ (C-O disconnection) acylium cation + 1-methylpiperidin-4-ol; FGC to acid chloride; FGC to 2-phenyl-3-methylpentanoic acid; further FGC to 3-methyl-2-phenylpentanenitrile; C-C disconnection to phenylacetonitrile anion + sec-butyl cation (2-bromobutane)]

Synthesis:

2-phenylacetonitrile —(2-bromobutane, NaNH$_2$)→ 3-methyl-2-phenylpentanenitrile —(NaOH)→ 2-phenyl-3-methylpentanoic acid —(SOCl$_2$)→ acid chloride —(1-methylpiperidin-4-ol, pyridine)→ **Pentapiperide**

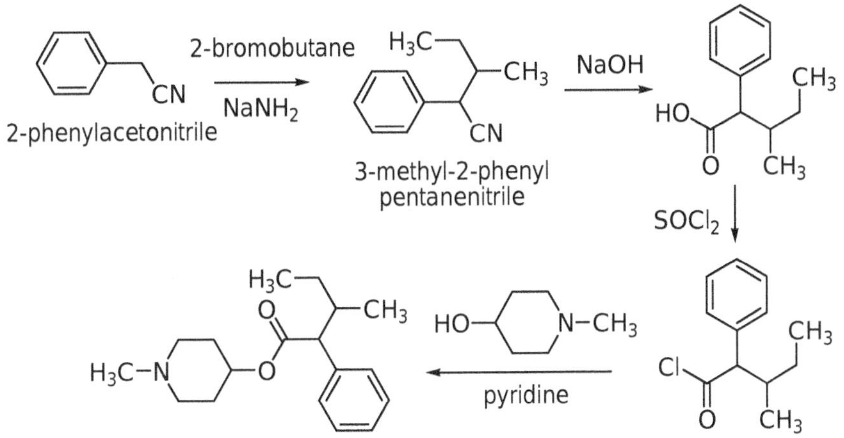

PENTIFYLLINE

Use: vasodilator

Analysis:

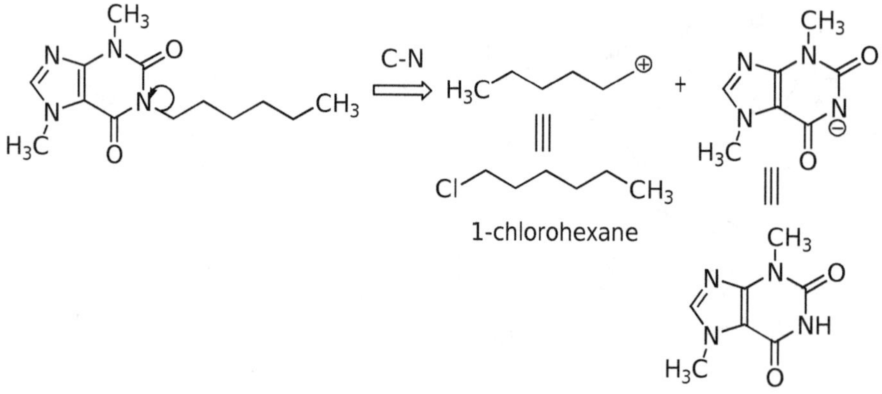
C-N
1-chlorohexane

Synthesis:

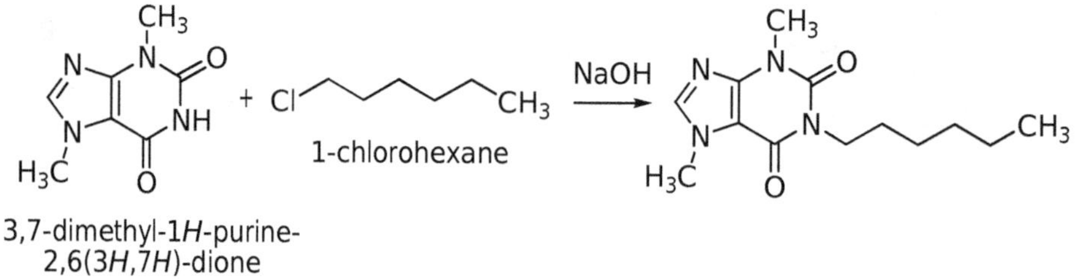
NaOH
1-chlorohexane
3,7-dimethyl-1*H*-purine-2,6(3*H*,7*H*)-dione

Pentifylline

PENTOXYVERINE

Use: antitussive

Analysis:

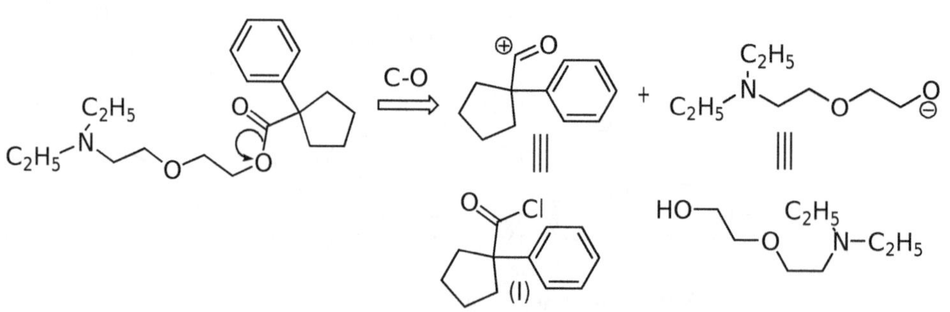
C-O
(I)

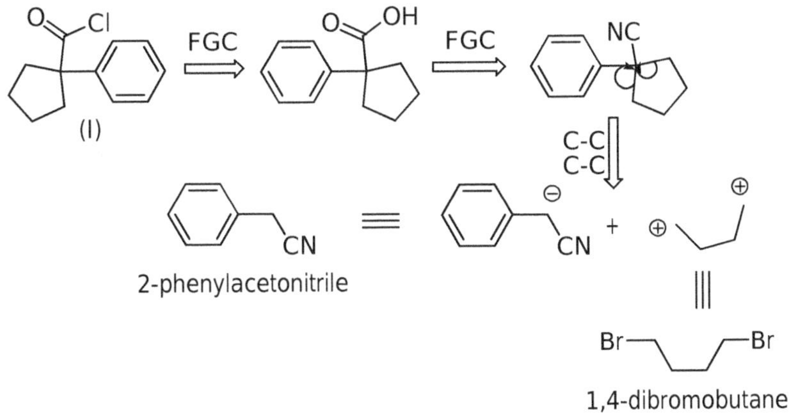

Retrosynthetic Analysis and Synthesis of Drugs

Synthesis:

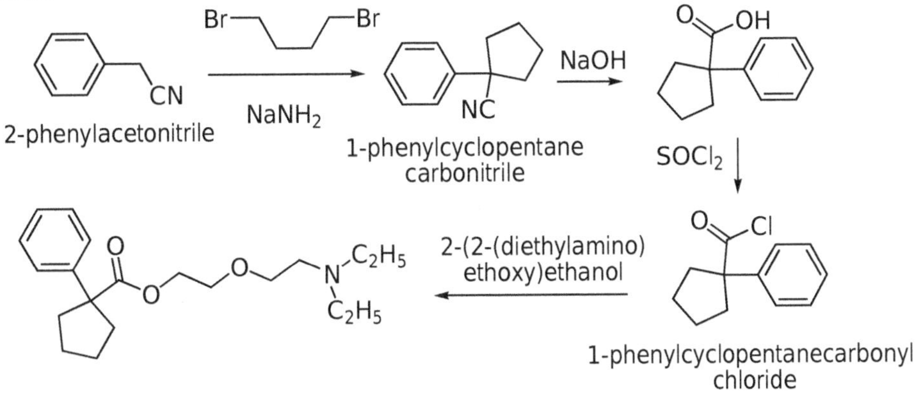

Pentoxyverine

PERAZINE
Use: psychosedative

Analysis:

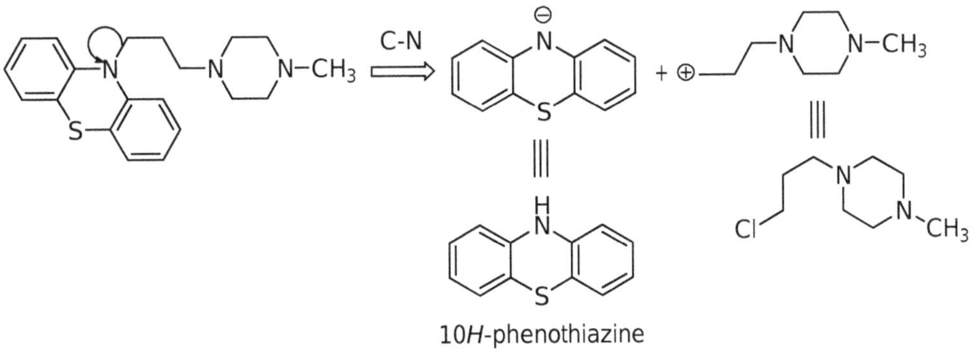

Synthesis:

10H-phenothiazine + 1-(3-chloropropyl)-4-methylpiperazine →(NaNH₂) **Perazine**

PERLAPINE
Use: hypnotic
Analysis:

Synthesis:

[Scheme: 2-benzylbenzenamine + COCl₂ (Phosgene), toluene → benzyl formanilide intermediate; AlCl₃, 1,2-dichlorobenzene → dibenzazepinone; (CH₃)₂N-C₆H₅, POCl₃ → chloro-dibenzazepine; H₃C-N-piperazine-NH → **Perlapine**]

PERPHENAZINE

Use: antiemetic, neuroleptic

Analysis:

[Retrosynthetic analysis: Perphenazine ⇒ (via C-N disconnection) piperazinylethanol anion + chloro-phenothiazine N-alkylated cation; equivalent to 2-(piperazin-1-yl)ethanol + 2-chloro-10H-phenothiazine with 1-bromo-3-chloropropane; further C-N disconnection to 2-chloro-10H-phenothiazine anion + chloropropyl cation]

2-(piperazin-1-yl)ethanol

2-chloro-10H-phenothiazine

Synthesis:

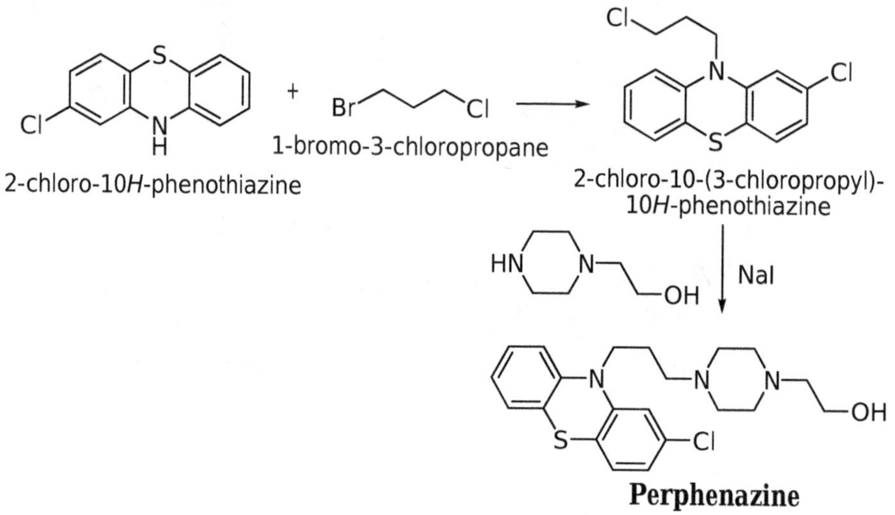

2-chloro-10H-phenothiazine + 1-bromo-3-chloropropane → 2-chloro-10-(3-chloropropyl)-10H-phenothiazine

↓ NaI, HN-piperazine-CH₂CH₂OH

Perphenazine

PETHIDINE

Use: analgesic, antispasmodic

Analysis:

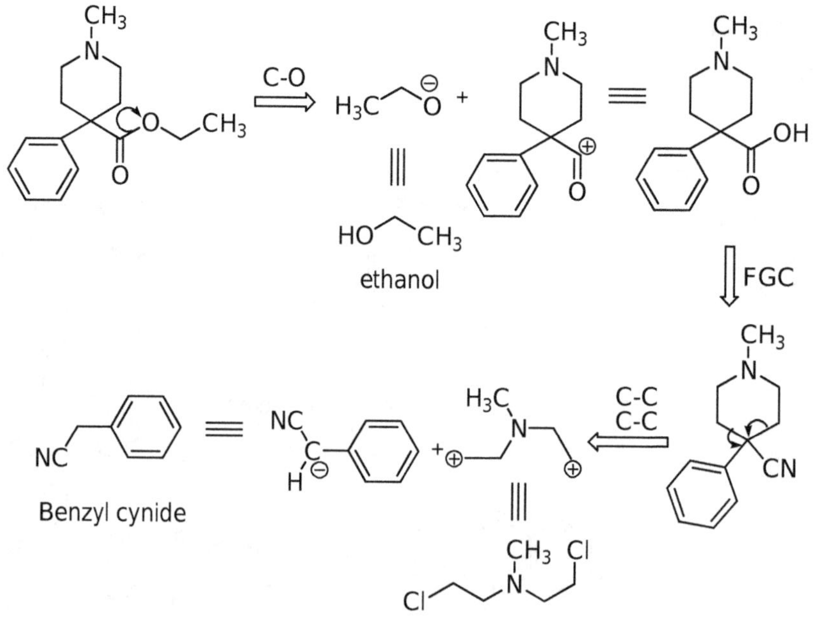

[Retrosynthetic scheme: pethidine ethyl ester ⇒ (C-O) ethoxide + acylium cation ≡ carboxylic acid; ethanol shown; FGC to nitrile intermediate; C-C, C-C disconnection to benzyl cyanide + bis(2-chloroethyl)methylamine]

Benzyl cynide

PHENACETIN

Use: analgesic, antipyretic

Analysis:

[Retrosynthetic scheme: Phenacetin → acetyl cation + p-phenetidine (or acetic anhydride); p-phenetidine ← reduction of 1-ethoxy-4-nitrobenzene ← 4-nitrophenoxide + ethyl cation (from chloroethane); 4-nitrophenol ≡ 4-nitrophenoxide]

Synthesis:

4-nitrophenol + chloroethane $\xrightarrow{NaOH}$ 1-ethoxy-4-nitrobenzene

$\xrightarrow{H_2/Pd-C \text{ or Raney-Ni}}$ 4-ethoxyaniline $\xrightarrow{\text{Acetic anhydride}}$ Phenacetin

PHENBUTRAZATE

Use: central stimulant

Analysis:

(I)

Synthesis:

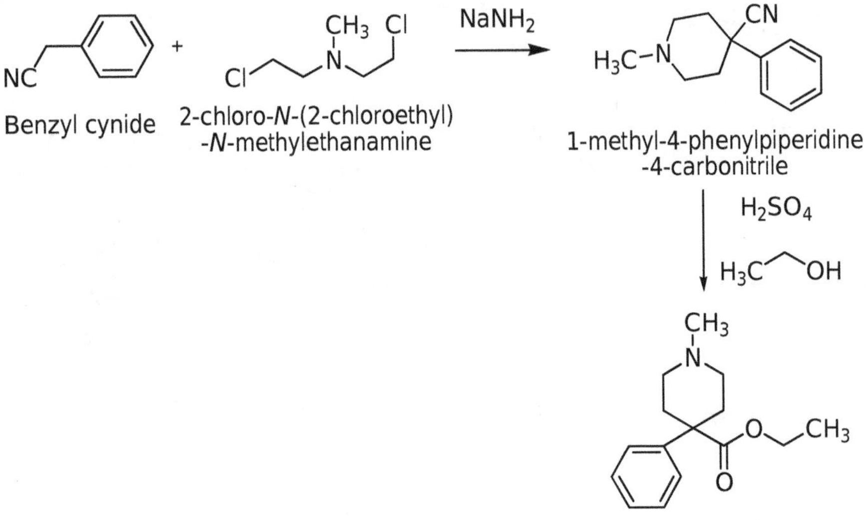

Benzyl cynide + 2-chloro-*N*-(2-chloroethyl)-*N*-methylethanamine →(NaNH₂) 1-methyl-4-phenylpiperidine-4-carbonitrile

→ (H₂SO₄, H₃C-CH₂-OH) **Pethidine**

PHENACEMIDE

Use: antiepileptic

Analysis:

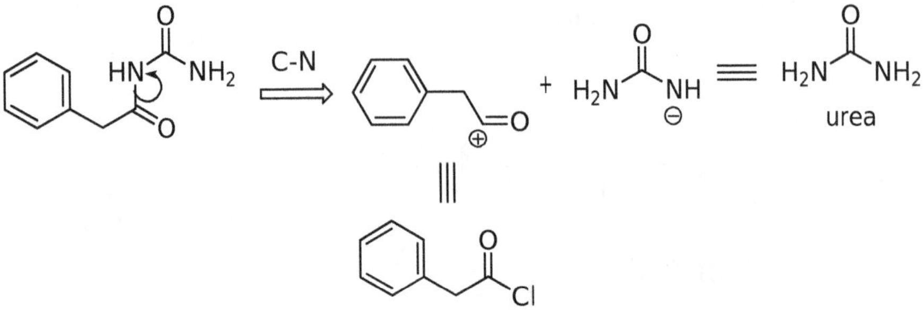

Phenacemide ⇒(C-N) 2-phenylacetyl cation + urea anion ≡ urea

≡ 2-phenylacetyl chloride

Synthesis:

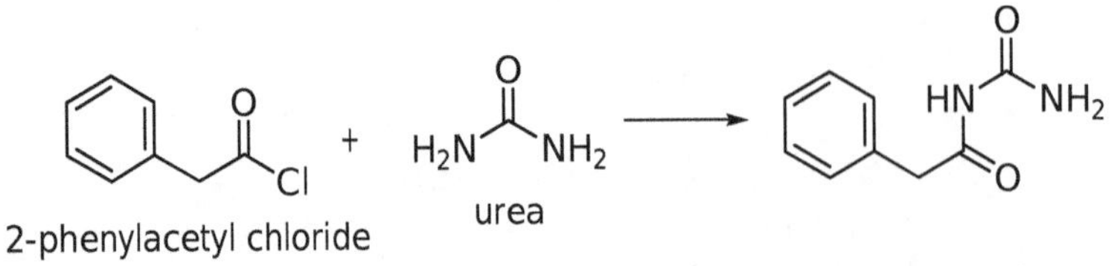

2-phenylacetyl chloride + urea → **Phenacemide**

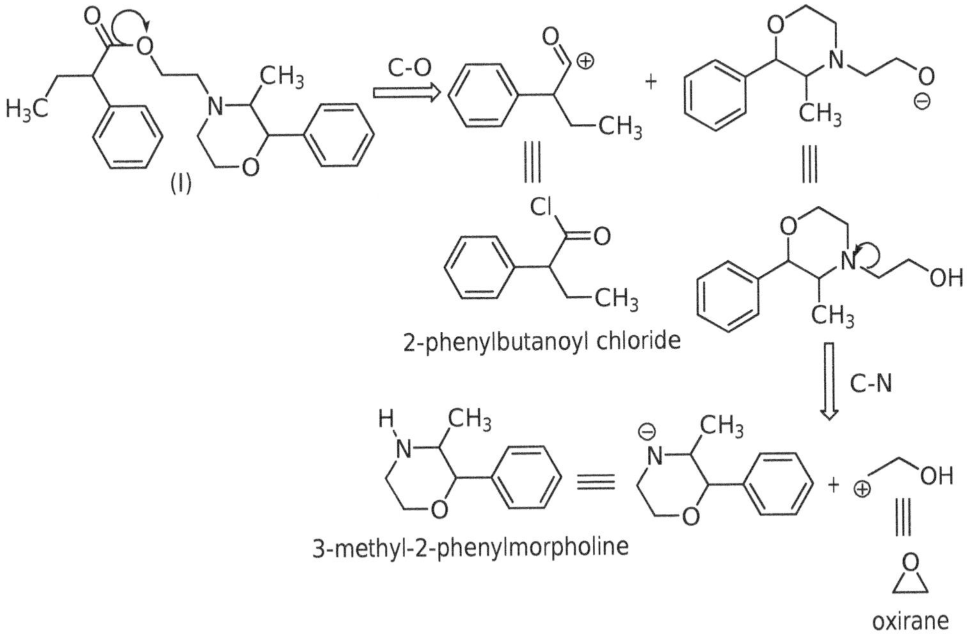

Synthesis:

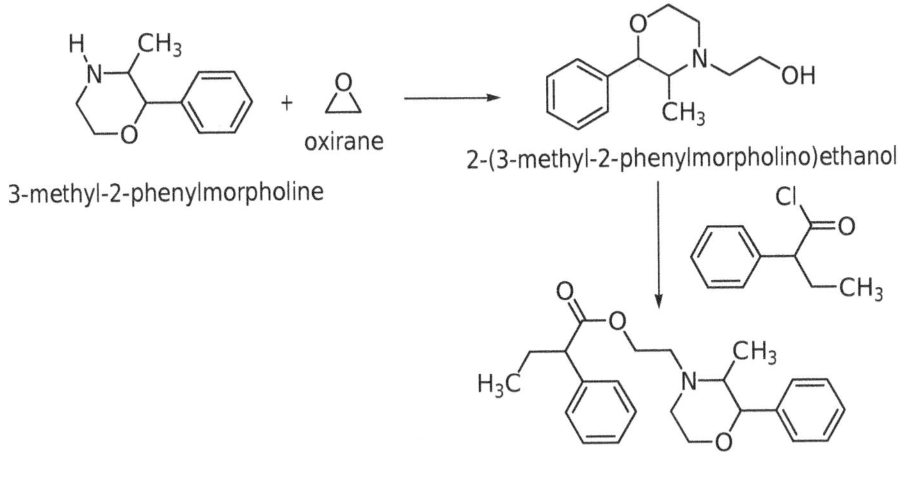

Phenbutrazate

PHENCARBAMIDE
Use: antispasmodic
Analysis:

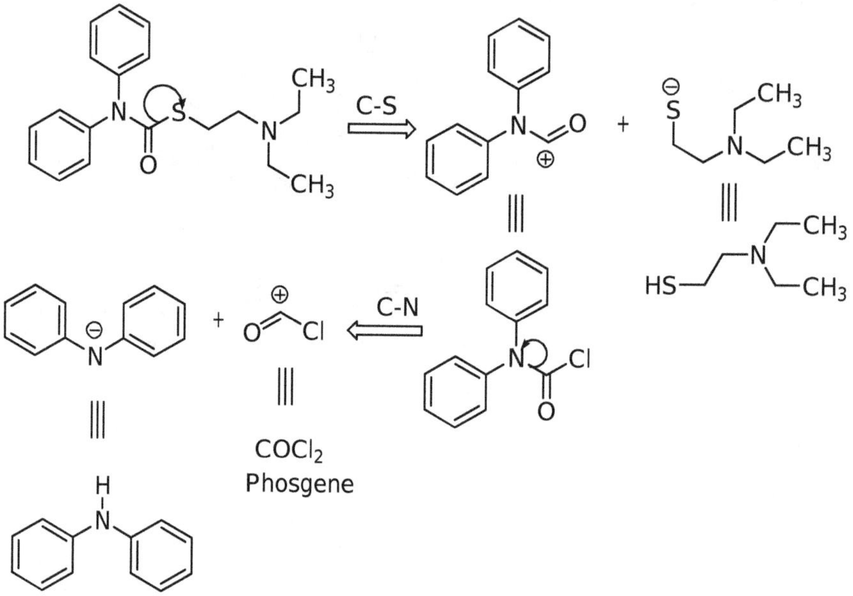

Synthesis:

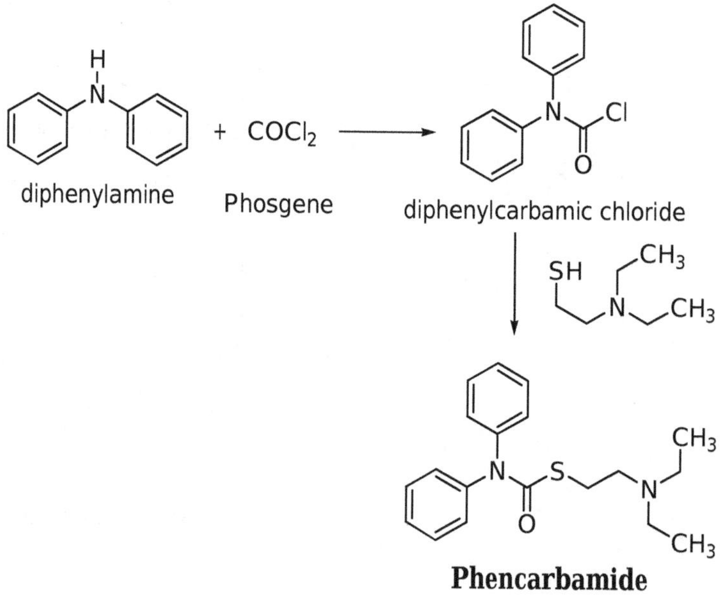

diphenylamine + COCl₂ (Phosgene) → diphenylcarbamic chloride

diphenylcarbamic chloride + HS-CH₂CH₂-N(CH₂CH₃)₂ → **Phencarbamide**

PHENELZINE
Use: MAO inhibitor, antidepressant
Analysis:

PhCH$_2$CH$_2$-NH-NH$_2$ $\xrightarrow{C-N}$ H$_2$N-NH$^\ominus$ + PhCH$_2^\oplus$ ≡ PhCH$_2$CH$_2$-Br

H$_2$N-NH$_2$ (hydrazine)

1-(2-bromoethyl)benzene

Synthesis:

PhCH$_2$CH$_2$-Br + H$_2$N-NH$_2$ → PhCH$_2$CH$_2$-NH-NH$_2$

1-(2-bromoethyl)benzene, hydrazine → **Phenelzine**

PHENETHICILLIN
Use: antibiotic
Analysis:

Phenethicillin structure $\xrightarrow{C-N}$ PhO-CH(CH$_3$)-C(=O)$^\oplus$ + 6-aminopenicillanic acid anion

≡ PhO-CH(CH$_3$)-C(=O)Cl + 6-aminopenicillanic acid (H$_2$N-)

$\Updownarrow$ FGC

PhO-CH(CH$_3$)-COOH

Synthesis:

2-phenoxypropanoic acid + 6-aminopenicillanic acid $\xrightarrow{N(C_2H_5)_3}$ **Phenethicillin**

PHENETURIDE
Use: antiepileptic
Analysis:

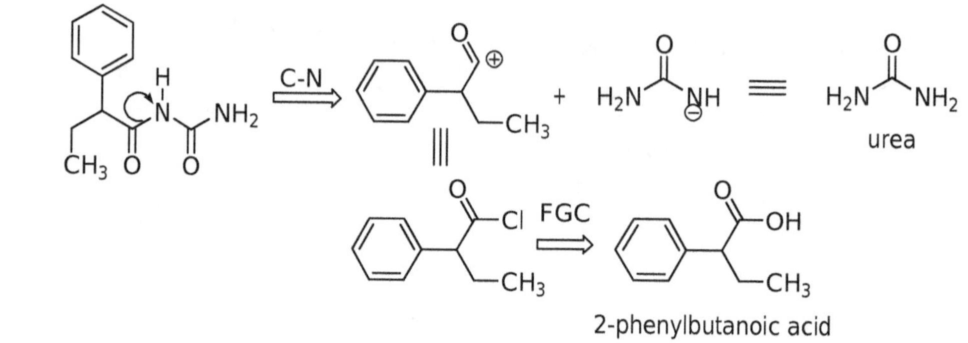

[Retrosynthetic analysis: pheneturide is disconnected at the C-N bond to give a 2-phenylbutanoyl cation and urea. FGC (functional group conversion) shows 2-phenylbutanoyl chloride derived from 2-phenylbutanoic acid.]

Synthesis:

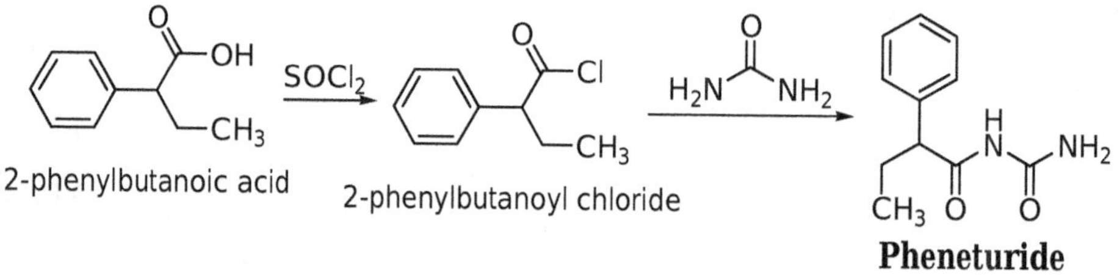

2-phenylbutanoic acid →(SOCl₂)→ 2-phenylbutanoyl chloride →(H₂N-CO-NH₂)→ **Pheneturide**

PHENIRAMINE
Use: antihistaminic
Analysis:

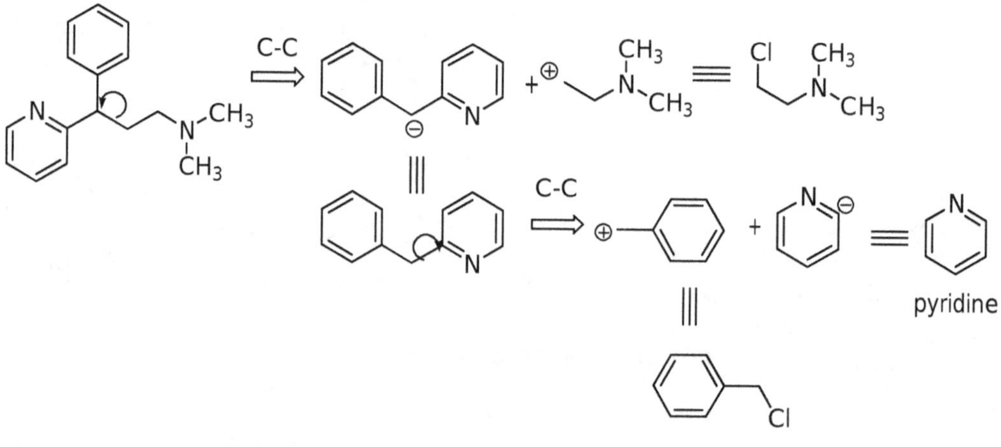

[Retrosynthetic analysis: pheniramine is disconnected at a C-C bond to give a 2-benzylpyridine carbanion and a 2-chloro-N,N-dimethylethylamine cation equivalent. Further C-C disconnection of 2-benzylpyridine gives phenyl cation + pyridine anion, equivalent to benzyl chloride + pyridine.]

Retrosynthetic Analysis and Synthesis of Drugs

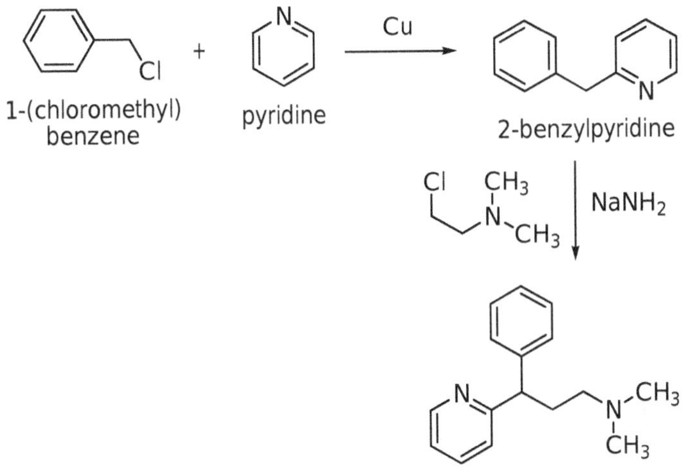

Synthesis:

1-(chloromethyl)benzene + pyridine →(Cu) 2-benzylpyridine

→ (Cl-CH₂CH₂-N(CH₃)₂ / NaNH₂) → **Pheniramine**

PHENPROBAMATE
Use: muscle relaxant, tranquilizer

Analysis:

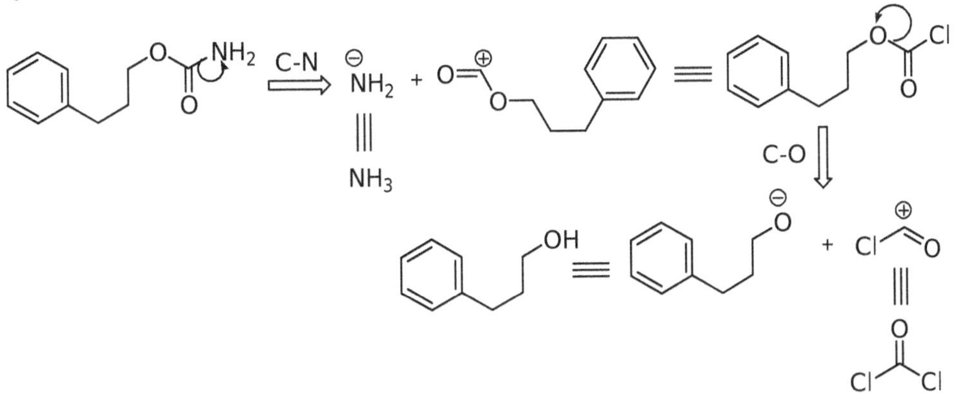

Phenprobamate ⇒(C-N) NH₂⁻ (≡ NH₃) + 3-phenylpropyl chloroformate cation

⇓ (C-O)

3-phenylpropan-1-ol (≡ alkoxide) + ClCO⁺ (≡ COCl₂)

Synthesis:

3-phenylpropan-1-ol →(COCl₂, NH₃) **Phenprobamate**

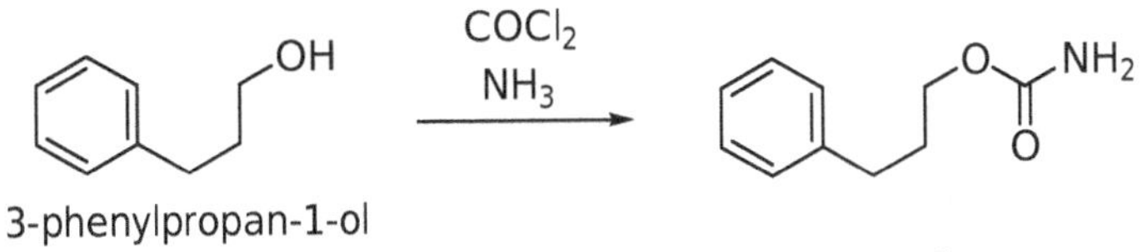

PHENTOLAMINE

Use: antihypertensive

Analysis:

[Retrosynthetic analysis scheme showing disconnection of phentolamine at C-N bond to give 2-methylimidazoline cation and 3-hydroxy-N-(p-tolyl)aniline anion; equivalent to 2-(chloromethyl)-4,5-dihydro-1H-imidazole and the secondary amine. Further C-N disconnection of the diarylamine gives phenol cation and p-toluidine anion, equivalent to 3-chlorophenol + p-toluidine; FCG to resorcinol.]

Synthesis:

resorcinol + p-toluidine → 3-hydroxy-N-(p-tolyl)aniline

2-(chloromethyl)-4,5-dihydro-1H-imidazole ↓

Phentolamine

PHENOXYBENZAMINE
Use: antihypertensive, vasodilator
Analysis:

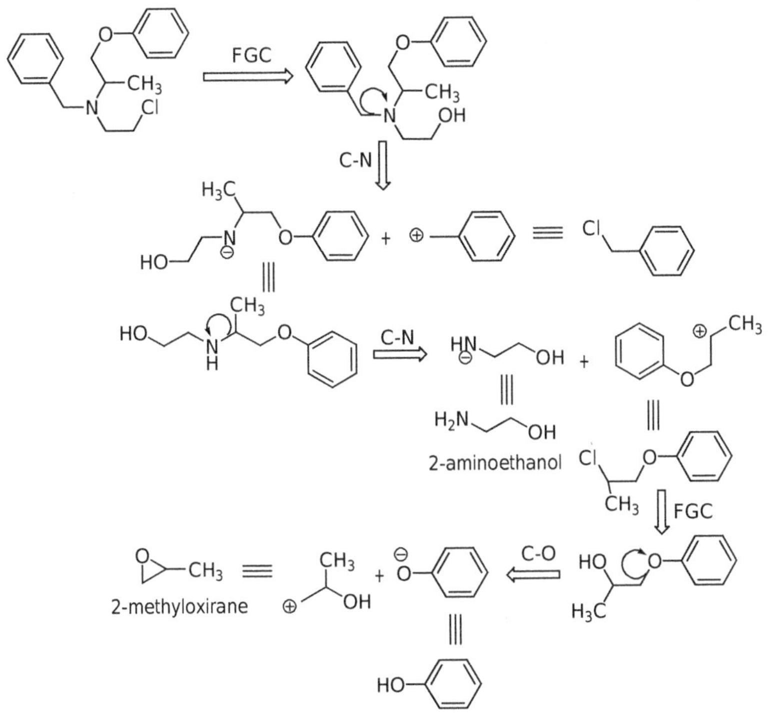

Synthesis:

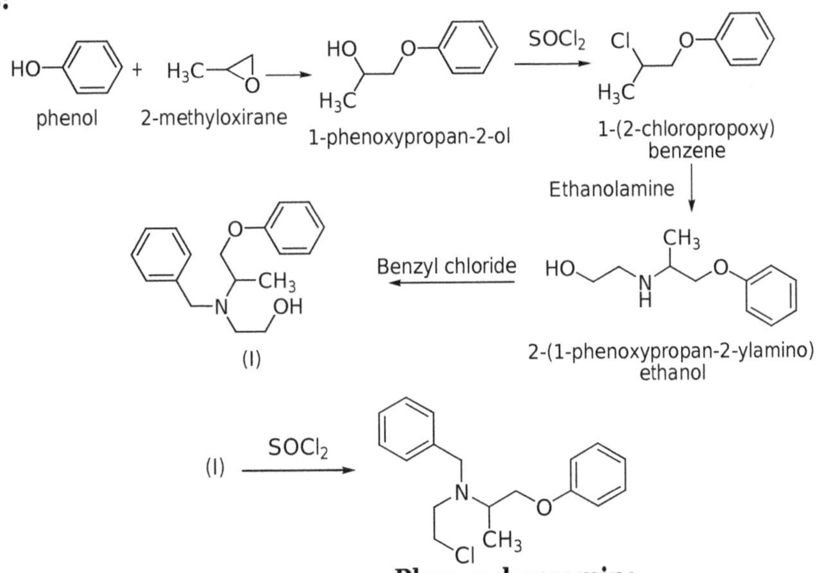

phenol + 2-methyloxirane → 1-phenoxypropan-2-ol →[SOCl$_2$] 1-(2-chloropropoxy)benzene →[Ethanolamine] 2-(1-phenoxypropan-2-ylamino)ethanol →[Benzyl chloride] (I)

(I) →[SOCl$_2$] **Phenoxybenzamine**

PHENYLBUTAZONE

Use: anti-inflammatory

Analysis:

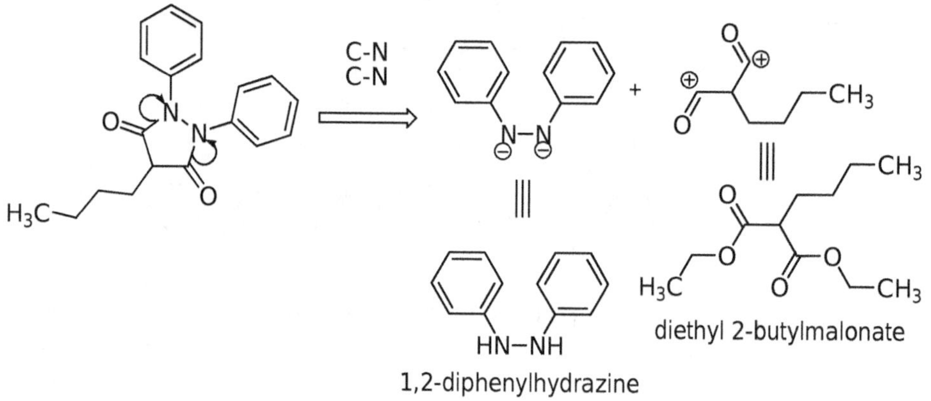

[Retrosynthetic scheme: phenylbutazone ⇒ (C-N, C-N disconnection) ⇒ 1,2-diphenylhydrazine + diethyl 2-butylmalonate]

Synthesis:

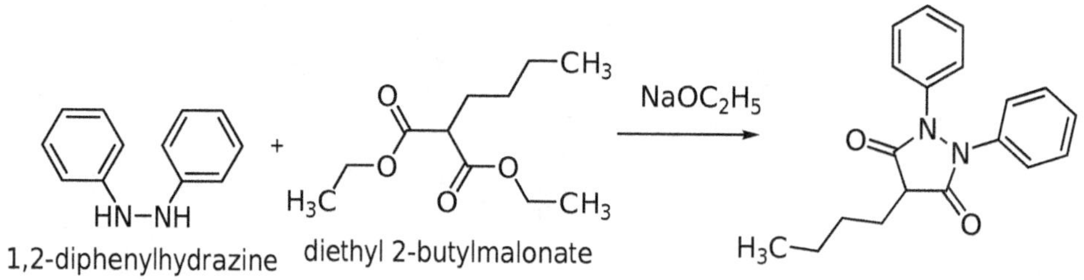

1,2-diphenylhydrazine + diethyl 2-butylmalonate → (NaOC₂H₅) → **Phenylbutazone**

PHENYLTOLOXAMINE

Use: antihistaminic

Analysis:

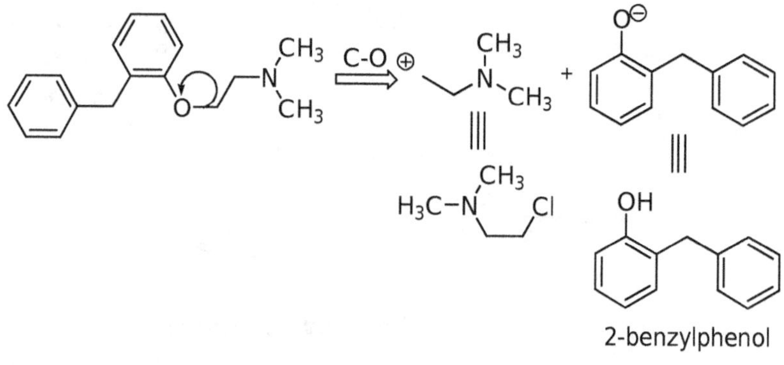

[Retrosynthetic scheme: phenyltoloxamine ⇒ (C-O disconnection) ⇒ H₃C–N(CH₃)–CH₂CH₂–Cl + 2-benzylphenol]

Retrosynthetic Analysis and Synthesis of Drugs

Synthesis:

2-benzylphenol + 2-chloro-N,N-dimethylethanamine →(NaOCH₃) **Phenyltoloxamine**

PIFOXIME
Use: anti-inflammatory
Analysis:

[Retrosynthetic scheme showing C–N disconnection of the oxime to give the ketone (I) and H₂N–OH (hydroxylamine); further C–N disconnection to piperidine + α-oxocarbenium intermediate; C–O disconnection of methyl ester (I) to give methanol + acyl cation, related to the acid chloride via FGC; C–O disconnection to HOOC–CH₂⁺ (from 2-chloroacetic acid) + 4-hydroxyacetophenone phenoxide]

piperidine

2-chloroacetic acid: Cl–CH₂–COOH

Synthesis:

1-(4-hydroxyphenyl)ethanone + 2-chloroacetic acid →(NaOH) HOOC-CH₂-O-C₆H₄-COCH₃ →(H₂SO₄, H₃C-OH) methyl ester intermediate →(piperidine) piperidine amide intermediate →(NH₂OH) **Pifoxime**

PIKETOPROFEN

Use: anti-inflammatory

Analysis:

Piketoprofen ⟹(C-N) 4-methylpyridin-2-amine anion + acylium cation

≡ 4-methylpyridin-2-amine (H₂N-pyridine-CH₃) + acid chloride (Cl-CO-CH(CH₃)-C₆H₄-CO-C₆H₅)

⟹(FGC) 2-(3-benzoylphenyl)propanoic acid (ketoprofen, COOH-CH(CH₃)-C₆H₄-CO-C₆H₅)

Synthesis:

[Reaction scheme: 2-(3-benzoylphenyl)propanoic acid + SOCl₂ → acid chloride; then 4-methylpyridin-2-amine, N(C₂H₅)₃ → **Piketoprofen**]

PIMEFYLLINE
Use: vasodilator

Analysis:

[Retrosynthetic scheme showing C–N disconnections of pimefylline into 7-(2-bromoethyl)-1,3-dimethylxanthine synthon + 3-(aminomethyl)pyridine, then further into 1,2-dibromoethane + theophylline anion]

Synthesis:

Theophylline + 1,2-dibromoethane —NaOH→ 7-(2-bromoethyl)-1,3-dimethyl-1H-purine-2,6(3H,7H)-dione

↓ 3-(aminomethyl)pyridine (pyridin-3-ylmethanamine, NH₂)

Pimefylline

PIMOBENDAN
Use: cardiotonic, vasodilator
Analysis:

Retrosynthetic Analysis and Synthesis of Drugs

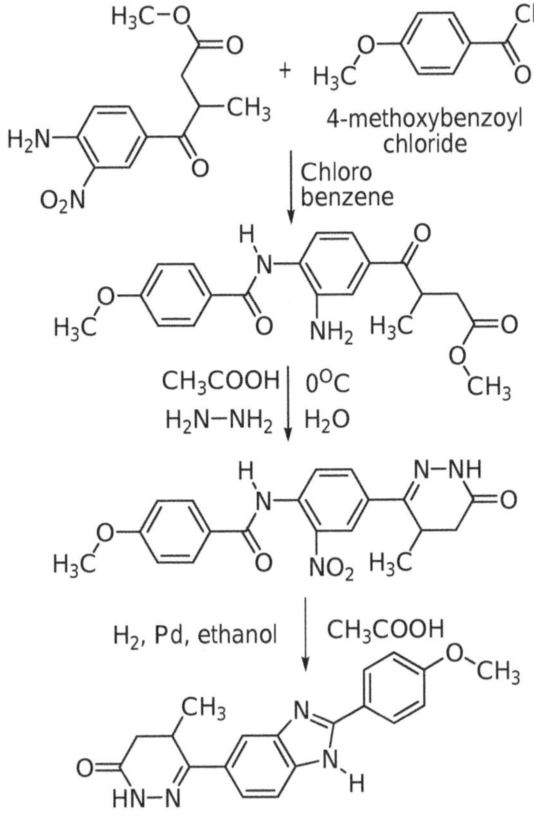

Synthesis:

[Scheme: synthesis of Pimobendan from methyl 3-(4-amino-3-nitrophenyl)-3-oxo-2-methylpropanoate + 4-methoxybenzoyl chloride in chlorobenzene; then CH₃COOH, H₂N–NH₂, 0°C, H₂O; then H₂, Pd, ethanol, CH₃COOH → **Pimobendan**]

PINDOLOL

Use: β-blocker

Analysis:

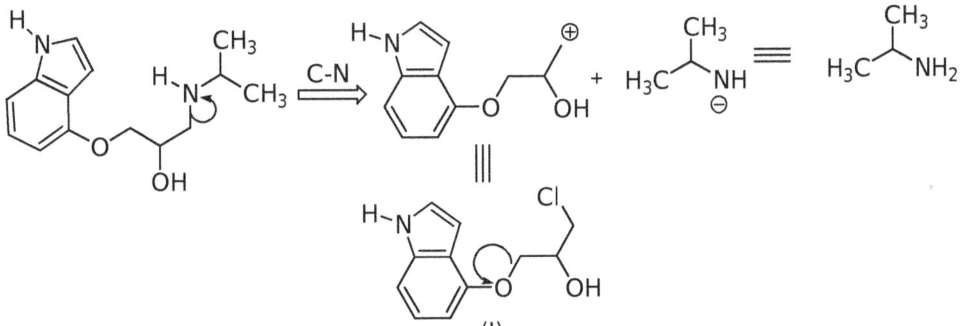

[Retrosynthetic analysis showing C–N disconnection of pindolol into 4-hydroxyindole-derived epoxide/chlorohydrin (I) and isopropylamine]

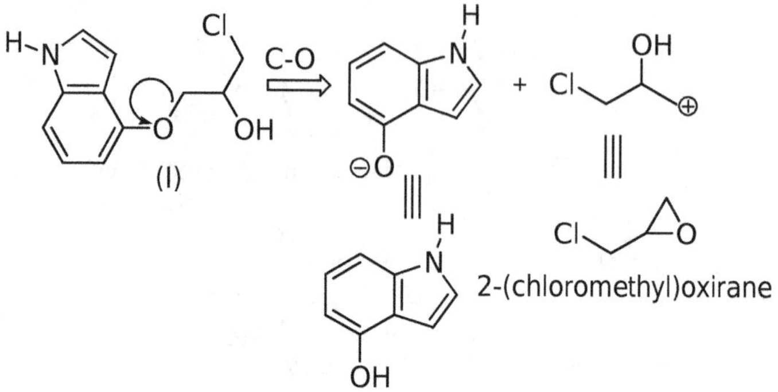

Synthesis:

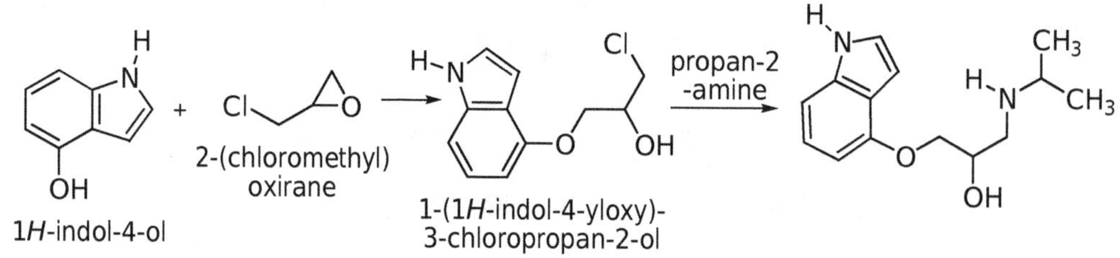

(Reaction scheme: 1H-indol-4-ol + 2-(chloromethyl)oxirane → 1-(1H-indol-4-yloxy)-3-chloropropan-2-ol → (propan-2-amine) → **Pindolol**)

PIPAMAZINE
Use: antiemetic
Analysis:

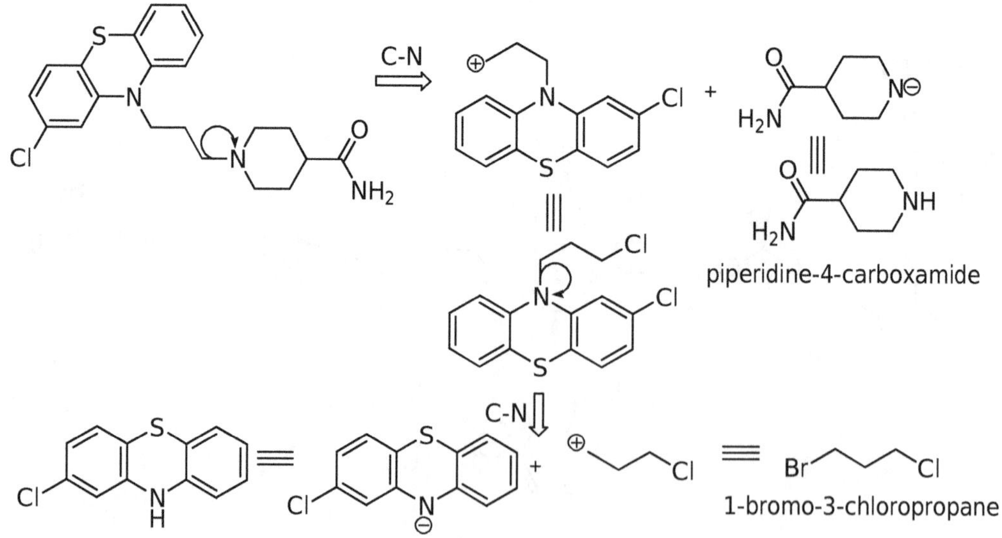

(Retrosynthetic analysis showing C-N disconnection to give 2-chloro-phenothiazine and piperidine-4-carboxamide, with intermediate 1-bromo-3-chloropropane)

Synthesis:

[Scheme: 2-chloro-10H-phenothiazine + 1-bromo-3-chloropropane, NaNH₂ → 2-chloro-10-(3-chloropropyl)-10H-phenothiazine; then piperidine-4-carboxamide, K₂CO₃, NaI → **Pipamazine**]

PIPAZETHATE

Use: antitussive

Analysis:

[Retrosynthetic scheme: C–O disconnection gives azaphenothiazine carbamoyl cation + 2-(2-piperidinoethoxy)ethanol; C–N disconnection gives 10H-pyrido-phenothiazine + phosgene (COCl₂)]

Synthesis:

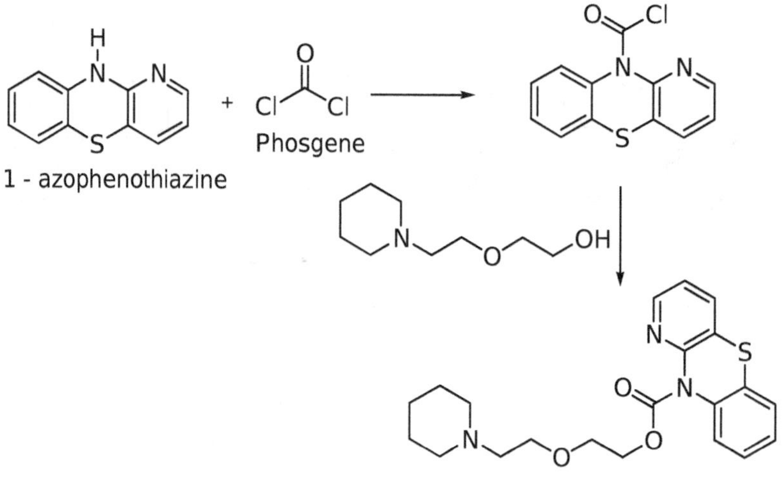

[Structure: 1-azophenothiazine + Phosgene → carbonyl chloride intermediate; then reaction with piperidinyl-ethoxy-ethanol gives **Pipazethate**]

PIPERACILLIN
Use: antibiotic
Analysis:

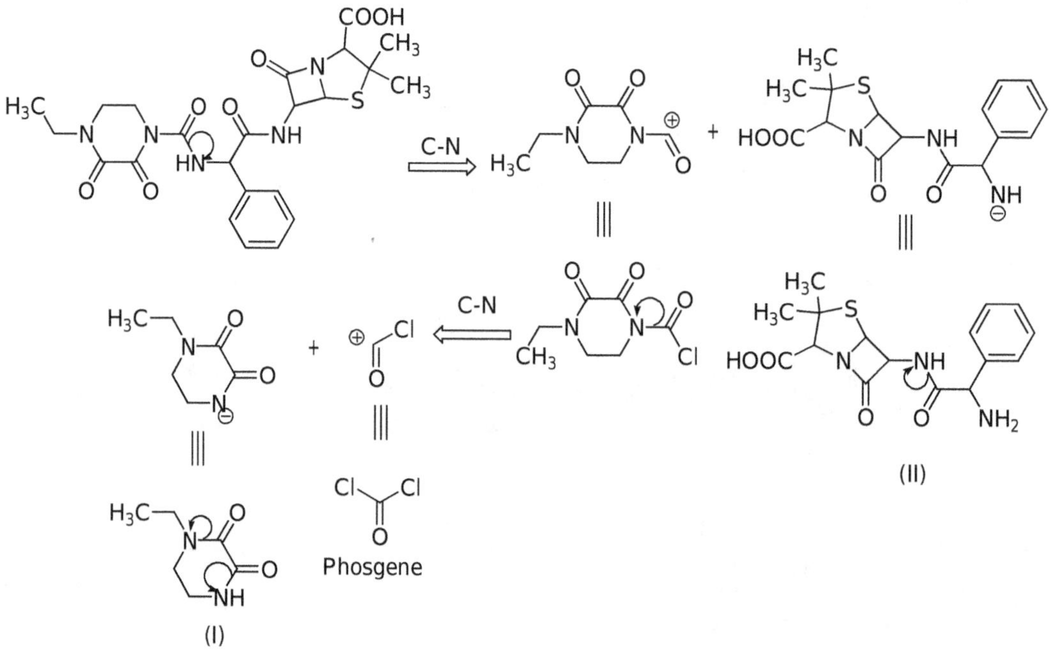

[Retrosynthetic analysis showing Piperacillin disconnected via C-N bond into acyl cation and anion fragment (II); further disconnection yielding piperazinedione fragment (I), phosgene, and 6-aminopenicillanic acid derivative with phenylglycine side chain.]

(I)

(II)

Phosgene

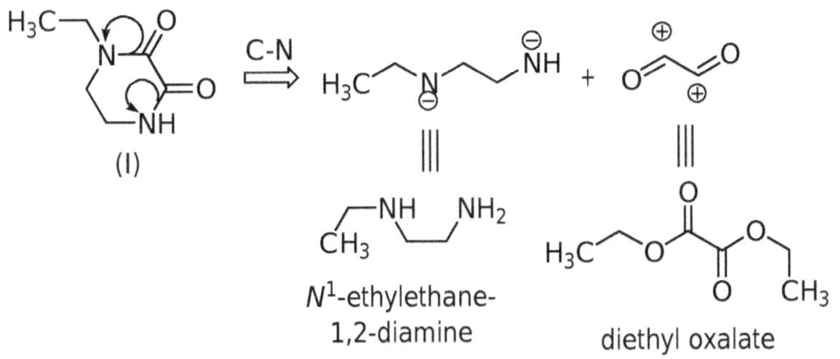

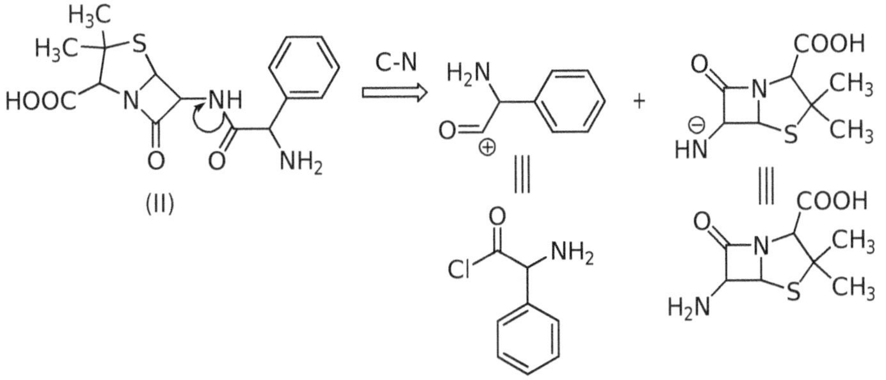

Retrosynthetic Analysis and Synthesis of Drugs

Synthesis:

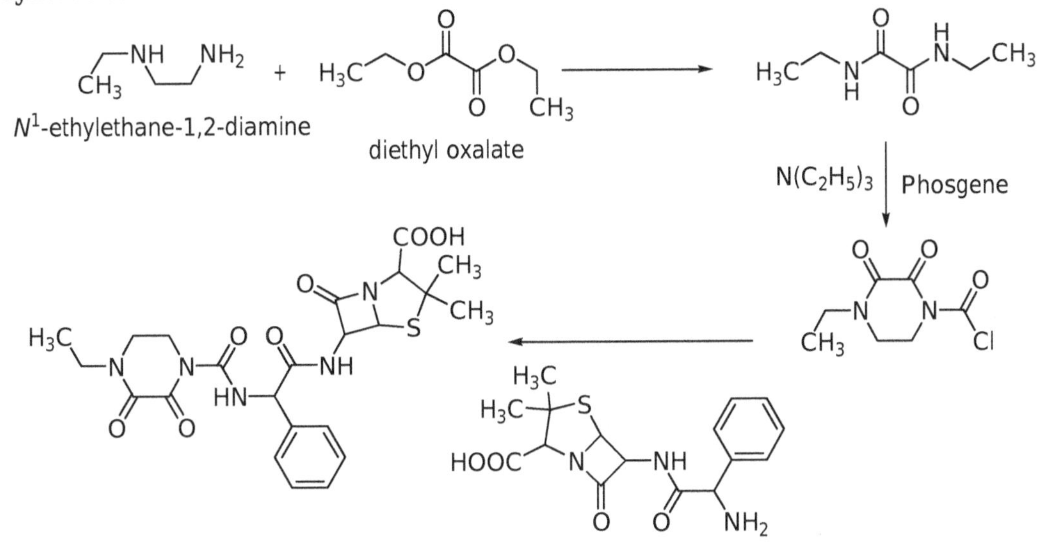

Piperacillin

PIPEROCAINE
Use: local anaesthetic
Analysis:

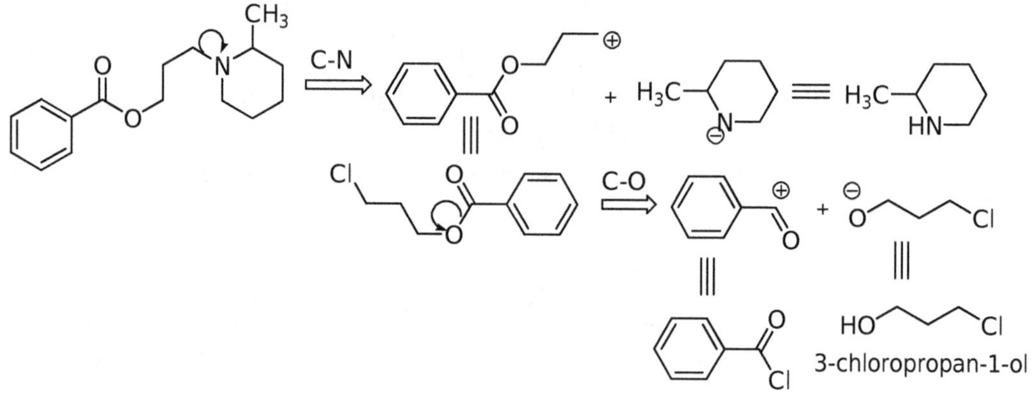

[Retrosynthetic analysis scheme: Piperocaine is disconnected at C-N bond to give 3-chloropropyl benzoate cation and 2-methylpiperidine anion (≡ 2-methylpiperidine). The 3-chloropropyl benzoate is further disconnected at C-O bond to give benzoyl cation (≡ benzoyl chloride) and 3-chloropropoxide (≡ 3-chloropropan-1-ol).]

Synthesis:

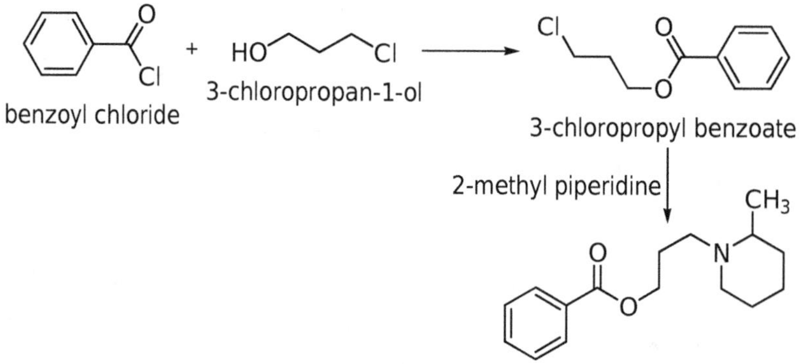

benzoyl chloride + 3-chloropropan-1-ol → 3-chloropropyl benzoate

3-chloropropyl benzoate + 2-methyl piperidine → **Piperocaine**

PIPOBROMAN
Use: antineoplastic
Analysis:

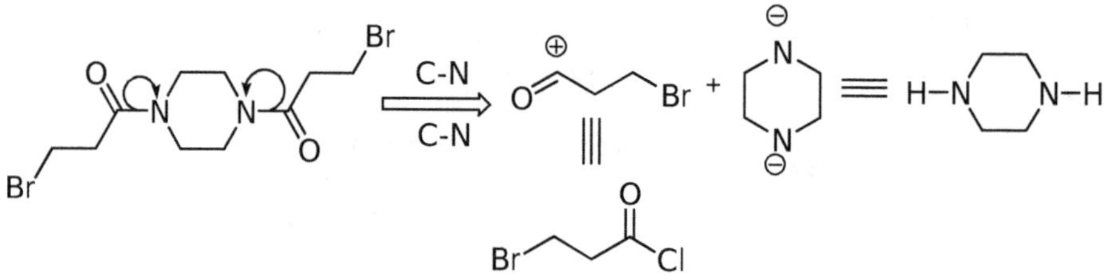

[Retrosynthetic analysis: Pipobroman is disconnected at both C-N bonds to give 3-bromopropanoyl cation (≡ 3-bromopropanoyl chloride) and piperazine dianion (≡ piperazine, H-N( )N-H).]

Synthesis:

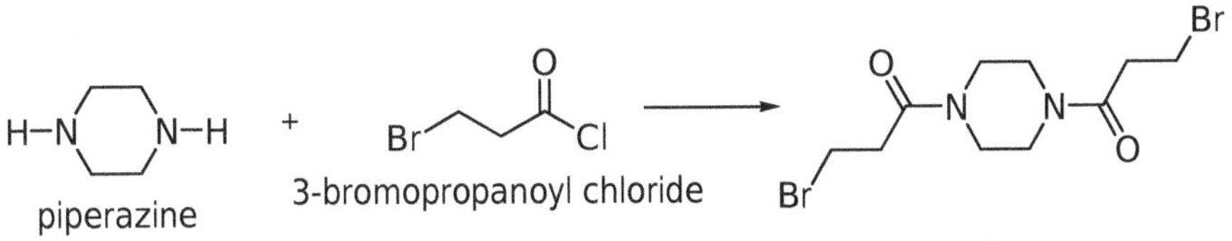

piperazine + 3-bromopropanoyl chloride → **Pipobroman**

PIRACETAM
Use: cerebro stimulant

Analysis:

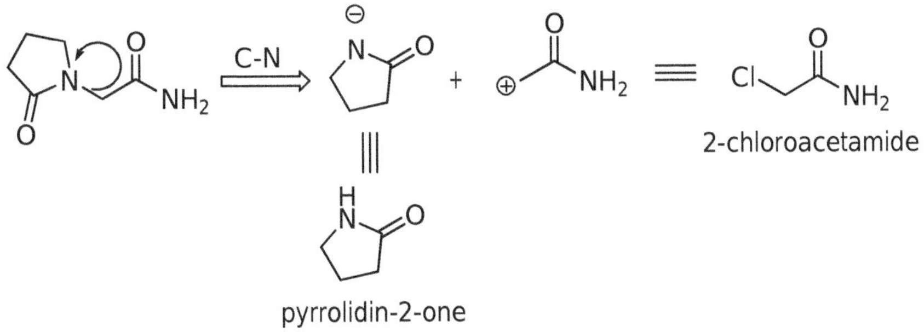

pyrrolidin-2-one + 2-chloroacetamide

Synthesis:

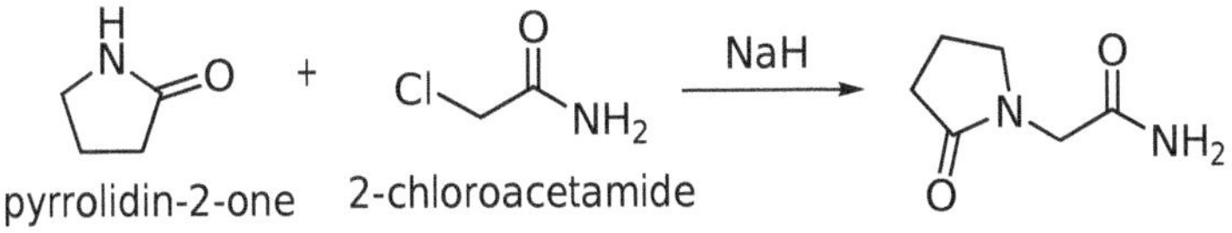

pyrrolidin-2-one + 2-chloroacetamide →(NaH) **Piracetam**

PIRETANIDE
Use: diuretic

Analysis:

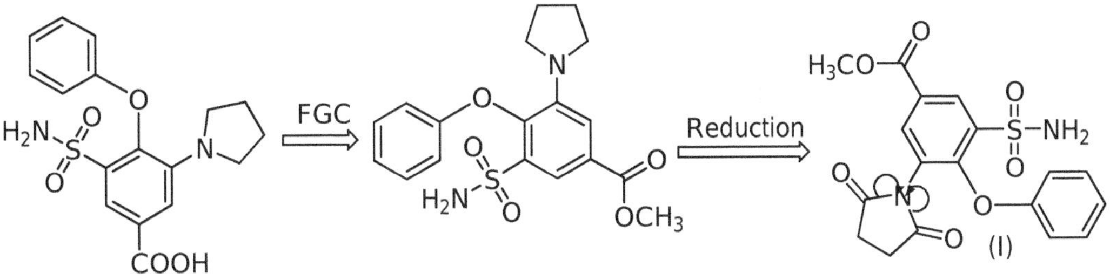

⇒(FGC) ⇒(Reduction) (I)

Synthesis:

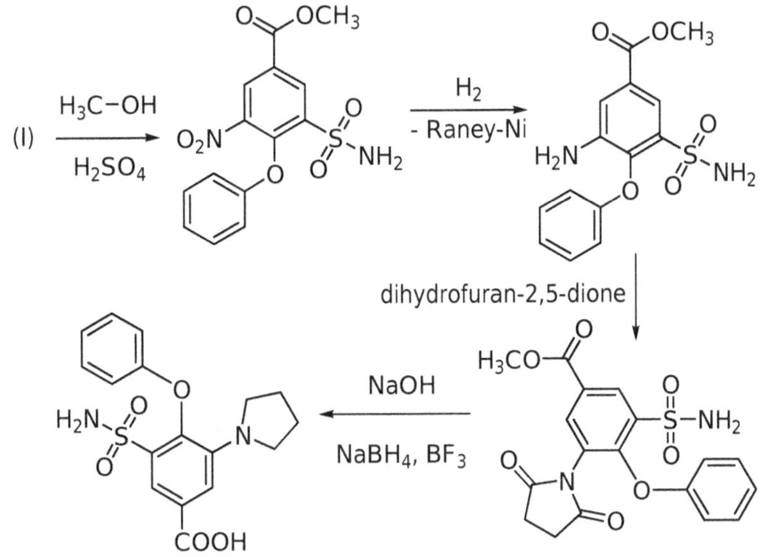

Retrosynthetic Analysis and Synthesis of Drugs

Piretanide

PIREZEPINE
Use: peptic ulcer therapeutic
Analysis:

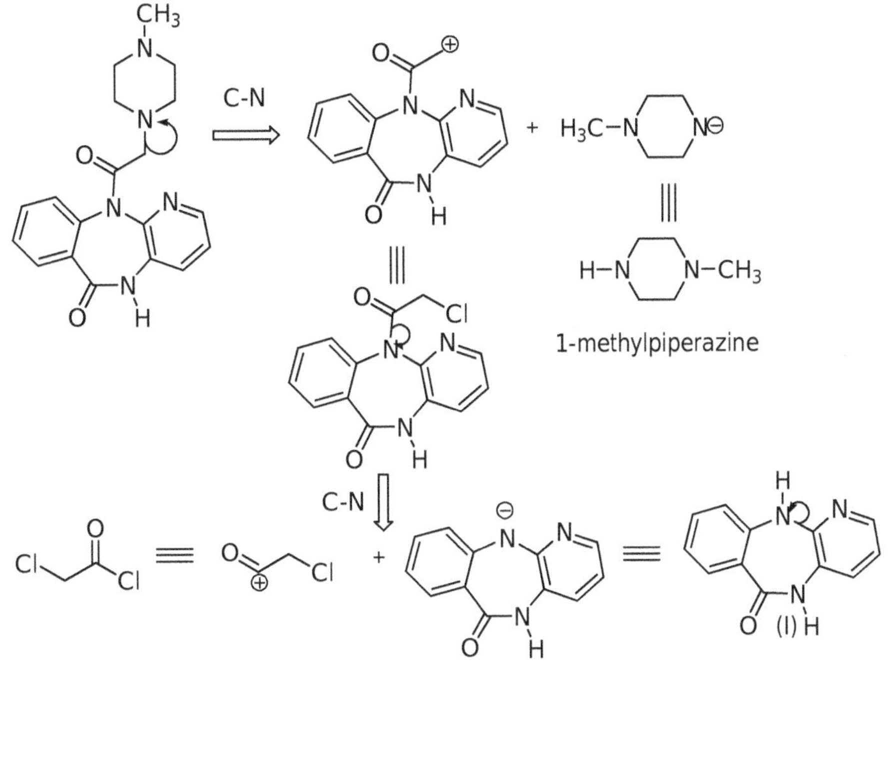

1-methylpiperazine

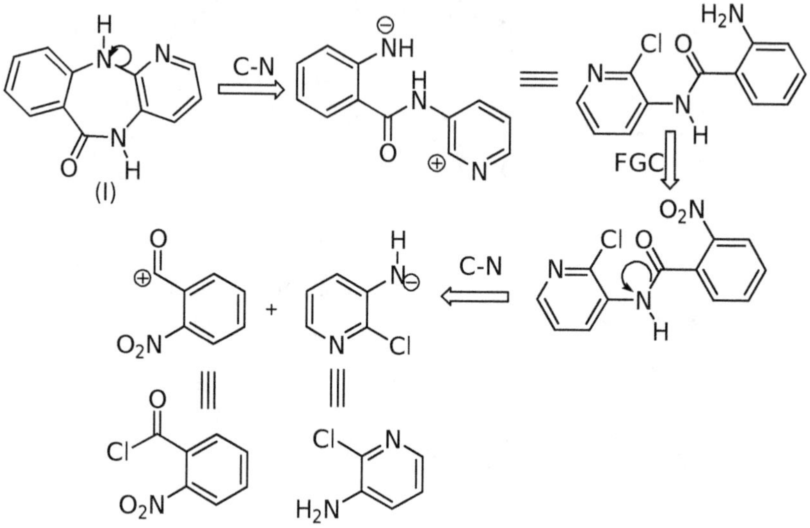

Retrosynthetic Analysis and Synthesis of Drugs

Synthesis:

2-nitrobenzoyl chloride + 2-chloropyridin-3-amine → N-(2-chloropyridin-3-yl)-2-nitrobenzamide

Raney-Ni, H_2

2-chloroacetyl chloride, $N(C_2H_5)_3$

200°C

1-methylpiperazine

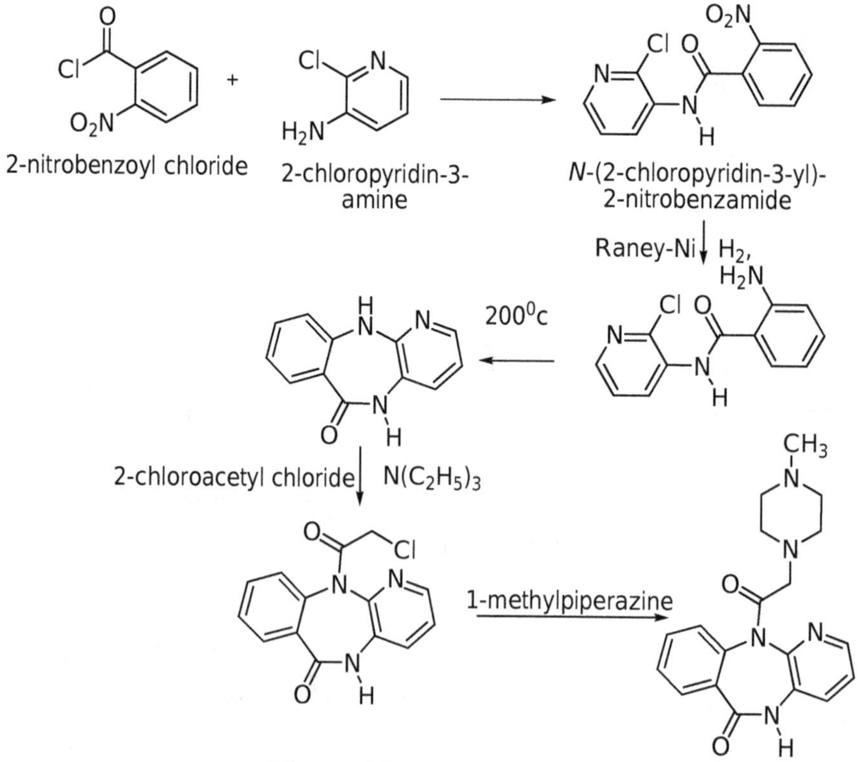

Pirenzepine

PIRIBEDIL
Use: vasodilator

Analysis:

Piribedil ⟹ [C-N disconnection] 2-chloropyrimidine + 1-((benzo[d][1,3]dioxol-5-yl)methyl)piperazine

Synthesis:

2-chloropyrimidine + 1-((benzo[d][1,3]dioxol-5-yl)methyl)piperazine ⟶ **Piribedil**

PIRITRAMIDE
Use: analgesic

Analysis:

Piritramide ⟹ [C-N disconnection] 3,3-diphenyl-3-cyanopropyl cation + 4-piperidino-4-carbamoylpiperidine

≡ 4-bromo-2,2-diphenylbutyronitrile + 4-piperidino-piperidine-4-carboxamide

Synthesis:

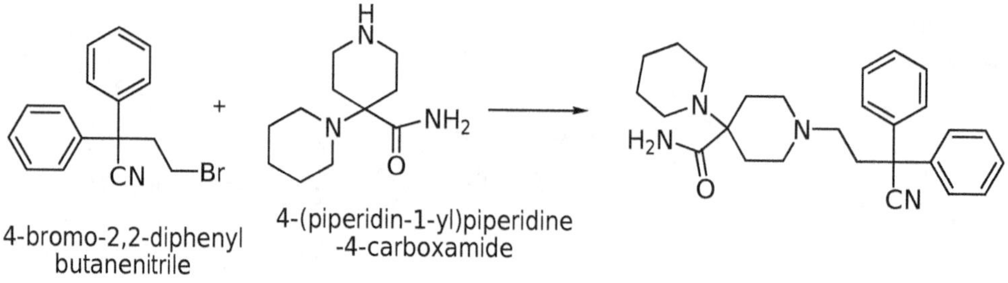

[Structures shown: 4-bromo-2,2-diphenylbutanenitrile + 4-(piperidin-1-yl)piperidine-4-carboxamide → **Piritramide**]

PIROXICAM
Use: anti-inflammatory
Analysis:

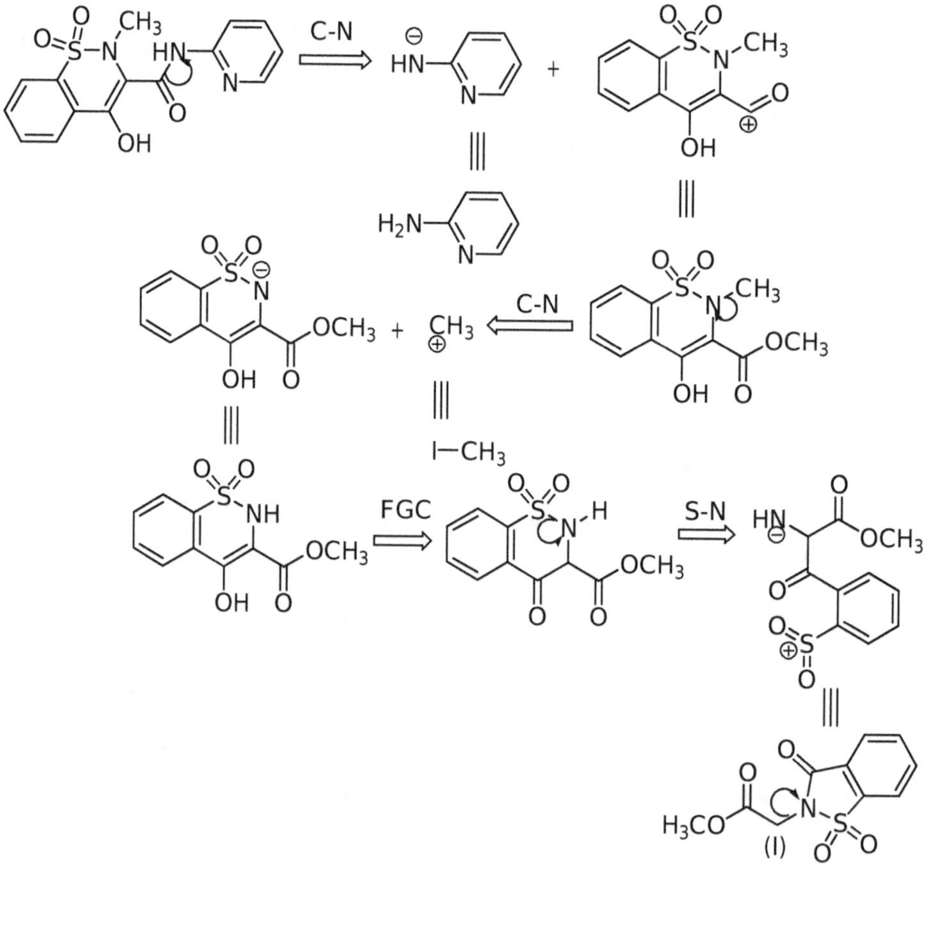

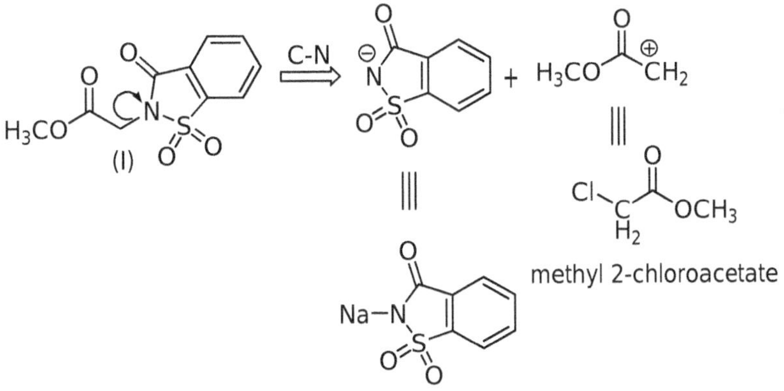

Retrosynthetic Analysis and Synthesis of Drugs

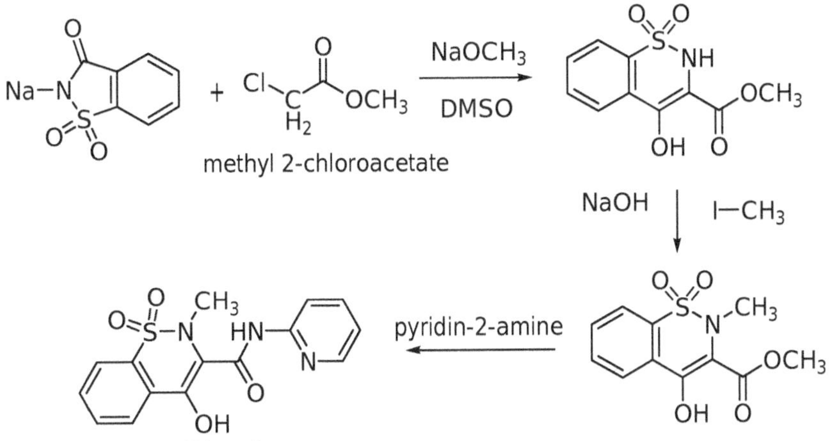

Synthesis:

PRAMOCAINE

Use: local anaesthetic

Analysis:

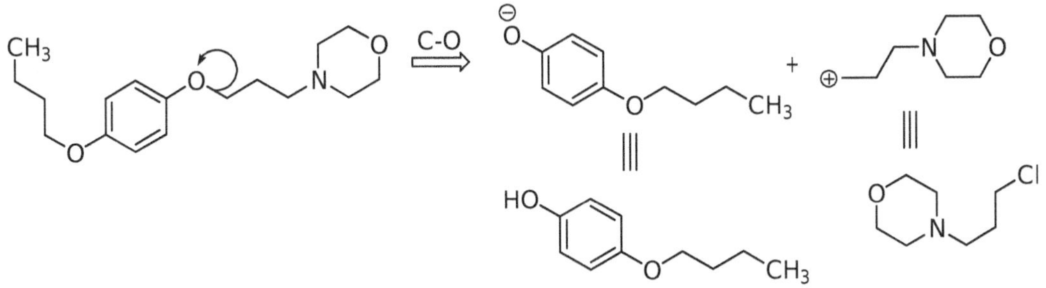

Synthesis:

4-butoxyphenol + 4-(3-chloropropyl)morpholine $\xrightarrow{KOH}$ **Pramocaine**

PRAZIQUANTEL
Use: anthelmintic

Analysis:

Retrosynthetic Analysis and Synthesis of Drugs

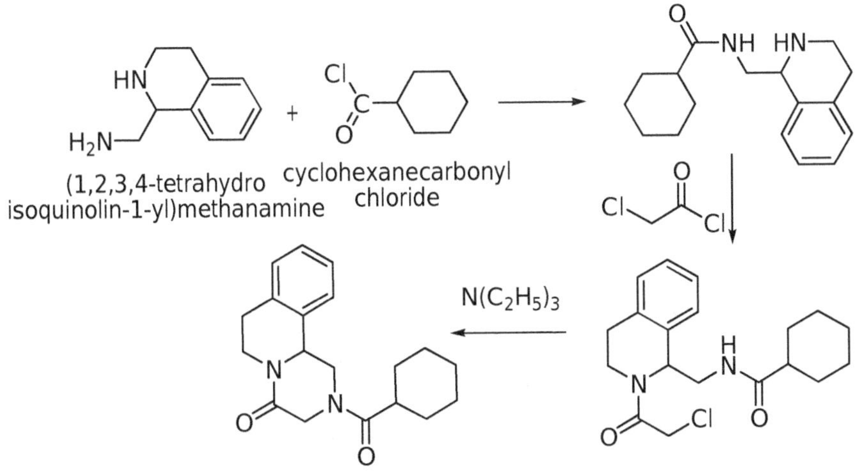

Synthesis:

[Scheme: (1,2,3,4-tetrahydroisoquinolin-1-yl)methanamine + cyclohexanecarbonyl chloride → amide intermediate → (with ClCH₂COCl) → chloroacetyl intermediate → (N(C₂H₅)₃) → **Praziquantel**]

PRAZOSIN
Use: antihypertensive
Analysis:

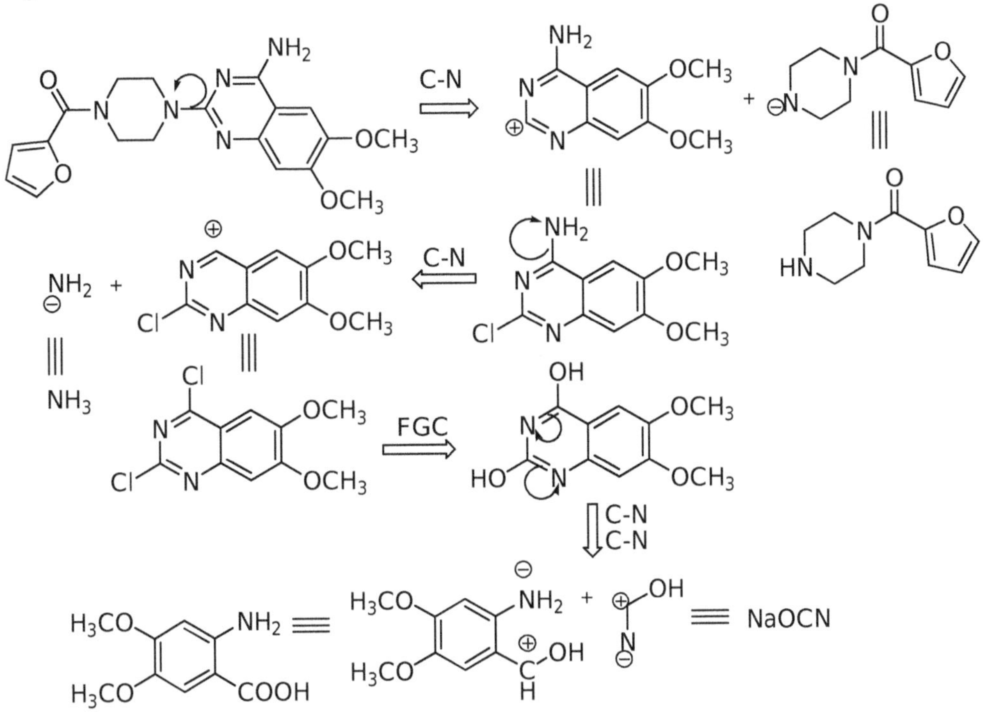

[Retrosynthetic scheme of Prazosin showing C-N disconnections giving 4-amino-6,7-dimethoxyquinazoline cation + 1-(2-furoyl)piperazine anion; further C-N disconnection giving 2-chloro-6,7-dimethoxyquinazoline + NH₂⁻ (≡ NH₃); FGC to 2,4-dichloro-6,7-dimethoxyquinazoline from 6,7-dimethoxyquinazoline-2,4-diol; C-N, C-N disconnections to 2-amino-4,5-dimethoxybenzoic acid (≡ acyl cation form) + NaOCN]

Synthesis:

[Scheme: 2-amino-4,5-dimethoxybenzoic acid + NaOCN (Sodium cyanate) → 6,7-dimethoxyquinazoline-2,4-diol → (POCl₃/PCl₅) → 2,4-dichloro-6,7-dimethoxyquinazoline → (NH₃) → 4-amino-2-chloro-6,7-dimethoxyquinazoline → ((furan-2-yl)(piperazin-1-yl)methanone) → **Prazosin**]

PRILOCAINE

Use: local anaesthetic

Analysis:

[Retrosynthetic analysis: Prilocaine ⟹ (C–N disconnection) acylium cation of N-(o-tolyl)acetamide + propan-1-amine (H₃C–CH₂–CH₂–NH₂); further disconnection ⟹ (C–N) o-toluidine + 2-bromopropanoyl bromide (Br–CH(CH₃)–C(=O)–Br)]

Synthesis:

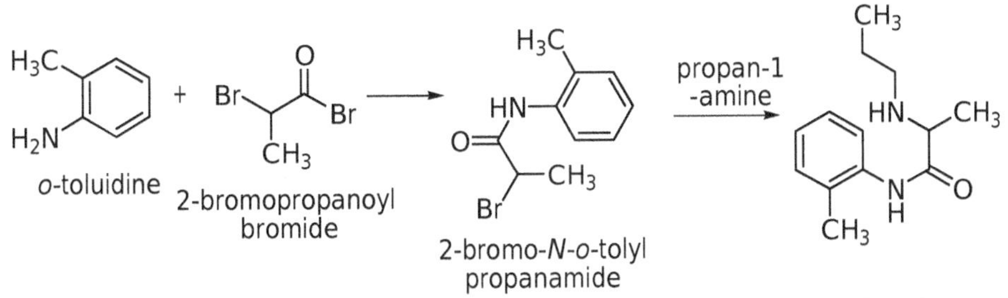

o-toluidine + 2-bromopropanoyl bromide → 2-bromo-N-o-tolyl propanamide →[propan-1-amine] **Prilocaine**

PRIMAPERONE

Use: vasodilator

Analysis:

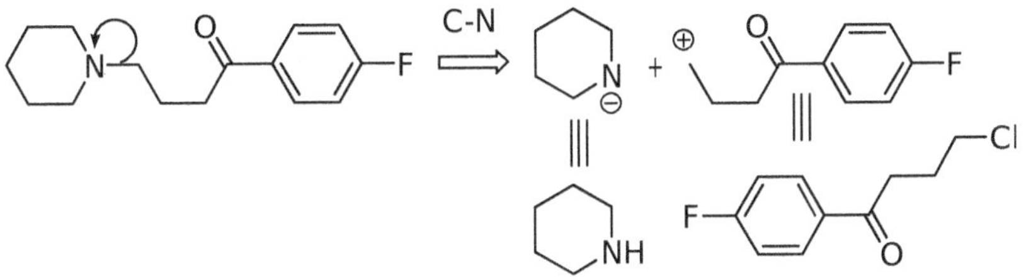

[retrosynthetic scheme: piperidine anion + 1-(4-fluorophenyl)-1-oxo cation ≡ piperidine (NH) + 4-chloro-1-(4-fluorophenyl)butan-1-one] via C–N disconnection

Synthesis:

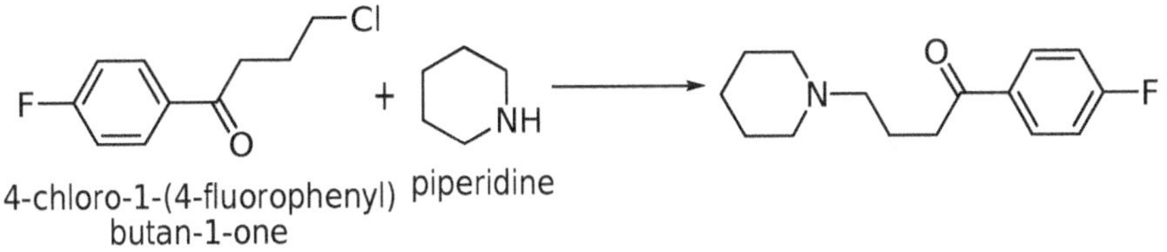

4-chloro-1-(4-fluorophenyl)butan-1-one + piperidine → **Primaperone**

PROBENECID

Use: uricosuric agent

Analysis:

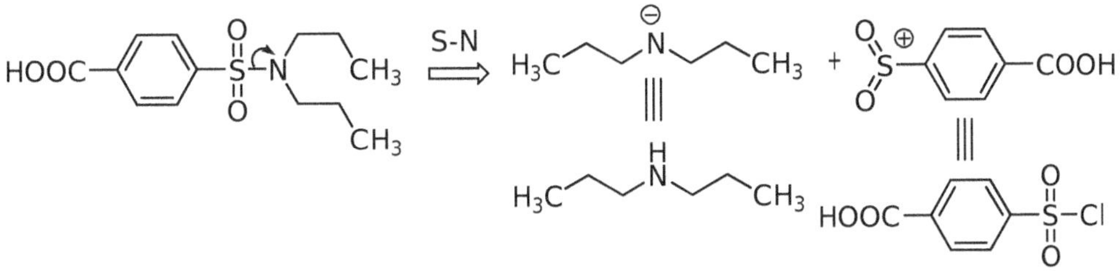

[4-(dipropylsulfamoyl)benzoic acid] ⇒[S–N] dipropylamine cation + 4-(chlorosulfonyl)benzoic acid sulfonyl anion ≡ dipropylamine + 4-(chlorosulfonyl)benzoic acid

Synthesis:

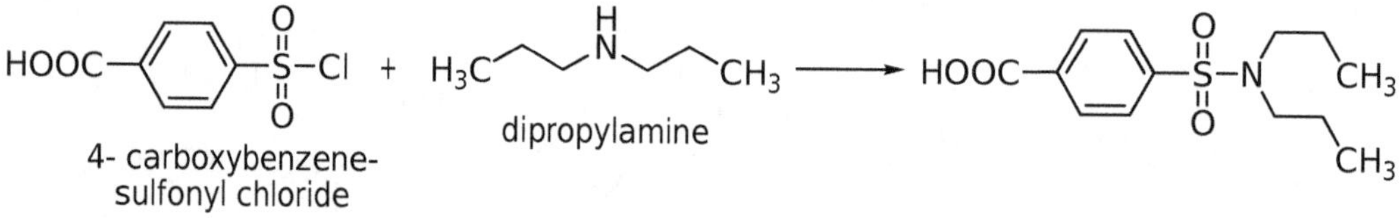

HOOC–C₆H₄–SO₂Cl (4-carboxybenzene-sulfonyl chloride) + H₃C-CH₂-NH-CH₂-CH₃ (dipropylamine) ⟶ HOOC–C₆H₄–SO₂–N(CH₂CH₂CH₃)₂

Probenecid

PROCAINAMIDE

Use: antiarrhythmic

Analysis:

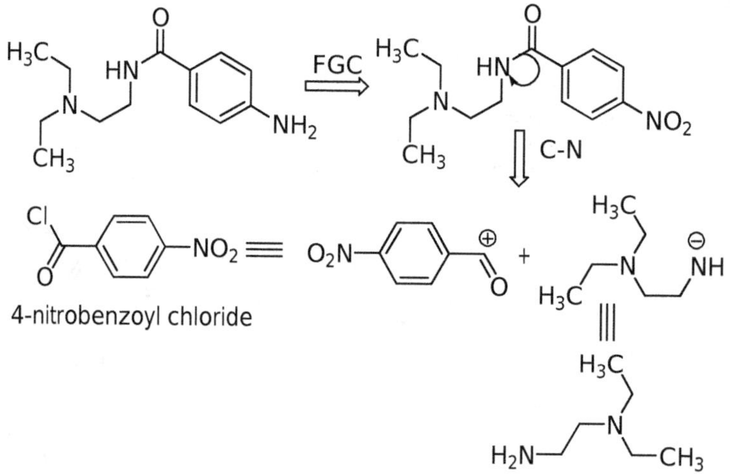

Et₂N-CH₂CH₂-NH-CO-C₆H₄-NH₂ ⟹ (FGC) Et₂N-CH₂CH₂-NH-CO-C₆H₄-NO₂ ⟹ (C-N)

4-nitrobenzoyl chloride (Cl-CO-C₆H₄-NO₂) ≡ O₂N-C₆H₄-CO⁺ + Et₂N-CH₂CH₂-NH⁻ ≡ H₂N-CH₂CH₂-NEt₂

Synthesis:

4-nitrobenzoyl chloride (Cl-CO-C₆H₄-NO₂) + H₂N-CH₂CH₂-N(Et)₂ (N^1,N^1-diethylethane-1,2-diamine) ⟶ Et₂N-CH₂CH₂-NH-CO-C₆H₄-NO₂

$\xrightarrow{H_2,\ Raney-Ni}$ Et₂N-CH₂CH₂-NH-CO-C₆H₄-NH₂

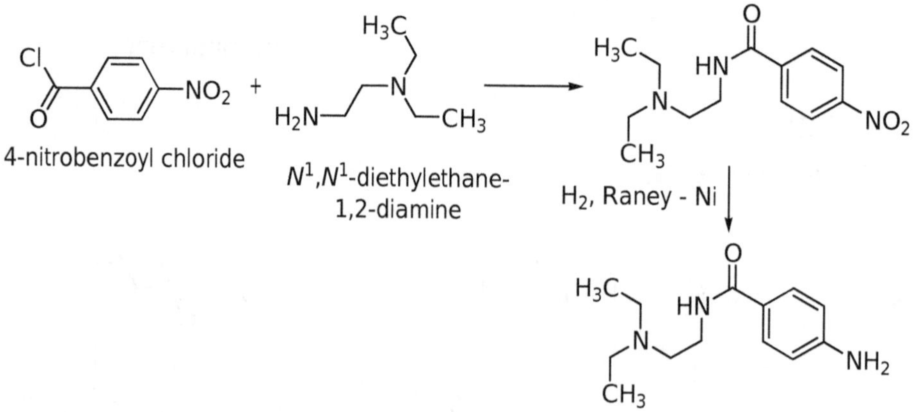

Procainamide

PROCAINE

Use: analgesic, local anaesthetic

Analysis:

[Retrosynthetic analysis: Procaine ⇒ (FGC) 2-(diethylamino)ethyl 4-nitrobenzoate ⇒ (C-O disconnection) 4-nitrobenzoyl cation + 2-(diethylamino)ethoxide; 4-nitrobenzoyl chloride ≡ 4-nitrobenzoyl cation; 4-nitrobenzoyl chloride ⇒ (FGC) 4-nitrobenzoic acid; alkoxide ≡ 2-(diethylamino)ethanol]

4-nitrobenzoic acid

Synthesis:

4-nitrobenzoic acid $\xrightarrow{SOCl_2}$ 4-nitrobenzoyl chloride $\xrightarrow{\text{2-(diethylamino)ethanol}}$ 2-(diethylamino)ethyl 4-nitrobenzoate $\xrightarrow{H_2,\ Raney-Ni}$ **Procaine**

PROCATEROL
Use: bronchodilator
Analysis:

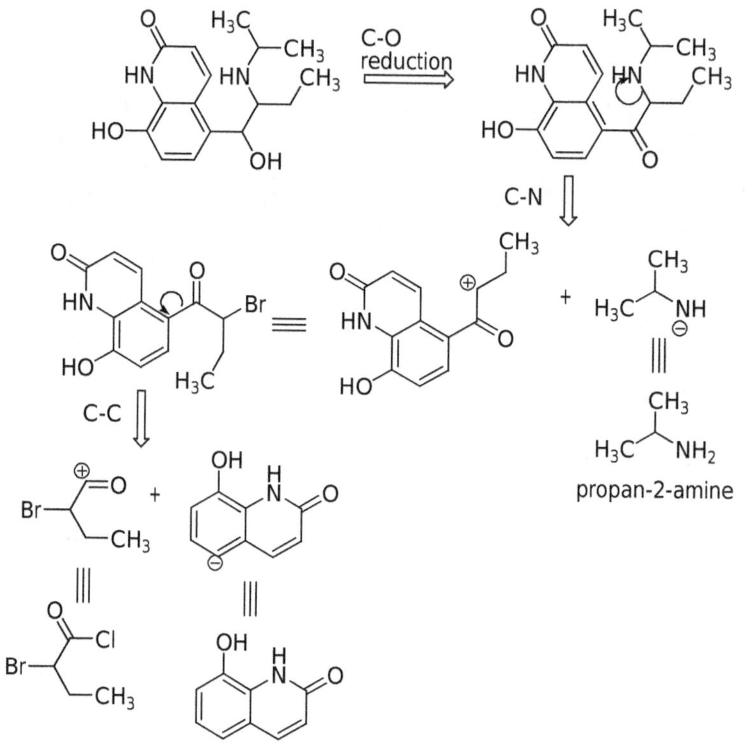

Synthesis:

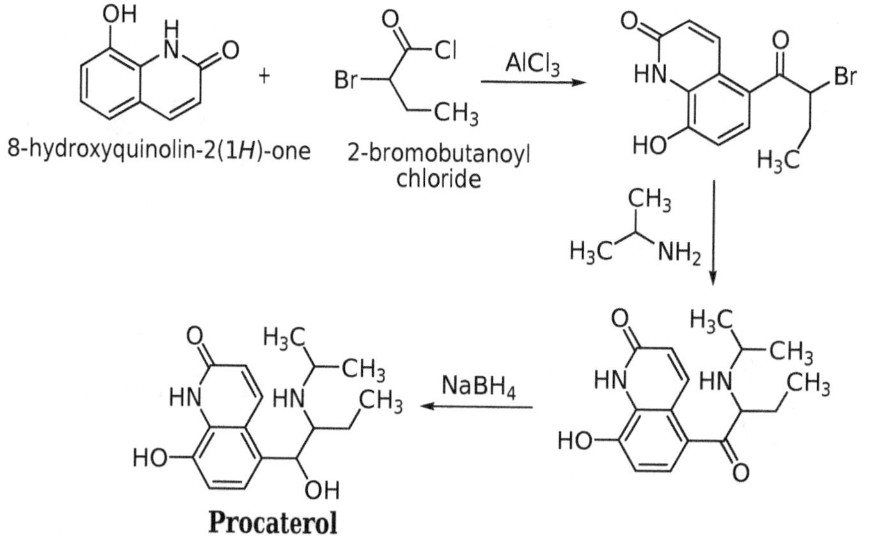

8-hydroxyquinolin-2(1H)-one + 2-bromobutanoyl chloride $\xrightarrow{AlCl_3}$ [intermediate] $\xrightarrow{H_3C-CH(NH_2)-CH_3}$ [amino ketone] $\xrightarrow{NaBH_4}$ **Procaterol**

propan-2-amine

PROCHLORPERAZINE

Use: antiemetic

Analysis:

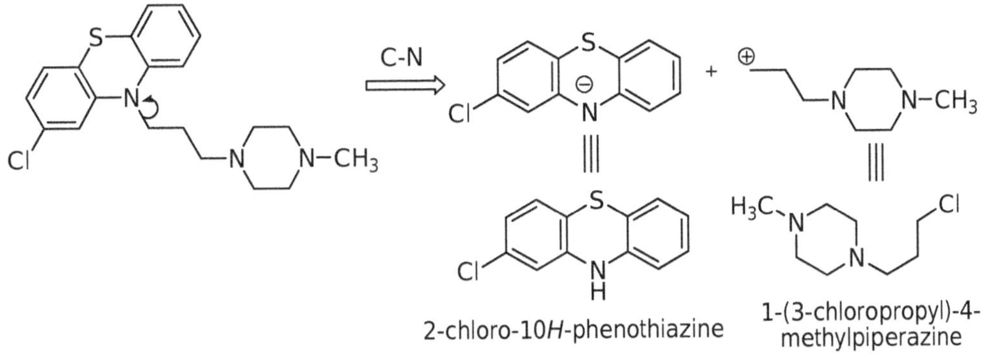

[Retrosynthetic analysis showing prochlorperazine disconnected at C-N bond to give 2-chloro-10H-phenothiazine and 1-(3-chloropropyl)-4-methylpiperazine]

Synthesis:

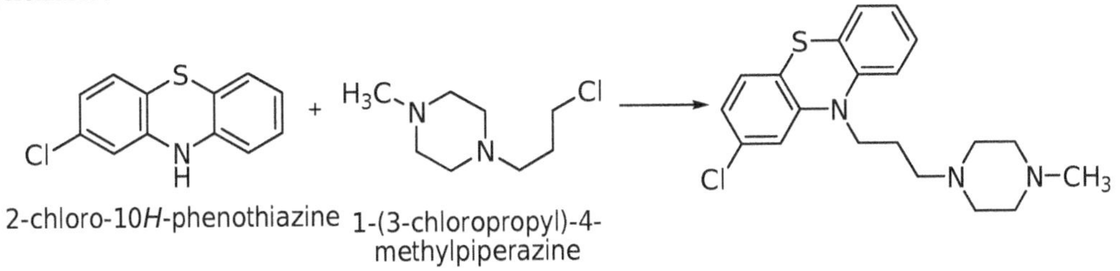

2-chloro-10H-phenothiazine + 1-(3-chloropropyl)-4-methylpiperazine → Prochlorperazine

PROMAZINE

Use: neroleptic, antiemetic

Analysis:

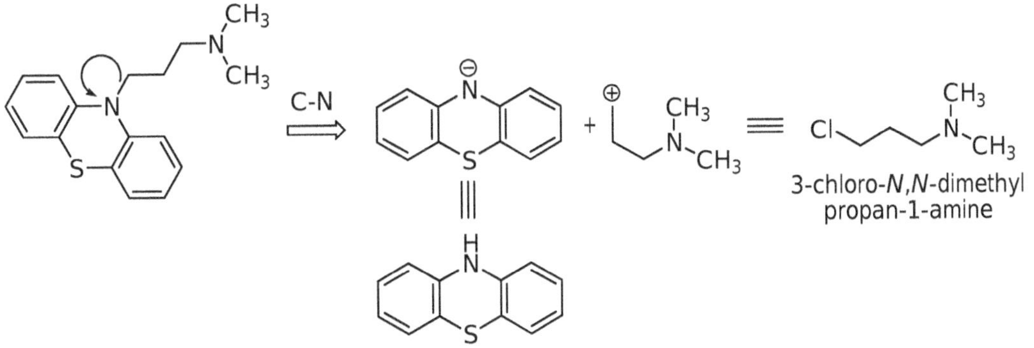

[Retrosynthetic analysis showing promazine disconnected at C-N bond to give 10H-phenothiazine and 3-chloro-N,N-dimethylpropan-1-amine]

Synthesis:

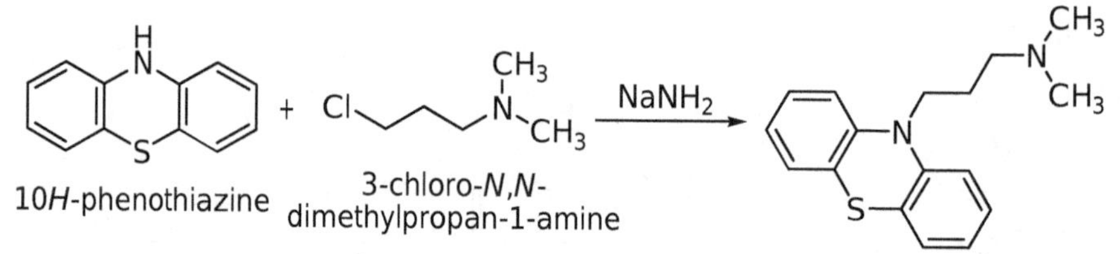

10H-phenothiazine + 3-chloro-N,N-dimethylpropan-1-amine →[NaNH₂] **Promazine**

PROPAFENONE
Use: antiarrhythmic

Analysis:

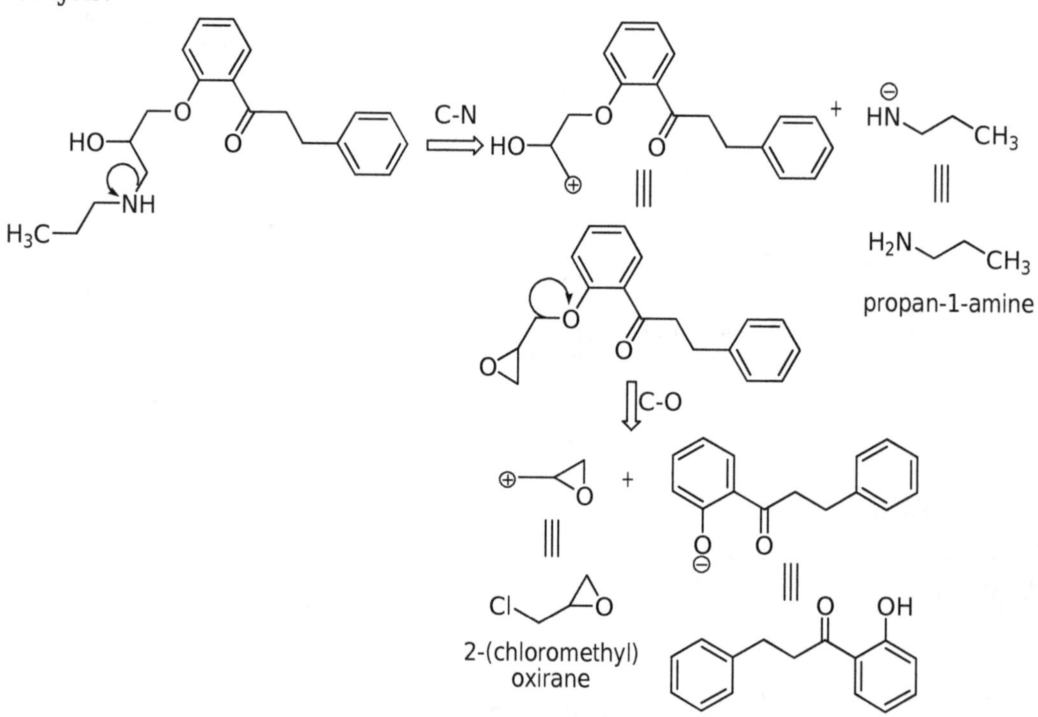

C-N ⟹ ... + propan-1-amine

⇓ C-O

2-(chloromethyl)oxirane + ...

Synthesis:

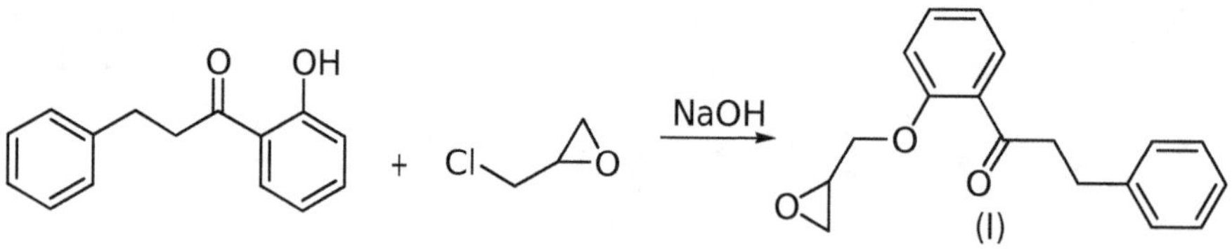

[2'-hydroxyphenyl 3-phenylpropyl ketone] + Cl–CH₂–(oxirane) →[NaOH] (I)

(I)
H2N
CH3
HO
O
O
NH
H3C

Propafenone

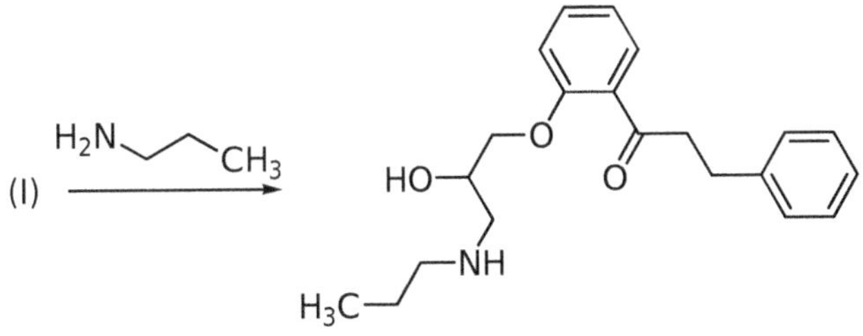

PROPALLYLONAL

Use: hypnotic

Analysis:

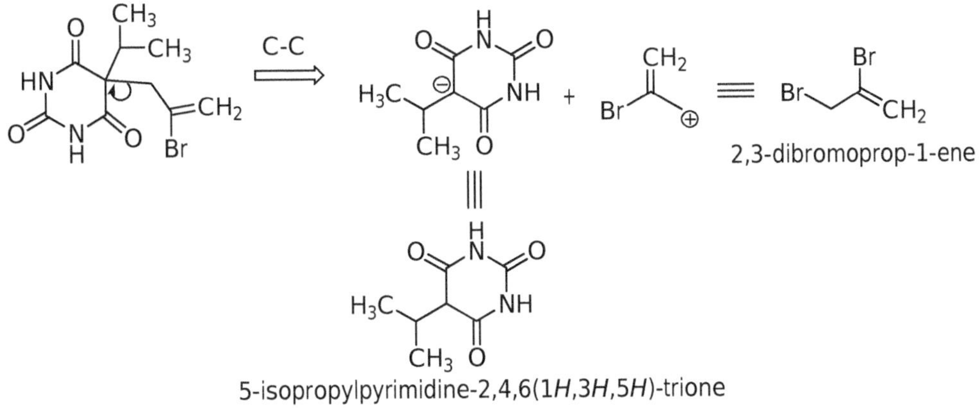

C-C
2,3-dibromoprop-1-ene
5-isopropylpyrimidine-2,4,6(1*H*,3*H*,5*H*)-trione

Synthesis:

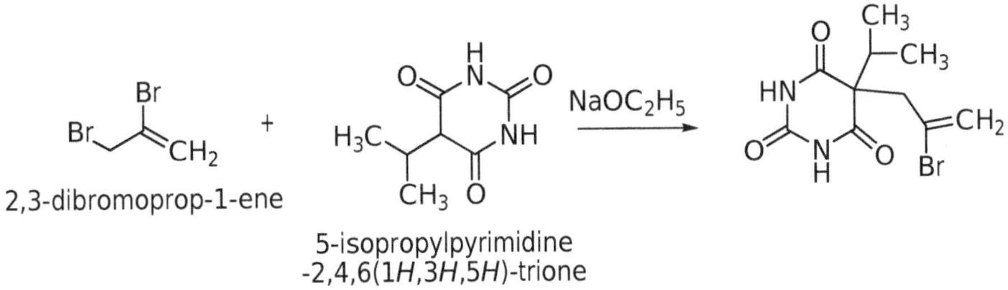

2,3-dibromoprop-1-ene
NaOC2H5
5-isopropylpyrimidine
-2,4,6(1*H*,3*H*,5*H*)-trione

Propallylonal

PROPANIDID
Use: anaesthetic
Analysis:

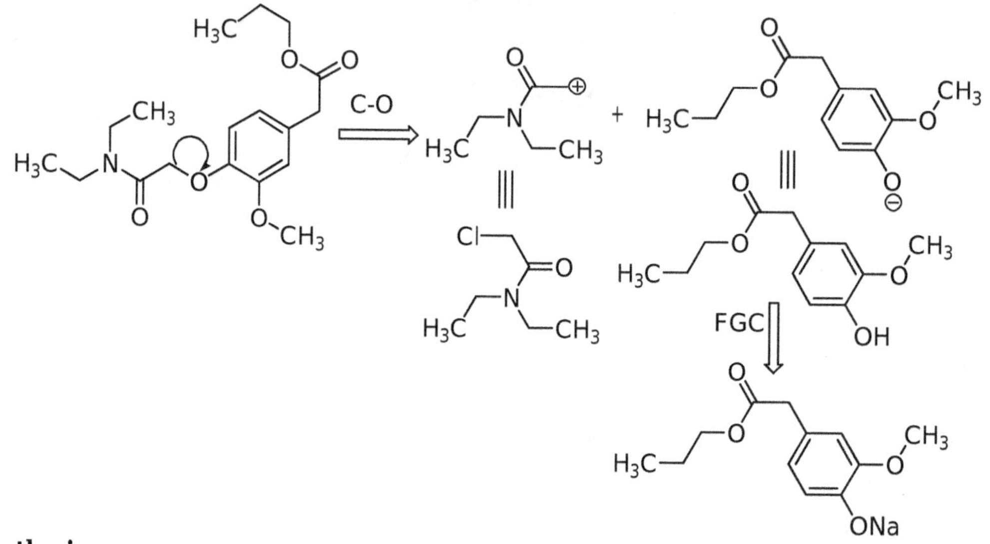

[Retrosynthetic analysis scheme showing C-O disconnection of propanidid into 2-chloro-N,N-diethylacetamide and the sodium phenoxide of propyl (4-hydroxy-3-methoxyphenyl)acetate, with FGC from the corresponding phenol.]

Synthesis:

[Scheme: sodium phenoxide of propyl (4-hydroxy-3-methoxyphenyl)acetate + 2-chloro-N,N-diethylacetamide → Propanidid]

2-chloro-N,N-diethyl acetamide

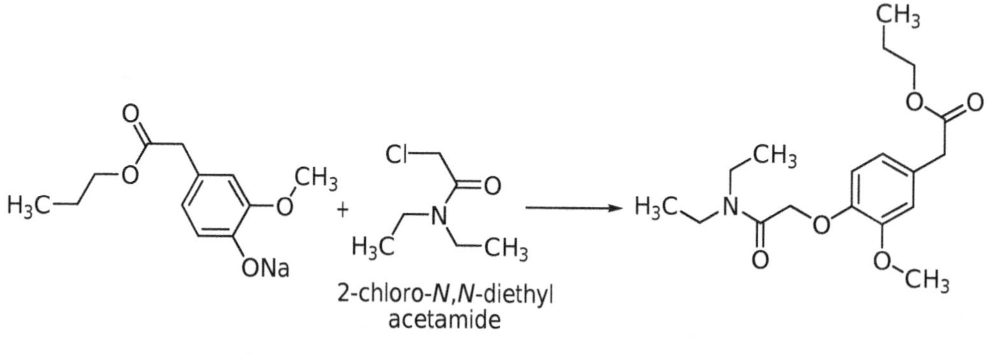

Propanidid

PROPICILLIN
Use: antibiotic
Analysis:

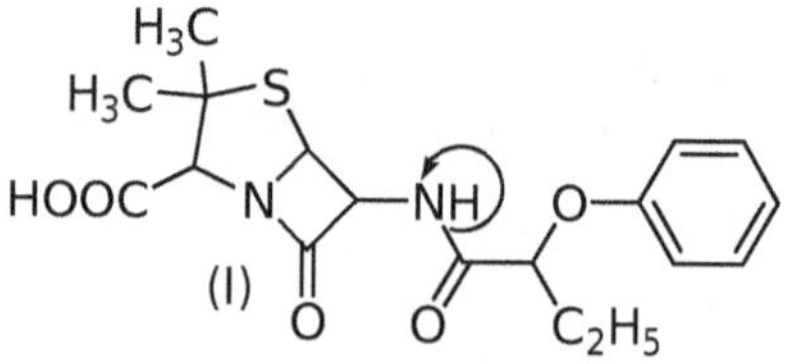

[Structure (I) of propicillin showing the penicillin nucleus with a 2-phenoxybutanamide side chain, with disconnection arrow at the NH amide bond.]

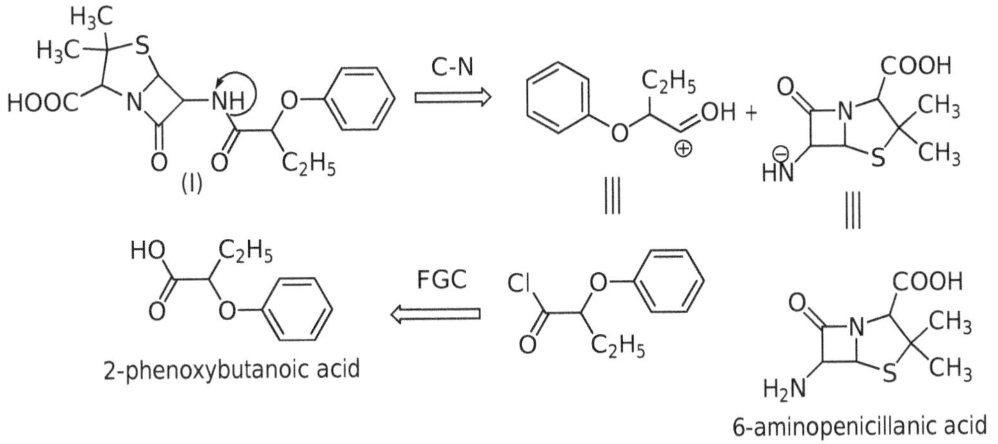

Retrosynthetic Analysis and Synthesis of Drugs

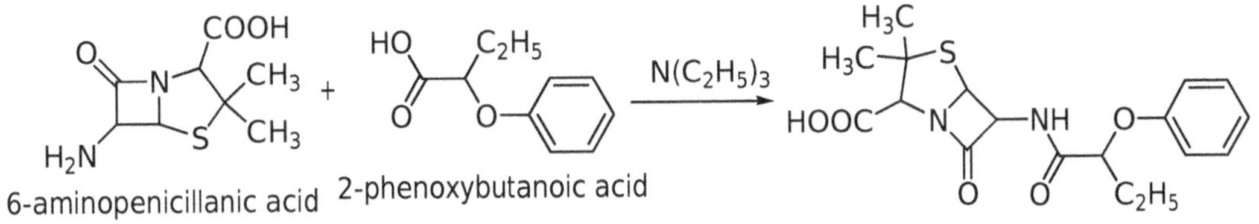

Synthesis:

6-aminopenicillanic acid + 2-phenoxybutanoic acid $\xrightarrow{N(C_2H_5)_3}$ **Propicillin**

PROPIRAM

Use: analgesic

Analysis:

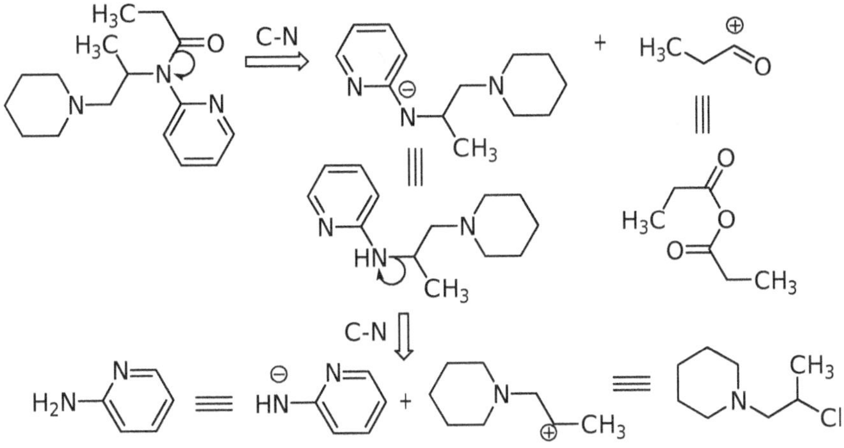

Synthesis:

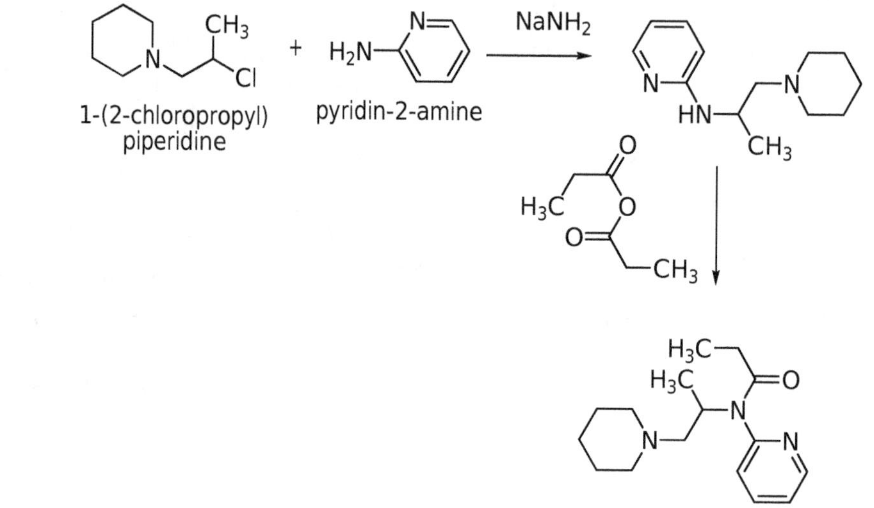

[Reaction scheme: 1-(2-chloropropyl)piperidine + pyridin-2-amine, NaNH₂ → intermediate, then propionic anhydride → propiverine]

1-(2-chloropropyl)piperidine + pyridin-2-amine

PROPIVERINE
Use: anticholinergic

Analysis:

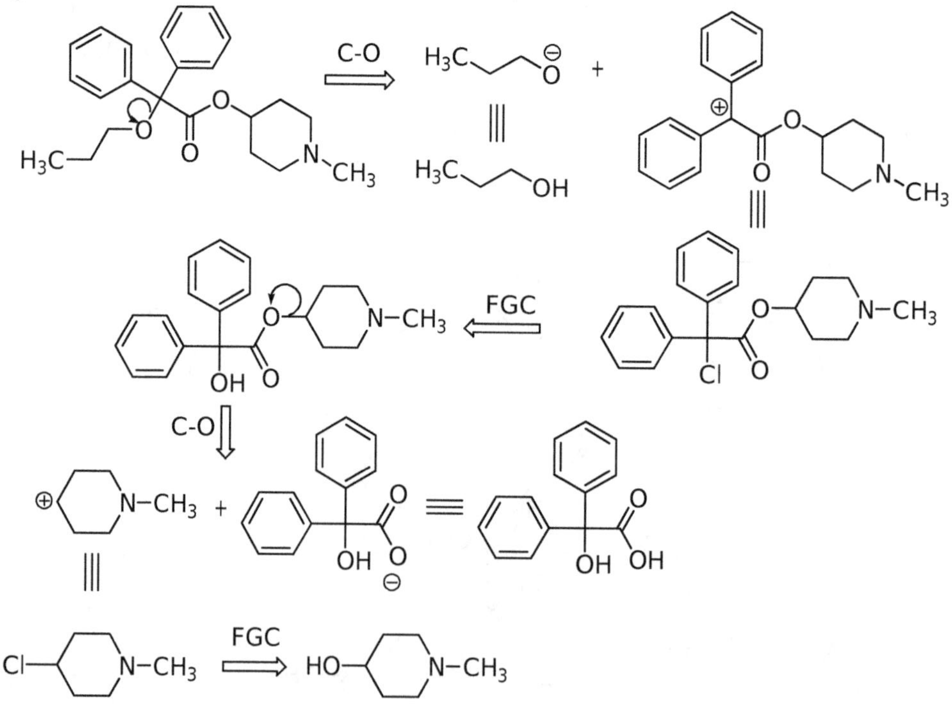

[Retrosynthetic analysis scheme showing C-O disconnection to propoxide + cation, FGC to chloride, C-O disconnection to N-methylpiperidine cation + benzilic acid, and FGC from 4-chloro-N-methylpiperidine to 4-hydroxy-N-methylpiperidine]

Synthesis:

[Scheme: 1-methylpiperidin-4-ol → (SOCl₂) → 4-chloro-1-methylpiperidine → (benzillic acid) → diphenyl(hydroxy)acetate ester of 1-methylpiperidin-4-ol → (SOCl₂) → chloro intermediate → (propan-1-ol) → **Propiverine**]

PROPRANOLOL

Use: β-blocker

Analysis:

[Retrosynthetic scheme showing propranolol disconnected via C–N to give naphthyloxy epoxide intermediate + isopropylamine; further C–O disconnection to naphthoxide + 2-(chloromethyl)oxirane; naphthoxide ≡ 1-naphthol]

2-(chloromethyl)oxirane

Synthesis:

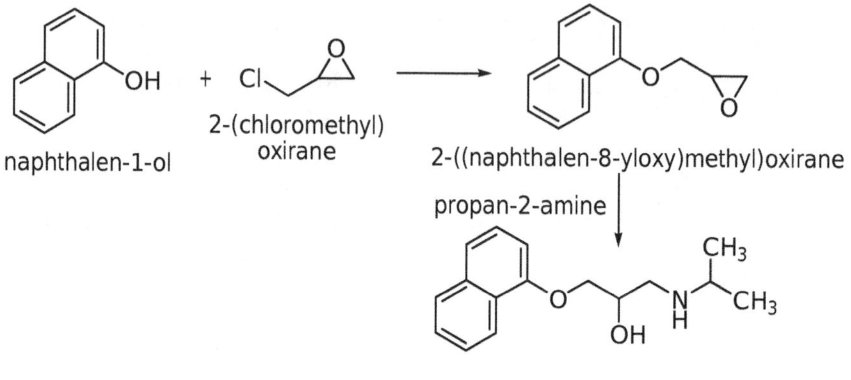

naphthalen-1-ol + 2-(chloromethyl)oxirane → 2-((naphthalen-8-yloxy)methyl)oxirane

propan-2-amine ↓

Propranolol

PROPYTHIOURACIL

Use: antithyroid agent

Analysis:

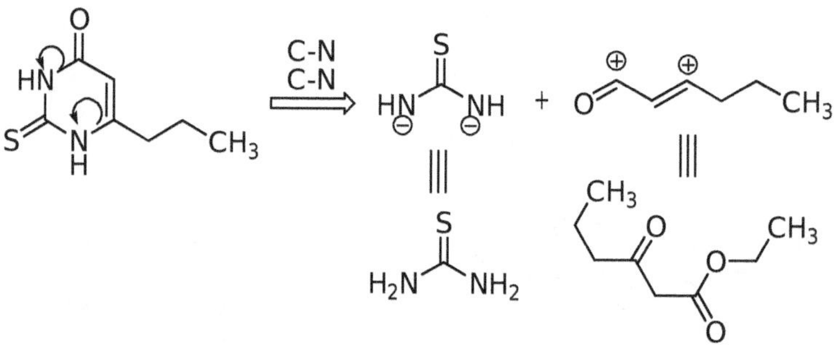

Propythiouracil ⟹ (C-N, C-N disconnection) thiourea + oxocarbenium synthon

≡ $H_2N-C(=S)-NH_2$ (thiourea) and ethyl 3-oxohexanoate

Synthesis:

ethyl 3-oxohexanoate + thiourea $\xrightarrow{NaOC_2H_5}$ **Propythiouracil**

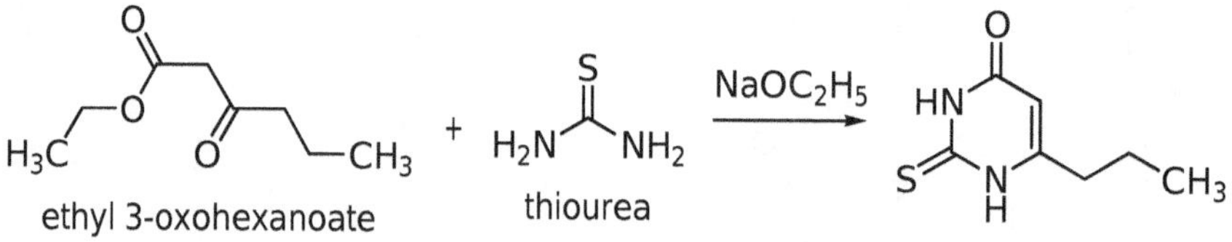

PROTHIPENDYL
Use: psychosedative, neuroleptic
Analysis:

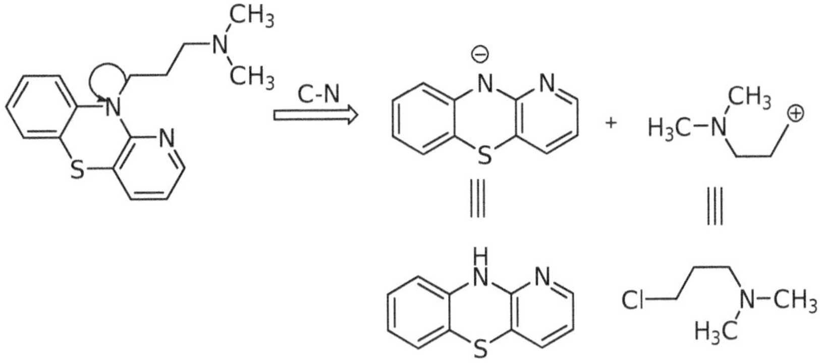

Synthesis:

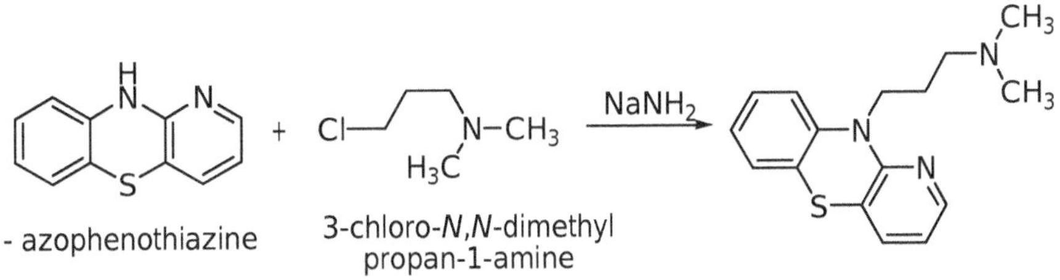

1 - azophenothiazine + 3-chloro-N,N-dimethyl propan-1-amine → (NaNH₂) **Prothipendyl**

PROTOKYLOL
Use: bronchodilator
Analysis:

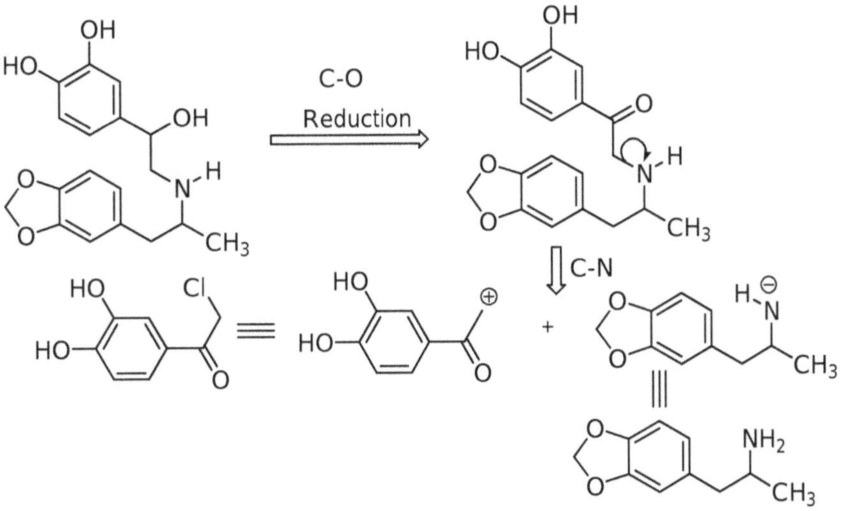

Synthesis:

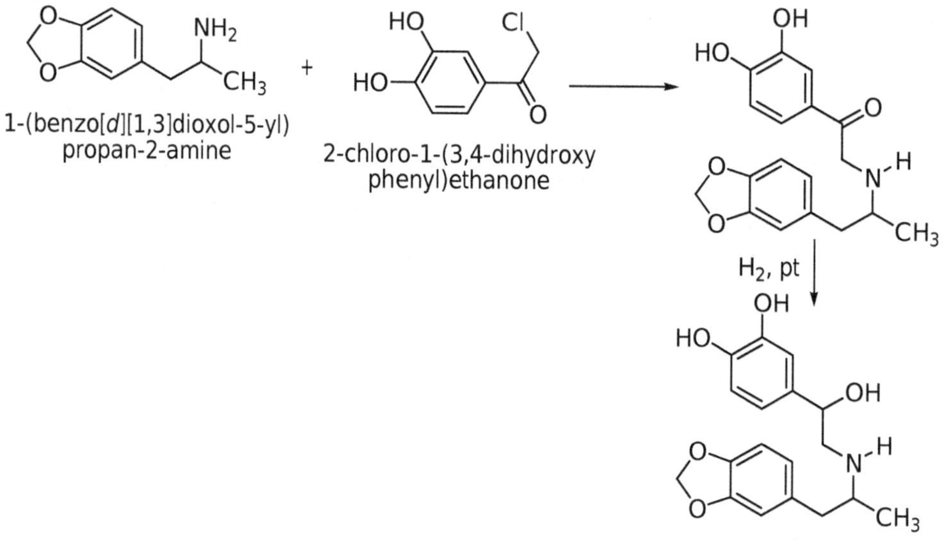

[Structure: 1-(benzo[d][1,3]dioxol-5-yl)propan-2-amine] + [Structure: 2-chloro-1-(3,4-dihydroxyphenyl)ethanone] → [Intermediate ketoamine]

H_2, pt ↓

Protokylol

PROXYPHYLLINE
Use: cardiotonic, bronchodilator

Analysis:

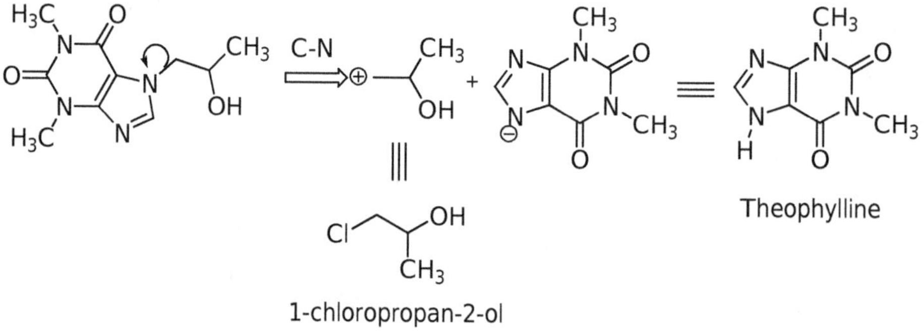

[Proxyphylline structure] ⟹ [cation with CH₃ and OH] + [Theophylline anion] ≡ **Theophylline**

||

[1-chloropropan-2-ol structure]

1-chloropropan-2-ol

Synthesis:

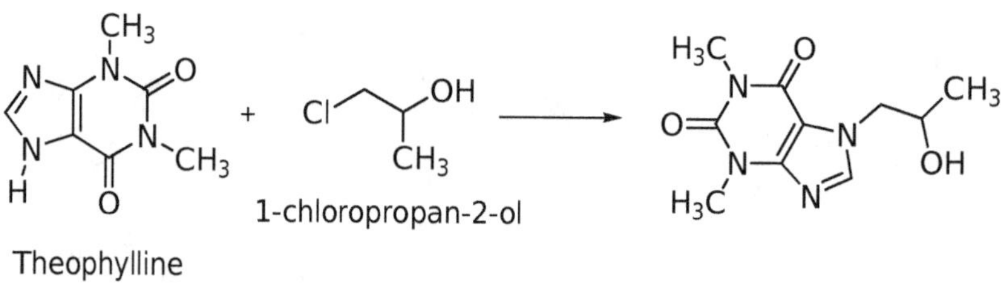

Theophylline + 1-chloropropan-2-ol → **Proxyphylline**

PYRAZINAMIDE

Use: tuberculostatic

Analysis:

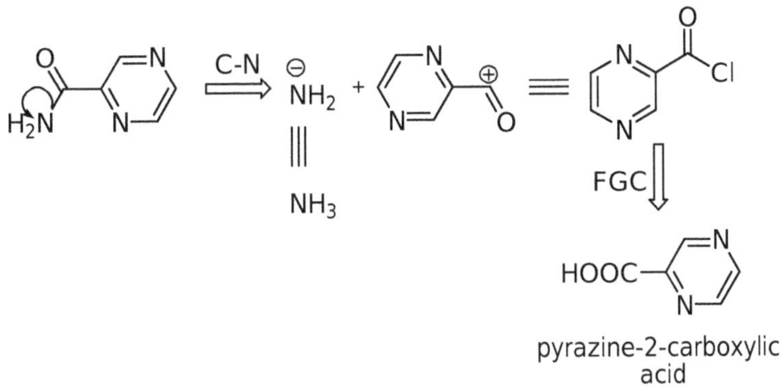

Synthesis:

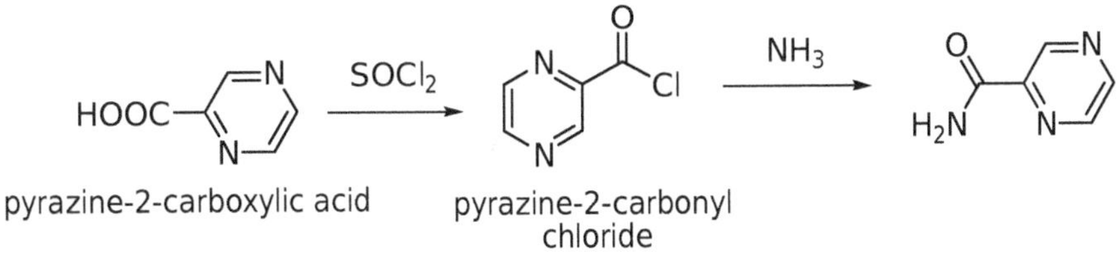

pyrazine-2-carboxylic acid → (SOCl$_2$) → pyrazine-2-carbonyl chloride → (NH$_3$) → **Pyrazinamide**

PYRIDINOL CARBAMATE

Use: antiarteriosclerotic

Analysis:

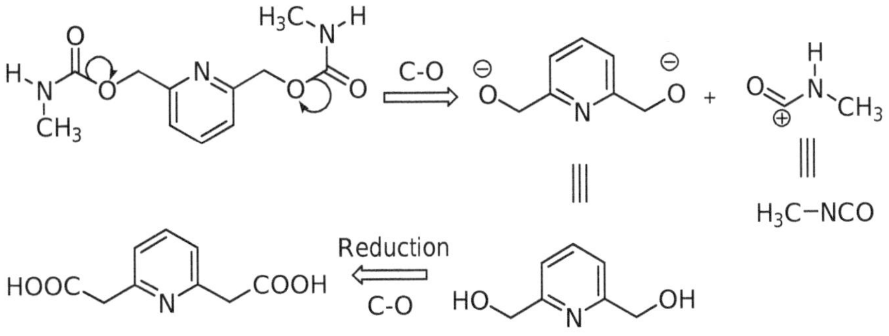

Synthesis:

Dipicolinic acid → (NaBH₄) → 2,6-bis(hydroxymethyl)pyridine → (H₃C-NCO) → **Pyridinol carbamate**

PYRIDOSTIGMINE BROMIDE

Use: parasympathomimetic

Analysis:

Pyridostigmine bromide ⇒ (C-N disconnection) pyridin-3-yl dimethylcarbamate + CH₃Br (≡ H₃C-Br)

⇓ (C-O disconnection)

pyridin-3-ol (≡ pyridin-3-olate) + dimethylcarbamoyl cation (≡ H₃C-N(CH₃)-C(O)Cl, dimethylcarbamic chloride)

Synthesis:

pyridin-3-ol + dimethylcarbamic chloride → pyridin-3-yl dimethylcarbamate

↓ CH₃Br

Pyridostigmine bromide

PYRROCAINE

Use: local anaesthetic

Analysis:

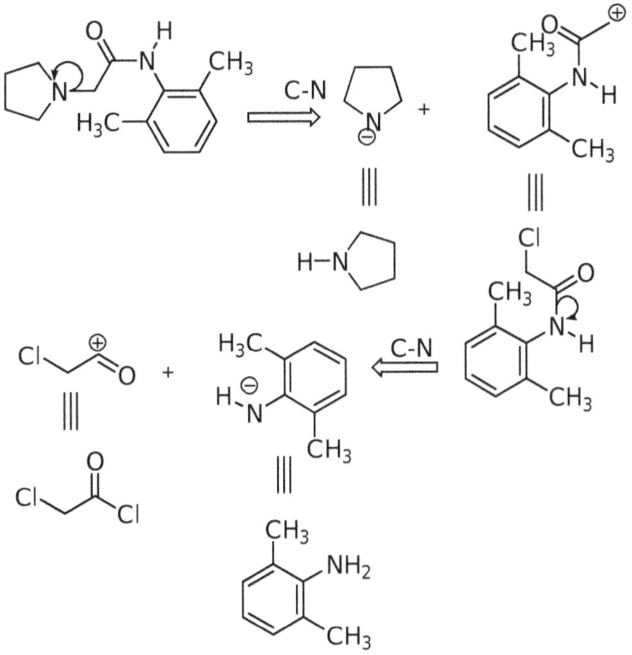

Synthesis:

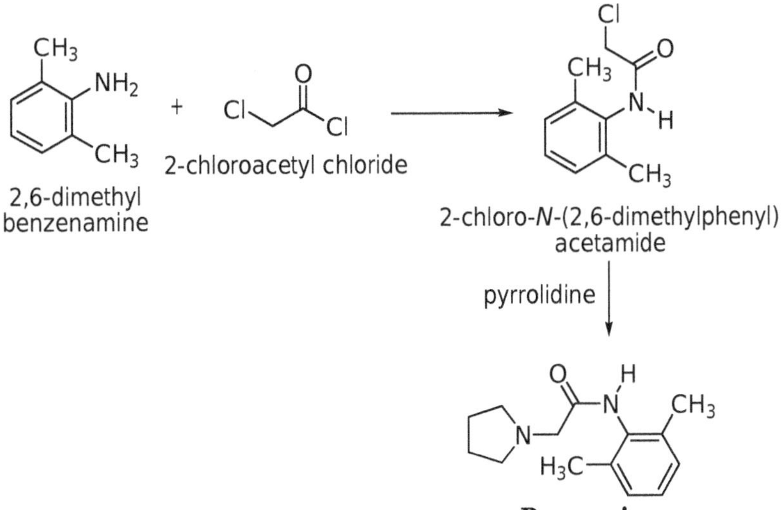

2,6-dimethyl benzenamine + 2-chloroacetyl chloride → 2-chloro-*N*-(2,6-dimethylphenyl)acetamide

↓ pyrrolidine

Pyrrocaine

RANITIDINE

Use: peptic ulcer therapeutic

Analysis:

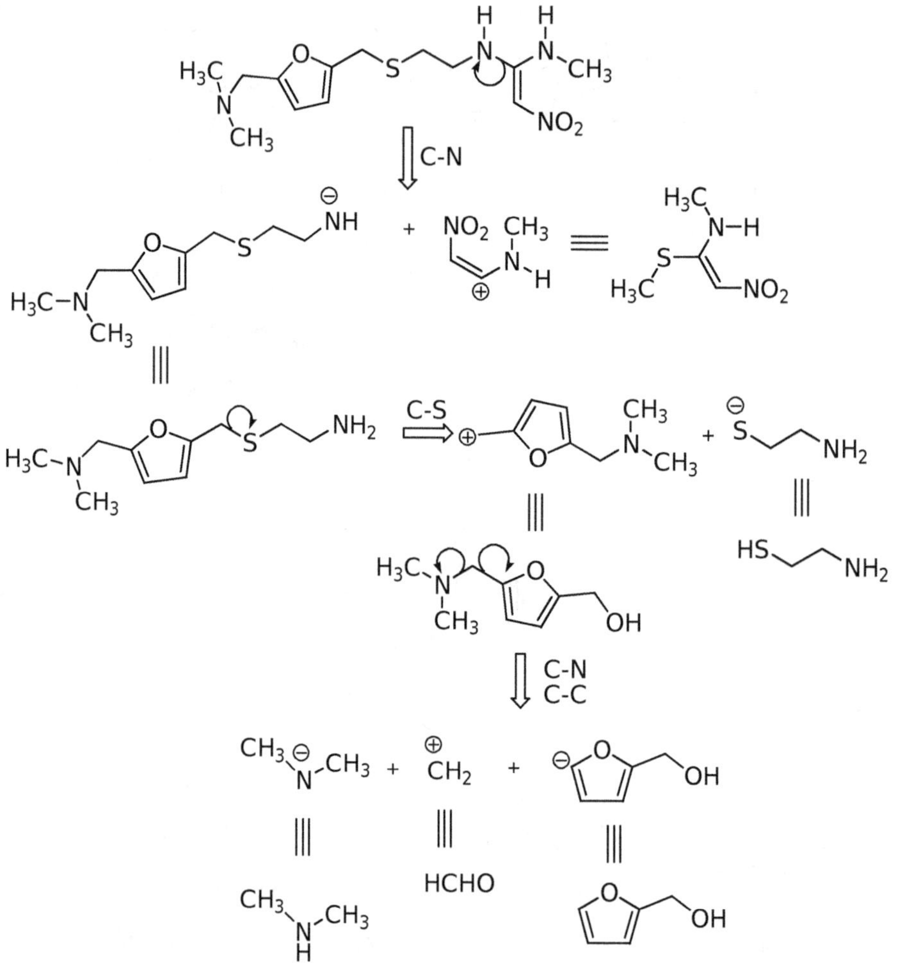

Synthesis:

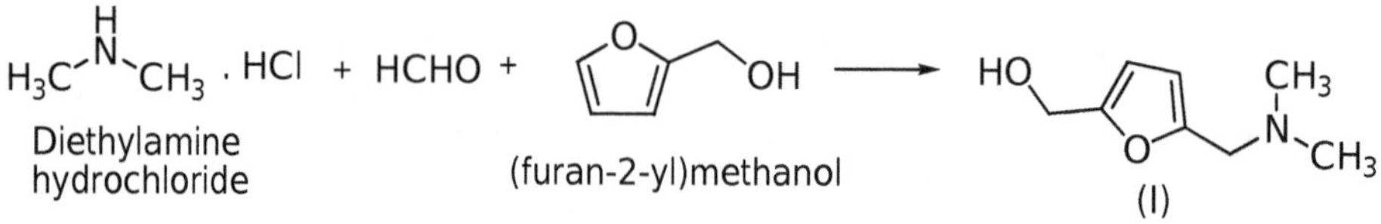

H₃C-NH-CH₃ · HCl + HCHO + (furan-2-yl)methanol ⟶ (I)

Diethylamine hydrochloride

REMOXIPRIDE
Use: neuroleptic
Analysis:

Synthesis:

[Scheme: 2,6-dimethoxybenzoic acid → (Br) → 3-bromo-2,6-dimethoxybenzoic acid → (SOCl₂) → acid chloride → (H₂N-CH₂-pyrrolidine-N-C₂H₅) → **Remoxipride**]

RILMENIDINE
Use: antihypertensive

Analysis:

[Retrosynthetic scheme: oxazoline of rilmenidine ⇒ (C-O) open-chain cation ≡ chloroethyl urea ⇒ (C-N) 1-chloro-2-isocyanatoethane + dicyclopropylmethylamine]

Synthesis:

[Scheme: dicyclopropylmethylamine + 1-chloro-2-isocyanatoethane (THF) → 1-(2-chloroethyl)-3-(dicyclopropylmethyl)urea → (Δ) → **Rilmenidine**]

ROSIGLITAZONE
Use: antidiabetic
Analysis:

Synthesis:

[Scheme showing synthesis of Rosiglitazone:
- 2-chloropyridine + 2-(methylamino)ethanol → 2-(N-methyl-N-(pyridin-2-yl)amino)ethanol (120°C)
- + 4-fluorobenzaldehyde, NaH, DMF → aldehyde intermediate
- + thiazolidine-2,4-dione, pyridine, CH₃COOH, toluene → arylidene intermediate
- Mg, I₂, CH₃OH → **Rosiglitazone**]

SALACETAMIDE

Use: antipyretic, antirheumatic

Analysis:

[Retrosynthetic scheme: salacetamide → C-N disconnection → acetyl cation (≡ acetic anhydride) + 2-hydroxybenzamide]

Retrosynthetic Analysis and Synthesis of Drugs

Synthesis:

acetic anhydried + 2-hydroxybenzamide →(NaOH) **Salacetamide**

SALMETEROL

Use: β-adrenoreceptor agonist

Analysis:

[Retrosynthetic scheme: Salmeterol undergoes C–N disconnection to give a phenethanolamine synthon (with HO, HOCH₂ on ring, and OH, CH₂NH⁻) plus a cationic ether chain synthon. Equivalents: the amine fragment corresponds to the aminoethanol-catechol derivative (NH₂, OH, CH₂OH, OH on ring), and the cation equivalent corresponds to Br-(CH₂)₆-O-(CH₂)₄-Ph. Further C–O disconnection gives 1,6-dibromohexane and 4-phenylbutan-1-ol.]

1,6-dibromohexane

4-phenylbutan-1-ol

Synthesis:

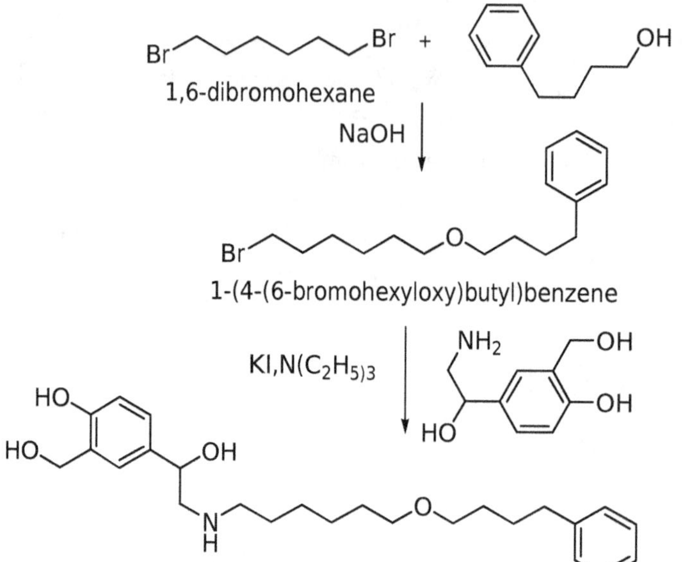

1,6-dibromohexane + 4-phenylbutan-1-ol →(NaOH) 1-(4-(6-bromohexyloxy)butyl)benzene →(KI, N(C₂H₅)₃, with 2-amino-1-(3-(hydroxymethyl)-4-hydroxyphenyl)ethanol) **Salmeterol**

SECNIDAZOLE

Use: amoebicide

Analysis:

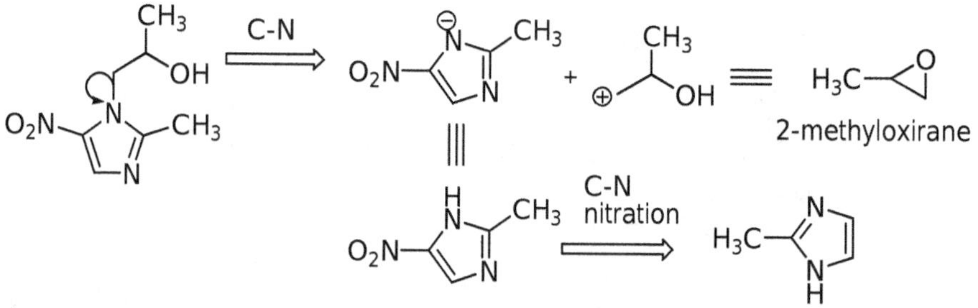

Secnidazole ⇒(C–N) 2-methyl-5-nitro-1H-imidazole anion + protonated 1-hydroxyethyl cation ≡ 2-methyloxirane (H_3C–oxirane)

2-methyl-5-nitro-1H-imidazole ⇒(C–N nitration) 2-methyl-1H-imidazole

Synthesis:

2-methyl-1H-imidazole →(H_2SO_4, HNO_3) 2-methyl-5-nitro-1H-imidazole →(2-methyloxirane, HCOOH) **Secnidazole**

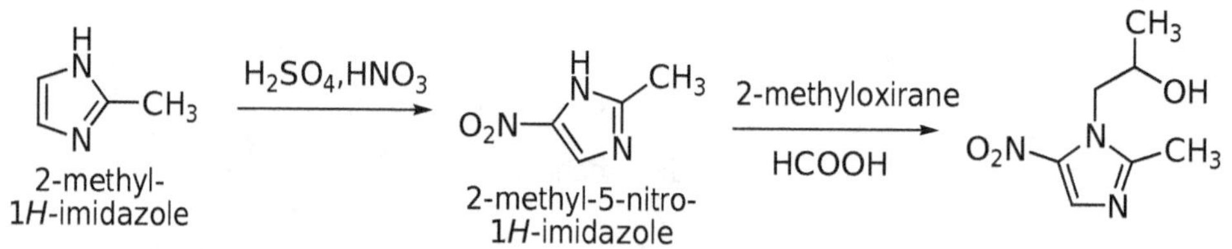

SECOBARBITAL

Use: hypnotics

Analysis:

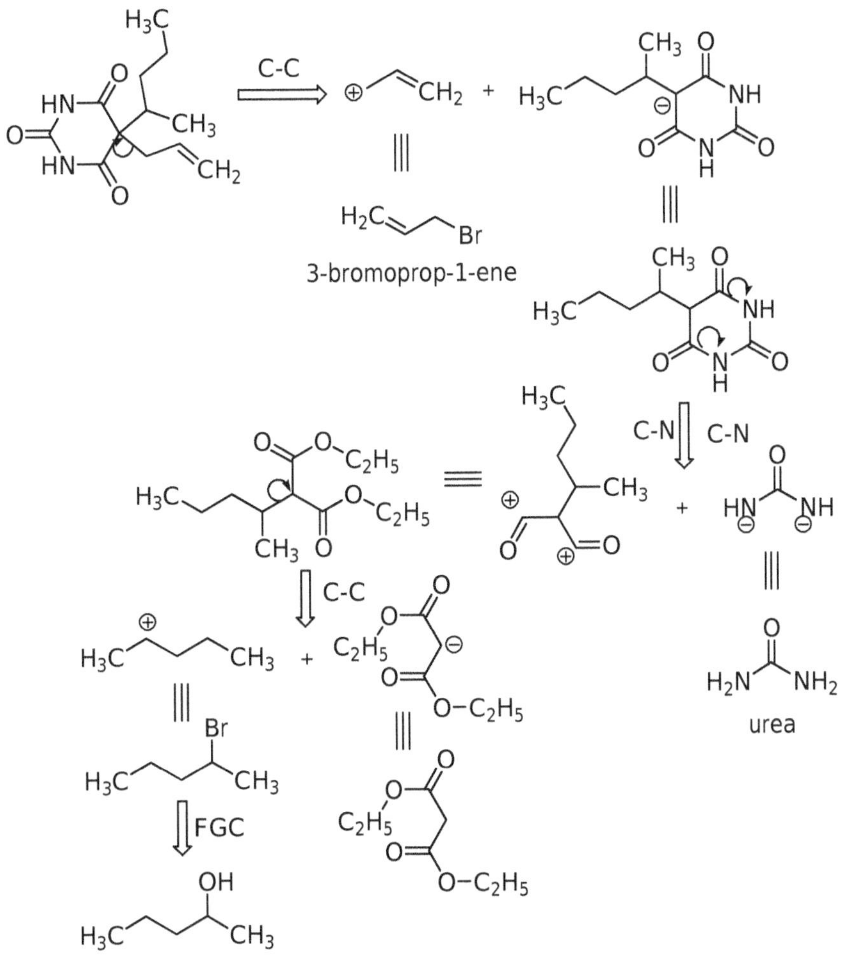

Synthesis:

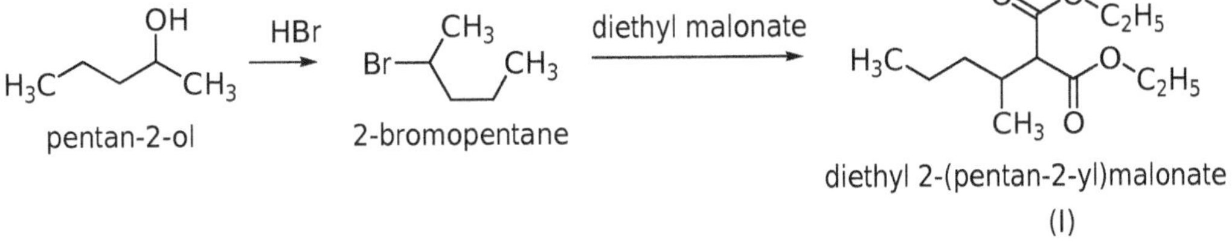

pentan-2-ol → (HBr) → 2-bromopentane → (diethyl malonate) → diethyl 2-(pentan-2-yl)malonate (I)

SERTACONAZOLE
Use: antifungal
Analysis:

Synthesis:

[Synthesis scheme for Sertaconazole: 2-chlorothiophenol + 1-chloropropan-2-one → 1-(2-chlorophenylthio)propan-2-one → (phosphoric acid) → 3-methyl-7-chlorobenzothiophene → (N-bromosuccinamide) → 3-bromomethyl-7-chlorobenzothiophene → (1-(2,4-dichlorophenyl)-2-(1H-imidazol-1-yl)ethanol) → **Sertaconazole**]

SOTALOL

Use: β-blocker, antihypertensive, antianginal

Analysis:

[Retrosynthetic analysis of Sotalol: C-O reduction of alcohol to ketone; C-N disconnection giving 4-(methanesulfonamido)-α-bromoacetophenone + propan-2-amine; C-C disconnection giving bromoacetyl bromide + methanesulfonanilide; S-N disconnection giving methanesulfonyl chloride + aniline]

propan-2-amine

Retrosynthetic Analysis and Synthesis of Drugs

Synthesis:

methanesulfonyl chloride + aniline → N-phenyl methanesulfonamide

→ (AlCl₃, CS₂, BrCH₂COBr) → 2-bromo-1-[4-(methanesulfonamido)phenyl]ethan-1-one

→ (H₂N-iPr) → 1-[4-(methanesulfonamido)phenyl]-2-(isopropylamino)ethan-1-one

→ (NaBH₄) → **Sotalol**

SPIPERONE
Use: neuroleptic
Analysis:

Spiperone ⇒ (C-N disconnection) → 4-fluorophenyl propan-1-one cation + spiro piperidine-imidazolidinone anion

≡ 4-chloro-1-(4-fluorophenyl)butan-1-one

≡ 1-phenyl-1,3,8-triazaspiro[4.5]decan-4-one

Synthesis:

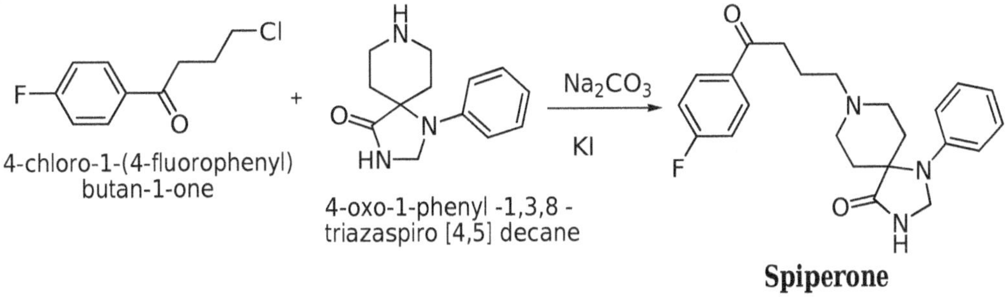

4-chloro-1-(4-fluorophenyl)butan-1-one + 4-oxo-1-phenyl-1,3,8-triazaspiro[4,5]decane $\xrightarrow{\text{Na}_2\text{CO}_3, \text{KI}}$ **Spiperone**

STEPRONIN

Use: hepatic protectant

Analysis:

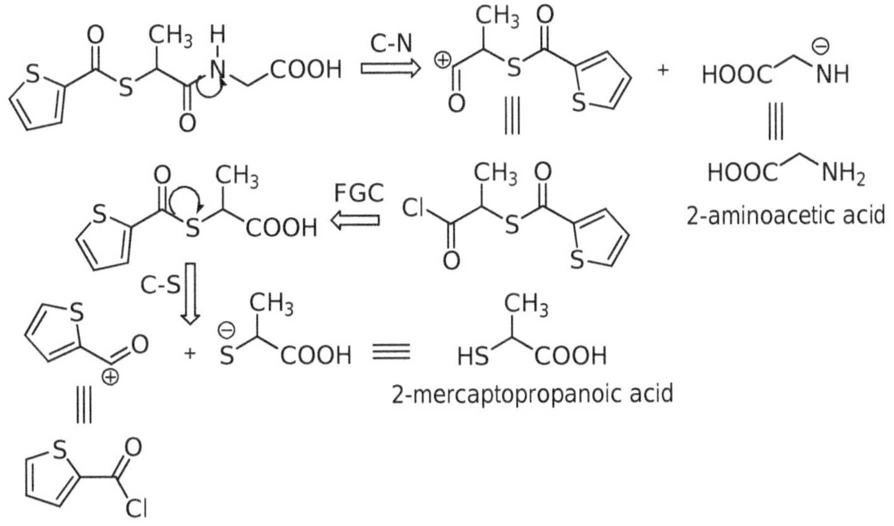

C-N disconnection gives acyl cation intermediate + HOOC-CH-NH⁻ ≡ HOOC-CH₂-NH₂ (2-aminoacetic acid)

FGC: acid chloride precursor

C-S disconnection: thiophene-2-carbonyl cation ≡ thiophene-2-carbonyl chloride + 2-mercaptopropanoic acid (HS-CH(CH₃)-COOH)

Synthesis:

thiophene-2-carbonyl chloride + 2-mercaptopropanoic acid (HS-CH(CH₃)-COOH) $\xrightarrow{\text{K}_2\text{CO}_3}$ thioester intermediate

Then: 2-aminoacetic acid, $SOCl_2$ → **Stepronin**

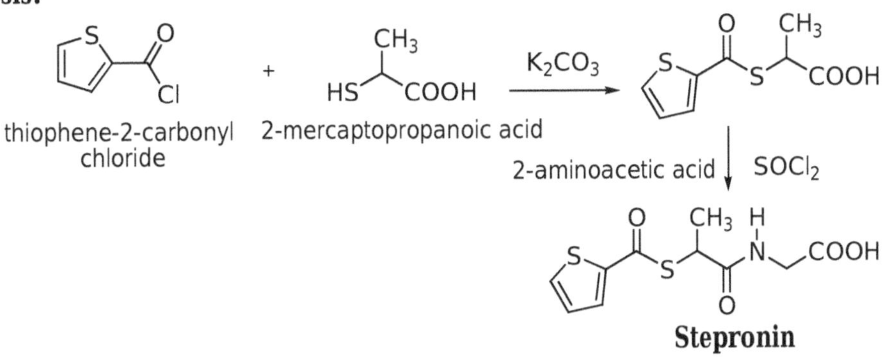

STYRAMATE
Use: muscle relaxant
Analysis:

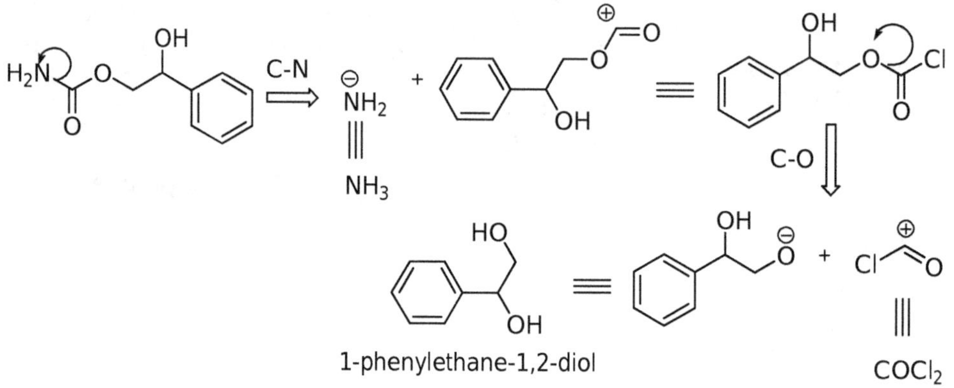

[Retrosynthetic analysis scheme: Styramate (H₂N-C(O)-O-CH₂-CH(OH)-Ph) is disconnected via C-N to give NH₂⁻ (≡ NH₃) + acyl cation intermediate (≡ 1-phenylethane-1,2-diol + COCl₂/phosgene) through C-O disconnection.]

Synthesis:

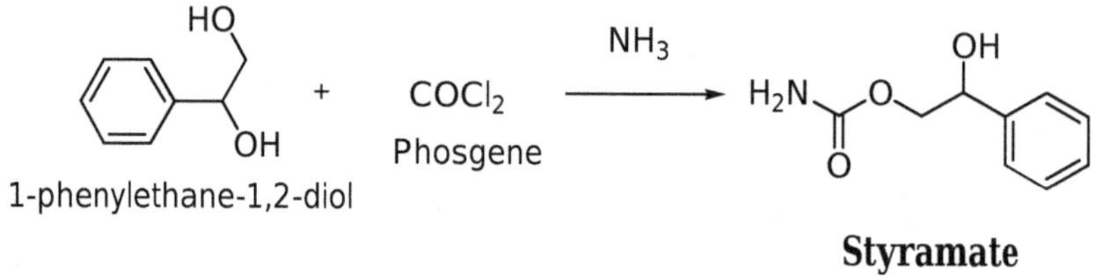

1-phenylethane-1,2-diol + COCl₂ (Phosgene) + NH₃ → Styramate (H₂N-C(O)-O-CH₂-CH(OH)-Ph)

SUCCINYLSULFATHIAZOLE
Use: antibacterial
Analysis:

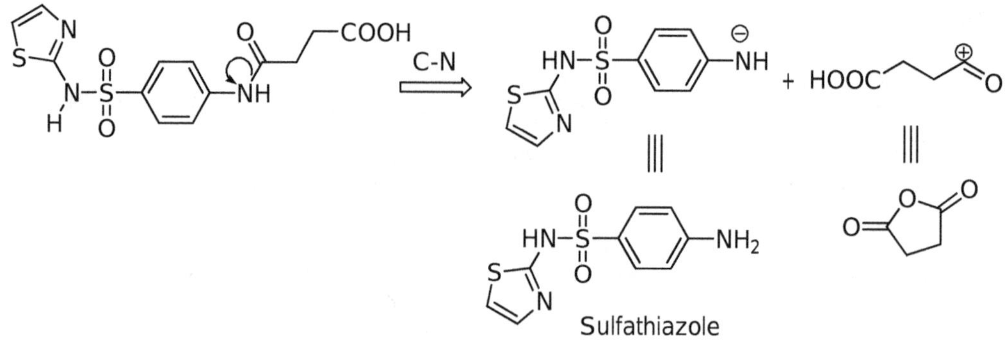

[Retrosynthetic analysis: Succinylsulfathiazole is disconnected via C-N to give sulfathiazole anion (≡ Sulfathiazole) + succinic acid acyl cation (≡ succinic anhydride).]

Synthesis:

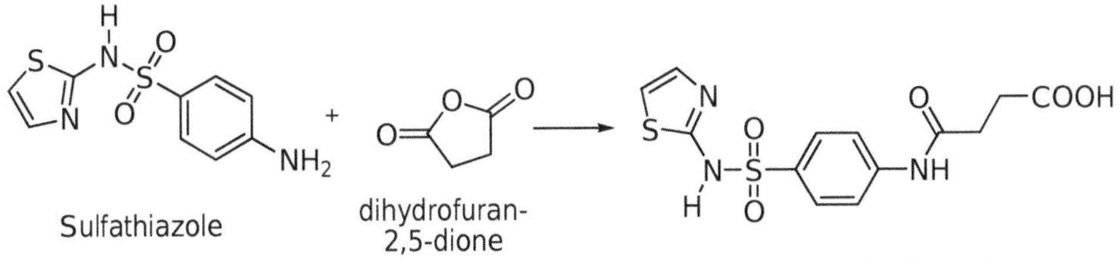

Sulfathiazole + dihydrofuran-2,5-dione → Succinylsulfathiazole

SULFACETAMIDE

Use: antibacterial

Analysis:

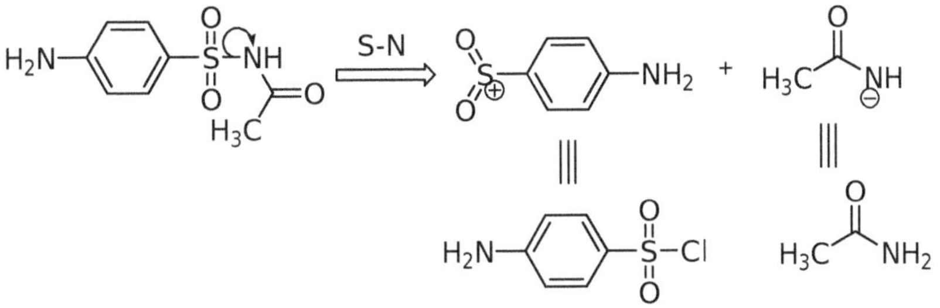

Sulfacetamide ⇒ (S-N disconnection) 4-aminobenzenesulfonyl cation + acetamide anion
≡ 4-aminobenzenesulfonyl chloride + acetamide

Synthesis:

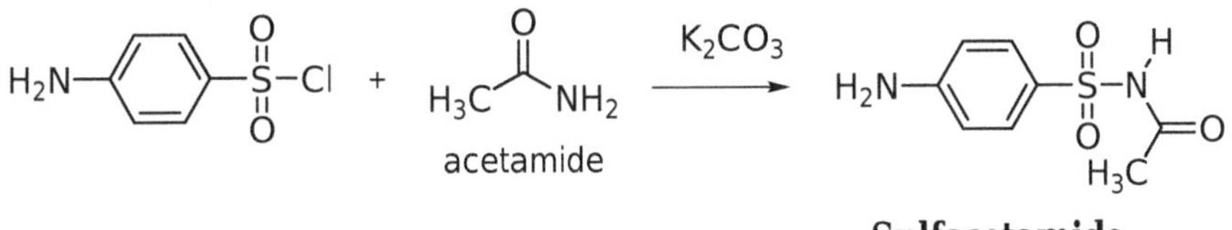

4-aminobenzenesulfonyl chloride + acetamide $\xrightarrow{K_2CO_3}$ Sulfacetamide

SULFACHLORPYRIDAZINE

Use: antibacterial

Analysis:

Sulfachlorpyridazine ⇒ (C-N disconnection) sulfanilamide anion + 3-chloropyridazinyl cation
≡ sulfanilamide + 3,6-dichloropyridazine

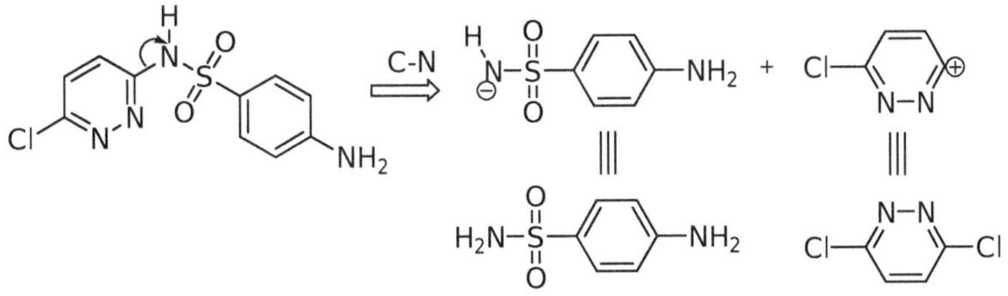

Synthesis:

[Scheme: 4-aminobenzene sulfonamide + 3,6-dichloropyridazine → (K₂CO₃) → Sulfachlorpyridazine]

4 - aminobnezene sulfonamide + 3,6-dichloropyridazine → **Sulfachlorpyridazine**

SULFADIAZINE

Use: chemotherapeutic

Analysis:

[Retrosynthetic scheme: Sulfadiazine ⟹ (FGC) acetamido-protected sulfadiazine ⟹ (S-N) 4-acetamidobenzenesulfonyl chloride + 2-aminopyrimidine]

Synthesis:

4-acetamidobenzene-1-sulfonyl chloride + pyrimidin-2-amine → acetamido sulfadiazine intermediate → (NaOH) → **Sulfadiazine**

SULFAGUANIDINE

Use: chemotherapeutic

Analysis:

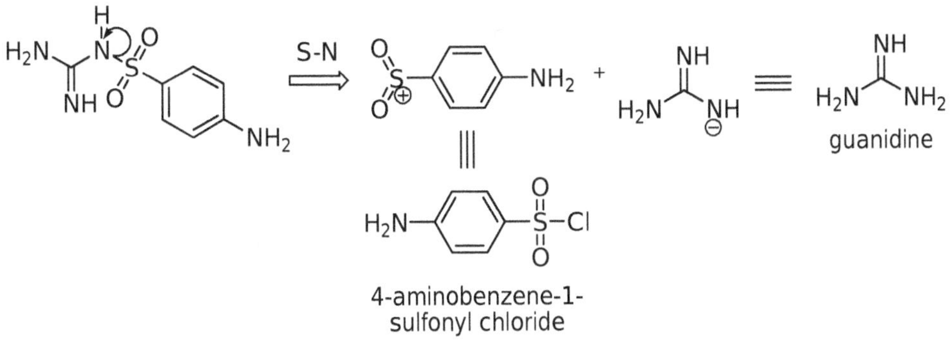

[Retrosynthetic analysis: Sulfaguanidine ⇒ (S-N disconnection) 4-aminobenzenesulfonyl cation + guanidine anion ≡ 4-aminobenzene-1-sulfonyl chloride + guanidine]

4-aminobenzene-1-sulfonyl chloride

guanidine

Synthesis:

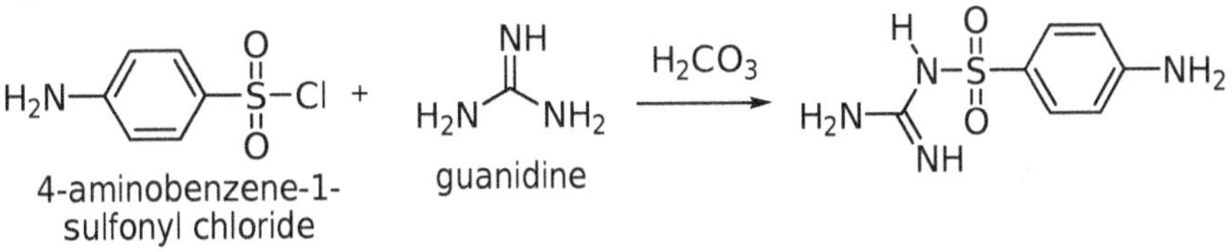

4-aminobenzene-1-sulfonyl chloride + guanidine $\xrightarrow{H_2CO_3}$ **Sulfaguanidine**

SULFAMETHIZOLE

Use: antibacterial

Analysis:

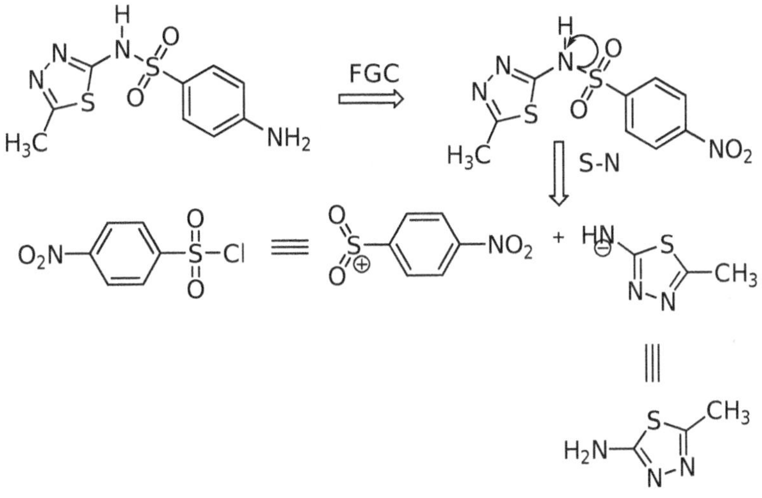

[Retrosynthetic analysis: Sulfamethizole ⇒ (FGC) nitro analog ⇒ (S-N disconnection) 4-nitrobenzenesulfonyl chloride + 2-amino-5-methyl-1,3,4-thiadiazole]

Synthesis:

4-nitrobenzene-1-sulfonyl chloride + 5-methyl-1,3,4-thiadiazol-2-amine → [intermediate with NO₂] → (Fe) → **Sulfamethizole**

SULFAMETHOXAZOLE

Use: chemotherapeutic

Analysis:

[Sulfamethoxazole] ⇒ (FGC) [N-acetyl protected sulfamethoxazole] ⇒ (S-N) [4-acetamidobenzenesulfonyl cation] + [5-methylisoxazol-3-amide anion]

≡ 4-acetamidobenzene-1-sulfonyl chloride   ≡ 5-methylisoxazol-3-amine

Synthesis:

4-acetamidobenzene-1-sulfonyl chloride + 5-methylisoxazol-3-amine → (I)

$$(I) \xrightarrow{\text{NaOH}} \text{H}_3\text{C}\underset{\text{O-N}}{\overset{}{\diagdown}}\text{N}-\overset{\text{H}}{\underset{\text{O}}{\overset{\text{O}}{\text{S}}}}-\text{C}_6\text{H}_4-\text{NH}_2$$

Sulfamethoxazole

TALINOLOL
Use: antihypertensive
Analysis:

[Retrosynthetic analysis scheme for Talinolol showing disconnections]

Starting from Talinolol structure (cyclohexyl-NH-C(=O)-NH-C6H4-O-CH2-CH(OH)-CH2-NH-C(CH3)3):

C-N disconnection gives:
H2N-C6H4-O-CH2-CH(OH)-CH2-NH-C(CH3)3 + cyclohexyl-NH-C(+)=O ≡ cyclohexyl-N=C=O

FGC:
H2N-C6H4-O-CH2-CH(OH)-CH2-NH-C(CH3)3 ⟹ O2N-C6H4-O-CH2-CH(OH)-CH2-NH-C(CH3)3

C-O disconnection:
ClCH2-CH(OH)-CH2-N(H)-C(CH3)3 ≡ (CH3)3C-NH-CH2-CH(OH)(+) + (−)O-C6H4-NO2

≡ HO-C6H4-NO2 (**4-nitrophenol**)

C-N disconnection:
ClCH2-CH(OH)(+) + H3C-C(CH3)2-NH(−) ≡ H3C-C(CH3)2-NH2

≡ ClCH2-CH(–O–)CH2 (chloromethyl epoxide / epichlorohydrin)

Synthesis:

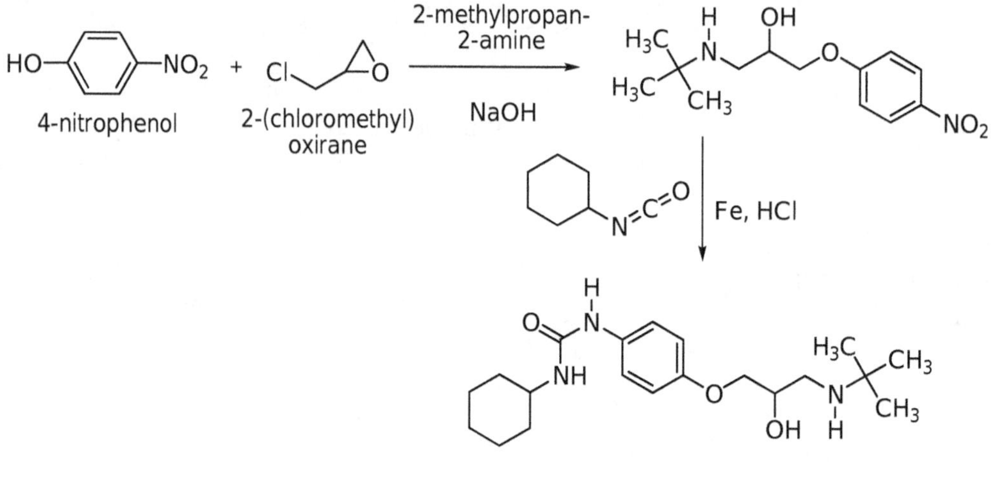

[Reaction scheme: 4-nitrophenol + 2-(chloromethyl)oxirane, with 2-methylpropan-2-amine and NaOH, gives the tert-butylamino-propanol-nitrophenyl ether intermediate; then cyclohexyl isocyanate with Fe, HCl yields Talinolol.]

Talinolol

TALIPEXOLE
Use: antiparkinsonian
Analysis:

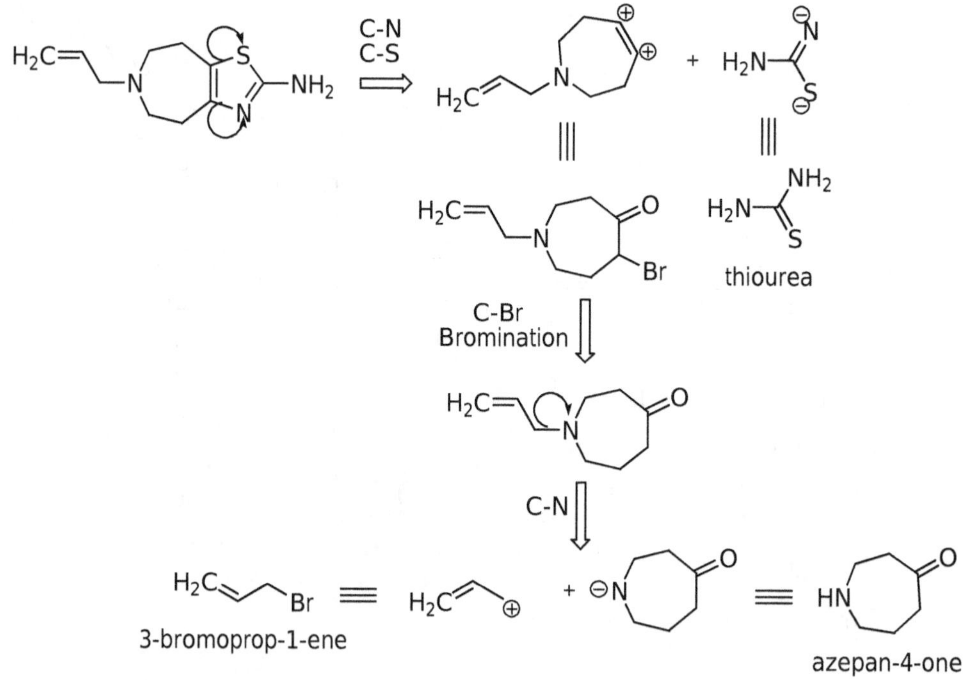

[Retrosynthetic scheme: Talipexole ⇒ (C–N, C–S disconnection) allyl-azepine cation + thiourea; ⇐ allyl-azepanone with α-Br (C–Br bromination) ⇐ allyl-azepan-4-one ⇐ (C–N) 3-bromoprop-1-ene (≡ H₂C=CH–CH₂⁺) + azepan-4-one anion ≡ azepan-4-one.]

3-bromoprop-1-ene

thiourea

azepan-4-one

Synthesis:

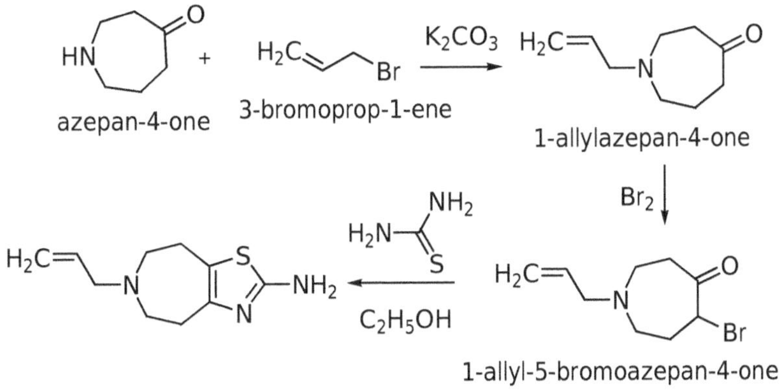

azepan-4-one + 3-bromoprop-1-ene →(K₂CO₃) 1-allylazepan-4-one →(Br₂) 1-allyl-5-bromoazepan-4-one →(thiourea, C₂H₅OH) **Talipexole**

TELMESTEINE

Use: mucolytic agent

Analysis:

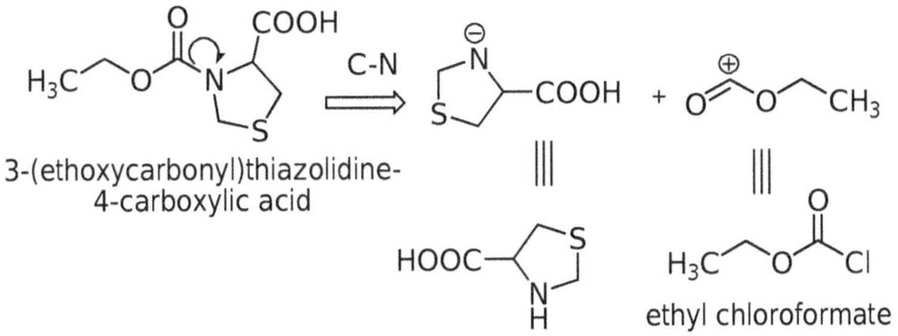

3-(ethoxycarbonyl)thiazolidine-4-carboxylic acid ⟹ (C–N) thiazolidine-4-carboxylic acid + ethyl chloroformate

Synthesis:

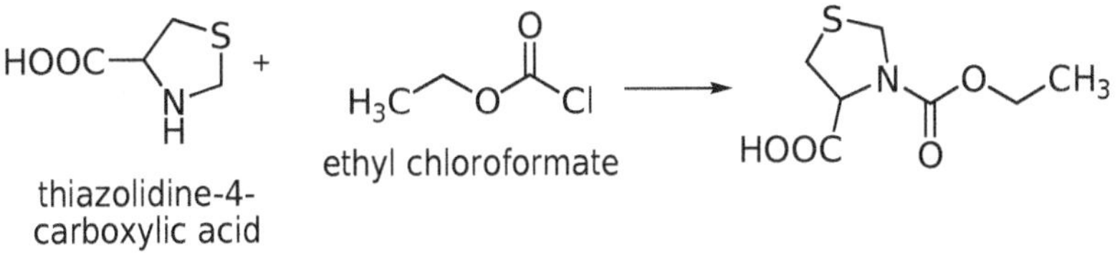

thiazolidine-4-carboxylic acid + ethyl chloroformate → **Telmesteine**

TENONITROZOLE
Use: antifungal
Analysis:

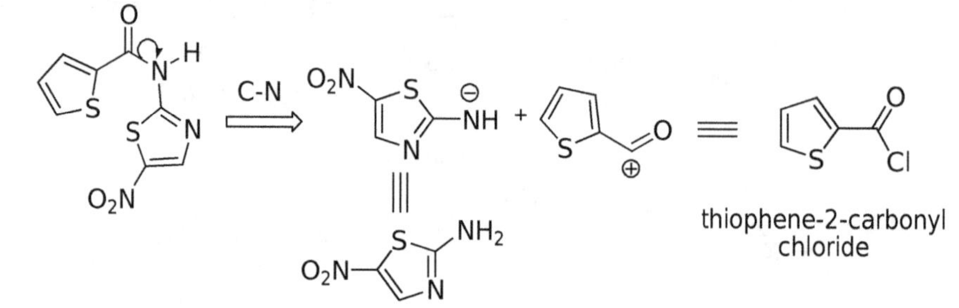

[Retrosynthetic analysis: Tenonitrozole (thiophene-2-carboxamide linked to 5-nitrothiazol-2-yl) disconnects via C–N bond to give 5-nitrothiazol-2-amine and thiophene-2-carbonyl cation, equivalent to thiophene-2-carbonyl chloride.]

Synthesis:

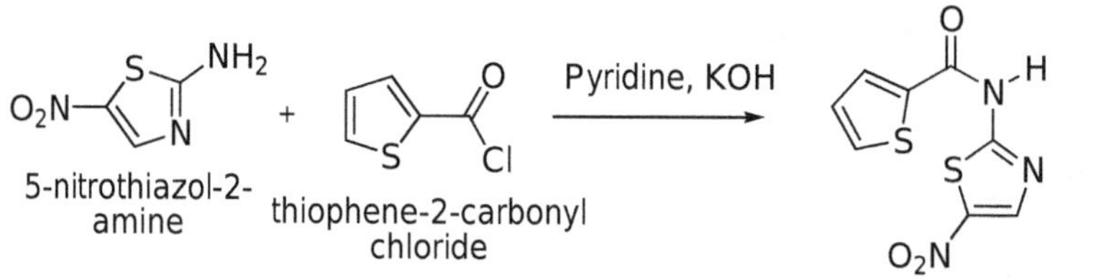

5-nitrothiazol-2-amine + thiophene-2-carbonyl chloride $\xrightarrow{\text{Pyridine, KOH}}$ **Tenonitrozole**

TERAZOSINE
Use: antihypertensive, α-blocker
Analysis:

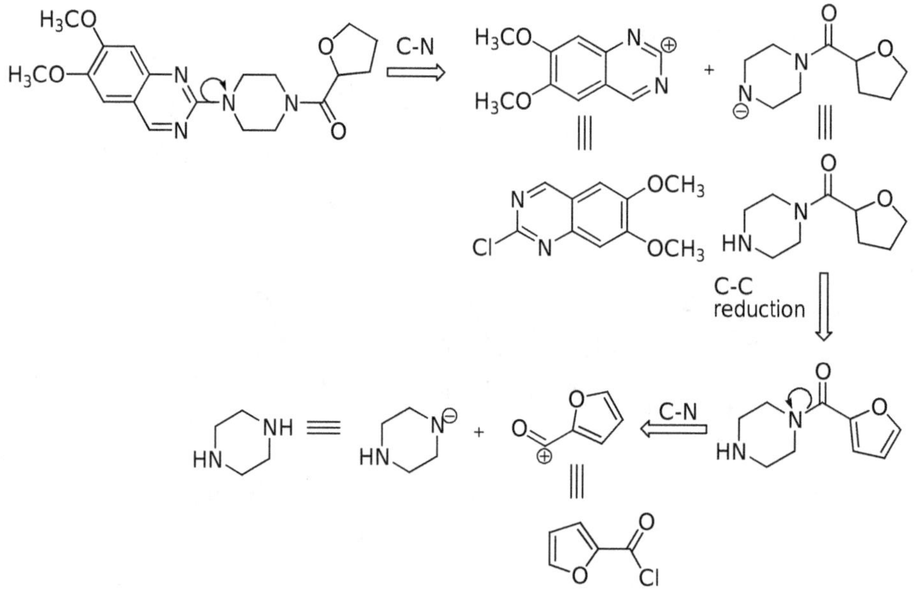

[Retrosynthetic analysis: Terazosine disconnects via C–N bond to give 6,7-dimethoxyquinazolin-2-yl cation (equivalent to 2-chloro-6,7-dimethoxyquinazoline) and 1-(tetrahydrofuran-2-carbonyl)piperazine. The latter by C–C reduction gives 1-(furan-2-carbonyl)piperazine, which disconnects via C–N to piperazine and furan-2-carbonyl cation (equivalent to furan-2-carbonyl chloride).]

Synthesis:

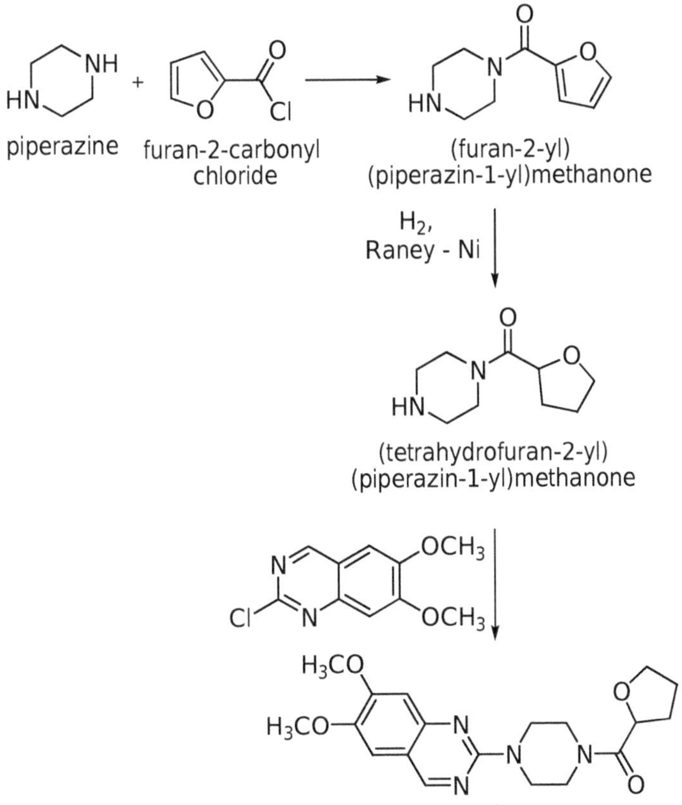

piperazine + furan-2-carbonyl chloride → (furan-2-yl)(piperazin-1-yl)methanone

↓ H₂, Raney - Ni

(tetrahydrofuran-2-yl)(piperazin-1-yl)methanone

↓ [2-chloro-6,7-dimethoxyquinazoline]

Terazosine

TERFENADINE
Use: antihistaminic
Analysis:

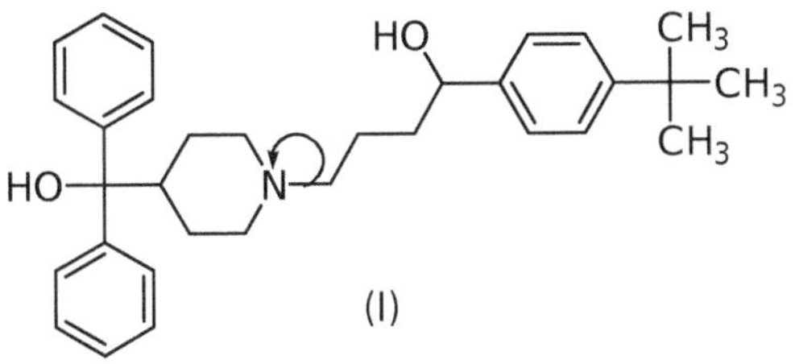

(I)

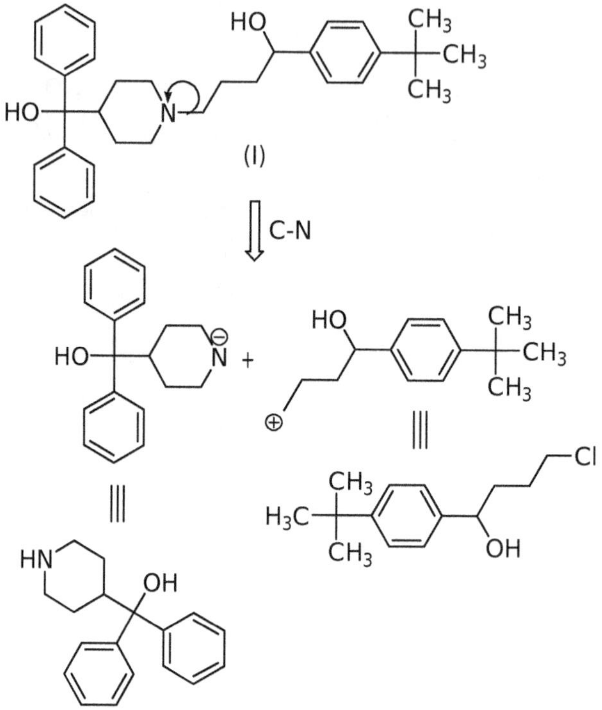

Retrosynthetic Analysis and Synthesis of Drugs

Synthesis:

diphenyl(piperidin-4-yl)methanol + 1-(4-*tert*-butylphenyl)-4-chlorobutan-1-ol

$KHCO_3$ | KI

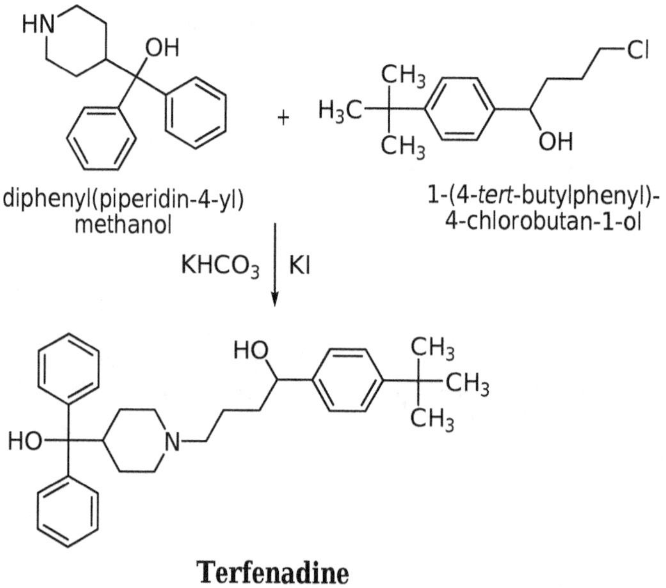

Terfenadine

TETRACAINE

Use: local anaesthetic

Analysis:

[Retrosynthetic analysis scheme: tetracaine disconnects via C-O to 4-(butylamino)benzaldehyde cation and 2-(dimethylamino)ethoxide; FGC to 4-(butylamino)benzoyl chloride + 2-(dimethylamino)ethanol; further to 4-(butylamino)benzoic acid; C-N disconnection to 4-aminobenzoic acid + butyl cation (≡ 1-bromobutane); equivalent to H₂N-C₆H₄-COOH (4-aminobenzoic acid).]

Synthesis:

4-aminobenzoic acid + 1-bromobutane → 4-(butylamino)benzoic acid

↓ SOCl₂

4-(butylamino)benzoyl chloride

+ HOCH₂CH₂N(CH₃)₂ → Tetracaine + HCl

Tetracaine

THIOPERAZINE

Use: antiemetic, neuroleptic

Analysis:

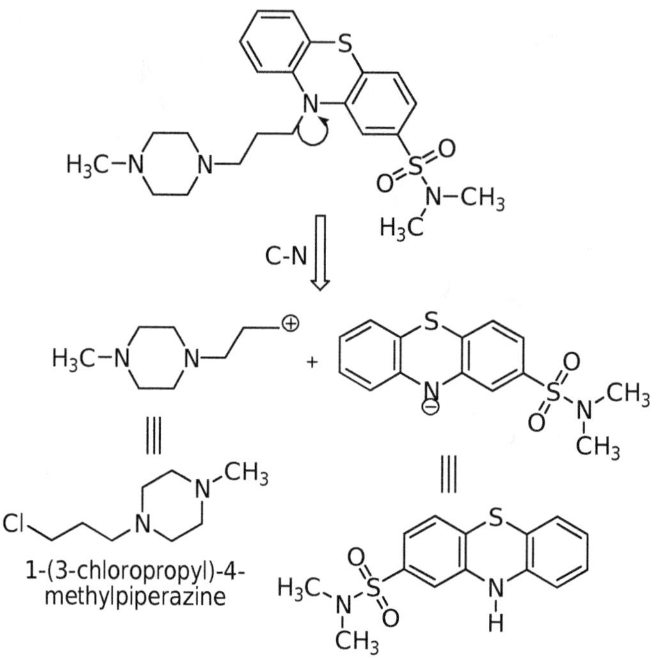

Synthesis:

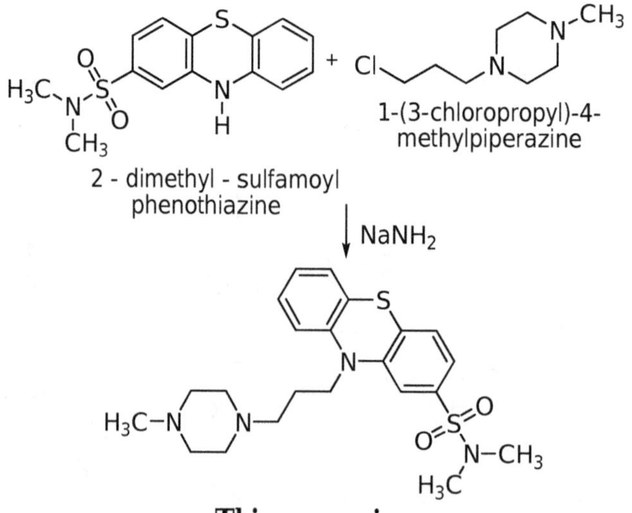

Starting materials: 2-dimethyl-sulfamoyl phenothiazine + 1-(3-chloropropyl)-4-methylpiperazine

Reagent: NaNH₂

Product: **Thioperazine**

THIOTEPA

Use: antineoplastic

Analysis:

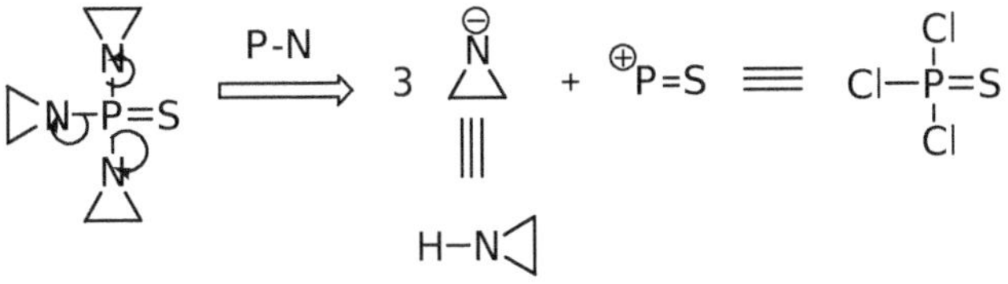

Synthesis:

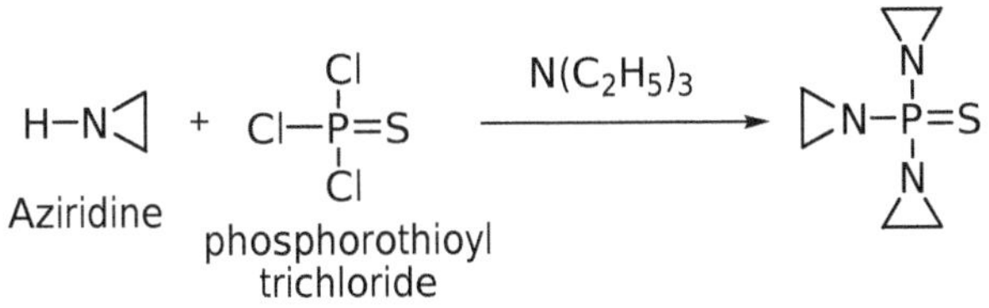

Aziridine + phosphorothioyl trichloride → Thiotepa (with N(C$_2$H$_5$)$_3$)

TICARCILLIN

Use: antibacterial, antibiotic

Analysis:

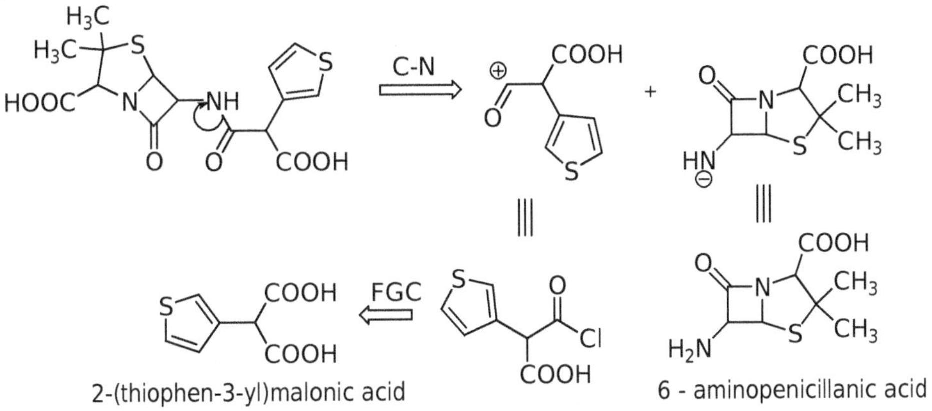

2-(thiophen-3-yl)malonic acid

6 - aminopenicillanic acid

Synthesis:

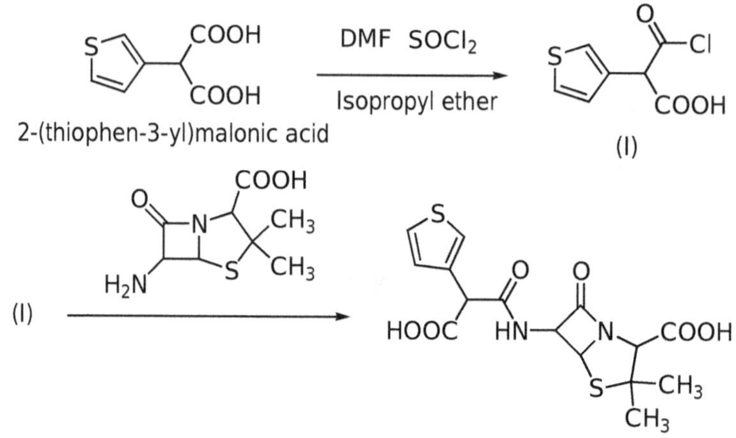

2-(thiophen-3-yl)malonic acid →(DMF, SOCl₂, Isopropyl ether)→ (I)

(I) + H₂N-[6-APA] → **Ticarcillin**

TICLOPIDINE

Use: platelet aggregation inhibitor

Analysis:

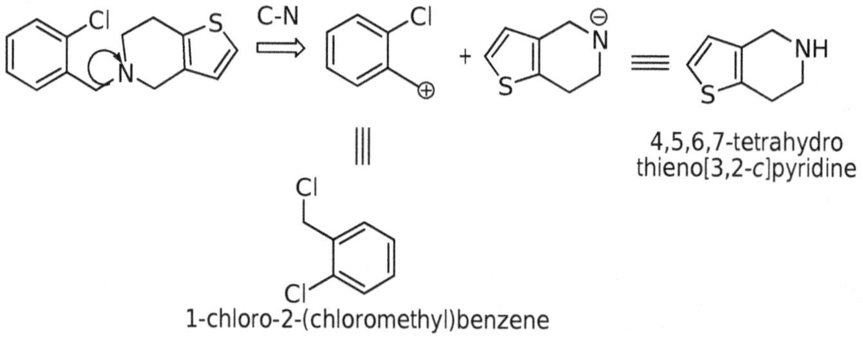

[Retrosynthetic scheme: Ticlopidine ⇒ 2-chlorobenzyl cation (≡ 1-chloro-2-(chloromethyl)benzene) + 4,5,6,7-tetrahydrothieno[3,2-c]pyridine anion (≡ 4,5,6,7-tetrahydrothieno[3,2-c]pyridine), C–N disconnection]

Synthesis:

4,5,6,7-tetrahydrothieno[3,2-c]pyridine + 1-chloro-2-(chloromethyl)benzene →(K₂CO₃, C₂H₅OH)→ **Ticlopidine**

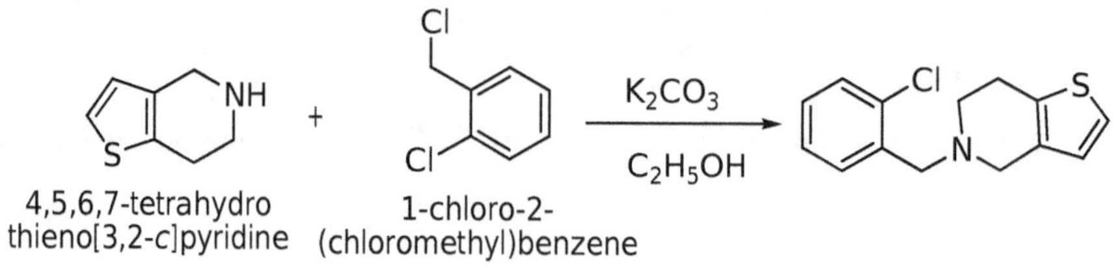

TIMOLOL
Use: β-blocker
Analysis:

Synthesis:

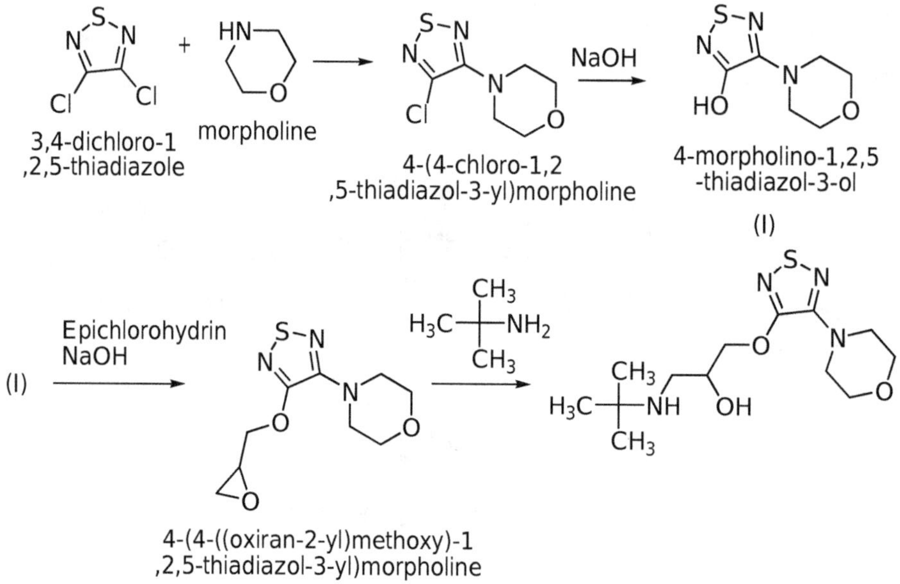

[Reaction scheme: 3,4-dichloro-1,2,5-thiadiazole + morpholine → 4-(4-chloro-1,2,5-thiadiazol-3-yl)morpholine → (NaOH) → 4-morpholino-1,2,5-thiadiazol-3-ol (I)]

[Reaction scheme: (I) + Epichlorohydrin/NaOH → 4-(4-((oxiran-2-yl)methoxy)-1,2,5-thiadiazol-3-yl)morpholine + tert-butylamine → **Timolol**]

TIOCONAZOLE

Use: antifungal

Analysis:

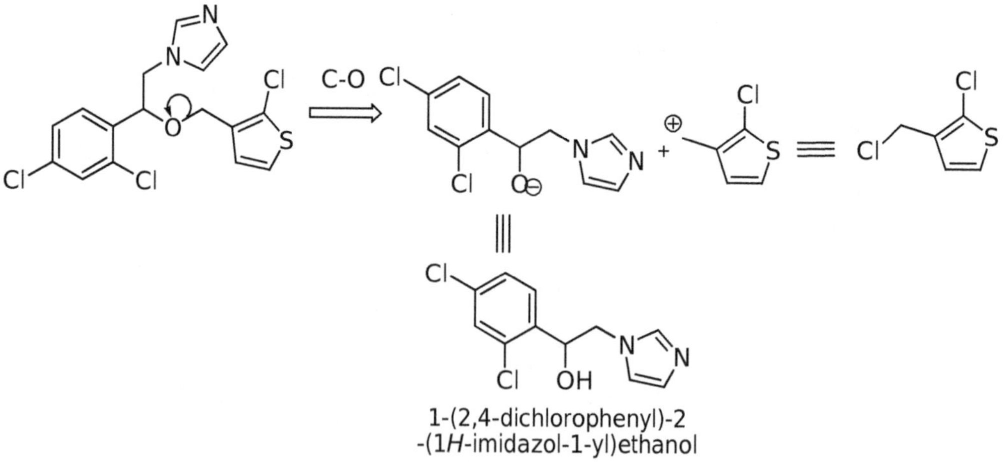

[Retrosynthetic scheme showing tioconazole disconnected (C–O) into 1-(2,4-dichlorophenyl)-2-(1H-imidazol-1-yl)ethanol (as alkoxide) and 2-chloro-3-(chloromethyl)thiophene cation]

1-(2,4-dichlorophenyl)-2-(1H-imidazol-1-yl)ethanol

Synthesis:

[Scheme: 1-(2,4-dichlorophenyl)-2-(1H-imidazol-1-yl)ethanol + 2-chloro-3-(chloromethyl)thiophene → (NaH) → **Tioconazole**]

TIOPRONINE
Use: hepatoprotectant
Analysis:

[Retrosynthetic analysis: Tiopronine disconnected via C–S bond to give NaSH and 2-bromopropanamidoacetic acid cation equivalent; further C–N disconnection yields 2-bromopropanoyl bromide and 2-aminoacetic acid (glycine).]

Synthesis:

[Scheme: 2-bromopropanoyl bromide + 2-aminoacetic acid → (NaHCO₃) → 2-(2-bromopropanamido)acetic acid → (NaSH) → **Tiopronine**]

TOCAINIDE
Use: antiarrhythmic

Analysis:

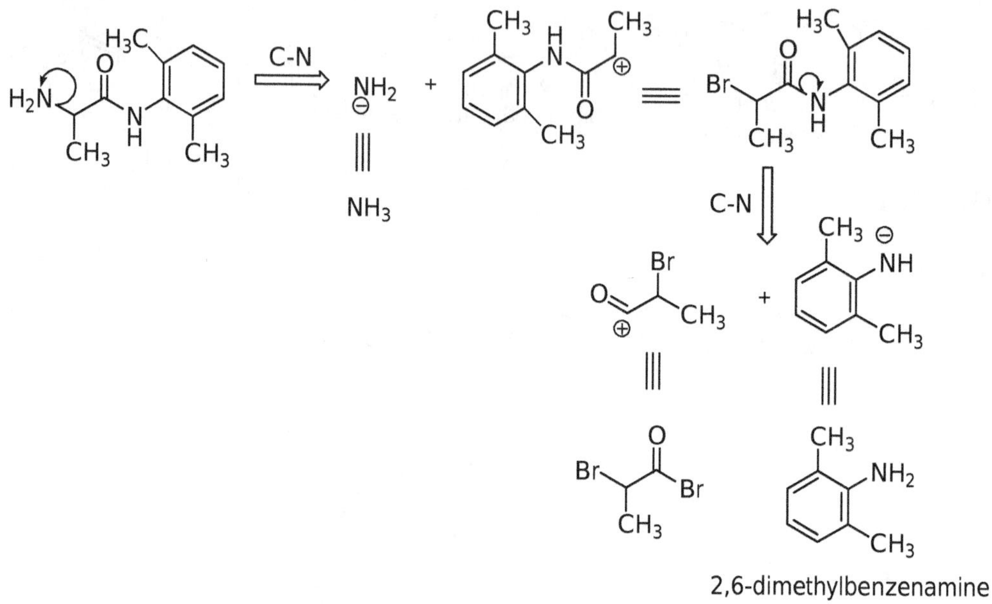

[Retrosynthetic analysis showing tocainide disconnected at C-N bond to give NH₃ and an acylium intermediate, equivalent to 2-bromopropanoyl bromide + 2,6-dimethylbenzenamine]

2,6-dimethylbenzenamine

Synthesis:

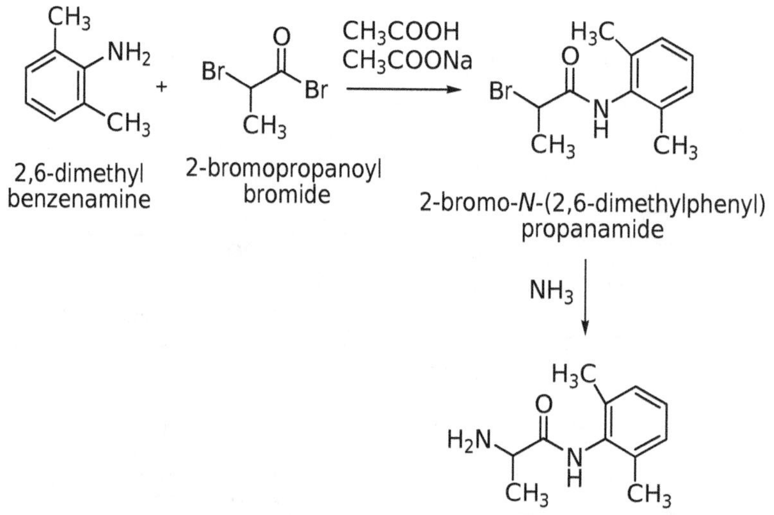

2,6-dimethyl benzenamine + 2-bromopropanoyl bromide → (CH₃COOH, CH₃COONa) → 2-bromo-N-(2,6-dimethylphenyl)propanamide

↓ NH₃

Tocainide

TODRALAZINE

Use: antihypertensive

Analysis:

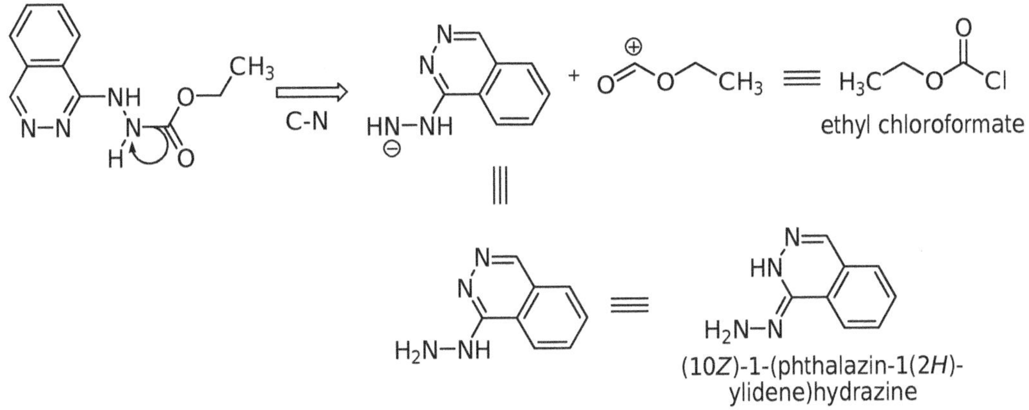
C-N
ethyl chloroformate
(10Z)-1-(phthalazin-1(2H)-ylidene)hydrazine

Synthesis:

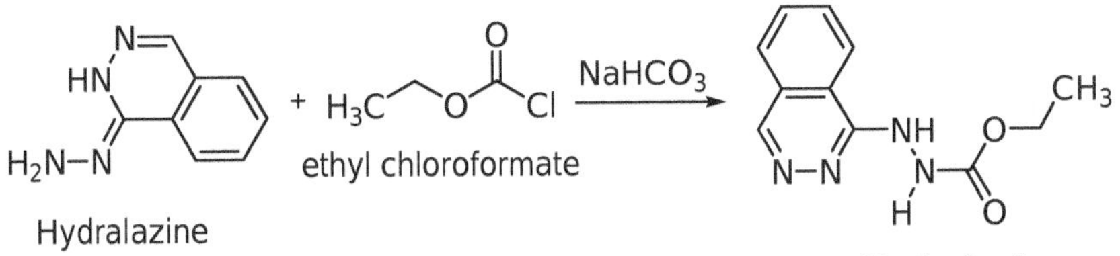
NaHCO3
ethyl chloroformate
Hydralazine

Todralazine

TOLAZAMIDE

Use: antidiabetic

Analysis:

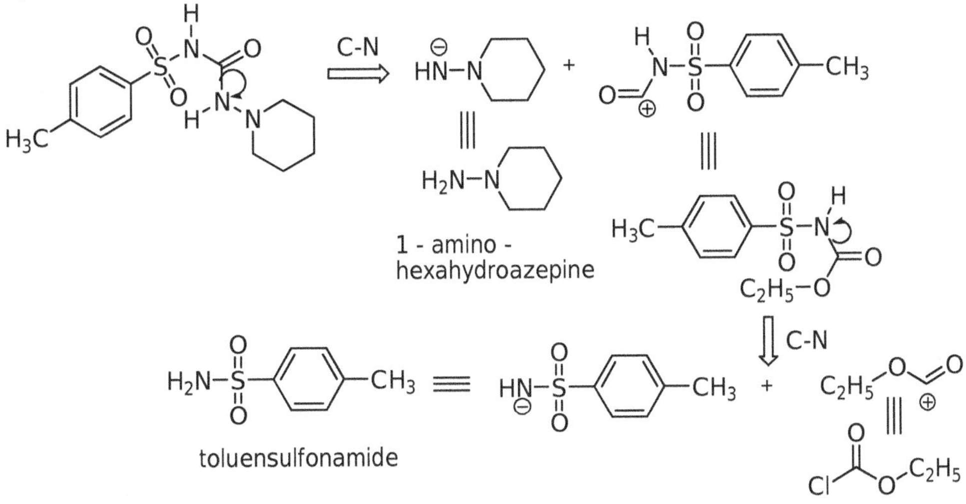
C-N
1 - amino -
hexahydroazepine
C-N
toluensulfonamide

Synthesis:

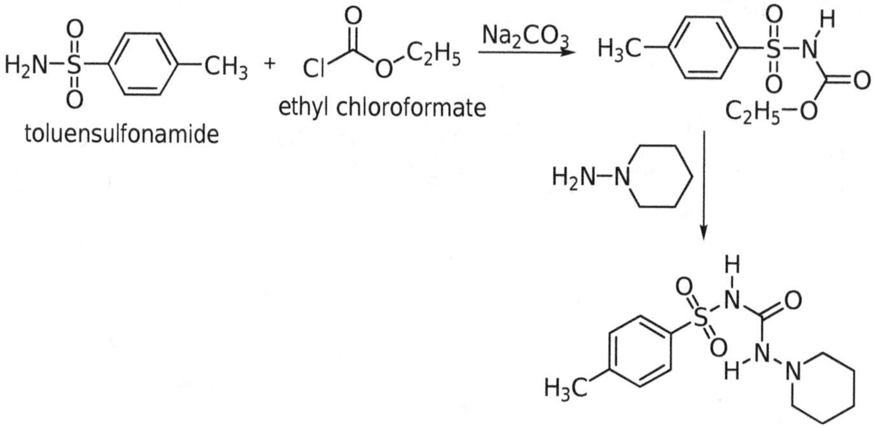

[Reaction: toluensulfonamide + ethyl chloroformate → (Na₂CO₃) → sulfonyl carbamate intermediate → (H₂N-N-piperidine) → **Tolazamide**]

TOLBUTAMIDE

Use: antidiabetic

Analysis:

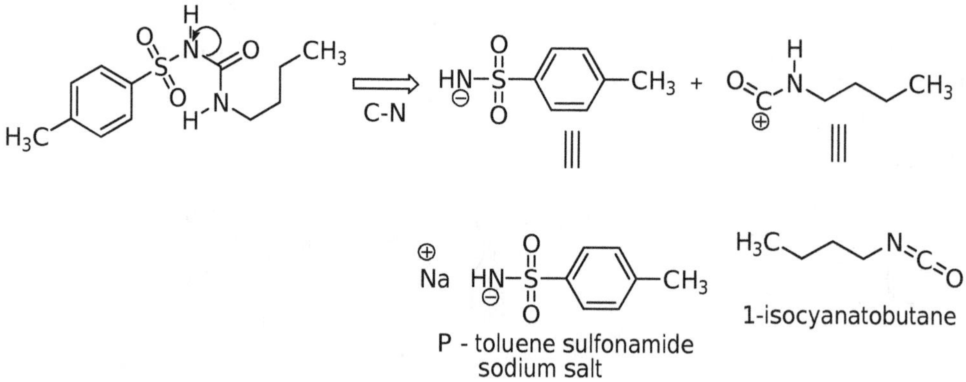

[Retrosynthetic analysis: tolbutamide ⇒ (C-N disconnection) → p-toluene sulfonamide sodium salt + 1-isocyanatobutane]

Synthesis:

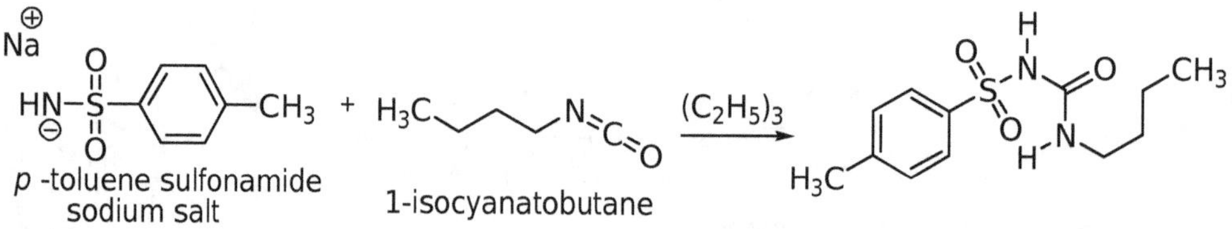

[p-toluene sulfonamide sodium salt + 1-isocyanatobutane → $(C_2H_5)_3$N → **Tolbutamide**]

TOLFENAMIC ACID
Use: anti-inflammatory
Analysis:

The C–N disconnection of tolfenamic acid gives HOOC-phenyl cation and chloro-methyl-aminophenyl anion, equivalent to **2-bromobenzoic acid** and **3-chloro-2-methyl benzenamine**.

Synthesis:

2-bromobenzoic acid + 3-chloro-2-methyl benzenamine $\xrightarrow{K_2CO_3}$ **Tolfenamic acid**

TOLIPROLOL
Use: antianginal, antihypertensive
Analysis:

C–N disconnection gives 3-methylphenoxy-hydroxypropyl cation + isopropylamine anion ≡ **propan-2-amine**.

C–O disconnection gives m-cresolate + epoxide ≡ m-cresol + epichlorohydrin.

m-cresol

Synthesis:

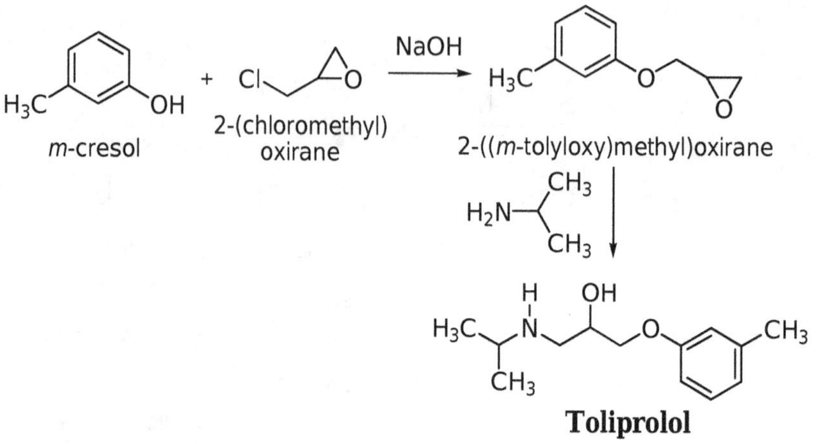

m-cresol + 2-(chloromethyl)oxirane →(NaOH) 2-((m-tolyloxy)methyl)oxirane →(H₂N-CH(CH₃)₂) **Toliprolol**

TOLNAFTATE
Use: fungicide, antimycotic
Analysis:

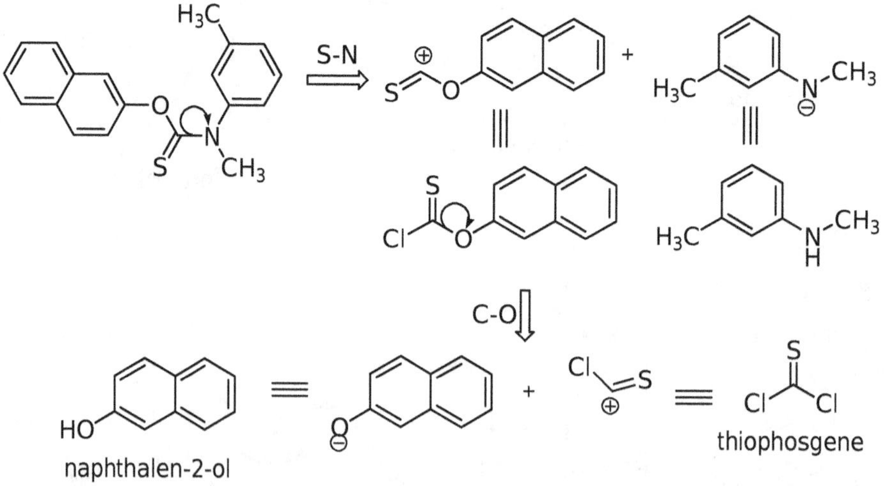

(S-N disconnection) → naphthalen-2-yl thiocarbonyl cation + N-methyl-m-toluidine anion ≡ naphthalen-2-yl thiochloroformate + N-methyl-m-toluidine

(C-O disconnection) → naphthalen-2-ol ≡ naphthalen-2-olate + thiocarbonyl cation ≡ thiophosgene

Synthesis:

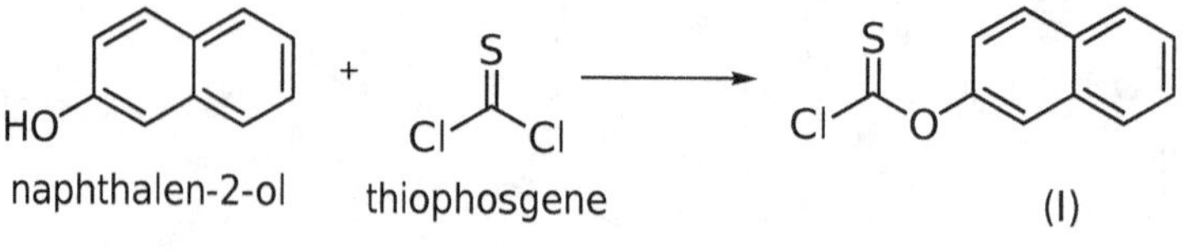

naphthalen-2-ol + thiophosgene → (I)

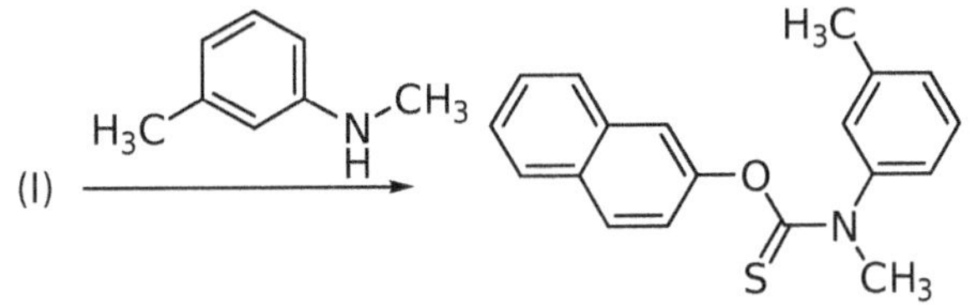

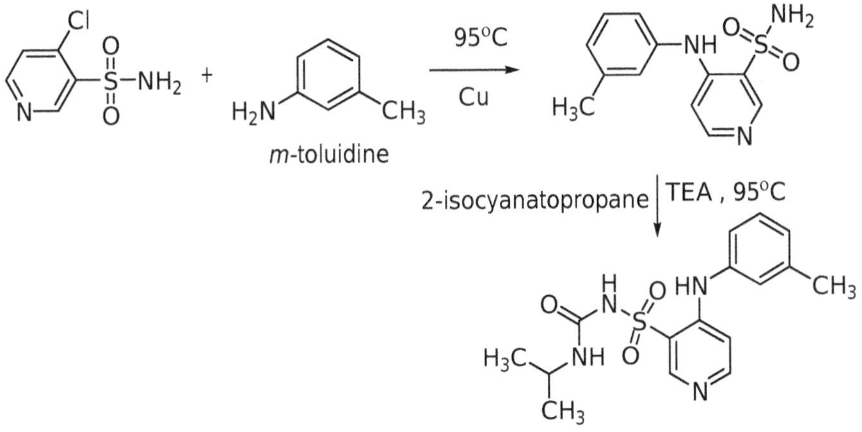

TORASEMIDE

Use: antihypertensive

Analysis:

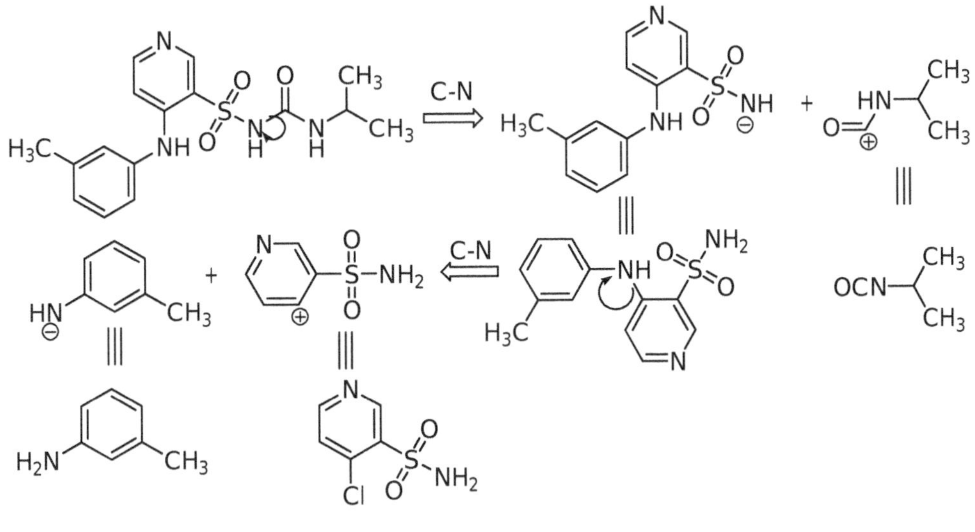

Synthesis:

TRANILAST
Use: antiallergic
Analysis:

[Retrosynthetic analysis: Tranilast ⇒ anthranilate anion + (E)-3-(3,4-dimethoxyphenyl)acryloyl cation; equivalent to anthranilic acid + (E)-3-(3,4-dimethoxyphenyl)acryloyl chloride, disconnection at C–N bond]

Synthesis:

Anthranilic acid + (E)-3-(3,4-dimethoxyphenyl)acryloyl chloride → **Tranilast**

TRIFLUPERAZINE
Use: neurosedative
Analysis:

[Retrosynthetic analysis: Trifluperazine ⇒ 2-(trifluoromethyl)phenothiazine anion + 1-methyl-4-(2-chloroethyl)piperazine cation; equivalent to 2-(trifluoromethyl)phenothiazine + 1-(2-chloroethyl)-4-methylpiperazine, disconnection at C–N bond]

Synthesis:

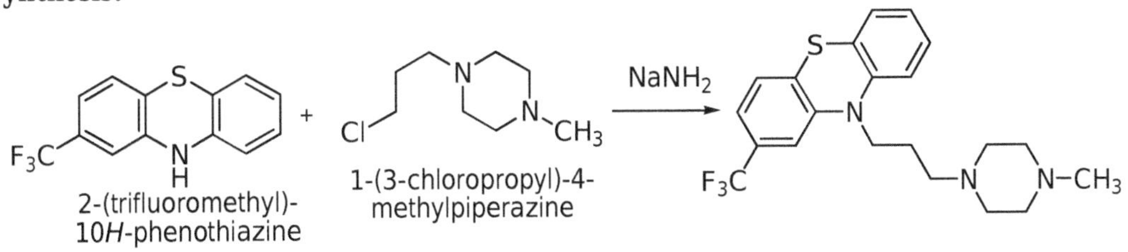

2-(trifluoromethyl)-10H-phenothiazine + 1-(3-chloropropyl)-4-methylpiperazine →[NaNH₂] **Trifluperazine**

TRIFLUPROMAZINE

Use: neuroleptic

Analysis:

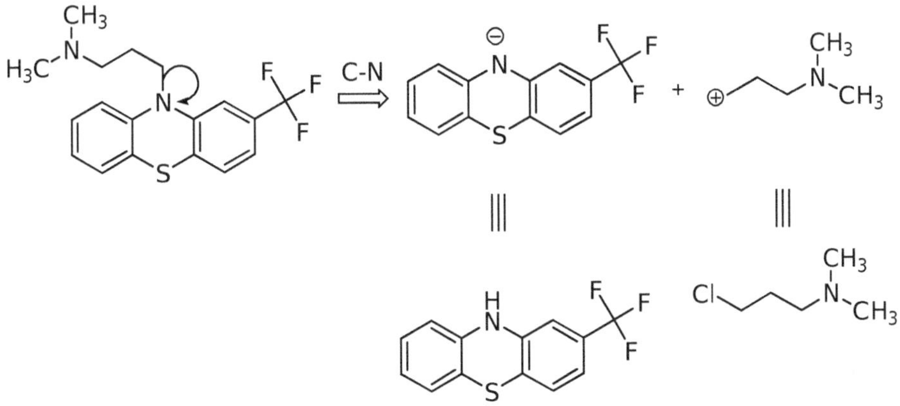

C-N disconnection gives phenothiazine anion (2-(trifluoromethyl)-10H-phenothiazine) + 3-chloro-N,N-dimethylpropan-1-amine cation equivalent.

Synthesis:

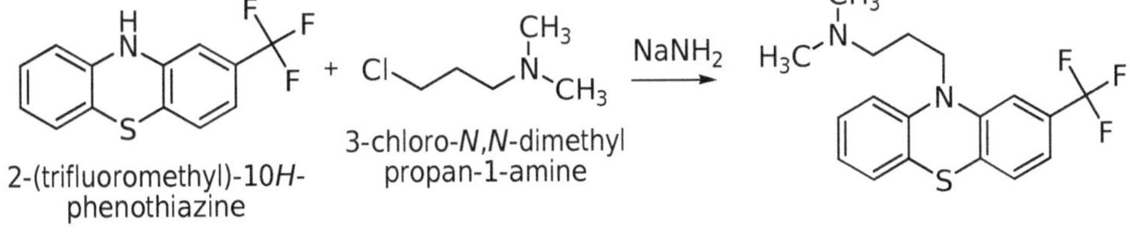

2-(trifluoromethyl)-10H-phenothiazine + 3-chloro-N,N-dimethyl propan-1-amine →[NaNH₂] **Triflupromazine**

TRIMEPRAZINE
Use: antihistaminic, psychosedative
Analysis:

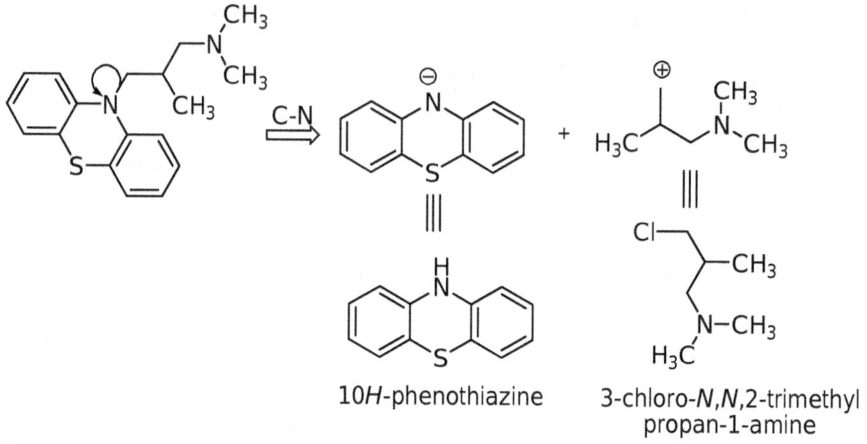

[Retrosynthetic scheme: Trimeprazine ⟹ (C-N disconnection) 10H-phenothiazine anion + 3-chloro-N,N,2-trimethylpropan-1-amine cation]

10H-phenothiazine   3-chloro-N,N,2-trimethyl propan-1-amine

Synthesis:

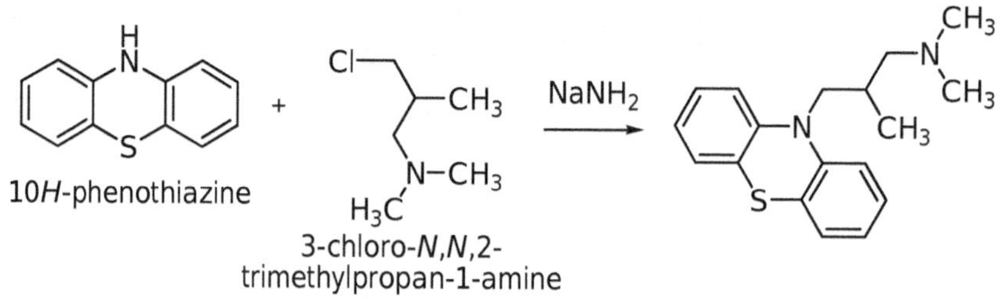

10H-phenothiazine + 3-chloro-N,N,2-trimethylpropan-1-amine $\xrightarrow{NaNH_2}$ **Trimeprazine**

TRIMETHOPRIM
Use: antibacterial
Analysis:

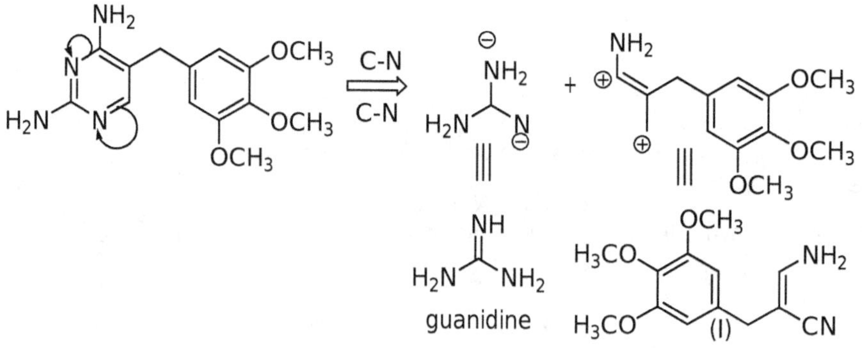

[Retrosynthetic scheme: Trimethoprim ⟹ (C-N, C-N disconnections) guanidine + intermediate (I)]

guanidine

(I)

Retrosynthetic Analysis and Synthesis of Drugs

Synthesis:

malononitrile + 3,4,5-trimethoxybenzaldehyde →(Piperidine) 2-(3,4,5-trimethoxybenzylidene)malononitrile →(H₂, Pd-C) intermediate (I) →(guanidine) **Trimethoprim**

TRIMETHOZINE
Use: neurosedative
Analysis:

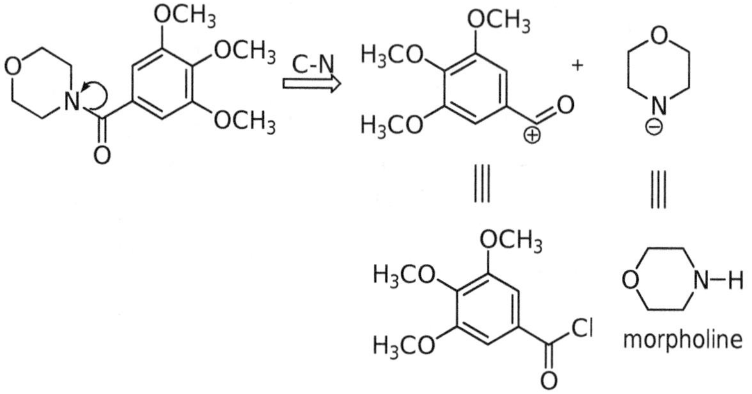

[Retrosynthetic analysis: trimethozine → 3,4,5-trimethoxybenzoyl cation + morpholine anion ≡ 3,4,5-trimethoxybenzoyl chloride + morpholine]

Synthesis:

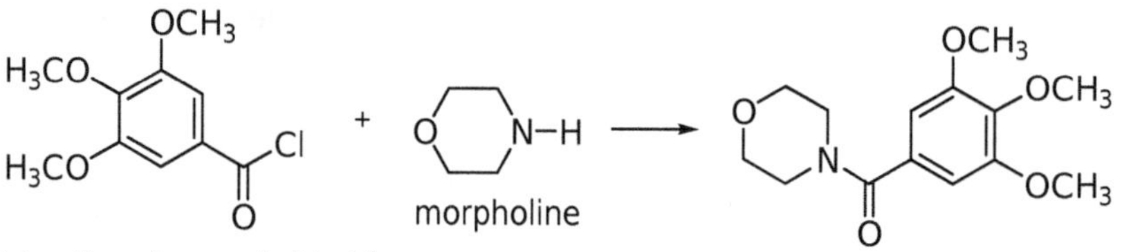

3,4,5-trimethoxybenzoyl chloride + morpholine → **Trimethozine**

TRIMIPRAMINE
Use: antidepressant
Analysis:

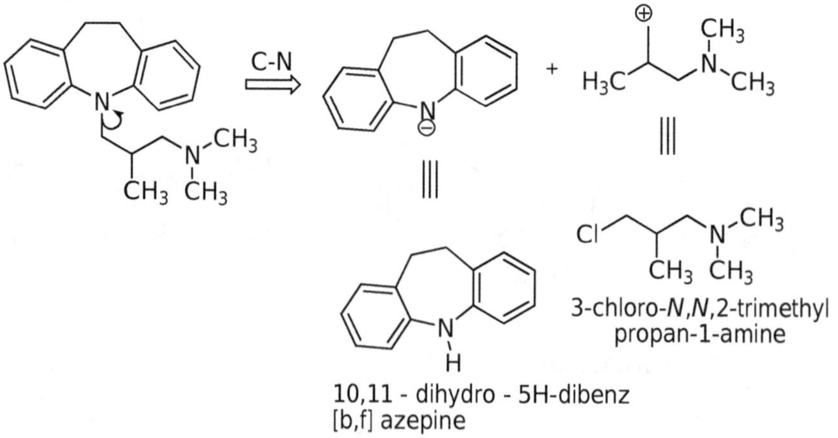

[Retrosynthetic analysis: trimipramine → dibenzazepine anion + 3-chloro-N,N,2-trimethylpropan-1-amine cation ≡ 10,11-dihydro-5H-dibenz[b,f]azepine + 3-chloro-N,N,2-trimethylpropan-1-amine]

Synthesis:

10,11 - dihydro - 5H-dibenz[b,f] azepine + ClCH₂CH(CH₃)CH₂N(CH₃)₂ → (NaNH₂) → **Trimipramine**

TRIPELENNAMINE

Use: antihistaminic

Analysis:

Tripelennamine ⟹ (C-N) N-benzylpyridin-2-amine anion + ⁺CH₂N(CH₃)₂

≡ N-benzylpyridin-2-amine + 2-chloro-N,N-dimethyl ethanamine

Synthesis:

N-benzylpyridin-2-amine + 2-chloro-N,N-dimethyl ethanamine → (NaNH₂) → **Tripelennamine**

URAMUSTINE
Use: antineoplastic
Analysis:

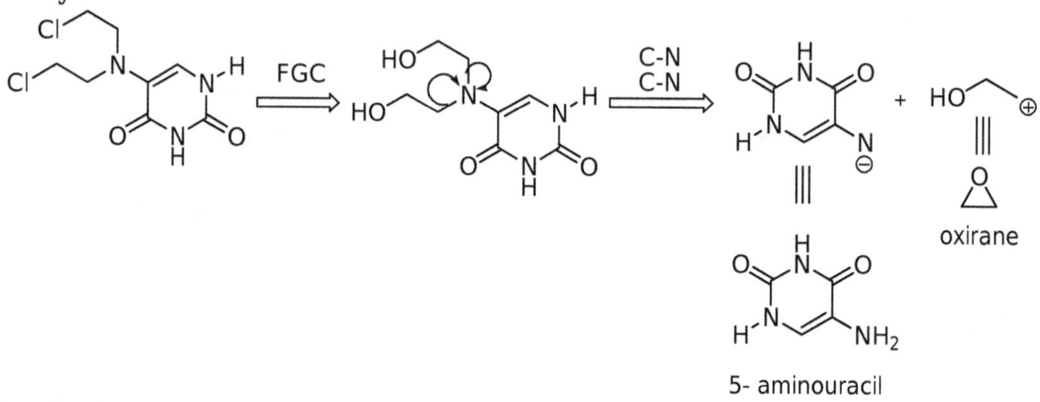

[Retrosynthetic analysis scheme: Uramustine ⟹ (FGC) bis(2-hydroxyethyl) intermediate ⟹ (C-N, C-N) 5-aminouracil (shown as diazonium-like) + HO-CH₂⁺ / oxirane; also shows 5-aminouracil]

Synthesis:

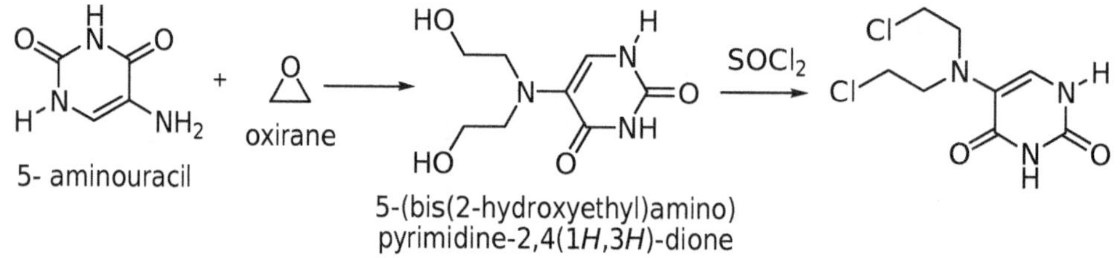

5-aminouracil + oxirane → 5-(bis(2-hydroxyethyl)amino)pyrimidine-2,4(1H,3H)-dione —SOCl₂→ **Uramustine**

VALETHAMATE BROMIDE
Use: antispasmodic
Analysis:

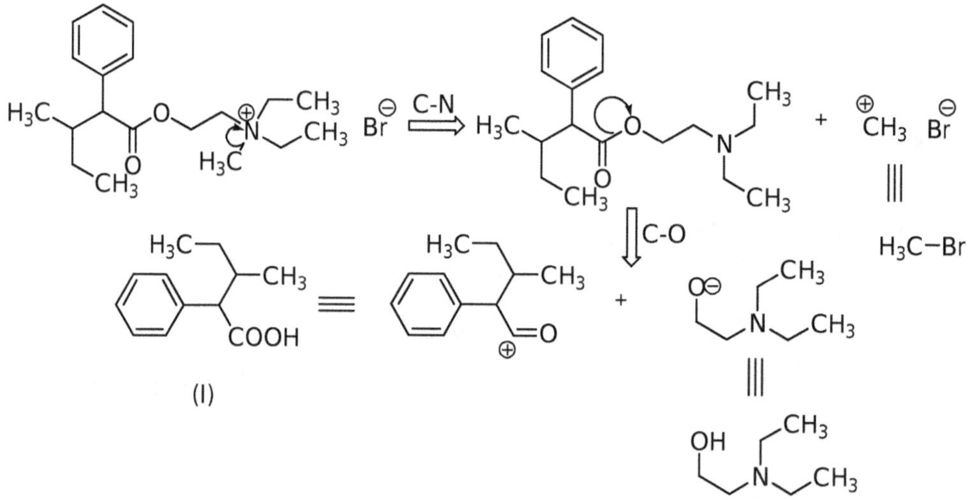

[Retrosynthetic analysis: Valethamate bromide ⟹ (C-N) tertiary amine ester + CH₃⁺ Br⁻ (H₃C-Br); ester ⟹ (C-O) acylium (from acid I: 2-phenyl-3-methylpentanoic acid / corresponding aldehyde) + alkoxide of 2-(diethylamino)ethanol (HO-CH₂CH₂-N(CH₂CH₃)₂)]

(I)

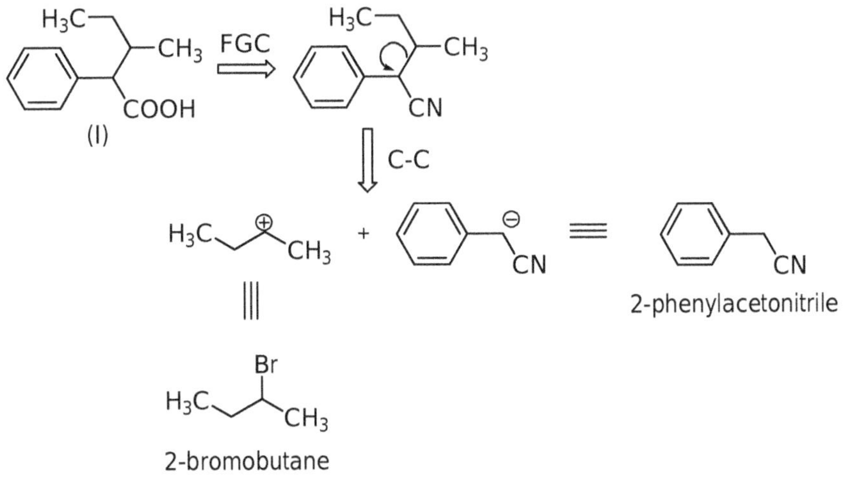

Synthesis:

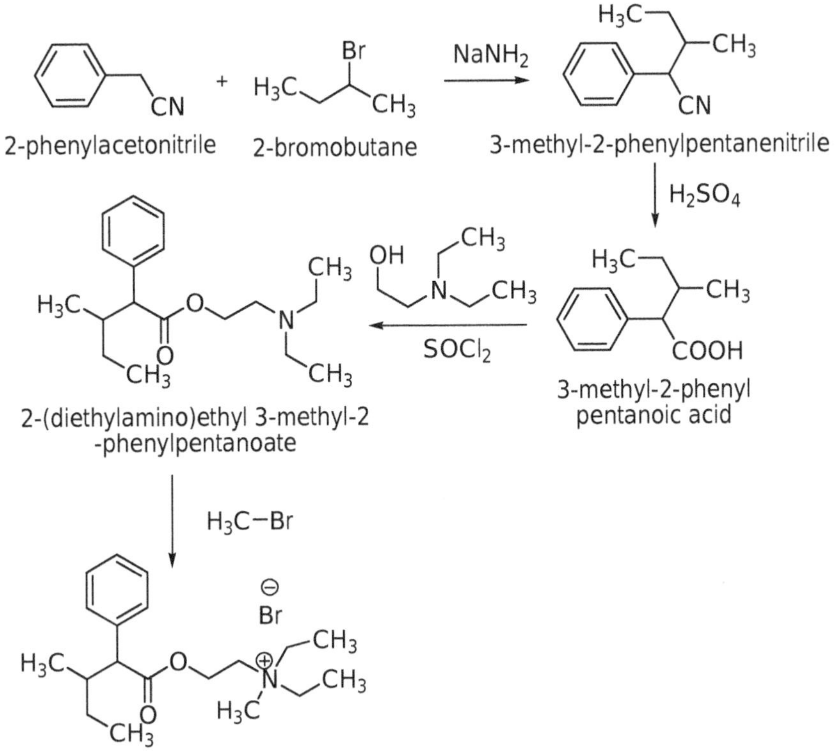

Valethamate bromide

VERAPAMIL

Use: coronary vasodilator

Analysis:

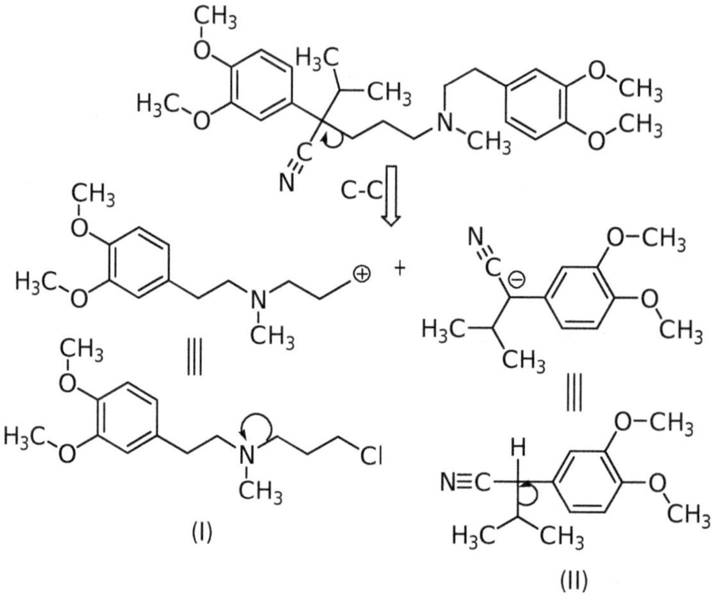

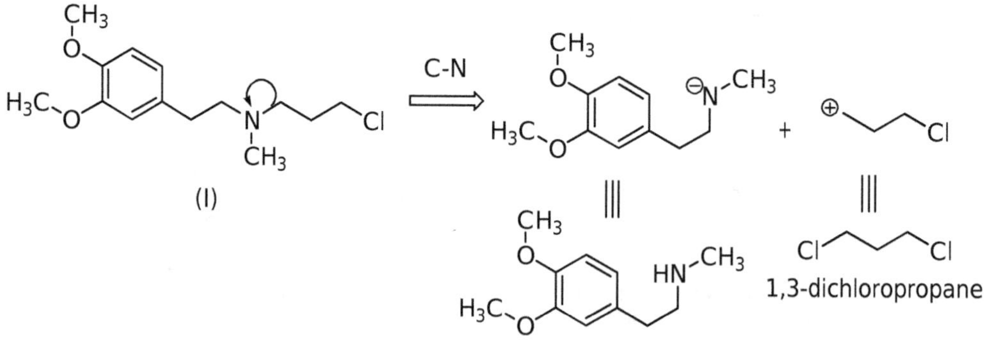

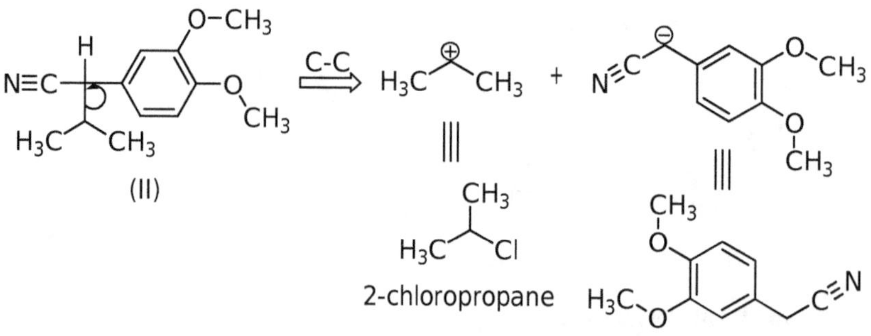

Retrosynthetic Analysis and Synthesis of Drugs

Synthesis:

[Scheme: 2-(3,4-dimethoxyphenyl)acetonitrile + 2-chloropropane (H₃C–CHCl–CH₃), NaNH₂ → Intermediate (I)]

[Scheme: 1,3-dichloropropane + 2-(3,4-dimethoxyphenyl)-N-methylethanamine → N-(3,4-dimethoxyphenethyl)-3-chloro-N-methylpropan-1-amine (II)]

(I) + (II) —NaNH₂→ **Verapamil**

WARFARIN

Use: anticoagulant

Analysis:

[Retrosynthetic scheme: Warfarin ⇒ 4-hydroxycoumarin anion + phenyl-substituted butanone cation ≡ benzylideneacetone (PhCH=CH–C(O)CH₃)]

[4-hydroxycoumarin structure shown]

Synthesis:

4-hydroxy-2H-chromen-2-one + (Z)-4-phenylbut-3-en-2-one → (Pyridine) → **Warfarin**

XATHINOL
Use: vasodilator

Analysis:

Xathinol ⇒ (C-N) Theophylline anion + cation intermediate ≡ Theophylline + chlorohydrin-amine ⇒ (C-N) 2-(chloromethyl)oxirane + 2-(methylamino)ethanol

Synthesis:

2-(chloromethyl)oxirane + 2-(methylamino)ethanol → HOCH$_2$CH$_2$N(CH$_3$)CH$_2$CH(OH)CH$_2$Cl (I)

(I) + Theophylline, Na$_2$CO$_3$ → **Xathinol**

XIBENOLOL
Use: β-blocker
Analysis:

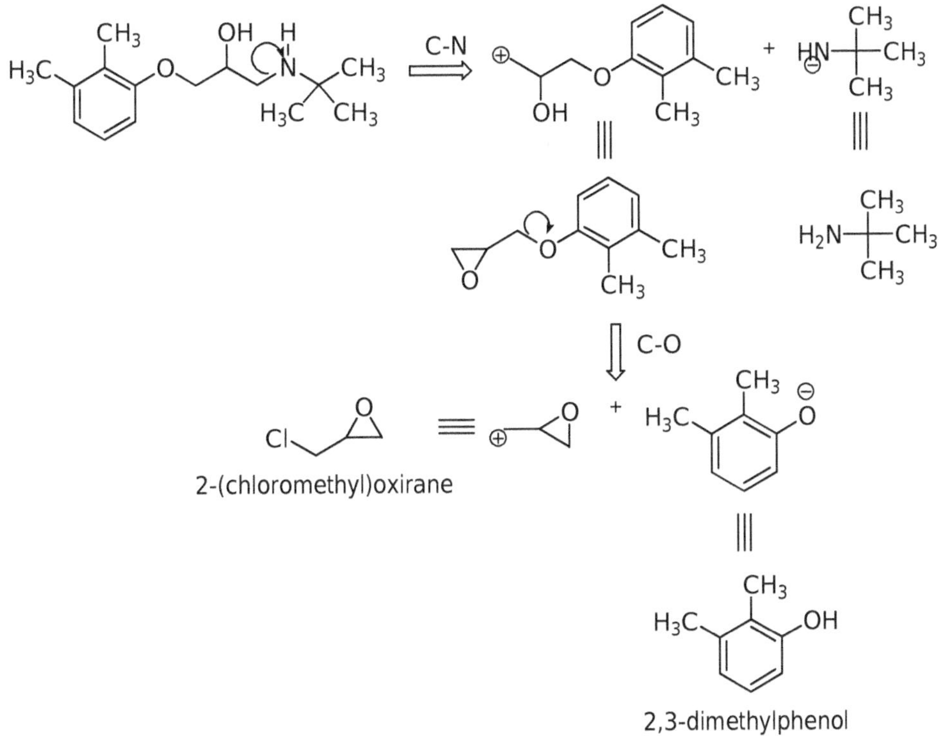

[Retrosynthetic analysis showing xibenolol disconnected at C-N bond to give epoxide intermediate and tert-butylamine, then disconnected at C-O bond to give 2-(chloromethyl)oxirane and 2,3-dimethylphenol]

2-(chloromethyl)oxirane

2,3-dimethylphenol

Synthesis:

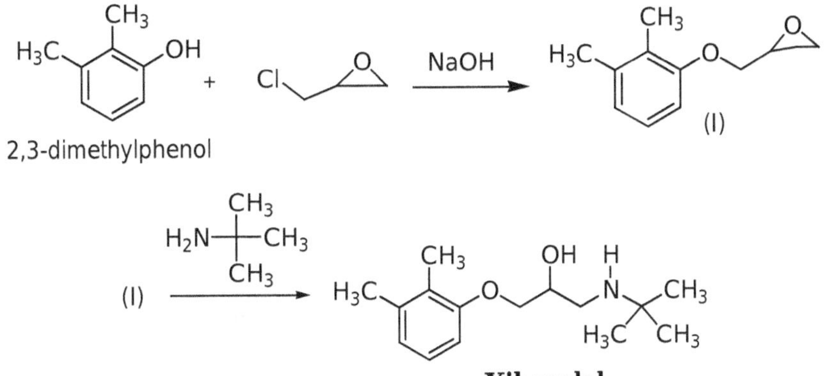

2,3-dimethylphenol + 2-(chloromethyl)oxirane $\xrightarrow{\text{NaOH}}$ (I)

(I) $\xrightarrow{\text{H}_2\text{N-C(CH}_3)_3}$ **Xibenolol**

XIPAMIDE
Use: diuretic
Analysis:

[Retrosynthetic scheme showing disconnection of xipamide: C-N amide disconnection to give acyl cation of 4-chloro-2-hydroxy-5-sulfamoylbenzoic acid and 2,5-dimethylbenzenamine anion; FGC to acid chloride form; S-N disconnection to sulfonyl cation and ammonia (NH₃); C-S chlorosulfonation disconnection to 4-chloro-2-hydroxybenzoic acid.]

Synthesis:

4-chloro-2-hydroxybenzoic acid + ClSO₃H → 2-hydroxy-4-chloro-5-(chlorosulfonyl)benzoic acid

→ NH₃ → 4-chloro-2-hydroxy-5-sulfamoylbenzoic acid (I)

(I) + 2,5-dimethylaniline (H₃C, CH₃ substituted aniline) / PCl₃ → **Xipamide**

DESIGN OF ORGANIC SYNTHESIS

The term *total synthesis* describes the complete chemical synthesis of organic molecules from simple, commercially available or natural precursors. Although this broad definition is sometimes confined to complex molecules such as alkaloids or steroids. The first conscious total synthesis of an organic compound is commonly considered to be that of urea (**1**) by Friedrich Wöhler in 1828, which is prepared accidentally in an attempt to make ammonium cyanate. The synthesis of urea marks the beginning of organic chemistry, disproving *vital force* theory by showing that organic compounds can be synthesized from inorganic materials. However, the idea of *vitalism* in chemistry was not completely abandoned until 1845, when Herrmann Kolbe, a student of Wöhler, achieved the synthesis of acetic acid (**2**) from its elements. Remarkably, Kolbe used the word *synthesis* for the first time when describing the process of assembling chemical compounds.

In 1850, Adolph Strecker accomplished the first synthesis of an α-amino acid, preparing alanine (**3**) by the condensation of acetaldehyde with ammonia and hydrogen cyanide, which remains, more than 150 years after its initial appearance, the most important method for the synthesis of α-amino acids. Also many other reactions, which still constitute the indispensable synthetic foundation of any organic chemist were discovered during that era, including the aldol reaction, the Friedel-Crafts alkylation and the Michael reaction. In 1890, Emil Fischer completed the total synthesis of (+)-glucose (**4**), which stands as another milestone in organic synthesis, due to the complexity of the target molecule, and inclusion of stereochemical elements for the first time. Also the birth of asymmetric synthesis dates from Fischer's work on carbohydrates in 1894, when he recognized that the addition of hydrogen cyanide to L-arabinose afforded one of the two possible diastereomeric cyanohydrins preferentially.

During the first part of the twentieth century, the molecular complexity of natural products that could be synthesized was slowly but surely increasing, some of the most prominent examples being the syntheses of haemin the red pigment of blood and the sex hormone equilenine (**5**).

[Structure 5: a steroid-like molecule with H₃C, =O, HO- and H substituents]

The discovery of new synthetic tools such as the Grignard reaction, the Claisen rearrangement and the Diels-Alder reaction conferred a deeper understanding of reaction mechanisms and the electronic nature of molecules and chemical bonding, constituting a great leap forward in terms of explaining and predicting chemical reactivity.

In a consequent manner Robert Burns Woodward applied these new concepts and ideas in organic synthesis. His total synthesis of quinine is often considered to mark the beginning of a new era in chemistry, elevating the science of organic synthesis into an intellectual and even more importantly, an artistic process. Perhaps his most spectacular synthetic achievement was the synthesis of Vitamin B_{12} in 1974, with Albert Eschenmoser, illustrating that organic chemists are capable of synthesizing any compound imaginable. Furthermore, it exemplified the impact organic synthesis has on the progress of organic chemistry itself: Woodward's analysis of a reaction problem during the synthesis of Vitamin B_{12} led in 1965 to the formulation of what are now known as the Woodward-Hoffmann rules. These represented a break through for quantum mechanical models of structures and predictive reactivity in organic chemistry.

During the second half of the twentieth century, organic chemistry and in particular natural product synthesis underwent an explosive growth as evidenced by inspection of the primary chemical literature. Furthermore, the original goal of total synthesis to confirm the structure of a natural product was more and more replaced with objectives related to the exploration of new technologies along the pathway. The discovery and invention of powerful new methodologies such as the Wittig reaction, palladium-catalyzed cross coupling reactions and olefin metathesis tremendously expanded the available synthetic tools. At the same time, the advances in chromatographic and spectroscopic techniques allowed the rapid purification and characterization of organic compounds with unparalleled facility and speed. Furthermore, the development of new synthetic strategies, models and theories led to an unprecedented degree of predictability making organic synthesis into the precise science.

During the last two decades, organic chemists were able to accomplish the synthesis of entirely new types of complex and densely functionalized structures, such as the powerful anti-cancer agent taxol and polyetherneurotoxins including brevetoxin A and B. A more recent example is the synthesis of haouamine, which nicely illustrates the continuing necessity for the development of new methodology. Even though the quest for the synthesis of molecules with a steadily increasing size and complexity, the challenge in organic synthesis today lies less in the synthesis of monstrous natural products than in the development of efficient, selective and environmentally benign transformations. Despite the immense number of organic transformations that have been developed since the days of Wöhler, organic synthesis is still in its early stages of development, compared to the powerful and selective synthetic tools available in nature.

Planning of Synthesis:

Organic synthesis is not only the phrase but it is a demanding science-art and suggest progress in our abilities to construct molecules of complexity with higher stereocontrol, faster analysis and greater prediction of eventual success. Now, we find ourselves familiar with methods of constructing a carbon skeleton for an organic molecule, how to introduce and transform functional groups and how to achieve the required selectivity. A chemist could almost expect the rich armory of existing methods that enable to solve practically any problem of synthetic chemistry, yet it is not quite so simple. It is essential to be skillful in planning a synthesis or design of synthesis.

In 1966, Corey presented plenary lecture entitled "General Methods for the Construction of Complex Molecules" at the IVth International IUPAC Symposium on the Chemistry of Natural Products in Stockholm. He was stated in this lecture *"The synthetic chemist is more than logician and strategist, the chemist is an explorer strongly influenced to speculate, imagine and even to create. These added elements provide to touch of artistry which can hardly be included in cataloging of basic principles of synthesis, but they are very real and important. The proposition can be advanced that many of most distinguished synthetic studies have entitled a balance between two different research philosophies, one embodying the ideal of deductive analysis based on known methodology and current theory, and the other emphasizing innovation and even speculation"*.

In 1990, the Nobel Prize in Chemistry was awarded to E. J. Corey for the development of the Theory and Methodology of Organic Synthesis. The essence of his research was in advancing the level of synthetic science by an approach consisting of three integral components;

1. The development of more general and powerful ways of thinking about synthetic problems.
2. The invention of new general reactions and reagents for organic synthesis and the design.
3. Execution of efficient multistep synthesis of complex molecules.

Theoretical analysis of the strategic problems in the total synthesis began to receive serious attention. In development of strategy for a specific synthesis, it is possible to encounter two extreme situations:

(a) The starting compound is given/ available and it is necessary to elaborate a route for its conversion into target structure.

(b) No specific starting compound is available, so the target compound must be analyzed to identify synthetic pathways from simple precursors.

Planning of Synthesis from Starting Material:

Planning a laboratory synthesis based on choice of well defined starting compounds is satisfactory in those cases where it is easy to identify structural fragments in the target molecule. Clear-cut example of this approach is found in the synthesis of biopolymers like proteins, polysaccharides and nucleic acids as these materials are constructed from relatively small monomeric blocks bound by heteroatomic bridges. The monomers in proteins and polypeptides are amino acids. An amidic bond serves as the bridge. Monosaccharides are the monomeric units of polysaccharides and these units are joined through oxygen by glycosidic bonds. In nucleic acids the individual units are nucleotides connected via phosphodiester bonds. The majority of polysaccharides have regular structure in polymeric chain which suggests that such a chain can be constructed from repeating mono or oligosaccharide links. The general strategy for their synthesis consist of polymerization or polycondensation of suitable monomers to form glycosidic bonds with the correct stereo and regiochemistry. The first synthesis of polysaccharide (**6**), is an analogue of the bacterial polysaccharide Dextrans. This biopolymer is composed of α-D-glucopyranosyl units linked by a → b bonds. D-Glucose (**7**) was an obvious starting material.

The main concern was to find a way to achieve the required region and stereo specificity in the formation of glycosidic bond. The cationic polymerization of 1,6-anhydro-β-D-glucopyranose derivative (**8**) having benzyl protected hydroxyl groups.

The cationic polymerization of monomer **8** occurs *via* the initial co-ordination of electrophilic initiator, PF_5, at the indicated ring oxygen atom to produce oxonium ion **9**, which is attacked by another molecule of **8** at its electrophilic site C_a, to form new oxonium ion **10**, repetition of this process leads to the consecutive formation of glycosidic bonds in a stereo specific fashion. Debenzylation of the final polymer **12** affords target product **6**.

There are generally two options available if a chemist is to avoid the complications in synthesis. One must find conditions that ensure either quantitative yield at the chemical stages of condensation and deprotection or guarantee a 100% purification of the product formed at each step. Furthermore, these conditions should be applicable for a peptide of any structure. The finding an errorless route of synthesis, is unrealistic, since for all practical purposes there are no simple organic reactions that will secure a 100% yield of product in every case. As we mentioned above, 100% purification of the products in the course of peptide synthesis is also far from being an easy task. In fact, it is a task of a formidable complexity. Therefore the first total synthesis of a peptide hormone, oxytocin (1953), consisting of only eight amino acids was evaluated as an outstanding achievement. In 1955, it brought the Nobel Prize to its originator, V. du Vigneaux. However, over the next two decades the synthesis of polypeptides of that complexity became routine and at the present time the preparation of a polypeptide of more than 100 amino acid units is not considered a prohibitively difficult task.

In the early 1960s a novel approach was devised to resolve the isolation and purification problems in a peptide synthesis. The discoverer of this approach, R. B. Merrifield, in his Nobel lecture said: "One day I had an idea how the goal of a more effective synthesis might be achieved. The plan was to assemble a peptide chain in a stepwise manner while it was attached at one end to a solid support". This idea turned out to be truly brilliant in terms of both its simplicity and initiative. The 'trick' of Merrifield's approach consists of chemically binding the growing polypeptide chain to an insoluble and inert polymer support. As a result, the separation and purification procedure is reduced to a simple filtration of the polymer-bound product and a careful washing to remove excess reactants and by-products. Such a mechanical operation can be made completely quantitative, is easily standardized and automated.

Planning from the Target Structure:

A general and more reliable approach involves the logistic application of sequential disconnections to the target molecule. As stated by Corey, 'retrosynthetic analysis is a problem-solving technique for transformating the structure of a target molecule to a sequence of progressively simpler structures along a pathway that ultimately leads to simple or commercially available starting materials for a chemical synthesis.

The retrosynthetic simplification of any target molecule involving a sequential rupture of bonds may be started from any bond and thus carried out to the simplest precursors along a multitude of retrosynthetic pathways. If this dismantling is carried out in an unsystematic fashion, the immense number of possibilities generated would make the approach useless for all practical purposes. On the other hand, a thoughtful retrosynthetic analysis governed by chemical logic and conducted in accordance with carefully chosen criteria represents a powerful approach to elaborate a sound synthetic strategy. Retrosynthetic analysis involves several more or less distinct steps; probably the most difficult and by far the most important, is the initial analysis of the synthetic target structure.

Before attempting the dissection of a target molecule it is useful to analyse the general synthetic task in order to identify and evaluate the complexity of a set of subtasks and then to determine an optimized order of solving these subtasks. The transformation of functional groups usually does not present a problem. The same refers to the attachment of alkyl pendants to the functionalized centers. Therefore, to a first approximation, the exact nature of functional groups introduced into specified positions of the intermediate products is irrelevant since these groups could be modified or removed in order to match the functionality of the target molecule. If the structure contains heteroatoms that are not a part of the heteroaromatic system, it makes sense to start the analysis by rupturing a carbon-heteroatom bond as the reverse reaction represents, essentially, a trivial transformation of functional groups. The presence of small ring fragments such as cyclopropane or epoxide rings in the structure of the target molecule almost automatically dictates the retrosynthetic scission of these moieties in the initial steps of retrosynthetical analysis, as both these groups can be easily introduced with the help of very reliable methods. The benefits of simplifying the target molecule are rather obvious. First of all, by doing this the final stages of the synthetic scheme relate to the more reliable and trouble-free reactions. The potentially risky steps are moved to the initial phases which, from the perspective of one's investment of time into a synthesis, carries obvious benefits. A second, but no less significant advantage of this approach is that it obviates the need to drag along highly reactive and labile groups in a multistep sequence. Quite often this approach may also greatly simplify selectivity problems in the course of a real synthesis. Thus, after splitting off side chains and removing or transforming 'extraneous' functional groups and other readily 'installable' moieties, the retrosynthetic analysis identifies the 'strategic core' of the original target molecule. The main focus of the planned synthesis, then becomes the assemblage of this strategic core.

The complexity of the key steps of a retrosynthetic analysis may differ dramatically, depending upon the overall structure of the strategic core, which can be conventionally divided into three main groups: acyclic, monocyclic and polycyclic.

The retrosynthetic analysis of acyclic systems usually does not require the formulation of special strategic concepts, as it usually can be based upon considering the positioning of functional groups and simple 'pendants'. This type of disconnection normally involves straightforward solutions derived from existing methods for creating C-C bonds.

As a rule, the dismantling of an acyclic chain can be carried out at almost any C-C bond and therefore, for even the simplest cases, one has to deal with a set of different retrosynthetic solutions. In fact, the number of options is even greater if one also takes into account that (i) more than one method may be feasible for the formation of a given C-C bond and (ii) within the limits of a given method, a set of fairly diverse reagents can be used. Rational selection among these options is determined by considering such factors as the availability of starting materials, the opportunity to exert rigorous control over the stereochemistry, the desire to minimize the number of steps and the ultimate purpose of the projected synthesis.

In regard to simple monocyclic systems, the basic principles of disconnection for the synthetic target molecule differ very little in essence from those of an acyclic system. In fact, here again the retrosynthetic analysis is more or less directly related to existing methods for the creation of rings.

The presence of a six-membered ring in the synthetic target molecule does not necessarily imply that its formation should be carried out as a result of ring forming reactions. In fact, this approach has two major strategic merits. First of all, it frees the chemist from creating the skeleton of the six-membered ring. Secondly, it may greatly simplify the problem of introducing the required functional substituent's on the ring carbons, as the preparation of the respective derivatives in the benzene series may be a more or less routine task. It is definitely worthwhile to consider the plausibility of these routes at the very beginning of a retrosynthetic analysis.

Selection of the Strategic Bond in a Target Molecule:

The exact reverse of the synthetic operations applied for the retrosynthetic disconnection of the bonds in a synthetic target structure is called a transform. A structural unit or set of functional groups that should be present in order to carry out a given synthetic reaction is called a retron. Thus, the presence of the required retron represents a mandatory prerequisite for the application of a given *transform* to simplify the target structure. The very first bond selected for disconnection determines the strategy of the entire synthetic scheme. Therefore, this bond should be considered as a strategic bond. Similar analysis aimed at the identification of the strategic bond could be also required for any intermediate structure generated in the course of the subsequent disconnection steps, leading ultimately to simple starting materials. In general, there are only a few bonds in the target molecule that can be reasonably considered as 'breakable' and even fewer of them as 'strategic'. The selection of the strategic bond will dictate the flavour of the rest of the dismantling down to suitable precursors and hence lead to synthetic plans as varied as those utilized for the syntheses.

Analysis of the Structure as a Whole:

The variations of the retrosynthetic analysis of synthesis based upon one general concept: "the sequential bond-after-bond disconnection of the core of the target molecule into a set of smaller fragments". Logistically it is an absolutely reliable approach, a consistent application of the retrosynthetic principles would inevitably produce a number of more or less reasonable pathways to synthesize the target molecule from available precursors. However, this reliable but overall rather lengthy procedure is not necessarily the most efficient mode of retrosynthetic analysis. The analysis of the target molecule as an integral entity can lead to the identification of peculiar structural characteristics that might prompt a much more economical route to its assembly. Such an in-depth examination is based upon both heuristic and logical considerations and, at times, the heuristic considerations might even be prevalent. This analysis of the molecule as a whole is aimed at the recognition of opportunities to put together the strategic core of the target molecule as a result of a single chemical operation or a very few operations and thus may be properly called a 'whole structure' strategy for the conception of a synthetic plan. An effective windfall upon retrosynthetic analysis does not happen very often. Nevertheless, it is generally recommended that the retrosynthetic analysis of polycyclic structures should be directed first to the search of pathways that lead to 'one stroke' framework assemblage. These possibilities can usually be accomplished with the help of cycloaddition reactions. In the course of the initial analysis, special emphasis should be given to identify structural features of the strategic core which might lead to the use of cycloaddition transforms. The validity of the conceived retrosynthetic plan was proven in its truly brilliant synthetic implementation. In fact, the synthesis of a rather complicated polycyclic framework containing three adjacent quaternary centers was achieved with record-breaking simplicity and efficiency. We do not want, however, to leave the reader with the impression that cycloadditions are some sort of 'golden key' that unlock the pathway to the creation of almost any cyclic system. Even reactions from this powerful arsenal can misfire and an otherwise brilliant retrosynthetic idea remains just that if it cannot be translated into a real synthesis. Taking advantage of the symmetry of the target structure often permits elaborating of the most economical pathways for assembling complicated frameworks. The direct application of a symmetry-guided retrosynthetic search is possible, though, only in the rare cases in which one has symmetrical target molecules. In any case, a thoughtful retrosynthetic analysis of even unsymmetrical structures may result in the disclosure of a 'masked' symmetry which might be made over by a retrosynthetical introduction or removal of extraneous fragments, skeletal rearrangements etc.

Synthetic Schemes: Linear and Convergent Mode

The simplest and most obvious composition of a synthetic plan is a linear sequence of steps leading to the construction of a target product **P** from the appropriate starting materials, as is shown in **Fig.1**.

$$R_0 + R_1 \longrightarrow R_0-R_1 \xrightarrow{R_2} R_0-R_1-R_2 \xrightarrow{R_3} R_0-R_1-R_2-R_3 \longrightarrow \longrightarrow$$
$$\longrightarrow \longrightarrow R_0-R_1-R_2-R_3----R_n$$

Fig. 1

The 'Achilles' heel' of this approach is the problem of achieving an acceptable overall yield. In consecutive reactions the final yield, of course, will depend upon the yields obtained in the intermediate stages. If the average yield per individual step is designated as Y, then the total yield of the product after the nth stage will be $Y_n = Y^n$. If Y is equal to 80%, a very acceptable yield, then the dependence of the overall yield on the number of steps would be as follows:

n	5	10	20	30	50	80
$Y_n(\%)$	33	11	1.2	0.12	1.4×10^{-3}	2.0×10^{-6}

In real life, the overall efficiency of multistep syntheses is usually even worse. A yield of 2.0×10^{-6}% implies that in order to obtain 20 mg of the final product one must begin with one tonne of starting material. This is the direct and unavoidable result of the detrimental work of the 'arithmetic demon'. To alleviate its effects, all synthetic plans strive to maximize the yields at every stage, as well as to minimize the number of steps required. The first task is directly related to developing a reliable, high-yield synthetic procedure. Careful planning may also reduce the number of such auxiliary steps as protection and deprotection, functional group interconversions etc., and thus shorten the entire sequence. As a result of these combined efforts, even a rather lengthy linear synthesis may be accomplished with an acceptable total yield.

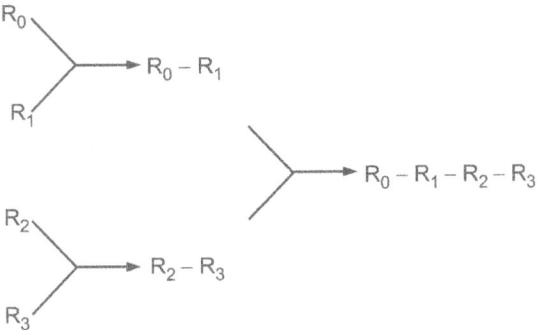

Fig. 2

Another entirely different way to increase the overall efficiency of a multistep synthesis is based on a convergent synthetic strategy; its essence illustrated in the model is given in Fig. 2. It is easy to show that in this case the dependence of the overall yield of the final product upon the total number of steps is expressed by the equation $Y_n = Y^{\log_2 n}$. If we again assume $Y = 80\%$, as the average yield per step, one can readily compare the relative effectiveness of the linear versus fully convergent routes for the assembling product P from the same fragments,

n	8	16	32	64	80
$Y_n(\%)$: Linear scheme	16.8	2.8	0.08	6×10^{-5}	2×10^{-6}
Convergent scheme	51.2	41	32.8	26	24.4

Assembling a target composed of 65 building blocks ($n = 64$) looks less than appealing if attempted via a linear route, as this route is virtually blocked by the 'arithmetic demon'. At the same time, though, the task does not look prohibitively complicated if a convergent route for its synthesis is feasible.

In addition to opening a way to 'defeat the arithmetic demon', the convergent route offers some additional benefits. First of all, convergent schemes are generally much more reliable. In fact, the failure of any single step of the convergent scheme does not invalidate the chosen pathway as a whole. It only indicates the necessity of surmounting this difficulty by finding a detour at some local point. On the other hand, the failure of one step of a linear approach may require a revision of the whole plan. Furthermore, in contrast to a linear approach, the question of compatibility between interfering functional groups is less likely to be a problem as the fragments bearing these groups can be treated on different branches of the synthetic tree which are joined in later steps. Owing to these features, the convergent scheme is also more suitable for the synthesis of a series of structural analogues. Finally, the extraordinary nature of these schemes provides an opportunity for simultaneous and independent studies aimed at elucidating the viability of all the entries ('branches') that lead to the point of convergency. Hence, the progress of the whole project may be greatly enhanced.

The idea of convergency undoubtedly constitutes one of the basic strategic principles of contemporary organic synthesis. It can be stated without too great an exaggeration that the wide utilization of this principle was responsible, to a substantial extent, for the stunning successes achieved in the syntheses of various complex organic compounds during the last decades. Moreover, the need to execute convergent schemes served as a powerful motivation for the development of novel synthetic methods specifically designed to achieve multicomponent one-pot coupling reactions.

Recommendations:

1. **Carry out a thorough examination of the target structure as a whole entity:**

   The main task at this initial stage of planning consists of the analysis of the general problem and sub-problems of the synthesis in order to identify the tasks of strategic importance. A thorough examination of the target structure as a whole molecular construction and not the sum of individual parts, it is sometimes possible to identify a very effective synthetic pathway.

2. **Select the strategic reaction:**

   The selection of a strategic reaction automatically dictates both the general composition and sequence of steps of the retrosynthetic analysis. The criteria for the selection of the optimal strategic reaction, generally speaking, can be very different, but convergency is most usually at the top of the priorities list. It is also good to remember that, with all other factors being equal, an intramolecular version of a reaction almost invariably is better than an intermolecular one. That is why, this popular avenue is taken so often in contemporary organic syntheses.

3. **Select the strategic bond:**

   This recommendation is especially important in those numerous cases in which the initial analysis does not identify an efficient strategic reaction and, hence, a sequential bond-by-bond dismantling of the structure becomes obligatory. The first bond in this sequence defines all subsequent steps in the retrosynthetic analysis.

   There are no rigorous rules for the unambiguous selection of the strategic bond. Moreover, no generally applicable and strictly defined criteria for its selection can be formulated as any molecular structure is, in essence, an individual assemblage of atoms. However, several criteria do exist that unquestionably simplify the task when a stepwise disassemblage of the target structure is required. It will be expedient to select in the role of a strategic bond, the bond that leads to the greatest simplification of structure. For example, with polycyclic systems this usually will mean finding the bond which upon breakage will produce a structure with the least number of side 'pendants', bridged cyclic fragments as well as medium-sized rings. It follows that the most likely candidate for a strategic bond should be looked for among the bonds in the bridged cycles as well as among the bonds to the centers common to several cycles.

Finally, the search for a strategic bond is always simplified when even a 'first glance' analysis leads to the identification of those bonds that clearly cannot be considered strategic. The latter include bonds in aromatic rings or heteroaromatic rings, as well as bonds which are located in readily available fragments.

4. **Carry out an initial retrosynthetic processing of the target structure:**

   This is also a very important step, essential to the above-mentioned procedures. It is mainly targeted at the identification of the shortest pathways for the retrosynthetic modification of the target structure in order to create the functionality pattern (retron) to secure the applicability of the chosen strategic transform.

   It is possible that preliminary retrosynthetic modifications of the target structure will implicate a few additional transformation steps that lengthen the whole scheme. However, the obvious gains provided by the opportunity to apply an efficient strategic reaction might well outweigh these expenses. It should also be kept in mind that, in the course of this step of the retrosynthetic analysis, not only the initial functional pattern but also the skeleton of the target itself need not be considered as fixed features. In fact, quite the contrary, the analysis of options suggested by various transformations of the basic framework might lead to truly imaginative solutions.

   A significant aspect of most preliminary examinations of a target structure involves the retrosynthetic removal of every part of the target molecule that is not essential for the elaboration of the strategic concept. As a result of these pursuits, a strategic core could be identified.

   The order in which we listed the above recommendations in no way should be considered as the preferential sequence of steps in a retrosynthetical analysis. For all practical purposes they must be considered simultaneously and, furthermore, throughout the entire sequence of dismantling down to the simple starting compounds. Such a systematic analysis will frequently lead to quite a number of possible routes. The selection among them can be dictated by very different reasons but, as we have already emphasized, the route that is tied together by a 'convergent knot' is almost invariably preferred. In general, the minimization of the number of steps is a significant aspect of any synthetic plan. In an ideal sequence, this implies that the intermediate product prepared at any stage is ready, without additional alterations, to serve as the precursor for the next constructive step.

The optimal route employs the most effective synthetic methods that ensure the highest yields and greatest selectivity. This consideration includes simplicity of the required operation of separation and purification which, as we have mentioned, can turn out to be the 'Achilles' heel' of an otherwise excellent synthetic scheme.

■■■

LIST OF DRUGS

1. Acepromazine, 8
2. Acetophenazine, 8
3. Acetylcholine chloride, 10
4. Adiphenine, 11
5. Almitrine, 11
6. Aminopromazine, 13
7. Amobarbital, 14
8. Amodiaquine, 15
9. Amoxycillin, 17
10. Ampicillin, 18
11. Anileridine, 19
12. Antazoline, 20
13. Aspirin, 20
14. Azapetine, 21
15. Bamifylline, 21
16. Beclobrate, 23
17. Benaprizine, 24
18. Benorylate, 25
19. Benserazide, 25
20. Bentiromide, 26
21. Benzphetamine, 27
22. Bethanechol, 28
23. Bevantolol, 29
24. Bisacodyl, 30
25. Bitolterol, 31
26. Bromdiphenhydramine, 32
27. Bromhexine, 33
28. Buclosamide, 34
29. Budralazine, 34
30. Bufetolol, 35
31. Buflomedil, 36
32. Bunitrolol, 37
33. Busulfan, 38
34. Butacaine, 38
35. Butalamine, 39
36. Butalbital, 40
37. Butamirate, 41
38. Butanilicanine, 41
39. Butethamine, 42
40. Butofilolol, 43
41. Cadralazine, 44
42. Captopril, 46
43. Carbachol, 47
44. Carbamazepine, 48

45. Carbenicillin, 49
46. Carfecillin, 50
47. Carmofur, 51
48. Carphenazine, 52
49. Carticaine, 53
50. Cefazolin, 54
51. Cephapirin, 55
52. Chloramphenicol, 56
53. Chlorcyclizine, 58
54. Chlorophenesin, 59
55. Chlorophenesin Carbamate, 59
56. Chloroprocaine, 60
57. Chloropyrilene, 61
58. Chloroquine, 61
59. Chlorzoxazone, 62
60. Chlorpheniramine, 63
61. Chlorpropamide, 64
62. Cidofovir, 65
63. Cilostazole, 66
64. Cimetidine, 67
65. Cinepazate, 68
66. Cinnamylephedrine, 69
67. Ciprofloxacin, 70
68. Clobazam, 71

69. Clofexamide, 74
70. Clonazepam, 74
71. Clopamide, 76
72. Cloperastine, 77
73. Clotrimazole, 77
74. Clozapine, 78
75. Cyclizine, 80
76. Cyclomethylcaine, 81
77. Cyclophosphamide, 82
78. Dapsone, 83
79. Diazepam, 84
80. Dibenzepine, 85
81. Dichlorphenamide, 86
82. Dicycloverine, 87
83. Diethylcarbmazine, 88
84. Diloxanide, 89
85. Diltiazem, 89
86. Dimethoxanate, 92
87. Diperodon, 92
88. Diphenoxylate, 93
89. Diphenylpyraline, 94
90. Dipivefrine, 94
91. Diprophylline, 96
92. Distigmine Bromide, 96

93. Dixyrazine, 98
94. Dofetilide, 99
95. Dopexamine, 101
96. Dropropizine, 103
97. Ebastine, 104
98. Econazole, 105
99. Edrophonium Chloride, 106
100. Emedastine, 106
101. Entacapone, 108
102. Epinephrine, 109
103. Epitizide, 110
104. Esmolol, 111
105. Ethambutol, 112
106. Ethotoin, 112
107. Etofibrate, 114
108. Etofylline, 115
109. Exalamide, 115
110. Febuprol, 116
111. Fenalcomine, 116
112. Fenbufen, 118
113. Fenethylline, 118
114. Fenofibrate, 119
115. Fenoprofen, 120
116. Fenoverine, 122
117. Fentanyl, 123
118. Floredil, 124
119. Fluanisone, 125
120. Flucoxacillin, 126
121. Flufenamic Acid, 127
122. Flunarizine, 128
123. Fluoxetine, 129
124. Flutamide, 129
125. Furasemide, 130
126. Gabexate, 131
127. Gallopamil, 132
128. Gefarnate, 134
129. Glibenclamide, 135
130. Glimepiride, 136
131. Glipizide, 138
132. Glybuzole, 140
133. Guaifenesin, 140
134. Histapyrrodine, 141
135. Homofenazine, 142
136. Hydroxyzine, 143
137. Ibopamine, 144
138. Ibuprofen, 144
139. Imipramine, 146
140. Indecainide, 146

141. Isoaminile, 147
142. Isoconazole, 148
143. Isoetarine, 149
144. Isoniazid, 151
145. Lactophenin, 152
146. Letrozole, 152
147. Levamisole, 153
148. Levobunolol, 155
149. Levodopa, 156
150. Lidoflazine, 156
151. Lobenzarit, 157
152. Lomifylline, 158
153. Lomustine, 158
154. Lonidamine, 159
155. Lopramine, 160
156. Losartan, 161
157. Mabuprofen, 162
158. Manidipine, 163
159. Mebendazole, 165
160. Meclofenoxate, 166
161. Mecloqualone, 167
162. Medibazine, 167
163. Medifoxamine, 168
164. Medrylamine, 169
165. Mefanamic Acid, 170
166. Mefexamide, 171
167. Mepacrine, 172
168. Mephenesin, 173
169. Meprobamate, 174
170. Meprylcaine, 174
171. Mesalazine, 175
172. Metahexamide, 175
173. Metformin, 176
174. Methdilazine, 177
175. Methicillin, 177
176. Methixene, 178
177. Methocarbamol, 179
178. Methyldopa, 179
179. Methylperone, 181
180. Methylphenidate, 181
181. Metoclopramide, 182
182. Metopimizine, 184
183. Metronidazole, 185
184. Miconazole, 186
185. Midazolam, 187
186. Minaprine, 188
187. Mirtazapine, 189
188. Moclobemide, 191

189. Mofebutazone, 191
190. Moroxydine, 192
191. Nabumetone, 193
192. Nafcillin, 194
193. Naftifine, 194
194. Naftopidil, 195
195. Nevirapine, 196
196. Niceritrol, 197
197. Niclosamide, 198
198. Nicotafuryl, 199
199. Nicotinamide, 199
200. Nifenalol, 200
201. Niflumic Acid, 200
202. Nikethamide, 201
203. Nimesulide, 201
204. Niridazole, 203
205. Nitrazepam, 203
206. Nitrefazole, 205
207. Nitrofurantoin, 205
208. Nomifensine, 206
209. Norfloxacin, 208
210. Notriptyline, 209
211. Octopamaine, 210
212. Omoconazole, 211
213. Opipramol, 212
214. Orphenadrine, 213
215. Oxaceprol, 214
216. Oxatomide, 214
217. Oxeladin, 215
218. Oxomemazine, 216
219. Oxybuprocaine, 217
220. Oxypendyl, 219
221. Paracetamol, 220
222. Parethoxycaine, 221
223. Pargyline, 222
224. Parsalmide, 222
225. Penbutolol, 224
226. Pentapiperide, 225
227. Pentifylline, 226
228. Pentoxyverine, 226
229. Perazine, 227
230. Perlapine, 228
231. Perphenazine, 229
232. Pethidine, 230
233. Phenacemide, 231
234. Phenacetin, 232
235. Phenbutrazate, 232
236. Phencarbamide, 234

237. Phenelzine, 235
238. Phenethicillin, 235
239. Pheneturide, 236
240. Pheniramine, 236
241. Phenprobamate, 237
242. Phentolamine, 238
243. Phenoxybenzamine, 239
244. Phenylbutazone, 240
245. Phenyltoloxamine, 240
246. Pifoxime, 241
247. Piketoprofen, 242
248. Pimefylline, 243
249. Pimobenden, 244
250. Pindolol, 245
251. Pipamazine, 246
252. Pipazethate, 247
253. Piperacillin, 248
254. Piperocaine, 250
255. Pipobroman, 250
256. Piracetam, 251
257. Piretanide, 251
258. Pirezepine, 253
259. Piribedil, 255
260. Piritramide, 255

261. Piroxicam, 256
262. Pramocaine, 257
263. Praziquantel, 258
264. Prazosin, 259
265. Prilocaine, 260
266. Primaperone, 261
267. Probenecid, 261
268. Procaine, 263
269. Procaterol, 264
270. Prochlorperazine, 265
271. Promazine, 265
272. Propafenone, 266
273. Propallylonal, 267
274. Propanidid, 268
275. Propicillin, 268
276. Propiram, 269
277. Propiverine, 270
278. Propranolol, 271
279. Propythiouracil, 272
280. Prothipendyl, 273
281. Protokylol, 273
282. Proxyphylline, 274
283. Pyrazinamide, 275
284. Pyridinol carbamate, 275

285. Pyridostigmine bromide, 276
286. Pyrrocaine, 277
287. Ranitidine, 278
288. Remoxipride, 279
289. Rilmenidine, 280
290. Rosiglitazone, 281
291. Salacetamide, 282
292. Salmeterol, 283
293. Secnidazole, 284
294. Secobarbital, 285
295. Sertaconazole, 286
296. Sotalol, 287
297. Spiperone, 288
298. Stepronin, 289
299. Styramate, 290
300. Succinylsulfathiazole, 290
301. Sulfacetamide, 291
302. Sulfachlorpyridazine, 291
303. Sulfadiazine, 292
304. Sulfaguanidine, 293
305. Sulfamethizole, 293
306. Sulfamethoxazole, 294
307. Talinolol, 295
308. Talipexole, 296
309. Telmesteine, 297
310. Tenonitrozole, 298
311. Terazosine, 298
312. Terfenadine, 299
313. Tetracaine, 301
314. Thioproperzine, 302
315. Thiotepa, 303
316. Ticarcillin, 303
317. Ticlopidine, 304
318. Timolol, 305
319. Tioconazole, 306
320. Tiopronine, 307
321. Tocainide, 308
322. Todralazine, 309
323. Tolazamide, 309
324. Tolbutamide, 310
325. Tolfenamic Acid, 311
326. Toliprolol, 311
327. Tolnaftate, 312
328. Torasemide, 313
329. Tranilast, 314
330. Trifluperazine, 314
331. Triflupromazine, 315
332. Trimeprazine, 316

333. Trimethoprim, 316

334. Trimethozine, 318

335. Trimipramine, 318

336. Tripelennamine 319

337. Uramustine, 320

338. Valethamate Bromide, 320

339. Verapamil, 322

340. Warfarin, 323

341. Xathinol, 324

342. Xibenolol, 325

343. Xipamide, 326.

■■■

(i)   (ii)   (iii)   (iv)

(v)   (vi)   (vii)   (viii)

(I)   (II)   (III)   (IV)

(V)   (VI)   (VII)   (VIII)

www.ingramcontent.com/pod-product-compliance
Lightning Source LLC
Chambersburg PA
CBHW081838230426
43669CB00018B/2748